Exam Ref 70-698
Installing and
Configuring Windows 10

Andrew Bettany
Andrew Warren

PUBLISHED BY
Microsoft Press
A division of Microsoft Corporation
One Microsoft Way
Redmond, Washington 98052-6399

Library of Congress Control Number: 2016934334
ISBN: 978-1-5093-0295-6

Printed and bound in the United States of America.

4   17

Microsoft Press books are available through booksellers and distributors worldwide. If you need support related to this book, email Microsoft Press Support at *mspinput@microsoft.com*. Please tell us what you think of this book at *http://aka.ms/tellpress*.

This book is provided "as-is" and expresses the author's views and opinions. The views, opinions and information expressed in this book, including URL and other Internet website references, may change without notice.

Some examples depicted herein are provided for illustration only and are fictitious. No real association or connection is intended or should be inferred.

Microsoft and the trademarks listed at *http://www.microsoft.com* on the "Trademarks" webpage are trademarks of the Microsoft group of companies. All other marks are property of their respective owners.

Acquisitions Editor: Karen Szall
Developmental Editor: Karen Szall
Editorial Production: Cohesion
Technical Reviewer: Randall Galloway; Technical Review services provided by Content Master, a member of CM Group, Ltd.
Copyeditor: Kerin Forsyth
Indexer: Lucie Haskins
Cover: Twist Creative • Seattle

Contents at a glance

	Introduction	*xlx*
CHAPTER 1	Prepare for installation requirements	1
CHAPTER 2	Install Windows 10	27
CHAPTER 3	Configure devices and device drivers	65
CHAPTER 4	Post-installation configuration	97
CHAPTER 5	Implement Windows in an enterprise environment	135
CHAPTER 6	Configure networking	161
CHAPTER 7	Configure storage	201
CHAPTER 8	Configure data access and usage	237
CHAPTER 9	Implement Apps	273
CHAPTER 10	Configure remote management	297
CHAPTER 11	Configure updates	319
CHAPTER 12	Monitor Windows	349
CHAPTER 13	Configure system and data recovery	385
CHAPTER 14	Configure authorization and authentication	419
CHAPTER 15	Configure advanced management tools	449
	Index	*467*

Contents

What do you think of this book? We want to hear from you!

Microsoft is interested in hearing your feedback so we can continually improve our books and learning resources for you. To participate in a brief online survey, please visit:

www.microsoft.com/learning/booksurvey/

Chapter 2   **Install Windows 10**   **27**

Chapter 3   **Configure devices and device drivers**   **65**

Chapter 9   Implement Apps   273

Chapter 14 Configure authorization and authentication   419

Chapter 15 Configure advanced management tools   449

Introduction

This book is intended for IT pros who are seeking certification in the 70-698 Installing and Configuring Windows 10 exam. These professionals typically administer and support Windows 10 devices in corporate, Windows Server domain-based environments with managed access to the Internet and cloud services. The book is also intended to provide skills for Enterprise Device Support Technicians (EDSTs), who provide Tier 2 support to users of Windows 10 in medium-to-large enterprise organizations.

To get the most from this book, you should have at least two years of experience in the IT field and should already have the following technical knowledge.

- Networking fundamentals, including Transmission Control Protocol/Internet Protocol (TCP/IP), User Datagram Protocol (UDP), and Domain Name System (DNS).
- Microsoft Active Directory Domain Services (AD DS) principles.
- Some experience with Windows Server 2016 or Windows Server 2012 R2.
- Experience with a Microsoft Windows client; for example, a working knowledge of Windows 7 or Windows 8.1.

Skills covered by reading this book include the following.

- Install, upgrade, and customize Windows 10.
- Manage apps.
- Configure storage.
- Configure network connectivity.
- Configure data security, device security, and network security.
- Maintain, update, and recover Windows 10.

We expect Windows 10 to continue evolving through regular upgrades, and you should ensure that your study is supplemented with practical experience, using the latest build of Windows 10, because new features are likely to be included in the exam.

This book covers every major topic area found on the exam, but it does not cover every exam question. Only the Microsoft exam team has access to the exam questions, and Microsoft regularly adds new questions to the exam, making it impossible to cover specific questions. You should consider this book a supplement to your relevant real-world experience and other study materials. If you encounter a topic in this book that you do not feel completely comfortable with, use the "Need more review?" links you'll find in the text to find more information and take the time to research and study the topic. Great information is available on MSDN and TechNet and in blogs and forums.

Organization of this book

This book is organized by the "Skills measured" list published for the exam. The "Skills measured" list is available for each exam on the Microsoft Learning website: *http://aka.ms/examlist*. Each chapter in this book corresponds to a major topic area in the list, and the technical tasks in each topic area determine a chapter's organization. If an exam covers six major topic areas, for example, the book will contain six chapters.

Microsoft certifications

Microsoft certifications distinguish you by proving your command of a broad set of skills and experience with current Microsoft products and technologies. The exams and corresponding certifications are developed to validate your mastery of critical competencies as you design and develop, or implement and support, solutions with Microsoft products and technologies both on-premises and in the cloud. Certification brings a variety of benefits to the individual and to employers and organizations.

> **MORE INFO**   **ALL MICROSOFT CERTIFICATIONS**
>
> For information about Microsoft certifications, including a full list of available certifications, go to *http://www.microsoft.com/learning*.

Acknowledgments

Andrew Warren   Writing any book is a collaborative effort, so I would like to thank my co-author, Andrew Bettany, for helping drive the project forward. Without the guiding hand of an experienced editor, it's doubtful any book would ever see the light of day, so thank you also to Karen Szall at Microsoft Press for ensuring that we kept to the deadlines and kept it brief.

Andrew Bettany   I am very grateful to both Karen Szall for providing a firm and steady guiding hand, and my coauthor, Andrew Warren, for his wealth of experience. The writing journey has been enjoyable and culminated in sitting and passing the 70-698 exam and obtaining my MCSA: Windows 10. This book is dedicated to Annette and Tommy. Mwah!

Free ebooks from Microsoft Press

From technical overviews to in-depth information on special topics, the free ebooks from Microsoft Press cover a wide range of topics. These ebooks are available in PDF, EPUB, and Mobi for Kindle formats, ready for you to download at:

http://aka.ms/mspressfree

Check back often to see what is new!

Microsoft Virtual Academy

Build your knowledge of Microsoft technologies with free expert-led online training from Microsoft Virtual Academy (MVA). MVA offers a comprehensive library of videos, live events, and more to help you learn the latest technologies and prepare for certification exams. You'll find what you need at *http://www.microsoftvirtualacademy.com*.

Quick access to online references

Throughout this book are addresses to webpages that the author has recommended you visit for more information. Some of these addresses (also known as URLs) can be painstaking to type into a web browser, so we've compiled all of them into a single list that readers of the print edition can refer to while they read.

Download the list at *http://aka.ms/ER698/downloads*.

The URLs are organized by chapter and heading. Every time you come across a URL in the book, find the hyperlink in the list to go directly to the webpage.

Errata, updates, & book support

We've made every effort to ensure the accuracy of this book and its companion content. You can access updates to this book—in the form of a list of submitted errata and their related corrections—at:

http://aka.ms/ER698/errata

If you discover an error that is not already listed, please submit it to us at the same page.

If you need additional support, email Microsoft Press Book Support at *mspinput@microsoft.com*.

Please note that product support for Microsoft software and hardware is not offered through the previous addresses. For help with Microsoft software or hardware, go to *http://support.microsoft.com*.

We want to hear from you

At Microsoft Press, your satisfaction is our top priority, and your feedback our most valuable asset. Please tell us what you think of this book at:

http://aka.ms/tellpress

We know you're busy, so we've kept it short with just a few questions. Your answers go directly to the editors at Microsoft Press. (No personal information will be requested.) Thanks in advance for your input!

Stay in touch

Let's keep the conversation going! We're on Twitter: *http://twitter.com/MicrosoftPress*.

CHAPTER 1

Prepare for installation requirements

The 70-698 Configuring Windows 10 exam focuses on preparing to install Windows 10, and this preparation requires careful consideration, especially when you plan to install Windows 10 on many devices in a large organization. This chapter explores the installation requirements and required preparation for the installation of Windows 10.

It is important to determine whether existing devices, such as desktop or laptop computers, and installed applications meet the installation requirements for Windows 10. If you plan to implement Windows 10 using existing devices, you must also consider whether to perform clean installations and then migrate user settings to those installations or perform in-place upgrades.

Another planning factor for the implementation of Windows 10 is to select the appropriate edition of Windows 10 for your users. Not only is Windows 10 available across many device types, including phones, tablets, laptops, and desktop computers, but it is also available in multiple editions and in both 32-bit and 64-bit versions. Choose the appropriate edition and architecture to provide the necessary feature set to your users, and remember that features such as Secure Boot, Client Hyper-V, Cortana, and others require specific hardware.

After determining which editions you want to install, consider how best to implement Windows 10. You can choose between simple interactive installations using local Windows 10 media, or deploying Windows 10 to your organization's devices by using one of several deployment technologies.

Skills covered in this chapter:

- Determine hardware requirements and compatibility
- Choose between an upgrade and a clean installation
- Determine appropriate editions by device type
- Determine requirements for particular features, including but not limited to Hyper-V, Cortana, Miracast, Virtual Smart Cards, and Secure Boot
- Determine and create appropriate installation media

Skill: Determine hardware requirements and compatibility

When planning to install Windows 10, to ensure proper functionality and adequate performance, make sure that any existing or new devices meet the minimum hardware requirements for Windows 10. It is also important to verify that existing hardware, such as printers, scanners, and other peripherals, are compatible with Windows 10. Finally, ensure that any applications in use within your organization that will be installed on Windows 10 devices are capable of running on the new operating system.

This section covers how to:

- Identify the minimum and recommended hardware required to support Windows 10
- Determine the compatibility of hardware for the installation of Windows 10
- Verify the compatibility of your existing application infrastructure with Windows 10

Identify hardware requirements for Windows 10

Windows 10 can run adequately on hardware of a similar specification to that which supports Windows 7. Consequently, most of the computers in use within organizations today are Windows 10–capable. However, to get the best from Windows 10, you might consider installing the operating system on the computers and devices that exceed the minimum specifications described in this section.

TABLE 1-1 Minimum hardware requirements for Windows 10

Component	Requirement
Processor	A 1-gigahertz (GHz) or faster processor
Memory	1 gigabyte (GB) or RAM on 32-bit versions and 2 GB for 64-bit versions
Hard disk space	16 GB for 32-bit versions and 20 GB for 64-bit versions
Graphics card	DirectX 9 or later with a Windows Display Driver Model (WDDM) 1.0 driver
Display resolution	800x600 pixels

Although the guideline specifications in Table 1-1 indicate hardware that will support Windows 10, to get the best experience from Windows 10, consider using computers and devices that exceed these requirements.

Determine hardware compatibility for Windows 10

After you have verified that any new or existing computers on which you intend to install Windows 10 meet the minimum hardware requirements, verify that the operating system also supports any existing hardware devices and peripherals.

If you are purchasing new computers preinstalled with Windows 10, take no further action. However, if you are using existing computers, or want to attach existing hardware peripherals to your new computers, verify compatibility of these older computers and peripherals.

> *NOTE* **THE GET WINDOWS 10 APP**
>
> If you are running a supported version of Windows 7 or Windows 8.1, you can use the Get Windows 10 app to help determine the compatibility of Windows 10 on your computer system and its connected devices. The Get Windows 10 app is automatically installed on upgradeable versions of Windows.

If you have only one or two computers and a few peripheral devices to check, the easiest, and probably quickest, solution is to visit the hardware vendor's website and check for compatibility of these devices and peripherals. You can then download any required drivers for the version of Windows 10—32-bit or 64-bit—that you intend to install.

EXAM TIP

If the vendor does not provide a Windows 10–specific driver for its hardware, you might be able to use a driver from an earlier version of Windows, such as Windows 8.1. Note that you must still obtain 32-bit drivers for 32-bit versions of Windows 10 and 64-bit drivers for 64-bit versions of Windows 10.

Verify hardware compatibility for multiple devices

When you have many computers to install or upgrade to Windows 10, it is not feasible to visit each computer and verify device and peripheral compatibility. In this situation, consider using a tool to help determine compatibility.

The Microsoft Assessment And Planning Toolkit (MAP), shown in Figure 1-1, enables you to assess the computer devices attached to your network. MAP can be used to:

- Determine feasibility to upgrade scanned devices to Windows 10.
- Determine your organization's readiness to move to Microsoft Azure or Office 365.
- Plan for virtualizing workloads to Hyper-V.

FIGURE 1-1 Microsoft Assessment And Planning Toolkit

> **NOTE** **DOWNLOAD MAP**
>
> You can download MAP from the Microsoft website at *https://www.microsoft.com/download* */confirmation.aspx?id=7826*.

Inventory and assess your devices

After you have downloaded and installed MAP, you can perform an analysis of the devices on your network. This process does not require an agent to be installed on the target devices. Use the following procedure to analyze devices on your network for feasibility.

1. Launch the Microsoft Assessment And Planning Toolkit.

2. When prompted, create a new inventory database to store the assessment.

3. In the navigation pane, click the Desktop node.

4. In the details pane, under Scenarios, under Windows 10 Readiness, click Collect Inventory Data to open the Inventory And Assessment Wizard.

5. On the Inventory Scenarios page, in the Choose Your Scenario list, select the computer types that you want to analyze and then click Next.

    For example, select Windows Computers.

6. On the Discovery Methods page, select how you want to connect to the devices you are scanning. (For example, select Use Windows Networking Protocols.) Click Next.

7. On the Windows Networking Protocols page, examine the workgroups and domains that are discovered and listed and click Next.

8. On the All Computers Credentials page, enter credentials that can be used to sign in to the target devices and then click Next.

9. On the Credentials Order page, select the order in which your defined credentials are used to connect to devices; click Next and then click Finish.

   The discovery and assessment begins, as shown in Figure 1-2.

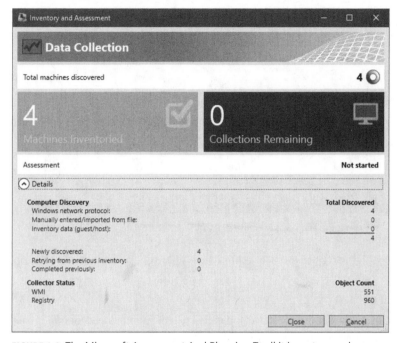

FIGURE 1-2 The Microsoft Assessment And Planning Toolkit inventory and assessment phase

10. When assessment is complete, click Close.

Analyze the report

After collecting the inventory, view and analyze the report by performing the following procedure.

1. In the Microsoft Assessment And Planning Toolkit dialog box, on the Desktop node, in the details pane, under Scenarios, click Windows 10 Readiness.

   Your report appears. You can choose to save the report as a Microsoft Excel spreadsheet.

2. Click Generate Windows 10 Readiness Report.

3. Click Close after the report is generated, and the report folder opens. Double-click the listed report file to open it in Microsoft Excel, as shown in Figure 1-3.

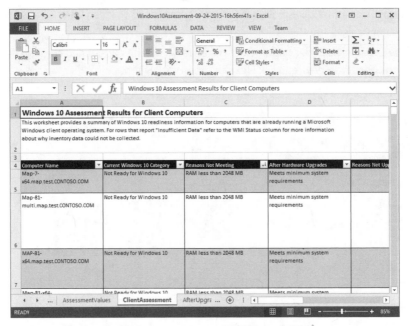

FIGURE 1-3 Viewing the MAP assessment report in Microsoft Excel

4. Click through the tabs to discover more details about the assessment. For example:

- Use the Summary tab to see how many machines are ready for Windows 10 and how many are not.

- The ClientAssessment tab shows individual machine details and identifies specific reasons for machines being assessed as not ready.

- The DiscoveredApplications tab shows the applications that are installed across your organization.

After you have completed your assessment, you can determine an appropriate course of action for the machines that have been identified as not ready for Windows 10. You might decide to upgrade the hardware to meet the requirements or to replace that hardware with new machines that meet the requirements for Windows 10.

Verify application compatibility for Windows 10

In addition to ensuring that your computer is compatible with Windows 10, it is also important to verify that all your organization's applications will run properly in Windows 10. Most applications that work correctly in Windows 7 work with little or no modification in Windows 10. However, some might experience minor issues, and others might not run properly at all.

Use the Application Compatibility Toolkit

You can download and use the Microsoft Application Compatibility Toolkit (ACT) to help determine whether your organization's installed applications will work correctly in Windows 10. ACT includes the following features.

- A database of known application issues and possible mitigations
- The Compatibility Administrator, shown in Figure 1-4, that you can use to create compatibility fixes to enable your applications to run properly

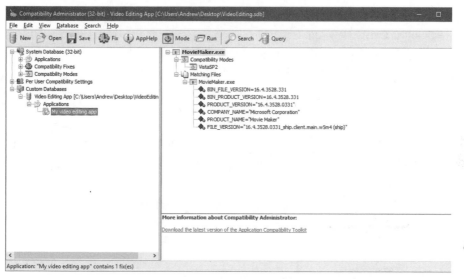

FIGURE 1-4 Analyzing and testing applications with Compatibility Administrator

- A setup analysis tool that helps identify issues with the installation process of your applications
- The Standard User Analyzer, which can help identify issues relating to running your application as a standard user

To test and fix an application, download the Windows Assessment and Deployment Kit (ADK) and then use the following procedure to test an application.

1. Build a Windows 10 computer that is representative of the configuration that you will use.
2. Install the required applications on this test workstation.
3. Run the applications and determine whether any have problems.
4. Install ACT on the test workstation. ACT requires access to a SQL Server database.

    You can use an existing instance of SQL Server on your network, or you can install SQL Server Express 2012 SP2 as part of the ACT installation and create the required database during setup. Note that when you install Windows ADK, you can choose to install the complete suite of tools, or select only the ACT.

5. Open Compatibility Administrator. Two versions are installed, one for 32-bit application testing and one for 64-bit application testing. Select the version appropriate to the architecture of your problematic application.

6. Create a custom database. This database holds information about your application during testing. In the navigation pane, under System Database, right-click Custom Databases and click New. Enter a meaningful name for your database, for example, **Video Editing App**.

7. Create a new application fix. Right-click your new database, point to Create New, and click Application Fix.

8. In the Create New Application Fix dialog box, enter the Name Of The Program To Be Fixed, the Name Of The Vendor Of This Program, and the Program File Location. This last entry is the executable file for your application. Click Next.

9. In the Compatibility Modes dialog box, shown in Figure 1-5, you can select a compatibility mode from a list. For example, you can choose to run the application as if it were running on Windows 95 or Windows Vista (Service Pack 2). Additional compatibility modes make specific adjustments to the behavior of the app, including running in 16BitColor mode or RunAsAdmin. After selecting the modes, click Next twice and then click Finish.

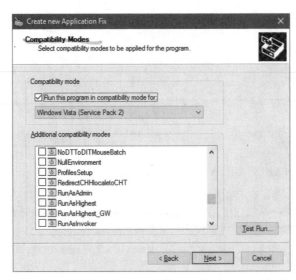

Figure 1-5 Configuring compatibility modes for an application fix

10. In the Compatibility Administrator console, on the toolbar, click Run and, in the Test Run Application dialog box, click OK.

    Your application loads within Compatibility Administrator.

11. Perform a series of standard tasks with the application. When you have finished testing the application, close it. If the application did not run successfully, repeat these steps until you find settings that do work. If the application did work with your settings, click Save on the toolbar.

12. Specify a location and name for the application compatibility fix. These are stored as .sdb files. Click Save.

13. You can then apply this fix file to the application within your organization by running the Sdbinst.exe command-line tool against the .sdb file. For example, at an elevated command prompt, type **sdbinst.exe d:\testapps\videoedit.sdb** and press Enter. You can also distribute the fix by using Group Policy Objects (GPOs) in an Active Directory Domain Services (AD DS) environment.

> *NOTE* **DOWNLOAD WINDOWS ADK**
> ACT is one of the tools in the Windows Assessment and Deployment Kit (Windows ADK). You can download the Windows ADK from the Microsoft website at *http://go.microsoft.com /fwlink/p/?LinkId=526740*.

Mitigate issues with application compatibility

If you discover compatibility issues with any of your existing applications, you have a number of possible solutions. You can:

- Use ACT to apply an application compatibility fix to the problematic application; this is sometimes also referred to as a *shim.*

- Determine whether updates exist for the application. Generally, updates are provided by software vendors for free or as part of a maintenance agreement.

- Determine whether upgrading to a more recent version of the application might resolve the compatibility issue. Software vendors normally charge for software upgrades.

- Build virtual machines based on an operating system environment in which the application works; for example, you could build a Windows XP guest operating system to support an old application.

Skill: Choose an upgrade or a clean installation

When considering how best to install Windows 10 on existing computers, you can choose between performing an upgrade and performing a clean installation. There are advantages and disadvantages to both approaches, and you should consider these carefully before you select a particular method.

Prepare an upgrade or migration strategy

It is important to understand the terminology used when describing the process of upgrading to Windows 10. *Upgrade* is often used generically to explain the licensing process of obtaining a version of Windows 10 that replaces an existing and supported upgradeable operating system, such as Windows 7 Home edition. This does not necessarily mean that you will perform an upgrade on an existing computer running Windows 7 and update that operating system to Windows 10.

When upgrading to Windows 10, you can choose between three methods. You can perform:

- **An in-place upgrade**   You can choose to update the existing operating system and perform what is called an *in-place upgrade* on existing hardware. User data and settings are retained.
- **A side-by-side migration**   In this scenario, the source and destination computers for the upgrade are different machines. You install a new computer with Windows 10 and then migrate the data and most user settings from the earlier operating system to the new computer.
- **A wipe-and-load migration**   In this scenario, the source and destination computer are the same. You back up the user data and settings to an external location and then install Windows 10 on the user's existing computer. Afterward, you restore user data and settings.

This section discusses all approaches to upgrading to Windows 10.

Supported upgrade paths

Performing an *in-place upgrade* can be the simplest option, especially when you have only a few computers to upgrade. However, you cannot perform an in-place upgrade on computers running a Windows version that does not share the same feature set as the edition of Windows 10 that you want to install.

Table 1-2 lists the supported upgrade paths based on the Windows edition.

TABLE 1-2 Supported upgrade paths to Windows 10

Earlier Windows version	Windows 10 Home	Windows 10 Pro	Windows 10 Enterprise
Windows 8/8.1	X		
Windows 8/8.1 Pro		X	

Earlier Windows version	Windows 10 Home	Windows 10 Pro	Windows 10 Enterprise
Windows 8/8.1 Enterprise			X
Windows RT			
Windows 7 Starter	X		
Windows 7 Home Basic	X		
Windows 7 Home Premium	X		
Windows 7 Professional		X	
Windows 7 Ultimate		X	
Windows 7 Enterprise			X

You will notice from Table 1-2 that direct upgrades between editions are not supported. That is, you cannot upgrade directly from Windows 7 Home to Windows 10 Enterprise.

> **NOTE** **UPGRADING FROM WINDOWS 7 HOME**
>
> If you want to upgrade from Windows 7 Home to Windows 10 Enterprise, you can achieve that in a two-stage process. First, upgrade to Windows 10 Home and then upgrade to Windows 10 Enterprise.

After you have determined whether your upgrade path is supported, choose how to perform the process of upgrading to Windows 10.

Considerations for performing an in-place upgrade

When determining whether to use the in-place upgrade method to upgrade to Windows 10, consider the following factors.

- It is a simple process and is ideal for small groups of computers.
- It provides for rollback to the earlier version of Windows.
- User and application settings and user data files are retained automatically.
- Installed applications are retained; however, retained applications might not work correctly after upgrading from an earlier Windows version.
- You do not need to provide for external storage space for data and settings migration.
- It does not allow for edition changes and is available only on supported operating systems (see Table 1.2).
- It does not provide the opportunity to start with a clean, standardized configuration.

Considerations for performing a migration

When determining whether to use one of the two migration methods to upgrade to Windows 10, consider the following factors.

- You have an opportunity to create a clean installation, free from remnant files and settings.
- You can reconfigure the existing disk partitions.
- You can upgrade to any Windows 10 edition, irrespective of the earlier Windows edition.
- Migration is a more complex process, and you must use migration tools such as USMT to migrate data and settings.
- You require storage space for user settings and files to be migrated.
- Applications are not retained, and you must manually reinstall these.

Perform an in-place upgrade to Windows 10

As you have seen, there are three ways to upgrade to Windows 10. The preferred method for small groups of computers is to use an in-place upgrade. Using an in-place upgrade enables you to retain all the users' applications, data files, and user and application settings. During the in-place upgrade, the Windows 10 setup program automatically retains these settings.

> *IMPORTANT* **BACK UP DATA FILES**
>
> It is important to perform a backup of user data files prior to launching an in-place upgrade to guard against possible data loss.

You perform an in-place upgrade to Windows 10 when your users will continue to use their existing computers. To perform an in-place upgrade, complete the following procedure.

1. Evaluate the user's computer to determine that it meets minimum hardware requirements for Windows 10 and that Windows 10 supports all hardware.
2. Verify that all applications work on Windows 10.
3. Optionally, back up the user's data files.
4. Run the **Setup.exe** program on the Windows 10 product DVD.
5. Choose Upgrade when prompted and complete the setup wizard.

In addition to installing the upgrade by using the Windows 10 product DVD and running Setup.exe, you can also obtain the upgrade from Windows Update automatically. Your computer must be up to date with service packs and additional updates for Windows Update to register your computer for this automatic upgrade.

Perform a migration to Windows 10

You perform a migration to Windows 10 when your users have new computers on which to install Windows 10. During the process, you perform the following high-level procedures.

1. Verify that all applications work on Windows 10.

2. If necessary, perform a clean installation of the appropriate edition of Windows 10 on the user's new computer.

3. On the new computer, install all the user's applications.

4. Back up the user's data files and settings from the old computer.

5. Restore the user's data files and settings on the new computer.

To perform the backup and restore of users' data and settings, use the User State Migration Tool (USMT). USMT is one of the tools in the Windows ADK.

Perform a side-by-side migration

When you opt to use the *side-by-side* migration strategy, illustrated in Figure 1-6, use the following procedure to complete the task.

1. Either obtain a computer with Windows 10 preinstalled or install Windows 10 on a new computer. When Setup.exe prompts you, choose Custom (Advanced). This is the destination computer.

2. Install the same applications on the destination computer as are presently on the source computer.

3. Create an external intermediate storage location, such as a file server shared folder, for the storage of user data and settings. This must be accessible from both the source and destination computers.

4. Use the USMT to collect the user's data and settings and store them in the external intermediate store.

5. Use the USMT to collect the user's data and settings from the external intermediate store and install them in the destination computer.

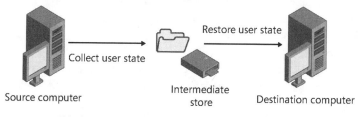

FIGURE 1-6 Side-by-side migration to Windows 10

Perform a wipe-and-load migration

When you opt to use the *wipe-and-load* migration strategy, illustrated in Figure 1-7, use the following procedure to complete the task.

1. Create an external storage location, such as a file server shared folder, for the storage of user data and settings.

2. Use the USMT to collect the user's data and settings and store them in the external location.

3. Install Windows 10 on the existing computer. When Setup.exe prompts you, choose Custom (Advanced).

4. Reinstall the applications on the computer.

5. Use the USMT to restore the user's data and settings from the external location.

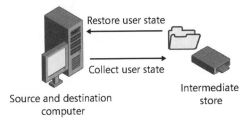

FIGURE 1-7 Wipe-and-load migration to Windows 10

Migrate user data and settings

As part of both migration strategies, you must migrate user data and settings to the destination computer. Consequently, it is important to determine where these data and settings reside and to select a tool to perform this migration.

> *NOTE* **WINDOWS EASY TRANSFER**
>
> For a small number of computers, consider using Windows Easy Transfer to migrate user data and settings between the source and destination computer. Windows Easy Transfer is not included on Windows 10, but you can copy the required files from the C:\Windows \system32\migwiz folder on a computer running Windows 7.

You should migrate all of the users' local data and settings. It is not necessary to migrate server-based data because this remains accessible after the migration. User data and settings consist of the following components.

- **User settings** This component contains all the configuration settings specific to a particular user.

- **User registry** The HKEY_CURRENT_USER hive of the registry contains user-specific settings.

- **Application data** The AppData folder contains the application-related settings that are not part of the registry.
- **User data** All user-specific folders and files are stored in subfolders beneath Documents, Favorites, Pictures, Videos, Music, and others.

You can use USMT to migrate user data and settings.

Quick check

- You want to upgrade a small number of computers to Windows 10. They all meet the minimum hardware requirements. Which upgrade strategy should you select?

Quick check answer

- You can choose either the wipe-and-load strategy, saving the user state to an intermediate storage location, or the in-place upgrade strategy, the easier option.

Skill: Determine editions by device type

Before you can deploy Windows 10 within your organization, you must select the appropriate edition of Windows 10. Your choice will be based on the form factor of the devices your users use and which specific features your users require.

This section covers how to:

- Select an appropriate edition of Windows 10
- Determine whether to implement 32-bit or 64-bit versions of Windows 10

Select a Windows 10 edition

Windows 10 is aimed at a wide audience of potential users, from individuals with a single device to large enterprise-level organizations with thousands of computers. The specific editions of Windows 10, listed in Table 1-3, are designed to address the varying needs of this diverse user base.

TABLE 1-3 Windows 10 editions

Edition	Features
Windows 10 Home	Designed primarily for home users and includes similar features to those found in Windows 8.1 Home, plus: ■ Microsoft Edge ■ Continuum tablet mode for touch-capable devices ■ Cortana ■ Windows Hello ■ Virtual desktops ■ A number of built-in universal Windows apps such as Photos, Maps, Mail, Calendar, Music, and Video Note that in Windows 10 Home, you cannot control updates as was possible on earlier Windows versions; these are received automatically.
Windows 10 Pro	Includes the same features as in Windows 10 Home but additionally provides: ■ Domain Join and Group Policy Management ■ Microsoft Azure Active Directory Join ■ BitLocker ■ Enterprise Mode Internet Explorer ■ Client Hyper-V ■ Windows Store for organizations ■ Enterprise Data Protection In Windows 10 Pro, updates are provided by Windows Update for Business. This provides for more control over updates than with Windows 10 Home. In addition, security updates are made available more quickly.
Windows 10 Enterprise	Windows 10 Enterprise builds on the features of Windows 10 Pro, providing additional features of relevance to larger organizations, including: ■ DirectAccess ■ Windows To Go Creator ■ AppLocker ■ Windows BranchCache ■ Start Screen Control with Group Policy ■ Credential Guard ■ Device Guard In addition to the ability to manage updates to Windows with Windows Update for Business, Enterprise customers can also access the Long-Term Servicing Branch (LTSB) as a special deployment.
Windows 10 Enterprise LTSB	This specialized edition of Windows 10 Enterprise receives security and other important updates in the normal way but does not receive feature updates. This enables organizations to know that their environment does not change over time. Windows 10 Enterprise LTSB does not include: ■ Microsoft Edge ■ Windows Store client ■ Cortana ■ Many built-in universal Windows apps

Edition	Features
Windows 10 Education	Provides the same features as Windows 10 Enterprise but does not offer support for LTSB. Windows 10 Education is only available through academic Volume Licensing.
Windows 10 Mobile	Designed for phones and smaller tablets, this edition offers broadly the same feature set as the Windows 10 Home desktop edition. It includes many of the same universal Windows apps as well as a touch-optimized version of Microsoft Office.
Windows 10 Mobile Enterprise	This edition offers features similar to Windows 10 Mobile. Windows 10 Mobile Enterprise provides security updates more quickly. It is available only to Volume Licensing customers.

Microsoft has also stated its intention to release a number of Windows 10 Internet of Things (IoT) editions. IoT editions will be made available after the release of Windows 10 desktop and mobile editions.

> **NEED MORE REVIEW?** **COMPARE WINDOWS 10 EDITIONS**
>
> To find out more about these Windows 10 editions, visit the Microsoft TechNet website at *http://aka.ms/k8iq7l.*

Choose the 32-bit or 64-bit versions

You can choose between 32-bit and 64-bit versions of all desktop editions of Windows 10. Generally, it would be usual to choose 64-bit versions unless there is a compelling reason to use 32-bit versions, such as because your hardware does not support the 64-bit architecture.

The features described in Table 1-3 for the various editions of Windows 10 are applicable for both 32-bit and 64-bit versions. However, 64-bit versions of Windows 10 do provide a number of advantages, including:

- **Memory**   Sixty-four-bit versions of Windows 10 can address more physical memory than 32-bit versions. Specifically, 32-bit versions are limited to 4 GB of RAM, whereas 64-bit versions have no such limitation.
- **Security**   Features such as Kernel Patch Protection, mandatory kernel-mode driver signing, and Data Execution Prevention (DEP) are available only in 64-bit versions of Windows 10.
- **Client Hyper-V**   This feature is only available on 64-bit versions of Windows 10. Your hardware must also support second-level address translation (SLAT).
- **Performance**   Sixty-four-bit processors can handle more data during each CPU clock cycle. This benefit is only realized when running a 64-bit operating system.

> **NOTE**   **16-BIT APPLICATIONS**
>
> Sixty-four-bit versions of Windows 10 do not support 16-bit applications directly. If your organization has 16-bit apps, consider using Client Hyper-V to run them.

Quick check

- It is important for your organization's computers to implement whole-drive encryption. It is also necessary for your users to be able to connect remotely using DirectAccess. Which edition of Windows 10 must you select?

Quick check answer

- Windows 10 Pro and Windows 10 Enterprise both support BitLocker drive encryption, but only Windows 10 Enterprise supports DirectAccess for remote connectivity. You must select Windows 10 Enterprise.

Skill: Determine requirements for particular features

A number of features in some editions of Windows 10 require specialist hardware or software configuration. This section explores those features and identifies any special hardware and configuration requirements.

This section covers how to:

- Identify hardware and configuration requirements for general Windows 10 features
- Identify hardware and configuration requirements for Windows 10 security features

 EXAM TIP

It is important to know that some of the new features of Windows 10 are available only on computers and devices that support specific hardware components.

General features

These features provide for general usability and functional improvements and include:

- **Client Hyper-V**   This enables you to create, manage, and run virtual machines that you can install with different guest operating systems to support, perhaps, earlier line-of-business (LOB) apps that will not run natively on Windows 10. Requirements of the Client Hyper-V feature are:

    - A 64-bit version of either the Windows 10 Pro or Windows 10 Enterprise edition.

    - A computer that supports SLAT.

    - Additional physical memory to support running the virtual machines. A minimum of 2 GB of additional memory is recommended.

To use Client Hyper-V to run virtual machines, you also need additional physical memory in your computer. It is recommended to add at least 2 GB of RAM to support this feature.

- **Cortana**   You can use Cortana as a digital assistant to control Windows 10 and perform tasks such as writing email, setting reminders, and performing web searches. Because Cortana is voice-activated and controlled, your Windows 10 device requires a microphone.

- **Continuum**   With Windows 10 available on a variety of devices types and form factors, with Continuum, Microsoft endeavors to optimize the user experience across device types by detecting the hardware on your device and changing to that hardware. For example, Windows 10 determines when you are using a non-touch desktop computer and enables traditional interaction with the operating system by use of a mouse. For users of hybrid devices, such as the new Microsoft Surface Pro 4, when you disconnect a keyboard cover, Windows 10 switches to tablet mode. When you use Windows 10 Mobile, Continuum enables you to use a second external display and optimizes app behavior on that display.

- **Miracast**   Windows 10 uses Miracast to connect your Windows device wirelessly to an external monitor or projector. The only thing needed is a Miracast-compatible external monitor or projector.

- **Touch**   Windows 10, like Windows 8 before it, is a touch-centric operating system. Although you do not need a touch device to use Windows 10, some features are made more usable through the use of touch. To implement touch, your tablet or display monitor must support touch.

- **OneDrive**   Users of Windows 10 are entitled to free online storage. OneDrive provides this storage. It is built into the Windows 10 operating system like any other type of storage, and consequently, it is easy to use. You must have a Microsoft account to use OneDrive.

- **Sync your settings**   When you use more than one Windows 10 device, it is convenient for your user settings to move with you to the new device. You can use the Sync Your Settings feature of Windows 10 to ensure that settings such as theme, Internet Explorer settings (including favorites), passwords, language, and ease of access are synchronized between your devices. You must have a Microsoft account to use this feature.

> **NOTE   ACTIVE STYLUS SUPPORT**
>
> Some touch devices have screens that support active stylus input. Active styluses provide for pressure-sensitive input and enable you to use your device for accurate note taking and drawing. Passive styluses are supported on all touch devices but do not support these more advanced features.

Security features

Windows 10 also includes a number of features that can help make your device more secure. These features include:

- **BitLocker**   A Trusted Platform Module (TPM) works with BitLocker to help protect against data theft and offline tampering by providing for whole-drive encryption. Requirements for BitLocker include:

  - A computer installed with either Windows 10 Pro or Windows 10 Enterprise.

  - Optionally, a TPM. Using a TPM with BitLocker enables Window to verify startup component integrity. You do not require a TPM in your computer to use BitLocker, but if you wish to use BitLocker with a TPM, the minimum requirement is TPM 1.2.

- **Device health attestation**   With the increase in use of users' own devices, it is important to ensure that Windows 10 devices connecting to your organization meet the security and compliance requirements of your organization. Device health attestation uses measured boot data to help perform this verification. To implement device health attestation, your Windows 10 devices must have TPM 2.0.

- **Secure Boot**   When Secure Boot is enabled, you can only start the operating system by using an operating system loader that is signed using a digital certificate stored in the UEFI Secure Boot DB. This helps prevent malicious code from loading during the Windows 10 start process. Requirements for Secure Boot include:

  - Computer firmware that supports Unified Extensible Firmware Interface (UEFI) v2.3.1 Errata B and for which the Microsoft Windows Certification Authority is in the UEFI signature database.

- **Two-factor authentication**   This is a process that provides for user authentication based on two factors: something the user knows, such as a password; and something the user has, such as a biometric feature (fingerprint or facial features); or a device, such as a cell phone. Requirements for two-factor authentication include:

  - A fingerprint reader, a cell phone, or an illuminated infrared camera.

  - Windows Hello   Windows Hello provides a more secure and improved sign-in experience for users. It has the following requirements.

  - Biometric devices that support the Windows Biometric Framework, for example, an illuminated infrared camera to enable facial recognition or iris detection, or a fingerprint reader.

- **Virtual Secure Mode**   This feature moves some sensitive elements of the operating system to *trustlets* that run in a Hyper-V container that Windows cannot access. This helps make the operating system more secure. Currently, this is only available in the Windows 10 Enterprise edition.

- **Virtual Smart card**   This feature offers comparable security benefits in two-factor authentication to that provided by physical smart cards. Virtual smart cards require a compatible TPM (version 1.2 or later).

Skill: Identify a strategy and prepare the installation media

You can choose from among a number of methods when considering how best to install Windows 10. Generally, the size of your organization and the number of devices that you must install will determine the strategy that you select. After selecting a strategy to install Windows, you must prepare the installation media to support your strategy.

This section covers how to:

- Select an installation strategy for Windows 10
- Determine the appropriate installation media to support your selected installation strategy

---

Select an installation strategy

You can choose from among a number of strategies when planning the installation of Windows 10. These strategies have different prerequisites, and some might require additional software components and configuration before you can begin installing Windows 10. Table 1-4 describes these strategies.

TABLE 1-4 Windows 10 installation strategies

Deployment option	Description
High-touch retail media deployment	Suitable for small organizations with few devices to install with Windows 10. Requires no specialist IT skills or additional services or components. All that is required is one or more copies of the Windows 10 installation media, which can be provided on a DVD, or the appropriate files can be accessed on a USB storage device or even from a network file server shared folder.
Low-touch deployment	Suitable for larger organizations that intend to install a few hundred devices, using limited installer intervention. Because the strategy relies on the use of image deployment and additional services, such as Windows Deployment Services (WDS) and, optionally, Microsoft Deployment Toolkit (MDT), some specialist IT skills are also required.
Zero-touch deployment	For very large organizations with thousands of devices. Requires a considerable investment in IT skills to facilitate this strategy. Also requires the use of MDT and Microsoft System Center Configuration Manager to deploy Windows 10, using no installer intervention.

Determine the appropriate installation media

Windows 10 uses an image-based installation and deployment model; that is, the Windows operating system installation files are packaged in an image file that is used as an installation source during the installation process.

A default installation image, Install.wim, is provided on the installation DVD in the \Sources folder. Although you can choose to use this default image, you can also configure it to create custom installation images that better suit the needs of your organization. Customizations might include:

- Selecting a particular edition of Windows 10.
- Choosing which Windows features are enabled.
- Including Wi-Fi profiles and virtual private network (VPN) profiles.
- Adding universal apps or desktop applications.

The Windows ADK contains a number of tools that you can use to create and manage Windows 10 images to support your installation needs. These are:

- **DISM**   The Deployment Image Servicing and Management (DISM) command-line tool enables you to capture, deploy, and manage Windows images. You can use the tool to manage both online and offline images.
- **Imaging and Configuration Designer**   This tool enables you to build and provision Windows 10 images; it provides both a graphical and a command-line interface.

You can then deploy these custom images to target computers within your organization that require Windows 10. You can perform this deployment in a number of ways and by using a variety of deployment technologies and tools, depending on the installation strategy you previously selected. Options include:

- **DVD installation**   You can use the default installation media, or you can use a customized image that you created. The device you are installing to requires an optical drive.
- **USB installation**   Once again, you can use the default or custom Windows images. This method is quicker, and although it does not require an optical drive, you might need to reconfigure your computer's BIOS or UEFI firmware settings to support startup from USB.

EXAM TIP

You can perform an unattended installation using this method, provided an unattended answer file is present on the USB device. Answer files are discussed in the following section.

- **WDS deployment**   To use this method, Dynamic Host Configuration Protocol (DHCP) must be available to network clients on your network, and your target computers running Windows 10 must support Pre-Boot Execution Environment (PXE). Combined with unattended answer files and custom images, you can use this method to deploy multiple images to multiple computers at the same time by using multicast.
- **Image-based installation**   By starting your computer into Windows Preinstallation Environment (Windows PE), you can use DISM to apply an image locally to the target computer. Alternatively, you can use MDT and System Center 2012 R2 Configuration Manager to deploy the image and desktop apps to the target devices.

- **Shared network folder installation** You can use Windows PE to start your computer and map a network drive to installation files and images on a network file shared folder. This is a comparatively inefficient method and has been replaced by the other methods previously described.

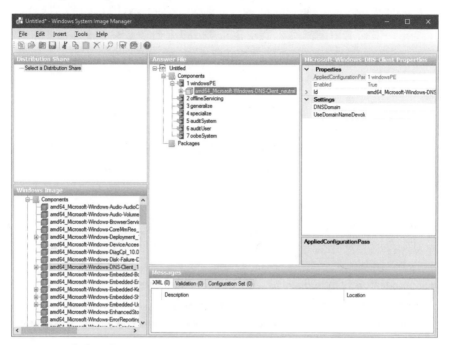

FIGURE 1-8 Windows System Image Manager

- **Windows SIM** The Windows System Image Manager (Windows SIM) enables you to create installation answer files for use in automated deployments. These answer files contain the configuration options used to install Windows 10. You can then:
    - Associate these answer files with a local copy of the installation media, perhaps on a USB memory stick. This provides for a semi-automated interactive installation.

> *NOTE* **NAMING THE ANSWER FILE**
>
> If you copy the answer file you create by using Windows SIM to a memory stick, call the file Autounattend.xml. Windows setup knows to search for this named file in the root of the installation media.

- Place the answer files on a deployment server, such as a Windows Server 2012 R2 server running the WDS server role, together with your Windows 10 deployment images. This provides for a light-touch deployment approach.

■ **Windows PE** Windows PE is used to start a computer that is being deployed with Windows 10. It enables access to Windows file systems and is, in essence, a partial Windows operating system. You can use the generic Windows PE provided on the product DVD, or you can customize it (using tools in Windows ADK) to address your specific deployment needs. You can then launch Windows PE from a DVD or a USB memory stick or across the network, using PXE.

Summary

- The Windows 10 hardware requirements are similar to those for Windows 8.1.
- You can use the MAP toolkit to assess your organization's hardware readiness for Windows 10.
- The ACT enables you to test application compatibility with Windows 10 and, where necessary, create compatibility fixes for problematic applications.
- You can choose between three upgrade strategies: in-place, side-by-side, and wipe-and-load.
- Different Windows 10 editions provide different feature sets, based on an organization's needs.
- Some features of Windows 10 require special hardware or additional configuration.
- You can use a number of tools in Windows ADK, including the Windows ICD, to create, customize, and distribute Windows 10 images for deployment throughout your organization.

Thought experiment

In this thought experiment, demonstrate your skills and knowledge of the topics covered in this chapter. You can find answers to this thought experiment in the next section.

A. Datum has 3,000 workstations currently running Windows 7 and Windows 8.1. Most of the computer hardware is of a similar specification. A. Datum wants to replace Windows 7 and Windows 8.1 with a unified client operating system: Windows 10 Enterprise. All computers must be running Windows 10 Enterprise at the end of the project.

As a consultant for A. Datum, answer the following questions.

1. What is the best method for A. Datum to upgrade to Windows 10?

2. How could you assess the readiness for the organization's computers to upgrade to Windows 10?

3. How could you determine what applications are in use throughout A. Datum?

4. You experience a number of problems with a graphics editing package in use in the Sales department at A. Datum. What could you do to resolve this?

Thought experiment answer

This section contains the solution to the thought experiment. Each answer explains why the answer choice is correct.

1. An in-place upgrade is the most straightforward option and is the preferred method.

2. You could use the MAP toolkit to assess computer readiness. The MAP report identifies the computers that do not meet the hardware or software requirements for Windows 10.

3. The MAP toolkit also reports on installed applications on inventoried computers.

4. If an application does not work in Windows 10, you can use the ACT in Windows ADK. This enables you to determine the cause of the problem and create a compatibility fix for the application. You can then distribute the fix throughout the organization by using Group Policy Objects (GPOs).

CHAPTER 2

Install Windows 10

There are multiple methods of installing or upgrading a device with Windows 10. This chapter reviews each method and focuses on the skills required to install and migrate the operating system in a number of scenarios, including native boot, installing to a virtual hard disk drive (VHD), and configuring additional regional and language support.

Skills covered in this chapter:

- Perform clean installations
- Upgrade by Windows Update
- Upgrade using installation media
- Configure native boot scenarios
- Migrate from previous versions of Windows
- Install Windows 10 onto a VHD
- Boot Windows 10 from VHD
- Install on bootable USB
- Install additional Windows features
- Configure Windows for additional regional and language support

Skill: Perform clean installations

Although the vast majority of PCs will be purchased preinstalled with Windows 10, most corporations will re-install the operating system to avoid the additional software that original equipment manufacturers (OEMs) include with their PCs. This software is often referred to as *bloatware* and can include utilities and tools or trial versions of software such as Microsoft Office or anti-spyware.

Installation media were created in Chapter 1, "Prepare for installation requirements," which you will need to perform a clean installation of Windows. You need to configure your BIOS or UEFI to enable you to boot to your installation media, such as a USB drive. This can be achieved by modifying the BIOS setting or choosing a custom boot order during the boot process.

There are several methods of installing Windows onto a device, as shown in Table 2-1, and you should familiarize yourself with each prior to taking the exam.

TABLE 2-1 Windows installation methods

Installation Method	Description
Install from DVD	You can use the installation media provided with a retail copy of the operating system, or you can use the downloadable media obtained from the Microsoft Volume Licensing Service (MVLS) or Microsoft Developer Network (MSDN) and burn it to optical media.
Install from USB	Use this method to install the operating system on one computer at a time. Installation from a USB device is quicker than using a DVD. You must modify BIOS or UEFI settings to enable boot from USB.
Install from Windows Deployment Services (Windows DS)	Requires Windows DS and Dynamic Host Configuration Protocol (DHCP) on a Windows-based server on the network. The target computer network card must support Pre-Boot Execution Environment (PXE). Using Windows DS allows automated installation of system images and deployment of Windows to multiple computers simultaneously by using multicast.
Install an image from Windows Preinstallation Environment (Windows PE)	Boot the device by using Windows PE and then use one of the following deployment options. 1. Use Deployment Image Servicing and Management (DISM) to apply the Windows image. 2. Use the Microsoft Deployment Toolkit (MDT) deployment solution. 3. Use the System Center 2012 R2 Configuration Manager (SCCM) deployment solution. Both MDT and SCCM are enterprise-level solutions that enable you to deploy Windows to hundreds or thousands of devices at once and configure lite-touch installation (LTI) or zero-touch installation (ZTI) for either minimal user interaction or no user interaction, respectively, during the deployment.
Install over the network	Start the computer by using Windows PE and connect to a copy of the installation files stored on a shared network folder. You would use this method when you are unable to use a USB device, Windows DS, MDT, or Configuration Manager.

During a clean installation on a new hard drive, perform the following steps to install Windows 10.

1. Insert the installation media and start the computer.

2. When the Windows Setup screen appears, choose the appropriate regional settings and then click Next.

3. In the Windows Setup window, click Install Now.

4. On the License Terms page, select the I Accept The License Terms check box and then click Next.

5. On the Which Type Of Installation Do You Want page, click Custom: Install Windows Only (Advanced).

6. On the Where Do You Want To Install Windows page, select the drive on which you want to install Windows and click Next.

   Windows will now complete the installation.

The Windows installer now continues without user input and performs the following stages.

- Copying Windows files
- Getting files ready for installation
- Installing features
- Installing updates
- Finishing up

Depending on your hardware performance, Windows should complete the clean install process within 15–20 minutes, and the machine will restart several times. A device with a solid-state drive (SSD) will outperform a slower Serial Advanced Technology Attachment (SATA) drive. During the final stages of installation, the Getting Ready notification appears while Windows installs device drivers specific to the hardware.

After Windows has completed the installation, the Get Going Fast page appears, as shown in Figure 2-1. This option enables you to customize Windows settings for personalization, location information, and various telemetry data relating to your browsing activity. Microsoft recommends that users allow these settings to be made; however, it is recommended that you ensure that you understand the implications of allowing the express settings option.

> **NOTE EXISTING OPERATING SYSTEM DRIVE**
>
> For a clean installation of Windows 10 on a device on which an operating system is already installed, erase this partition either by formatting or deleting any partitions present during the setup process.

After the Get Going Fast page, you create an administrative user account for the PC and protect it with a password. Windows 10 will then complete the installation process, which will include:

- Creating a user profile.
- Setting up your apps.
- Updating default apps.

On completion, you are presented with the default Windows 10 desktop with the illuminated Windows logo.

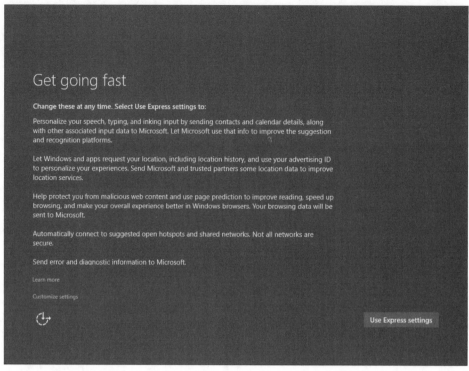

FIGURE 2-1 Get Going Fast

Skill: Upgrade by using Windows Update

With Windows 10, you can upgrade using physical installation media or directly over the Internet, using Windows Update. Only Windows 7 Service Pack 1 (SP1) or Windows 8.1 editions can be upgraded directly. The device must be connected to the Internet to perform this upgrade. The process is relatively fast and, where possible, the Windows installer uses the Background Intelligent Transfer Service (BITS) to optimize the file download to the device.

> **This section covers how to:**
> - Identify editions that can be upgraded by using Windows Update
> - Perform the upgrade
> - Go back to a previous version of Windows
> - Block upgrading to Windows 10

Identify editions that can be upgraded by using Windows Update

Not all editions of Windows 7 or 8.1 can be upgraded using Windows Update; the data shown in Table 2-2 lists the upgrade possibilities.

TABLE 2-2 Suitability for Windows Update upgrade to Windows 10

SKU to be upgraded	Windows Update
Windows 7 Pro	No
Windows 7 Enterprise	No
Windows 7 Pro with SP1	Yes, with update KB 2952664 installed
Windows 7 Enterprise with SP1	No
Windows 8 Pro	No
Windows 8 Enterprise	No
Windows 8.1 Pro	Yes, with updates KB 2919355 and KB 2976978 installed
Windows 8.1 Enterprise	No
Windows 10 Pro (1507)	Yes (if not activated using Key Management Service (KMS)
Windows 10 Enterprise (1507)	Yes (if not activated using KMS)

From Table 2-2, you can see that the Enterprise editions of Windows 7, Windows 8, and Windows 8.1 are not eligible for upgrading using Windows Update.

The future servicing methodology of Windows 10 relies on the ability to disseminate and install upgrades by using Windows Update. The promotional period has therefore been an extremely beneficial pilot of the upgrade technology built into this version of Windows.

If the device is running Windows 7 or 8.1, in theory it should allow the upgrade to proceed. However, you should ensure that the device has the minimum hardware requirements, especially if you suspect the device has previously been upgraded. Windows 8.1 devices must have the Windows 8.1 Update (KB2919355) installed before upgrading to Windows 10.

> **NOTE** **SYSTEM REQUIREMENTS**
>
> If you are upgrading a device, consider checking whether the device hardware supports Windows 10 by reviewing the system requirements at *https://www.microsoft.com/windows /windows-10-specifications?OCID=win10_null_vanity_win10specs*.

Perform the upgrade

When you are ready to upgrade to Windows 10, you need to be connected to the Internet. The operating system can then download the latest Windows updates. When the system is up to date, Windows can download the Get Windows 10 (GWX) notification utility that enables you to upgrade directly to Windows 10. The GWX app is installed in C:\Windows\System32 \GWX and can be seen running in Task Manager with the process called GWX.exe.

After the GWX tool has been installed, it is very persistent at reminding you to upgrade, and many consumers discovered that it was not easy to disable or remove the Get Windows 10 icon that appears in your notification area.

> **NOTE GWX NOT APPEARING**
>
> If you are using Windows 7 SP1 or Windows 8.1 and the GWX app is not installed, you can check Windows Update to see whether the KB3035583 update has been hidden. If the update is not found, you can review the instructions at *https://support.microsoft.com /kb/3035583*.

From time to time, the notification icon might display a larger prompt telling you to upgrade to Windows 10. Clicking the Windows icon that appears in the notification area opens a dialog box that encourages you to upgrade now or to start the download and upgrade later, as shown in Figure 2-2.

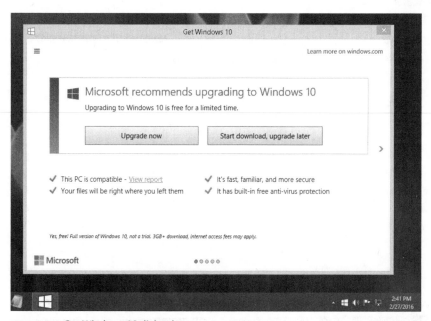

FIGURE 2-2 Get Windows 10 dialog box

If you perform a clean install of Windows 8.1, you will be prompted to upgrade to Windows 10 even before you log on to the device, as shown in Figure 2-3.

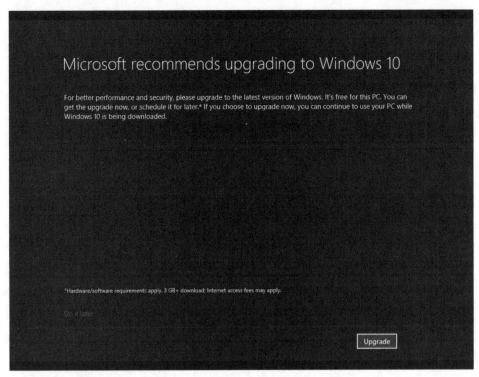

FIGURE 2-3 Windows 10 upgrade during Windows 8.1 installation

Windows Update will list Windows 10 as an optional update, which you can install as shown in Figure 2-4. To perform the installation, which is a 2604.5 MB download, you must have administrative privileges. You must also accept the Microsoft software license terms when you agree to the upgrade. Rather than download a Windows Image (WIM) file or ISO file, Windows 10 uses the new Electronic Software Download (ESD) file format and downloads the image .esd file to the C:\Windows\SoftwareDistribution\Download folder. During the initial installation phase, the installer copies the Install.esd file to the C:\$Windows.~BT\Sources folder.

> *NOTE* **NEW ESD FILE FORMAT**
>
> The ESD file is a compressed and encrypted version of the traditional WIM file format. The imaging file contains the Windows operating system in a protected container to ensure that it is not tampered with during delivery. The compression used allows the ESD disk image file to be approximately 30 percent smaller than the corresponding native WIM image, which makes it a better choice for use when updating over the Internet.

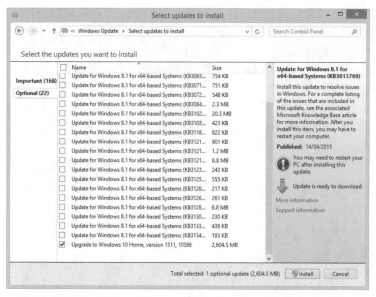

FIGURE 2-4 Windows Update Upgrade to Windows 10

After downloading, the installation is prepared. As part of the upgrade process, a backup of the current operation system is made and stored in the Windows.old folder on the system drive. If the device is low on disk space or has only a small drive, you might see a message, "Windows Needs More Space," as shown in Figure 2-5. Windows allows you to store the Windows.old backup folder on an external drive such as an external USB drive and Windows Setup to use it to back up the previous version of Windows to the USB external drive. The upgrade dialog box will advise how large the external drive must be, and this can be 8–10 GB, depending on the version of Windows being upgraded.

If you attach an external hard drive or USB drive as shown in Figure 2-5, click Refresh to advance the upgrade process.

The saved version of Windows enables the user to revert to the previous version of Windows, and Windows retains it for 30 days after the upgrade. This is only possible while Windows 10 has access to the Windows.old folder on the PC or external hard drive.

After the device has created a backup of the current installation to a temporary folder named $WINDOWS.~TMP, Windows announces it is ready to install the upgrade, as shown in Figure 2-6. After the upgrade has been downloaded and a backup created, the upgrade can be completed or scheduled for a later time. If you click Schedule It For Later in the dialog box shown in Figure 2-6, you will be able to choose and confirm the date and time for a future upgrade appointment or start the upgrade now.

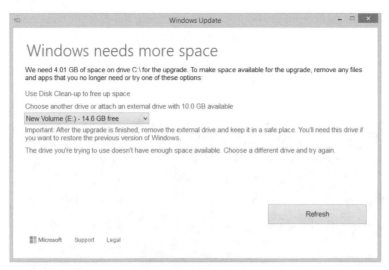

FIGURE 2-5 Windows Update, requiring more space

***NOTE* UPGRADE APPOINTMENT TIME CANNOT BE CHANGED AFTER SCHEDULING**

If you choose to defer and schedule the upgrade of a device to Windows 10, you cannot change the time you specified for the upgrade. The upgrade will commence automatically. If the PC is turned off at the scheduled time, the upgrade will start the next time the device is turned on.

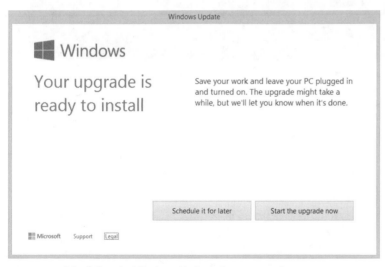

FIGURE 2-6 Scheduling the Windows Update after preparation

Windows restarts several times during the upgrade process. During the upgrade, you see a status screen that details the various activities, as shown in Figure 2-7. The key stages are:

- Copying files.
- Installing features and drivers.
- Configuring settings.

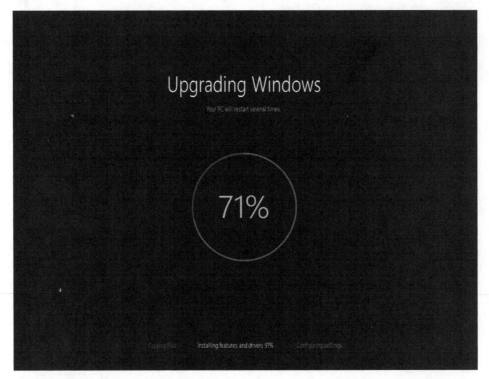

FIGURE 2-7 Windows 10 upgrading status

The Windows Recovery Environment (WinRE) provides the platform for installing the upgrade. Windows 10 is installed to a new temporary folder called $WINDOWS.~BT\NewOS, and all the existing folders from the down-level operating system, such as Windows, Program Files, Users, and Perflogs, are moved to the Windows.old folder so that, if necessary, you can recover the system at a later stage.

During the second stage of the process, the drivers are installed in the drivers store. Then, as part of the final stage, the Windows files stored in $WINDOWS.~BT\NewOS are moved to the root of the system drive. When completed, Setupact.log will have been moved to C:\Windows\Panther directory, and the Setupapi log files, which are useful for troubleshooting driver installation issues, will be stored in C:\Windows\INF\.

When the percentage reaches 100 percent, the upgrade process presents a new screen, which announces "Welcome to Windows 10!" and requires you to enter the password for the user who initiated the upgrade. If you use this user, the upgrade process will continue, using this user. When the credentials have been verified, the Get Going Fast screen appears, as shown in Figure 2-1.

As you progress through the Windows 10 onboarding process, you are presented with options to enable features such as Cortana, as shown in Figure 2-8. The wording of the dialog box encourages you to accept the default, and the option to deviate from the default is tucked away and labeled Not Now.

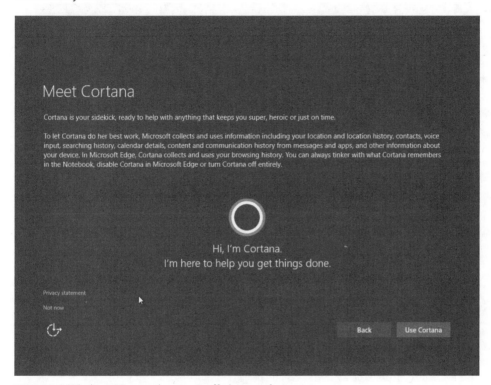

FIGURE 2-8 Windows 10 upgrade process offering new features

As part of the upgrade, the user is shown new apps that have been included in Windows 10. In the Windows 10 10586 version, the following apps have been upgraded.

- Photos
- Groove Music
- Microsoft Edge
- Films & TV

After the final restart, the device initiates the out-of-box-experience (OOBE) sequence, which informs you that the PC has been upgraded, all files are exactly where you left them, and Windows 10 has some exciting new features.

The new Windows 10 desktop, as shown in Figure 2-9, then appears.

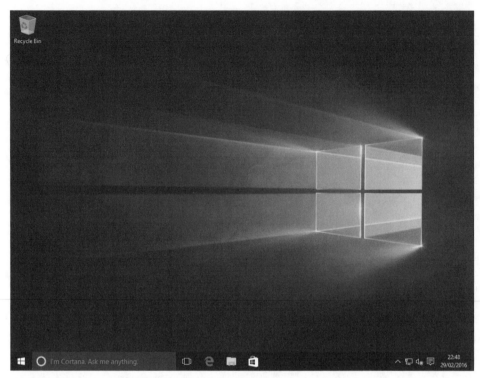

FIGURE 2-9 Windows 10 desktop after the upgrade process has succeeded

Go back to previous version of Windows

When the upgrade is complete, you can confirm the existence of the Windows.old folder. This will be stored on the C drive or a removable hard drive if this was necessary during the upgrade. The Windows.old folder is not a hidden or system folder. This folder will be deleted to recover disk space after 30 days.

If, during the initial month after the upgrade, you want to revert to the previous version of Windows, select Get Started in the Recovery section titled Go Back To Windows 8.1, as shown in Figure 2-10.

If you choose Go Back to Windows 8.1, Microsoft offers a short survey by which you can provide feedback about why you are reverting to the previous version, or you can launch a Microsoft Support app to troubleshoot problems directly with a Microsoft Answer Tech or schedule a return telephone call.

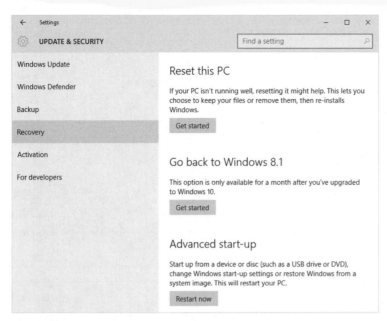

FIGURE 2-10 The Recovery tab showing how to go back to the previous operating system

> **NOTE GO BACK TO THE PREVIOUS OPERATING SYSTEM**
>
> Do not delete the Windows.old folder; otherwise, you will not be able to reverse the upgrade process. After a month, a built-in scheduled task will automatically remove the Windows.old folder; this utility can be found in Scheduled Tasks at \Microsoft\Windows \Setup\SetupCleanupTask.

Block upgrading to Windows 10

About six months after initial release of Windows 10, Microsoft released a fix for users who wanted to block the GWX system tray icon and prevent the Windows 10 upgrade in Windows Update. This fix involves making modifications to the system registry; it is therefore essential for a valid backup of the system, including the current registry, to be available prior to implementing the following fix.

For Pro and Ultimate editions of Windows 7 and Pro versions of Windows 8.1, modify the Group Policy Object as follows.

1. Open Group Policy editor by typing **gpedit.msc**.
2. Click Computer Configuration.
3. Click Administrative Templates and then click Windows Components.
4. Click Windows Update.

5. Double-click Turn Off The Upgrade To The Latest Version Of Windows Through Windows Update.

6. Click Enable as shown in Figure 2-11.

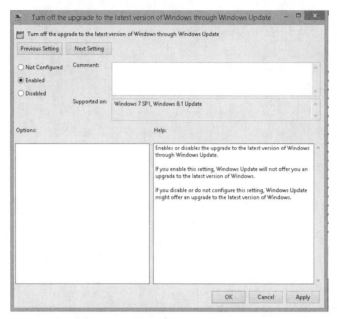

FIGURE 2-11 Disabling prompt to upgrade to Windows 10

The setting of the GPO will be configured never to detect, download, or install the upgrade, and it will prevent the GWX utility from appearing. On a system that is not able to upgrade to Windows 10, for example on a Windows RT 8.1 or Windows RT device, or a Windows 10 machine, the GWX icon and the GPO will not be available.

> **NOTE WINDOWS UPDATES**
>
> If you do not find the GPO shown in Figure 2-11, check whether Windows is up to date. Open Windows Update and click Check For Updates. After the latest updates are installed, the new GPO should be available.

By setting the Turn Off The Upgrade To The Latest Version Of Windows Through Windows Update to Enable, Windows creates a new registry key on the system that blocks the Windows 10 upgrade through Windows Update.

The ability to modify the Group Policy setting is not available for devices on which non-Enterprise or Ultimate versions of Windows 7 or Windows 8.1 are installed. You can manually create the required registry key as follows.

1. Open the Windows Registry by typing **Regedit.exe.**

2. If you receive the UAC prompt, click Yes.

3. Navigate to HKLM\SOFTWARE\Policies\Microsoft\Windows\WindowsUpdate.

4. Right-click the WindowsUpdate subkey and select New DWORD (32-bit) Value.

5. Type **DisableOSUpgrade** as the new DWORD name.

6. Double-click the DisableOSUpgrade key and enter **1** as the value.

7. Close the registry editor and restart the device.

> *NOTE* **DISABLE THE GWX NOTIFICATION ICON**
>
> If you prefer not to see the GWX icon in the notification area on your non-Enterprise version of Windows 7 or Windows 8.1, you can edit the following entries in the Windows registry: Subkey: HKLM\Software\Policies\Microsoft\Windows\Gwx and create the DWORD value: DisableGwx = 1. Finally, restart your system for the settings to take effect.

Skill: Upgrade using installation media

If you have practiced the skills mentioned in the previous sections, you have seen that the in-place upgrade process works well. Although other methods, such as wipe-and-load, are still available, the upgrade is now the recommended deployment method Microsoft suggests for existing devices such as Windows 7 or Windows 8.1.

An enterprise will normally obtain Windows 10 media by downloading it from the Volume Licensing Center (VLC) at *https://www.microsoft.com/licensing/servicecenter/default.aspx*. VLC media use a generic product key during the installation process, which is activated by a KMS that is tied to the enterprise license agreement.

Alternatively, purchased retail media can be used, which can be supplied on a USB thumb drive or by a direct download from the online Microsoft Store.

Another option is to use the Media Creation Tool (MCT), which generates a ready-to-use, bootable USB flash drive or an ISO file. Media created with the MCT cannot be used for upgrading a Windows Enterprise edition client.

> *NOTE* **MEDIA CREATION TOOL (MCT)**
>
> You can download the MCT at *http://go.microsoft.com/fwlink/?LinkId=691209*.

If you encounter issues while upgrading, inspect the installation log file found at C:\windows\Panther\UnattendGC\SetupAct.log. If you are trying to use the wrong media, there should be an entry such as the following:

```
Info [windeploy.exe] OEM license detected, will not run SetupComplete.cmd
```

With all upgrades, you must ensure that you have at least 2 GB RAM and enough disk space. In the exam, you could face scenarios in which the current system drive has insufficient disk space. For previous versions of Windows, you would recommend one of the following resolutions for Windows systems needing more space to complete the upgrade.

- Run Disk CleanUp Wizard, remove any unwanted files, and empty the Recycle Bin.
- Uninstall apps, files, and language packs that you do not need.
- If possible, expand the volume by using the Disk Management tool.
- Move personal files off the system drive and onto another drive or external drive.

If the system fails during the upgrade due to a compatibility issue, you can troubleshoot the cause by reviewing the setuperr.log found at C:\$Windows.~BT\Sources\Panther \setuperr.log. Some of the most common codes are shown in Table 2-3.

TABLE 2-3 Setuperr.log errors relating to upgrading

Error Code	Description
CsetupHost::Execute result = 0xC1900200	PC not meeting the system requirements for Windows 10
CsetupHost::Execute result = 0xC190020E	Insufficient free hard drive space
CsetupHost::Execute result = 0xC1900204	Wrong Windows 10 SKU or architecture
CsetupHost::Execute result = 0xC1900210	No issues found

If you want to check the system for compatibility only, you can run Setup.exe with a command-line switch, which will check for compatibility but not perform the upgrade.

An example command is:

```
Setup.exe /Auto Upgrade /Quiet /NoReboot /DynamicUpdate Disable /Compat ScanOnly
```

Windows 8.1 supports mounting an ISO disc image directly in File Explorer to enable you to download the Windows 10 ISO and upgrade without first having to create installation media such as a DVD or bootable USB. For Windows 7, you must use bootable media, extract the files contained in the ISO, or use a third-party tool to mount the ISO.

A major advantage of upgrading rather than performing a clean installation (sometimes referred to as a *wipe-and-load* scenario) is that all the applications, settings, and data on the PC are retained during an upgrade. This often results in a much quicker process, and the device can be returned to the user in the shortest possible time.

> ***NEED MORE REVIEW?*** **WINDOWS 10 ENTERPRISE: FAQ FOR IT PROFESSIONALS**
>
> This TechNet resource is useful to obtain answers to common questions about installation for Windows 10 Enterprise. Visit *https://technet.microsoft.com/windows /dn798755#administration*.

As part of the upgrade, Windows 10 will check the following.

- If UEFI is used, this is UEFI v2.3.1 or later if Secure Boot is used.
- System Host is not configured to boot from VHD.

- The system is not installed as a Portable Workspace (i.e., using Windows To Go).

Details of the setup compatibility checks can be reviewed in the log file found at C:\$WINDOWS.~BT\Sources\Panther\setupact.log.

The installation process proceeds in the same way as the in-place upgrade using Windows Update.

Skill: Configure native boot scenarios

You have seen that Windows 10 can be installed from either a clean installation or an upgrade. Later in this chapter, you see how to boot directly to an operating system installed inside a VHD, but first, review the boot configuration of Windows 10 and how you can modify this configuration to enable you to dual boot with other operating systems.

EXAM TIP

Review the terms *boot* and *system partitions,* which relate to the volumes on a hard disk that Windows 10 uses to start and load the operating system. These terms have been around for many years, and they are not named intuitively.

- The system partition contains files required to boot Windows 10.
- The boot partition contains Windows 10 system files.

This section covers how to:

- View configuration information
- Multiboot Windows

View configuration information

You can use various tools such as Windows PowerShell, Disk Management, or BCDEdit to identify which partition is the boot or system partition. The Disk Management snap-in gives you a graphical method to view the configuration information, as follows.

1. Right-click the Start button and choose Disk Management.
2. Expand the width of the Status column.

You should now see the status of the partitions, and the drive letters. if provided.

- The system partition is indicated by (System) (no drive letter in this example).
- The boot partition is indicated by (Boot) (C drive in this example, as shown in Figure 2-12).

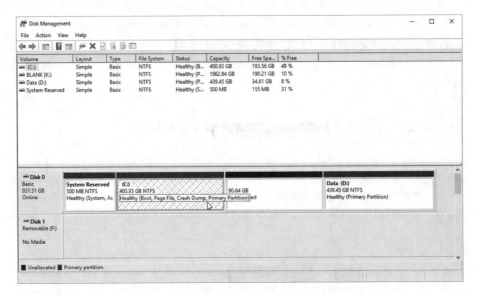

FIGURE 2-12 Boot and system partition information shown in Disk Management

In Windows PowerShell, you can use the Get-Volume -FileSystemLabel "System Reserved" cmdlet to list the system partition.

The Boot Configuration Data (BCD) Store maintains the configuration parameters for loading Windows, and the primary tool for working with the actual boot records is the command-line tool BCD Editor (Bcdedit.exe).

To view the contents of your boot configuration, use the following steps.

1. Open an elevated command prompt or administrative Windows PowerShell console.

2. Type **BCDEdit /v** and then press Enter.

3. Review the output.

In a multiple boot system, the command prompt output should be similar to the contents shown in Figure 2-13.

In Figure 2-13, you see the Windows Boot Manager and the Windows Boot Loader sections. The boot entries relate to a Windows 8.1 and Windows 10 description. Each operating system stored in the BCD has its own globally unique identifier (GUID). In the example shown in Figure 2-13, the two GUIDs are as follows.

- Windows 8.1: {37e47a93-6808-11e5-b2f0-83e8e58e54e8}

- Microsoft Windows 10: {37e47a8f-6808-11e5-b2f0-83e8e58e54e8}

If you want to change the displayed name of the operating system setting, you can use the following command.

```
BCDEdit /set {37e47a8f-6808-11e5-b2f0-83e8e58e54e8} description "Windows 10 1511"
```

FIGURE 2-13 Displaying the boot configuration using BCDEdit

Multiboot Windows

Multibooting your computer is possible with Windows 10 and enables you to install multiple operating systems on the same computer. For example, a helpdesk technician might need to support both Windows 7 and Windows 10 and must be able to switch quickly between the two operating systems. By multibooting Windows, the user can reboot and select an alternate version of Windows without needing to swap devices.

Other scenarios for implementing multiboot configuration include the following.

- **Testing application compatibility** Earlier applications might not be compatible with a new operating system and might require access to physical rather than virtualized hardware. Issues found when testing application compatibility should be reported to your in-house software development team or a third-party independent software vendor (ISV) to resolve issues that are blocking your adoption of the new operating system.

- **Testing a new operating system** Testing is commonly performed in a multiboot configuration. Multibooting a new operating system enables testers to test-drive it on physical devices so that you can evaluate whether it is compatible.

- **Multiple users** By employing a multiboot configuration, one computer can be used by multiple users; each user will have either the same operating system version or different versions installed. When each user requires a physically different configuration, such employees could be working at different times of the day on a single PC and require special or earlier applications that are incompatible with the other user configuration.

To multiboot Windows 10, you must first install Windows 10. It is best practice to keep the operating systems on logically separate partitions on your computer. If you do not have a spare partition, create one. In the following example, you use Disk Management first to shrink the primary partition to free up space, and then you create a second partition to install Windows in a multiboot environment, using the following steps.

1. Type **diskmgmt.msc** into the Search box and press Enter.

2. Locate the primary partition, which is marked (Boot, Page File, Crash Dump, Primary Partition); this is normally the C drive.

3. Right-click the primary partition drive (C) and select Shrink Volume.

4. In the Shrink C: dialog box, type the size in MB to which you want to shrink the drive, such as 40960 MB, and click Shrink.

   The Windows installation program formats the 40.00 GB partition.

5. Close Disk Management.

You are now ready to install the second operating system on the newly created partition as follows.

1. Insert your installation media, such as a DVD or bootable USB drive.

2. Reboot your system and press any key when the system detects the bootable USB drive or DVD.

3. After the setup program loads, proceed with the setup as for a clean installation and select the newly created Unallocated Space (40.0 GB drive in the preceding example) for the location to install Windows and click Next.

4. Allow the Windows installation to complete and then configure the additional version of Windows.

To switch between the two operating systems, you must reboot your system and choose your desired version of Windows in the boot menu, as shown in Figure 2-14.

EXAM TIP

The new advanced boot options have multiple screens and levels of options. Ensure that you have explored each tool and configured Windows 10 in a multiboot scenario before you take the exam.

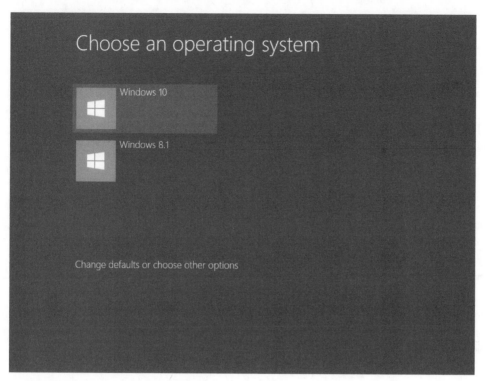

FIGURE 2-14 Multiboot choices at boot time

Skill: Migrate from previous versions of Windows

When upgrading from an older operating system, it is very common for the user to be presented with a new device running the new version of Windows after the old device is removed. This can sometimes cause significant loss of productivity while the user becomes familiar with the updated operating system and reconfigures settings to their preferences.

This user personalization of the device can sometimes be overlooked within an enterprise. Consider the following examples of customization and personalization.

- Desktop appearance, sounds, themes, backgrounds
- Start-menu customization
- Icons, file associations
- Files and folders stored locally
- Device and power settings
- Application settings, such as autotype, template locations

This section covers how to:

- Migrate applications by using User Experience Virtualization (UE-V)
- Perform a user state migration

Migrate applications by using User Experience Virtualization

You might have encountered occasions when users are unhappy if they lose application settings that were stored with the application or in the user profile. For example, most Outlook users appreciate the autocomplete list feature that displays suggestions for names and email addresses as you begin to type them. If the user profile is stored separately from the PC, such as on a file server, most settings can be migrated to the new device after the user logs on. If the device is standalone, the profile and application settings will not be transferred to the new PC.

Enterprises can use roaming profiles to retain some application customization, which synchronizes the profile data during logon and logoff. For a more comprehensive roaming solution for application settings, consider using Microsoft User Experience Virtualization (UE-V) to enable the capture and centralization of users' application settings and Windows 10 settings.

UE-V is licensed through the Microsoft Desktop Optimization Pack and includes the ability to:

- Specify which application and desktop settings are to be synchronized.
- Deliver the settings to users' workstations throughout the enterprise.
- Enable UE-V to record and monitor setting changes to non-Microsoft, third-party applications.
- Recover settings after hardware replacement or upgrade.

> **NEED MORE REVIEW?** **UE-V VERSION 2.X**
>
> This TechNet resource provides more in-depth information to enterprises seeking to employ UE-V 2.x: *https://technet.microsoft.com/library/dn458926.aspx*.

Previous versions of Windows provided a GUI tool such as Windows Easy Transfer to assist the transfer of settings from an old computer to the new one. Microsoft has not included Windows Easy Transfer with Windows 10 and instead recommends an in-place upgrade, which will maintain all apps and settings.

Despite the unavailability of Windows Easy Transfer, Microsoft has partnered with Laplink, a third-party software reseller, to offer its tool, PCmover Express (Personal use) for free. This tool provides functionality similar to Windows Easy Transfer and assists the transfer of selected files from your old Windows-based PC to your new PC running Windows 10. You can find more information relating to PCmover Express at *http://windows.microsoft.com /en-gb/windows-10/windows-easy-transfer-is-not-available-in-windows-10*.

Perform a user state migration

When computers are being replaced or refreshed on a large scale, the loss of productivity can be significant. In this scenario, you can use the User State Migration Tool (USMT) 10.0. For systems that are not being upgraded, the USMT is available as part of the Windows Assessment and Deployment Kit (Windows ADK). You should always use the latest version of the Windows ADK, which is available from the TechNet website at *https://technet.microsoft.com/windows /mt240566?f=255&MSPPError=-2147217396*.

User state migration is performed in two phases as follows.

1. Settings and data are captured (collected) from the source and stored in a secure migration store using the ScanState tool.

2. Captured settings and data are restored on the destination computer, using the LoadState tool.

USMT is a command-line tool that can be scripted to capture and migrate data efficiently and securely and is intended for performing large-scale automated deployments. You choose which data is captured, and these settings are stored in migration XML files as follows.

- MigApp.xml
- MigDocs.xml
- MigUser.xml
- Custom XML files that you can create

The XML files provide the migration rules that USMT needs to process.

> **IMPORTANT**   **INSTALL APPLICATIONS**
>
> It is important to ensure that any applications you require are already installed on the destination computer so that the captured app settings can be reinstated. USMT does not migrate the applications themselves, only supported applications' settings.

The types of data that USMT can capture and migrate are shown in Table 2-4.

TABLE 2-4 Data types accessible by USMT

Data Type	Example	Description
User data	My Documents, My Video, My Music, My Pictures, Desktop files, Start menu, Quick Launch settings, and Favorites	Folders from each user profile.
	Shared Documents, Shared Video, Shared Music, Shared Desktop files, Shared Pictures, Shared Start menu, and Shared Favorites	Folders from the Public profiles.

Data Type	Example	Description
	File	USMT searches fixed drives, collecting files that have any of the file name extensions that are defined in the configuration XML file.
	Access control lists (ACLs)	USMT can migrate the ACL for specified files and folders.
Operating system components	Mapped network drives, network printers, folder options, users' personal certificates, and Internet Explorer settings.	USMT migrates most standard operating system settings.
Supported applications settings	Microsoft Office, Skype, Google Chrome, Adobe Acrobat Reader, Apple iTunes, and more	USMT will migrate settings for many applications, which can be specified in the MigApp.xml file. Version of each application must match on the source and destination computers. With Microsoft Office, USMT allows migration of the settings from an earlier version of an Office application.

NEED MORE REVIEW? **USMT MIGAPP.XML SUPPORTED APPLICATIONS**

This TechNet resource provides the list of applications that you can specify in the MigApp.xml file for USMT to migrate the settings. Visit *https://technet.microsoft.com/library /hh825238.aspx?f=255&MSPPError=-2147217396#BKMK_2*.

The following settings are not migrated when you use USMT.

- Local printers, hardware-related settings
- Device drivers
- Passwords
- Customized icons for shortcuts
- Shared folder permissions
- Files and settings if the operating systems have different languages installed

After you have installed the USMT included in the Windows ADK, you have the following components as described in Table 2-5.

TABLE 2-5 USMT components

Component	Description
ScanState	Scans a source computer and collects files and settings, writing them to a migration store. (The store file can be password protected and can be compressed and encrypted if required, although you cannot use the /nocompress option with the /encrypt option.) You can turn off the default compression with the /nocompress option.
LoadState	Migrates the files and settings from the migration store to the destination computer.

Component	Description
USMTUtils	Compresses, encrypts, and validates the migration store files.
Migration XML files	MigApp.xml, MigUser.xml, or MigDocs.xml files, and custom XML files USMT uses to configure the process.
Config.xml	Used with /genconfig to exclude data from a migration.
Component manifests	Controls which operating system settings are to be migrated. These manifests are specific to the operating system and are not modifiable.

To initiate the collection of the files and settings from the source computer, use the following steps.

1. Ensure that you have a backup of the source computer.

2. Close all applications.

3. Run ScanState, using an account with administrative privilege and the command similar to:

   ```
   ScanState \\remotelocation\migration\mystore /config:config.xml / i:migdocs.xml
   /:migapp.xml /v:13 /l:scan.log
   ```

4. Run UsmtUtils with the /verify switch to ensure that the migration store is not corrupted, using UsmtUtils /verify C:\mystore\storename.img.

5. On the destination computer, install the operating system, install any applications that were on the source computer, and then close any open applications.

6. Run the LoadState command, specifying the same .xml files that you used when you ran ScanState using the command similar to:

   ```
   LoadState \\remotelocation\migration\ /config:config.xml / i:migdocs.xml
   /i:migapp.xml /v:13 /l:load.log
   ```

7. Restart the device and verify whether some of the settings have changed.

Earlier, you saw that when you deploy Windows 10 on a device that contains a modern version of Windows, it creates a Windows.old folder. By using the ScanState tool, you can migrate user settings from an offline Windows system including the Windows.old folder. This can be advantageous in the following scenarios.

- Improved performance if the Windows.old folder is local

- Simplified end-to-end deployment process by migrating data from Windows.old by enabling the migration process to occur after the new operating system is installed

- Improved success of migration because files will not be locked for editing while offline

- Ability to recover and migrate data from an unbootable computer

NEED MORE REVIEW? **USMT TECHNICAL REFERENCE**

TechNet has updated the technical reference relating to USMT 10.0; you can find it at *https://technet.microsoft.com/library/mt299211(v=vs.85).aspx.*

Skill: Install Windows 10 to a VHD

We discussed earlier in this chapter how to multiboot Windows 10. There is a newer method of using multiple operating systems on a single device without repartitioning the drive; it involves installing Windows 10 inside a virtual hard disk (VHD) that has been configured to behave as though it is natively booting. Native boot indicates that there is no parent operating system.

VHDs can be used in both a virtual (for example, Hyper-V) or physical environment. This section discusses the ability to install Windows 10 directly onto a VHD. After the initial configuration of the VHD has completed, for the purposes of normal operations, Windows will not be able to distinguish between a physical and a virtual drive.

VHD boot is still relatively new and thought of as quite specialist; expect to see VHD boot or Native Boot included on the exam.

> **This section covers how to:**
>
> - Create and configure a Native Boot VHD
> - Use Disk Management to attach a VHD
> - Install Windows inside a VHD

Create and configure a native boot VHD

The steps required to prepare a VHD must be performed carefully; otherwise, the VHD will not be present during the installation process. To prepare a native boot VHD, first create and configure it so that Windows will install into it.

Perform the following steps.

1. Type **diskmgmt.msc** into the search area or right-click the Start button and click Disk Management.

2. In Disk Management, click Action and then click Create VHD.

3. In the Create And Attach Virtual Hard Disk dialog box, provide the parameters for your VHD.

    An example VHD is:

    - Location C:\VHD\Windows10vhd.vhd.
    - Virtual hard disk size: 40 GB.
    - Virtual hard disk format: VHD.
    - Virtual hard disk type: Fixed size.

4. Click OK to create your VHD.

    Because fixed type was selected, this might take several minutes to complete, and you will see the creation progress in the bottom right of the Disk Management dialog box.

Your new VHD should automatically attach to the system. If it does not, you can use Disk Management to attach it.

Use Disk Management to attach a VHD

Your new VHD should automatically be attached to the system but if not, use Disk Management to attach the drive as follows.

1. Click Action and then click Attach VHD, browse to your new VHD, and choose the VHD to attach.

2. If you prefer to use the command line, you can also use the DiskPart tool and type **create vdisk file= C:\VHD\Windows10vhd.vhd maximum=40960 type=fixed** to achieve the same result.

3. Leave the VHD drive in the Not Initialized state; this updates when Windows installs to it.

Windows can now install to the VHD file.

Install Windows inside a VHD

To install Windows inside your VHD file, follow these steps.

1. Insert your Windows media (or ISO if you are using a virtual machine) in your computer and boot from it.

2. Follow the onscreen prompts, providing the appropriate information until the Where Do You Want To Install Windows screen appears.

3. Press Shift+F10 to launch an administrative command prompt window.

4. In the administrative command prompt window, type **DiskPart**.

5. In DiskPart, type **List disk**.

6. Locate the VHD disk that you have created and type **select vdisk file=D:\VHD\ Windows10vhd.vhd**. (Notice that the drive letter has been changed.)

7. In DiskPart, type **attach vdisk** and press Enter.

8. Type **Exit** to close DiskPart and then close the administrative command prompt window.

9. On the Where Do You Want To Install Windows page, click Refresh.

   Your VHD disk should now appear.

10. Select the VHD drive and allow Windows to install normally.

After rebooting the machine, you should see the ability to choose an operating system during boot time, as shown in Figure 2-15.

After proper configuration, Windows 10 does not differentiate between physical and virtual hard drives and behaves as if it is running natively and not virtually.

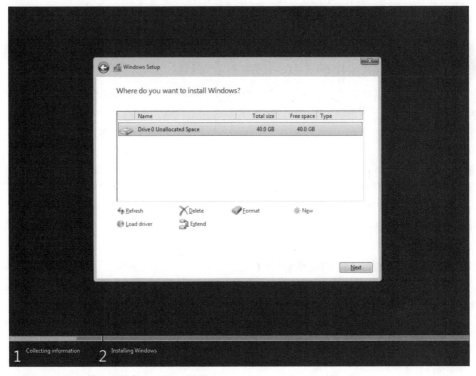

FIGURE 2-15 Installing Windows onto a VHD

A few features are not supported when Windows 10 is booted from a VHD. These include the following.

- Windows 10 does not support hibernation when started from a VHD, although sleep mode is supported.

- The version of Windows 10 on the VHD cannot be upgraded to a newer version.

- You cannot enable BitLocker on the Windows 10 volume contained on a native-boot VHD.

- You cannot boot to Windows 10 from a VHD stored on a remote share or USB flash drive.

- Only Windows 10 Enterprise and Windows 10 Education edition licensing supports starting from a VHD natively.

> *NEED MORE REVIEW?*   **DEPLOY WINDOWS ON A VHD (NATIVE BOOT)**
>
> This TechNet resource provides more depth to this topic: *https://msdn.microsoft.com/library /windows/hardware/dn898535(v=vs.85).aspx.*

Skill: Boot Windows 10 from VHD

Sometimes you want to multiboot your computer so that it can boot to a secondary Windows environment such as a preview version of Windows 10. You could use the multiboot procedure that you saw earlier or configure your system to boot to Windows 10 running inside a VHD. This can be the only way to multiboot if your second hard disk uses the GUID Partition Table (GPT), which is required for partitions larger than 2 terabytes (TB), because the secondary Windows environment will not install to a partition on the GPT disk.

You review how to use a virtual hard disk (VHD) to provide a boot volume that uses the MBR partition style inside a VHD located on the GPT drive. You then apply the installation image to the VHD and configure the computer to boot to the second Windows environment. Three key stages are required to configure your computer to boot from VHD; they are described in this section.

> **This section covers how to:**
>
> - Create an MBR-partitioned VHD
> - Apply the Windows Image to the VHD
> - Configure boot options

Create an MBR-partitioned VHD

You need to create a new VHD to store the Windows 10 image that will become your second Windows environment. You can use Disk Management, Windows PowerShell, or DiskPart to create VHDs in Windows 10. The Disk Management steps are as follows.

1. Right-click the Start button and select Disk Management from the menu.
2. Select Create VHD from the Action menu.
3. In the Create And Attach Virtual Hard Disk dialog box, specify the desired location of the VHD folder.
4. Specify the desired size of the created VHD.
5. Specify VHD or VHDX format.
6. Specify Fixed Size or Dynamically Expanding. (If you have the available space, choose a fixed size drive because this will provide the best performance).
7. After the drive is created, the VHD is automatically attached.
8. Locate the new VHD drive in the lower-left navigation pane, right-click the disk, and select Initialize Disk.
9. Specify the MBR partition style for the disk.
10. When the disk is initialized, right-click in the unallocated space in the pane on the right side and select New Simple Volume to launch the New Simple Volume Wizard.

11. Allow the volume size to be the default value and assign the drive letter V to the volume.

12. Format the partition as NTFS and label it **VHDBoot**.

13. Close Disk Management.

Apply the Windows Image to the VHD

Now that you have created an empty VHD for your second Windows environment, you are ready to use the DISM command-line tool to apply your Windows 10 image to the new volume. The DISM steps are as follows.

1. Insert or mount the installation media for the secondary environment; this can be a Windows 10 DVD, Windows 10 bootable USB drive, mounted ISO, or customized deployment image.

2. Right-click the Start button and select Command Prompt (Admin) from the menu.

3. Type the following command, which will apply the Install.wim file located in the Sources folder of the installation media to the VHD mounted at drive letter V:

   ```
   DISM /Apply-Image /ImageFile:D:\Sources\install.wim /Index:1 /ApplyDir:V:\
   ```

4. Close the Command Prompt (Admin) window.

> **NOTE** **DEPLOYMENT IMAGE SERVICING AND MANAGEMENT (DISM)**
>
> You will use the Deployment Image Servicing and Management (DISM) tool, which is built-in in the Windows 10.

Configure boot options

With Windows 10 now applied to the VHD, you must update the boot options so that the current Windows environment is aware of the additional Windows environment on the VHD. The BCDboot command-line tool enables you to manage system partition files, including configuring the boot options. You can add your second Windows environment to the current boot menu by completing the following steps. The command-line steps using BCDBoot are as follows.

1. Right-click the Start button and select Command Prompt (Admin) from the menu.

2. In the command prompt window, type the following command and press Enter.

   ```
   CD V:\Windows\System32
   ```

3. Verify that the command prompt now displays V:\Windows\System32.

4. Type the following command to configure the Windows environment on the VHD to add its boot files to the system partition for multi-boot.

   ```
   BCDBoot V:\Windows
   ```

5. Close the command prompt and restart your computer.

6. When the computer retarts, you should be presented with a prompt to select between the existing operating system and the secondary Windows environment when the computer starts.

NOTE **BOOT FROM VHD**

Only the Pro, Enterprise, and Education editions of Windows 10 are licensed to boot from VHD.

Skill: Install on bootable USB

With the performance and capacity benefits achievable with USB drives, Microsoft now sells Windows 10 installation media on USB drives. You can also download the Windows 10 image, so that you can either upgrade your current Windows system or create your own bootable USB flash drive containing the Windows 10 installation media to install Windows 10 on another PC.

This section covers how to:

- Install on bootable USB, using the Media Creation Tool (MCT)
- Manually create a Windows 10 bootable USB

Install on bootable USB, using the Media Creation Tool

You saw earlier that Microsoft provides a downloadable Media Creation Tool (MCT), which enables you to generate a ready-to-use Windows 10 bootable USB flash drive. The MCT can't be used with the Windows Enterprise edition client. One advantage of using the MCT Wizard is that it downloads the required Windows 10 edition and architecture based on your selections and copies this directly to your USB drive.

To create a bootable USB, using the MCT so that you can perform a clean installation of Windows 10, use these steps.

1. Download the MCT at *http://go.microsoft.com/fwlink/?LinkId=691209*.

2. Run the Media Creation Tool.

3. Select Create Installation Media For Another PC.

4. Select the language, edition, and architecture (64-bit or 32-bit) for Windows 10 and click Next.

5. On the Choose Which Media To Use page, select USB Flash Drive and click Next.

6. On the Select A USB Flash Drive page, select your removable drive and click Next.

7. After the MCT has downloaded Windows 10 and copied it to your removable drive, click Finish.

The USB flash drive can now be used to install Windows 10.

Manually create a Windows 10 bootable USB

If you already have downloaded the correct edition of Windows 10 or you have other installation media, such as a DVD containing Windows 10, you can manually create a bootable USB. Insert the installation media or mount the Windows 10 ISO before performing this task.

You can manually create a bootable USB that can be used with any edition of Windows by preparing a USB removable drive, using the following steps.

1. Right-click the Start button and select Command Prompt (Admin); accept the UAC prompt.

2. Insert the USB drive that you want to make a bootable Windows 10 installation USB.

3. Type **diskpart** and press Enter to launch the DiskPart command-line utility.

4. Type **listdisk** to display the list of storage drives.

5. Identify the disk number of the USB drive that you are using; you should be able to find it by looking at the Size column.

6. Type **select disk _X_** to select the USB drive, where _X_ is the disk number of your USB drive.

7. Type **clean** to erase the USB drive.

8. Type **create partition primary** to create a primary partition on the USB drive.

9. Type **select partition 1** to select the newly created partition.

10. Type **active** to make the partition active.

11. Type **format fs=ntfs quick** to format the partition.

12. Type **assign** to instruct Windows to allocate a drive letter to the USB drive.

13. Type **exit** to leave Diskpart.

14. You can use the built in command line tool Xcopy to copy the contents of your mounted Windows 10 ISO or DVD to the USB drive by typing **xcopy g:*.* /s/e/f h**: and pressing Enter. You must change the drive letters to match your source files location (G) and removable drive (H).

> **NOTE   UEFI**
>
> If your system supports UEFI, format the USB flash drive as FAT32 rather than as NTFS. To format the partition as FAT32, type **format fs=fat32** quick and then press Enter.

Skill: Install additional Windows features

Similar to Windows 8.1, you can add and remove Windows features as required without the need to revert to the installation media.

> **This section covers how to:**
> - Use the Windows Features app
> - Use DISM to add or remove Windows features

Use the Windows Features app

To launch the Windows Features app as shown in Figure 2-16, which allows you to turn Windows features on or off, perform one of the following three methods.

- Type **OptionalFeatures.exe** into the search bar and press Enter.
- Navigate to Control Panel > Programs > Programs And Features and select Turn Windows Features On Or Off.
- Right-click the Start button and select Programs And Features and select Turn Windows Features On Or Off.

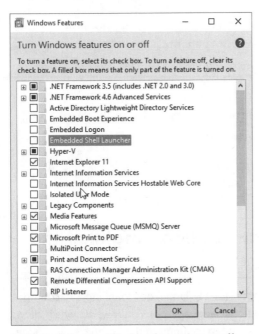

FIGURE 2-16 Turning Windows features on or off

Use DISM to add or remove Windows features

If you prefer to use the command prompt, or need to automate the process, you can also use the Deployment Image Servicing and Management (DISM) tool. DISM is a command-line tool that you use to modify Windows; it's also included in the Windows ADK. One feature of DISM is the ability to enable or disable Windows features directly from the command prompt. The Windows installation can be online on a running operating system or offline in a WIM or VHD file.

If you are not sure of the name of the Windows feature, you can use the following command to list all the features available in the operating system.

```
Dism /online /Get-Features
```

After you know the name of the Windows feature, you can enable a specific feature by using DISM. You can use the /All argument to enable all the parent features in the same command. For example, type:

```
Dism /online /Enable-Feature /FeatureName:TFTP /All
```

> **NEED MORE REVIEW?** **ENABLE OR DISABLE WINDOWS FEATURES BY USING DISM**
>
> TechNet provides a useful technical reference relating to DISM, which can be found at
> *https://technet.microsoft.com/library/hh824822.aspx*.

In Windows 10, you can also run DISM within Windows PowerShell or use native Windows PowerShell commands for many of the functions DISM performs.

The equivalent commands in Windows 10, using Windows PowerShell, are:

```
Get-WindowsOptionalFeature -Online
```

which lists all the features available in the operating system, and:

```
Enable-WindowsOptionalFeature -Online -FeatureName TFTP -All
```

To disable the TFTP feature, type:

```
Disable-WindowsOptionalFeature -Online -FeatureName TFTP
```

Skill: Configure Windows for additional regional and language support

When Windows 10 was released, it offered support for 111 languages spanning 190 countries and regions. You can download any of the additional languages for Windows 10, which allows users to view menus, dialog boxes, and other user interface items in their preferred language.

To add an input language to your PC, perform the following steps.

1. Open Settings > Time & Language > Region & Language.

2. Under Languages, select Add A Language.

3. Select the language you want to use from the list, as shown in Figure 2-17.

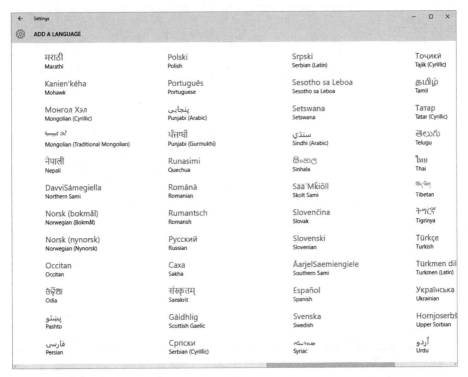

FIGURE 2-17 Select language

Windows 10 searches Windows Update for the language and then downloads the language and installs it. Language packs are typically about 5–10 MB in size, but for complex languages, this can be higher. While downloading and installing the language, Windows displays a notification that it is adding some new features to Windows.

After the language is installed, you can set it to be the default language for your PC or remove the language. You can also use an Options button to add additional regional keyboard layouts. Depending on the hardware of your device, other settings might also be in this Options app for configuring features such as region-specific fonts, handwriting and pen settings, typing, and optical character recognition (OCR) to your PC.

You can also use the Lpksetup command prompt to perform unattended or silent-mode language pack operations, such as:

```
lpksetup.exe /i * /p <path>
```

This example installs all language packs that are located on installation media specified in the *<path>* location. The full command-line options for Lpksetup.exe are shown in Table 2-6.

TABLE 2-6 Lpksetup.exe command-line options

Option	Description
/i	Installs the specified language packs. If you do not include * or language after /i, you are asked to continue the install through the user interface (UI).
*	Wildcard character that represents all language packs found in language_pack_path or the directory where lpksetup.exe is located.
Language-region	Specifies the language pack or packs to be installed or uninstalled.
/u	Uninstalls the specified language packs. If you do not include * or language after /i, you are asked to continue the uninstall through the user interface (UI).
/r	Suppresses the need to restart after an operation is complete.
/p language_pack_path	Indicates the path of the language packs to install.
/s	Performs a silent and unattended operation that requires no user input.
/f	If the computer is required to restart, forces a restart even if other users are logged on to the computer.

EXAM TIP

The parent language is the language selected during the installation of Windows 10. The only method of changing the parent language is to reinstall Windows 10 and select a different language.

Summary

- There are multiple methods of obtaining Windows 10, including clean installs and upgrading a prior version of Windows.
- Windows Update can automatically download and deploy Windows with minimal user interaction.
- Enterprise editions of Windows 7 and Windows 8 cannot be upgraded using Windows Update.
- After upgrading to Windows 10, you can revert to the prior version at any time, although the Windows.old folder on the device will be deleted after one month.
- Windows 10 can be multibooted with other operating systems.

- You can install Windows 10 in a VHD, which behaves like a native-booted operating system.

- You can migrate user and application settings from one device to another, using the USMT.

- USMT uses ScanState and LoadState to migrate data and can use compression or encryption during the migration process.

- You can add or remove Windows features by using Control Panel, DISM, or Windows PowerShell.

- Windows 10 supports 111 languages, and you can add and remove language support in the Settings app or with the Lpksetup command.

Thought experiment

In this thought experiment, demonstrate your skills and knowledge of the topics covered in this chapter. You can find answers to this thought experiment in the next section.

You need to upgrade company devices from Windows 8.1 Pro to Windows 10 Pro. There are 50 devices in total. Twenty-five of these devices are Surface 3 Pro tablets. The remainder are desktop PCs. Members of the software testing and development team require Hyper-V to be installed on their workstations.

You need to ensure that the Surface tablets are made available to the sales team in the shortest possible time.

The company has commissioned a short introduction to Windows 10 that is available on the company intranet and offline. All users must view the training prior to using Windows 10.

Answer the following questions for your manager:

1. How will you provision Windows 10 to the Surface tablets?

2. You want all desktop users to self-upgrade after they view the online training module. How will they initiate the upgrade?

3. How will you make Hyper-V available to the software testing and development team?

Thought experiment answer

This section contains the solution to the thought experiment.

1. The Surface tablets already contain a modern operating system that can be upgraded to Windows 10. The quickest method of provisioning Windows 10 would be to insert a USB drive containing the Windows 10 ISO or installation files and run Setup.exe. You could upgrade by using Windows Update, but this would not be the quickest method.

2. Instruct the users to click the Get Windows 10 icon in the notification area to initiate the upgrade of their system to Windows 10 through Windows Update over the Internet.

3. Answers might vary. The software testing and development team should run the OptionalFeatures.exe or type **Turn Windows features on or off** in the search area. After the Turn Windows Features On Or Off screen appears, select Hyper-V and click OK. If the team members do not have the necessary administrative privileges, they should ask the help desk to enable this setting for them. Another possible solution would be to turn the Hyper-V feature on using the DISM command: DISM /online / Enable-Feature /FeatureName: Microsoft-Hyper-V.

CHAPTER 3

Configure devices and device drivers

Windows 10 identifies and configures hardware during the initial installation. Upon delivery of a device running Windows 10, the user will typically want to add their own hardware and peripherals such as a printer, a Bluetooth mouse, or web cam. In this chapter, you learn how Windows 10 installs drivers for new devices and hardware and how you can maintain these drivers, upgrade them, and resolve driver issues that might occur.

Skills covered in this chapter:

- Install devices
- Update, disable, and roll back drivers
- Resolve driver issues
- Configure driver settings
- Driver signing
- Manage driver packages
- Download and import driver packages
- Use Deployment Image And Service Management tool (DISM) to add packages

Skill: Install devices

When you install a hardware component on Windows 10, the operating system requires a device driver to be installed so that you can use it. After it's configured, the device driver loads automatically and is available for Windows to use. This section explains how Windows 10 automatically installs devices and locates the device driver from the Windows Component Store, from Windows Update, or directly from you.

> **This section covers how to:**
> - Install devices
> - Manage devices and printers

Install devices

For hardware to function properly, it requires special software designed for Windows 10 to communicate with it. This software is referred to as a device driver, and when Windows 10 detects new hardware, the system automatically attempts to install one of the built-in drivers included as part of the operating system, located within the Windows 10 Driver Store, or download them through Windows Update, from the Internet. New and updated hardware device drivers are regularly submitted to Microsoft by the equipment vendor for testing and cataloguing. If the Windows Update feature is enabled, Windows 10 automatically detects the presence of new device drivers, downloads them, and installs them.

New hardware is typically installed automatically when it's added to Windows 10, with the operating system detecting and identifying the new hardware through the Plug and Play feature. Windows 10 supports new hardware connected through a variety of connection methods, including USB (1.0 through 3.1), Wi-Fi, and Bluetooth. In addition to backward compatibility for existing and earlier hardware, emerging technologies such as near-field communication (NFC) and Miracast for wireless displays also have built-in support in Windows 10.

For advanced users or for managing or troubleshooting a hardware device issue, you can use Device Manager. Device Manager provides information about each device, such as the device type, device status, manufacturer, device-specific properties, and device driver information.

There are multiple ways to load the Device Manager, including:

- Right-clicking the Start button and selecting Device Manager.
- Typing **Device Manager** into Search.
- Opening Control Panel, selecting Hardware And Sound, and then selecting Device Manager.

The Device Manager default view (devices by type) is shown in Figure 3-1.

You can expand and explore each node in Device Manager and then select a device. All devices have properties, and these can be viewed by right-clicking the desired device and selecting the properties. The Properties dialog box for a device is shown in Figure 3-2.

FIGURE 3-1 Device Manager showing the devices by type view

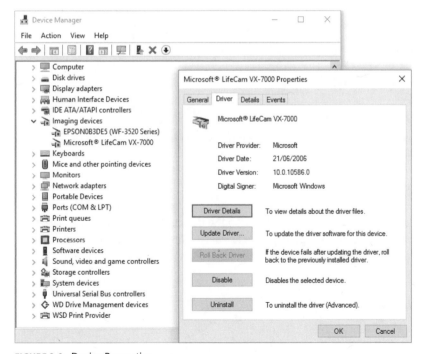

FIGURE 3-2 Device Properties

If you added a new peripheral and Windows 10 does not immediately recognize it, first check that the device is connected properly and that no cables are damaged. You should ensure that the external device is powered on and not in sleep or standby mode. You can also open Device Manager and launch the Scan For Hardware Changes Wizard from the Action menu, which will locate previously undetected hardware and then configure it for you.

Manage devices and printers

Device Manager provides one method of managing devices within Windows 10. Another way to add and manage devices is by using the Devices And Printers app within Control Panel. This Devices And Printers app enables you to add devices and printers by clicking the menu item at the top of the screen. This launches an easy-to-use wizard that searches for devices and walks the user through the process of installing devices, as shown in Figure 3-3.

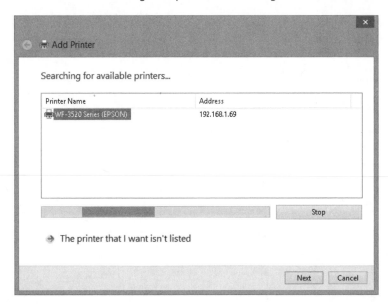

FIGURE 3-3 Add Printer Wizard

After a piece of hardware is installed, you can view it in the Devices And Printers app, and Windows displays photorealistic icons to help you recognize the devices. If you click and open one of the icons, a new view appears that focuses on the device. This window is the device stage and is shown in Figure 3-4. The type of functionality found in the device stage depends on the support provided by the manufacturer of the device that is installed alongside the device driver.

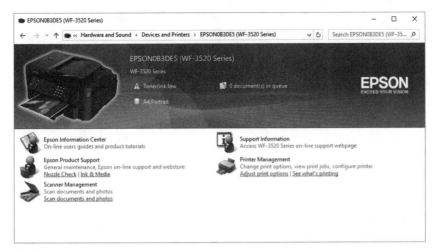

FIGURE 3-4 Device stage

Skill: Update, disable, and roll back drivers

Most computers that you'll work with have different hardware components, such as motherboards, disk controllers, graphics cards, and network adapters. Fortunately, Windows 10 is designed to work with an extensive list of hardware devices and benefits from Plug And Play, which tries to detect new devices automatically and then installs the correct driver software.

If Windows has a problem with a device, you must troubleshoot the cause, and this can involve locating the correct or updated device drivers and installing them. In this chapter, you focus on working with devices and drivers and the corrective and preventive actions you can take to help ensure that the devices you configure are free from problems.

> **This section covers how to:**
>
> - Update device drivers
> - Prevent driver updates over metered connections
> - Disable individual driver updates or Windows Updates
> - Turn on or off automatic device driver installation in Device Installation Settings
> - Perform a driver rollback

Update device drivers

Windows 10 automatically attempts to install a device driver and, if one is not available locally, attempts to locate one through Windows Update. For most systems, devices and their associated drivers remain constant and require no further administrative effort. In the following instances, you might need to update, disable, or reinstate a previous driver.

- Windows 10 detects that a newer driver is available through Windows Update.
- You want to install a newer device driver manually, typically obtained from the manufacturer's website.
- The device is not performing or functioning correctly with the current driver.
- A new or beta version of a driver is causing stability issues.

To update a specific driver, select the device in Device Manager and select Update Driver Software from the context menu.

Windows 10 offers you two choices for updating the driver.

- Search Automatically For Updated Driver Software.
- Browse My Computer For Driver Software.

Typically, most users allow Windows to locate, download, and install an updated device driver automatically if one is available through Windows Update. This is the default method.

If you have the installation media that came with the hardware, you can use the browse feature to locate the correct driver. The Windows 10 Update Driver Software Wizard can automatically search through the subfolders in the media and locate all the relevant drivers for the device.

If you have already downloaded a specific device driver from the manufacturer, for example, a video driver from NVIDIA or AMD/ATI, you might need to run the driver installation wizard included in the download files, which includes additional software besides the device driver.

If Windows determines that the current driver is the most up to date or best driver available, you can confirm the version number of the driver by viewing the properties of the driver in Device Manager. If you have a more recent driver that you want to use, you must manually uninstall the current driver and then manually install the more recent driver.

Prevent driver updates over metered connections

Windows 10 enables you to prevent new or updated drivers from being downloaded while the device is connected on a metered connection.

You can check your settings for this behavior by completing the following steps.

1. Open Settings and click Devices.
2. In Printers & Scanners, scroll down to Download Over Metered Connections.
3. The setting should be set to Off by default, as shown in Figure 3-5.

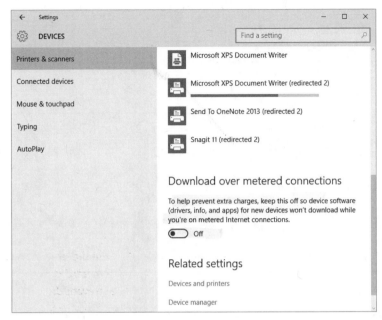

FIGURE 3-5 Configuring the Download Over Metered Connections setting

4. The same setting can also be found in the Connected Device section, which is below the Other Devices section.

5. Close Settings.

Windows 10 should automatically detect whether your connection is metered. If you are connecting to the Internet by tethering or a Wi-Fi hotspot, you can manually configure the connection to be a metered connection by using the following steps.

1. Connect to the metered Wi-Fi connection.

2. Open Settings and choose Network & Internet.

3. Under the Wi-Fi section, choose Advanced Options.

4. Under Metered Connection, select the On status for the toggle switch.

Disable individual driver updates or Windows Updates

Sometimes it is important to remove a device driver completely from the system. It might be corrupted or incompatible with your system. If Windows determines that the driver is valid and up to date, it is impossible to use another device driver while the current driver is present. To uninstall an unwanted device driver, use the following steps.

1. Open Device Manager.

2. Locate the device with the problem driver, right-click it, and choose Uninstall.

3. In the Uninstall dialog box, select the Delete The Driver Software For This Device check box, if this option is available, as shown in Figure 3-6.

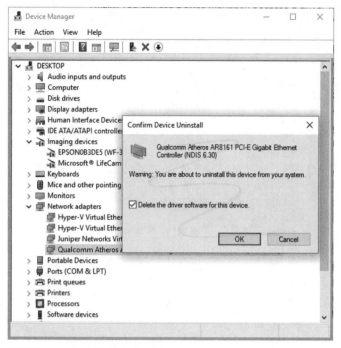

FIGURE 3-6 Uninstalling device driver software

If the item relates to an unwanted Windows Update, use the following steps.

1. Type **View Installed Updates** in the Search box and then click View Installed Updates – Control Panel in the Search results.

2. Locate and uninstall the unwanted update by selecting it from the list and then clicking Uninstall.

If the driver is reluctant to be uninstalled, try restarting the computer and attempting the procedure again. Only as a last resort should you try to delete the software manually. You can use the PnPUtil.exe command-line tool and remove the .inf files that are associated with the device as shown.

```
PnPUtil.exe -a -d <path to the driver> \<drivername>.inf
```

The use of the PnPUtil.exe command-line tool is discussed later in this chapter.

> **NOTE** **DRIVER INSTALLATION AND REMOVAL ARE ADMINISTRATIVE FUNCTIONS**
> You must use administrative privileges to install or uninstall a device or driver package by using Device Manager.

Because different hardware types have different functions and features, review the tabs in the properties screen. Not all devices have the same tabs, and some devices do not offer the ability to view or modify the device driver.

Turn on or off automatic device driver installation in Device Installation Settings

Sometimes installing an updated driver can cause your computer to lose functionality, and you might decide to uninstall the driver. Windows 10 automatically attempts to reinstall the driver, which is not desirable. In this situation, you might want to turn off the automatic device driver installation setting by using the following steps.

1. Open Control Panel; under Hardware And Sound, click Devices And Printers.

2. Under Devices, right-click the icon that represents your computer—it should have your computer name—and click Device Installation Settings, as shown in Figure 3-7.

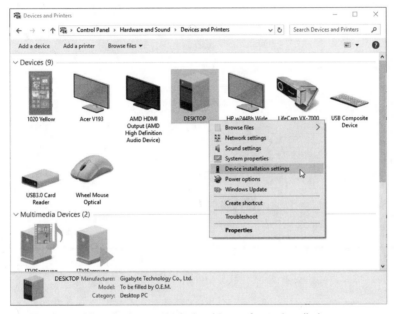

FIGURE 3-7 Disabling the automatic device driver software installation

3. In the Device Installation Settings dialog box, choose No, (Your Device Might Not Work As Expected). (Yes is the default setting.)

4. A further set of choices is presented, offering:

   - Always Install The Best Driver Software From Windows Update (default setting).
   - Never Install Driver Software From Windows Update.
   - Automatically Get The Device App And Info Provided By Your Device Manufacturer (selected by default).

5. Click Save Changes.

Perform a driver rollback

Sometimes a driver problem can cause the system to become unstable. In Device Manager, you can roll back an updated driver to its previous version. If the system allows you to start normally, you can perform this task by using the following steps.

1. Open Device Manager.

2. Right-click the device that you want to roll back and then click Properties.

3. In the Properties dialog box, click the Drivers tab and then click Roll Back Driver.

4. In the Driver Package Rollback dialog box, click Yes as shown in Figure 3-8.

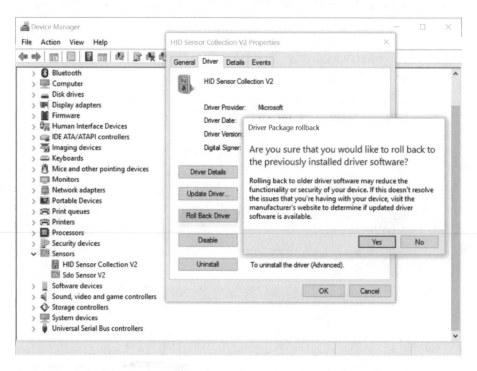

FIGURE 3-8 Device Driver Package Rollback

The Driver Package Rollback feature can only be used to revert to a previously updated driver. If you have not installed a later driver, the option in Device Manager will be unavailable.

> **NOTE NO DRIVER ROLLBACK FOR PRINTERS**
> Although Printers and Print queues appear in Device Manager, you cannot use Driver Package Rollback for these devices.

If your system is unstable or won't start up properly because of a faulty driver, such as a video driver, you might need to restart the computer in Safe Mode to access Device Manager and perform the driver rollback. Windows 10 automatically detects startup failures and should boot into the advanced startup menu.

Microsoft removed the ability to restart in Safe Mode by using Shift+F8 in Windows 10 so that the boot process could be quicker.

You can force Windows 10 still to respond to Shift+F8 by enabling the feature by typing the following command within an elevated command prompt.

```
BCDEdit /set {default} bootmenupolicy legacy
```

The command should complete successfully and, the next time you restart your PC, the boot process will take a little longer while Windows 10 checks to see whether you are pressing F8 to invoke the Safe Mode boot experience; follow these steps.

1. When your PC restarts, select Troubleshoot from the Choose An Option menu.

2. Select Advanced Options.

   Select Startup Settings and click Restart. You see the Advanced Boot Options screen as shown in Figure 3-9.

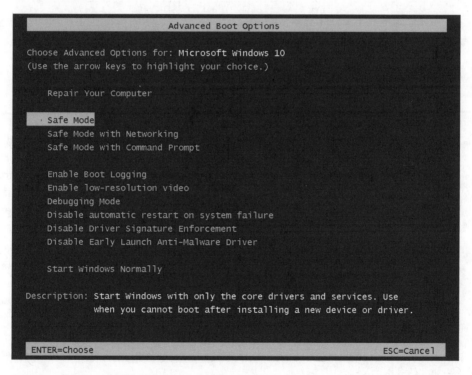

FIGURE 3-9 Windows 10 Advanced Boot Options screen

3. Select Safe Mode and press Enter.

4. Log on to the system and roll back the driver as described earlier.

The rollback feature remembers only the last driver that was installed and doesn't keep copies of multiple drivers for the same device.

Skill: Resolve driver issues

One of the most common issues with device drivers relates to users attempting to install a driver designed for an earlier operating system or a different architecture. In some cases on previous versions of Windows, it might have been possible to install a Windows 7 driver on a Windows 8–based computer, but this is not a supported operation for Windows 10 and should be avoided in a production environment. As is the case with other software installations, you can't use a 32-bit driver for a 64-bit resource. You can't use a 64-bit driver to communicate with a 32-bit resource, either.

In this section, you review how to disable specific device driver updates and tools you can use to verify the drivers on your system.

This section covers how to:

- Disable updates
- Use driver verification tools

Disable updates

Sometimes a specific update or driver will not be compatible with your system. Although all updates and drivers should be thoroughly checked before they are made available for installation, it is almost impossible to test every combination of software and hardware that can coexist on a computer. In some configurations, the new software might produce unsatisfactory results. You saw earlier that one method to avoid this situation is to turn off updates completely.

Disabling automatic driver updates might have a more widespread effect than you want, especially if you only need to disable or prevent the installation of a single driver. To enable you to block a specific update, Microsoft has released the Show Or Hide Updates troubleshooter package, available from the Microsoft Download Center at *https://support.microsoft .com/kb/3073930*.

This troubleshooter, shown in Figure 3-10, searches for available driver and Windows updates and then enables you to hide them, which prevents Windows from automatically installing them.

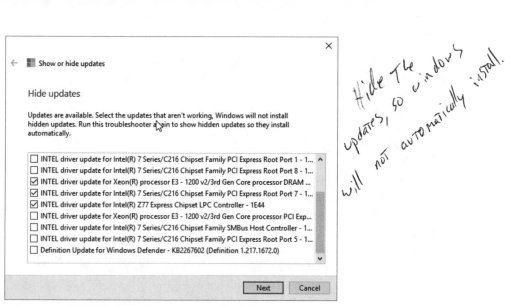

FIGURE 3-10 Show Or Hide Updates troubleshooter

(handwritten note) Hide The windows updates, so windows will not automatically install.

Each time you experience an issue with a driver or update that you don't want installed, you can run this troubleshooter and select the updates that you want to disable.

> **NOTE** **DEVICE MANAGER ERROR TROUBLESHOOTING**
>
> Device Manager marks a device that is not operating normally with a yellow exclamation point. When troubleshooting a device, you can check the error that Device Manager reports. For a detailed list of errors that Device Manager reports, see the article at *https://msdn.microsoft.com/library/windows/hardware/ff541422(v=vs.85).aspx.*

Use driver verification tools

If you encounter issues with drivers that seem to relate to malware or missing drivers, you can use a command-line tool called Sigverif.exe, which checks whether any drivers have been installed on the computer that have not been signed. The check can take several minutes to complete. To run this tool, perform the following steps.

1. Open a command prompt. (Standard user privilege level is OK.)

2. Type **sigverif.exe** and press Enter.

    The File Signature Verification Tool appears.

3. Review the Advanced options.

4. Click Start and view the results, as shown in Figure 3-11.

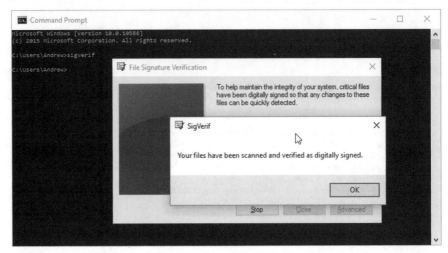

FIGURE 3-11 File Signature Verification tool

The sigverif tool is useful if you need to locate an unsigned driver, but there is a more powerful driver verification tool built into Windows 10, called the Driver Verifier Manager.

EXAM TIP

In the advanced settings of the Signature Verification tool is the file name of the log file, a good thing to know for the exam. Review the log file found at %SystemRoot%\Sigverif.txt after the operation has completed.

With the enhanced kernel mode operation and reliance on signed drivers, Windows 10 should be less prone to frequent Stop errors. Although less likely, even signed drivers can cause problems, especially if you have an exotic combination of hardware inside your computer. If you do encounter instability then, use the built-in Driver Verifier to discover whether a faulty driver is causing the problem.

Driver Verifier Manager can help you troubleshoot, identify, and resolve common device driver problems, and you can then remove, reinstall, or roll back the offending driver with Device Manager.

To run the series of driver tests, follow these steps.

1. Open a command prompt (Admin), using administrative privileges.

2. Type **verifier.exe** and press Enter.

   The Driver Verifier tool appears.

3. Review the settings in the tool.

   Depending on which option you choose, you might need to restart your machine for the tool to recognize all loaded drivers.

4. After you have selected drivers to be tested, restart the computer, restart the application, and then select Display Information About The Currently Verified Drivers.

Driver Verifier Manager tests each specified driver at startup and then enables you to perform live test of each loaded driver by a range of tests, as shown in Figure 3-12. If it detects a problem, the tool can identify the driver, and then you can disable it.

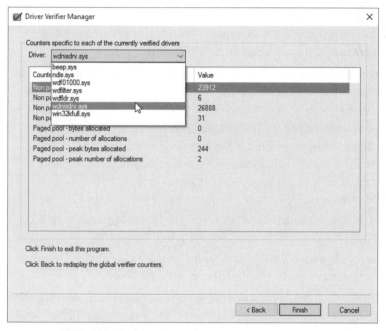

FIGURE 3-12 Driver Verifier Manager tool

Skill: Configure driver settings

Device drivers provide Windows 10 with the information required to populate the device details that you find in Device Manager. If only a few details are available to view, the device might have been installed using the built-in driver, and you might be able to install a driver from the manufacturer's website, which will give additional information through Device Manager.

In this section, you explore Device Manager, configure driver settings that are available for installed devices, and look at how to view and configure settings for older hardware.

> **This section covers how to:**
> - View device settings
> - Support older hardware

View device settings

The default Device Manager screen enables users to work directly in the Properties dialog box of a device and provides information about the device that the hardware and device driver provide. The following is a review of Device Manager features that you can use to explore the available information so that you can configure the driver settings.

In Device Manager, explore these four menu options.

- **File**   This menu enables you to exit the console and optionally delete the record of the console customizations you make to the console settings.

- **Action**   This menu enables you to access the action-specific tasks relating to the highlighted hardware, including Update Driver Software, Disable, Uninstall, Scan For Hardware Changes, Add Legacy Hardware, Properties, and Help.

- **View**   This menu enables you to change how the console view displays advanced information relating to the devices listed in Device Manager. You can view devices by device type or connection or resources by type or connection. Some hardware is also hidden from normal view, and this option can be set to show hidden devices. The Customize option enables you to show or hide items within the console.

- **Help**   This menu offers access to help topics relating to Device Manager and the console, plus a link to the Microsoft TechCenter website, which is part of TechNet.

There are several advanced views in Device Manager that standard users do not normally use. These include the connection type and hidden device views, as follows.

- **Show Hidden Devices**   In previous versions of Windows, printers and non–Plug and Play (PnP) devices could be marked by the device manufacturer as a NoDisplayClass type of device, which prevents it from automatically being displayed in the Device Manager. Devices that have been removed from the computer but whose registry entries are still present can also be found in the hidden devices list.

- **Devices By Type**   This is the default view and shows devices grouped by familiar device name such as Network Adapters, Ports, and Disk Drives. Each node can be expanded by selecting the > symbol to the left of the node name.

- **Devices By Connection**   You can view devices based on the hardware connection, such as physical or virtual.

- **Resources By Type**   Use this option to view resources organized by how they connect to system resources, including Direct Memory Access (DMA), Input/Output (IO), Interrupt Request (IRQ), and Memory. Unless your BIOS allows you to declare that you are not using a Plug And Play–compliant operating system, you will not be able to modify these settings.

- **Resources By Connection**   This view is for advanced users only and is not particularly useful on a modern system. Viewing the device hardware resources by DMA, IO, IRQ, and Memory were useful for earlier versions of Windows prior to the introduction of Plug And Play, which allowed the operating system to manage automatically the resources required by devices.

Support for older hardware

Some of the advanced settings in Device Manager are seldom used but have been retained for backward compatibility with older devices that do not support Plug And Play. Modern hardware peripherals must support Plug And Play, which allows Windows 10 to assign hardware resources automatically to new devices. If you look on the Resource tab of a device Properties dialog box in Device Manager, you see that a check box is selected indicating that Windows 10 is using automatic settings, as shown in Figure 3-13. The setting is dimmed and not changeable unless you disable the BIOS/UEFI setting, which declares that the operating system is Plug And Play–compliant.

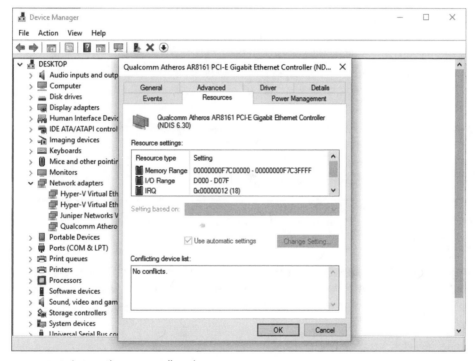

FIGURE 3-13 Automatic resource allocation

The Plug And Play standard for connecting devices to Windows is nearly two decades old. Some hardware still exists that requires the administrator to install it manually. In Device Manager, the Add Hardware Wizard enables you to install hardware that does not support Plug And Play. To install such hardware, perform the following steps.

1. Open Device Manager.
2. On the Action tab, click Add Legacy Hardware.

3. On the Welcome To The Add Hardware Wizard page, click Next.

4. Select one of these options:

   - Search For And Install The Hardware Automatically (Recommended)

   - Install The Hardware That I Manually Select From A List

5. Follow the wizard prompts to finish the configuration of the hardware and provide the driver when requested.

> **NOTE NON-PNP (OLDER) DEVICES ARE NOT SHOWN IN WINDOWS 10**
>
> Since Windows 8 and Windows Server 2012, non-PnP devices have not been represented in Device Manager as viewable nodes.

Skill: Driver signing

One of the reasons Windows 10 is more secure than earlier versions of Windows is that kernel mode drivers must now be submitted to and digitally signed by the Windows Hardware Developer Center Dashboard portal. Windows 10 will not load kernel mode drivers that the portal has not signed.

To ensure backward compatibility, drivers that are properly signed by a valid cross-signing certificate will continue to pass signing checks on Windows 10.

> **NEED MORE REVIEW? DRIVER SIGNING CHANGES IN WINDOWS 10**
>
> This MSDN resource provides more depth on driver signing changes in Windows 10 at *https://blogs.msdn.microsoft.com/windows_hardware_certification/2015/04/01/driver-signing -changes-in-windows-10/.*

Windows 10 also introduces a new Universal Windows driver, which is designed to work on all OneCoreUAP-based editions of Windows, such as Windows 10 for desktop editions (Home, Pro, Enterprise, and Education), Windows 10 Mobile, and Windows 10 Internet of Things Core (IoT Core).

A Universal Windows driver has access to the trusted kernel and has a very limited range of the interfaces that are available to a Windows driver. OEMs can supplement the driver functionality by including additional software, but this will be external to the driver. Windows 10 security is more robust by locking down the kernel to signed drivers and encouraging developers to use the Universal Windows driver model,

For information about how to build, install, deploy, and debug a Universal Windows driver for Windows 10, see Getting Started With Universal Windows Drivers.

If you have a specific need to install an unsigned driver—for example, if you are a developer and work with drivers, and you want to test the driver functionality without having to sign the driver digitally each time—you can invoke a special boot-time configuration setting that bypasses the security the Windows 10 driver enforcement model provides. To load an unsigned driver (not recommended), you can follow these steps.

1. Log out of Windows 10.

2. On the logon screen, click the Power button, hold down the Shift key, and click Restart.

3. On the Choose An Option screen, choose Troubleshoot.

4. Choose Advanced Options.

5. On the Advanced Options screen, select Startup Settings and click Restart. Advanced Boot Options appears.

6. Choose Disable Driver Signature Enforcement, as shown in Figure 3-14.

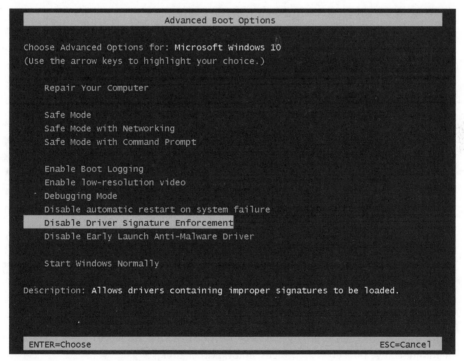

FIGURE 3-14 Disable Driver Signature Enforcement

7. Install the unsigned driver and then restart the computer.

Skill: Manage driver packages

When device drivers are created by the original equipment manufacturer (OEM), they are deployed with the hardware in a driver package that includes all the files and information required for Windows 10 to communicate with the hardware. You see how driver packages are managed and how to install, provision, and import driver packages on Windows 10 devices.

> **This section covers how to:**
> - Use the driver store
> - Use PnPUtil.exe to manage driver packages

Use the driver store

You saw earlier that the driver package can include an information file (.inf file), any files that the .inf file references, and a .cat file that contains the digital signature for the device driver. Windows 10 uses the Driver Store to hold device drivers that have been installed or pre-staged.

All Windows 10 kernel mode drivers must be digitally signed by the Windows Hardware Developer Center Dashboard portal. Windows 10 will prevent the loading of new kernel mode drivers that are not signed by the portal. This is an important change from previous versions of Windows and will make the operating system more secure. Previously, it could be possible for a hacker to gain unauthorized access to a system by using a flaw in an unsigned device driver. Ensuring that all drivers are digitally signed will remove the ability for a hacker to add or modify device driver contents.

If you are creating a custom installation image, or if you build and deploy many computers, you can speed up the driver installation process by pre-loading the Windows 10 driver store with the specific drivers for the peripheral devices that your devices will be using. When Windows 10 finds the drivers it needs in the driver store, located in %SystemRoot%\System32\DriverStore, it uses these local drivers and does not download them from Windows Update.

Pre-installing a driver is a two-stage process, and the first stage must be carried out with administrator credentials. You need to add the driver package to the driver store and then ensure that the hardware is attached; Windows 10 then automatically locates and installs the local driver.

There are a few ways to deploy drivers to the driver store, and the most appropriate method will depend on your physical network infrastructure, network connectivity, and level of administrative privileges on devices, among other things.

Use PnPUtil.exe to manage driver packages

To pre-stage the installation of a specific hardware device, you can install a driver manually before connecting the device, by using the PnPUtil.exe command-line tool. This could be useful when distributing a laptop to a remote user who you know has a local printer or scanner. Standard users cannot normally install device drivers, but if the driver package is already in the driver store, this is possible.

Run the PnPUtil.exe command by using administrative privileges, and you can use it to manage the Driver Store, adding, deleting, and listing driver packages. You saw earlier that a driver package consists of all the information Windows 10 requires to install and trust the driver, including the following.

- **Driver files** Dynamic link library (DLL) files with the .sys file extension.
- **Installation files** Text files containing all the information needed to install a driver. These .inf files include information such as driver name and location, driver version information, and registry information. These files are copied to the %SystemRoot%\Inf directory during installation. Every installed device must have an .inf file.
- **Driver Catalog file** Contains a cryptographic hash of each file in the driver package. These hashes are used to verify that the package was not altered after it was published (created). Digitally signing the catalog file proves the file has not been altered, because only the digital signature owner can sign the file.
- **Additional files** These are files such as a device installation application, device icon, device property pages, and additional files.

For enhanced security, Windows 10 now uses a single kernel model across all editions of Windows 10 and is encouraging the use, now, of a new universal driver model. This universal .inf file is required when deploying device drivers to an offline system image, such as when building a Windows 10 Mobile system (which does not support Plug And Play).

The syntax for the PnPUtil.exe command-line tool is as follows.

```
PnPUtil.exe -a <path to the driver> \<drivername>.inf
```

The full list of parameters is shown in Table 3-1.

TABLE 3-1 PnPUtil.exe parameters

Parameter	Description
-a	Adds a driver package to the driver store
-d	Removes a driver package from the driver store
-e	Lists the driver packages that are currently in the driver store
-f	Forces the deletion of the specified driver package from the driver store; cannot be used with the -i parameter.
-i	Installs the driver package on matching devices that are connected to the system. Cannot be used with the -f parameter
/?	Displays help

An example command to add the INF file specified by MyDevice.inf to the driver store (located at %SystemRoot%\System32\DriverStore) is:

```
PnPUtil.exe –a C:\Temp\MyDevice.inf
```

EXAM TIP

After a driver has been added to the driver store, the driver is referenced in the store through its published name, which might be different from the driver package (.inf) name. You can review the published name by viewing the contents of the .inf file.

In addition to the PnPUtil.exe tool, you can use the following Windows PowerShell cmdlets.

- **Get-PnpDevice**   Displays information about PnP devices
- **Get-PnpDeviceProperty**   Displays detailed properties for a PnP device
- **Enable-PnpDevice**   Enables a PnP device
- **Disable-PnpDevice**   Disables a PnP device

An example Windows PowerShell command to enable the device with an instance ID of 'USB\VID_5986&;PID_0266&;MI_00\7&;1E5D3568&;0&;0000' is as follows.

```
PS C:\> Enable-PnpDevice –InstanceId 'USB\VID_5986&;PID_0266&;MI_00\7&;1E
5D3568&;0&;0000'
```

For more information about, or for the syntax of, any of the Windows PowerShell cmdlets, you can use the Get-Help *<cmdlet name>* cmdlet such as the following.

```
Get-Help <cmdlet name> –Examples
```

Skill: Download and import driver packages

Drivers are packaged together; each driver package consists of all the software components that are needed for your device to work with Windows.

Most drivers are obtained directly by using built-in tools such as Windows Update, but if you are provisioning systems, you might want to deploy the PC with the required drivers already imported and configured.

> **This section covers how to:**
> - Download driver packages
> - Deploy driver packages by using the Windows Imaging and Configuration Designer
> - Import driver packages

Download driver packages

Device drivers can be accessed to perform a malicious attack on your systems. Therefore, you should ensure that driver packages are sourced only from reputable locations such as the manufacturer's own website. You should avoid third-party driver repository websites because some sites repackage drivers and include spyware or freeware products in the installation files.

The built-in Windows 10 driver packages are often just the core drivers created by your device manufacturer and provided by Microsoft through the Windows Hardware Quality Labs (WHQL), which tests and digitally signs the drivers. Video drivers often include additional software support and hardware functionality. For example, drivers sourced directly from NVIDIA or AMD for their graphics cards include the NVIDIA Control Panel or the AMD Catalyst control panel, respectively.

If you are seeking the most up-to-date or even beta version of a device driver, you must download this directly from your device manufacturer. In most cases, you will not need to upgrade your device driver after Windows 10 is installed. If everything is working properly, you probably don't need to install extra hardware drivers.

If you are a gamer, it can be beneficial to ensure that your graphics card drivers are using the latest versions so that they support the latest PC games.

You should consider downloading new driver packages in the following scenarios.

- **If you play PC games**   Install the latest graphics drivers directly from your graphics card manufacturer because they are often required to play the latest games. Newer versions can also improve graphics performance.

- **When you need a hardware utility**   Install the latest version if the manufacturer-provided driver package includes a hardware utility, such as a network configuration tool or ink monitor for your printer.

- **To resolve a bug**   Bugs can be found in released drivers and will often be fixed in the most up-to-date version.

- **To install hardware manually**   If Windows Plug And Play does not automatically detect and install the hardware, you might need to download the driver package from the manufacturer and install the device driver.

Deploy driver packages by using the Windows Imaging And Configuration Designer

A new method of deploying customized Windows devices (or applying customizations to an already deployed device) is by using the new Windows Imaging And Configuration Designer (ICD) tool available in Windows 10. This tool is part of the Windows Assessment And Deployment Kit (ADK) for Windows 10, which is available at *http://go.microsoft.com /fwlink/?LinkId=526803*.

> ***NOTE*** **DOWNLOAD THE LATEST VERSION OF THE WINDOWS ADK FOR WINDOWS 10**
>
> **You must ensure that the Windows ADK for Windows 10, language packs, and Feature-On-Demand (FOD) files are all from the same build with a matching build number.**

After you have installed the Windows ADK for Windows 10, you can open the ICD and create a new provisioning package (with the .ppkg file extension), which can then be deployed to the devices requiring customization. You can email the .ppkg file or deploy it physically on a USB drive through Microsoft Intune or Group Policy, or you can build it directly into a new system image if you have not yet deployed the computer.

To deploy a device driver by using the Windows ICD, create a new project but use the following steps.

1. Click Start, type **ICD**, and launch Windows Imaging And Configuration Designer.
2. Accept User Account Control (UAC) if prompted.
3. Click New Provisioning Package.
4. On the Enter Project Details page, name the project **Deploy Scanner Driver**.
5. On the New Project page, select the Common To All Windows Desktop Editions, click Next, and click Next again.
6. On the Available Customizations page, expand Deployment Assets and then click Drivers.
7. In the middle pane, next to the Driver folder path, click Browse.
8. Browse to your INF-based driver, select the driver, and then click OK.

    The driver .inf file should show up in the Drivers box. (You might need to extract driver files if they have been packaged as .zip or .exe files.)
9. In the Name box, type the friendly name for the driver, as shown in Figure 3-15.

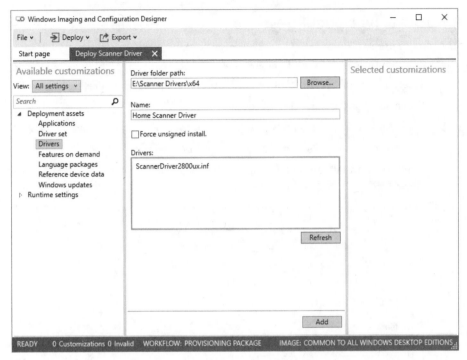

FIGURE 3-15 Windows Imaging And Configuration Designer (ICD) tool

10. Select the Force Unsigned Install check box only if the driver is unsigned.

11. Click Add to add the customization.

This now appears in the right pane. The driver's descriptive name should appear in the Selected Customizations pane. To complete the process, the provisioning package is created by using the following steps.

1. On the menu bar, click Export.

2. Select Provisioning Package.

3. On the Describe The Provisioning Package page, review the information, modify Owner to be IT Admin, and then click Next.

4. On the Select Security Details For The Provisioning Package page, click Next.

5. Choose the default name and location or provide a path and file name for the provisioning package to be created and click Next.

6. On the Build The Provisioning Package page, review the information and then click Build.

7. When it is complete, click Finish.

8. After the provisioning package has been built, use the links provided to locate the created files. You can deploy these files to your remote users on removable media such as USB drives.

Import driver packages

The remote users will import the driver package contained in the provisioning package to their computer by completing the following steps.

1. Insert a removable drive containing the provisioning package files (in the media root).

2. Open Settings and then click Accounts.

3. Click Work Access and then click Add Or Remove A Package From Work Or School.

4. On the Provisioning Packages page, click Add A Package.

5. On the Choose A Method page, select Removable Drive from the Add From drop-down list.

6. Select the package that you want to install and click Add, as shown in Figure 3-16.

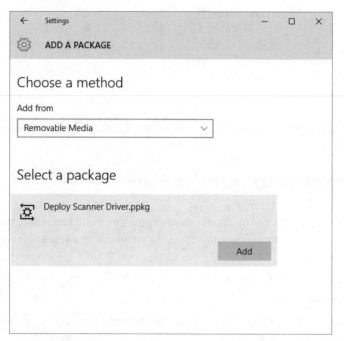

FIGURE 3-16 Adding a provisioning package

7. On the UAC page, click Yes.

8. On the Is This Package From A Source You Trust page, click Yes, Add It.

   The package will install in the background.

Skill: Use Deployment Image Servicing And Management tool to add packages

You saw earlier that the Deployment Image Servicing and Management (DISM) tool is now included as part of the Windows 10 operating system. It is useful for offline image servicing. DISM is a command-line tool that you can use to maintain images and apply them with Windows Updates. It is also used to add and remove Windows features, including language packs, and to manage device drivers.

> **This section covers how to:**
> - Add packages by using DISM
> - Manage driver packages with DISM

Add packages using DISM

If you have a custom Windows 10 image, you can use DISM to modify it, and the changes will be visible when you next deploy the image. This can be useful when you know that a driver has been updated since you built the deployment image. Using DISM to inject the new driver saves you from having to rebuild the whole image. Using DISM is similar to using a file compression tool such as WinRAR, whereby you add or remove new files and then WinRAR reseals the .wim, .vhd, or vhdx file ready for deployment.

When you use DISM to install a device driver to an offline image, the device driver is added to the driver store. When the image is booted, Plug And Play (PnP) runs, looks for drivers in the store, and associates them with the corresponding devices on the computer they're being installed on.

To add drivers to an offline image by using DISM, use these steps.

1. Right-click the Start button and select Command Prompt (Admin).

2. Establish the name or index number for the image that you are servicing by typing:

    ```
    Dism /Get-ImageInfo /ImageFile:C:\test\images\install.wim
    ```

3. Mount the offline Windows image by typing the following.

    ```
    Dism /Mount-Image /ImageFile:C:\test\images\install.wim /Name:"Windows Offline
    Image" /MountDir:C:\test\offline
    ```

4. You can now add the driver, located in the C:\Drivers folder, to the image by typing:

```
Dism /Image:C:\test\offline /Add-Driver /Driver:C:\drivers\New_driver.inf
```

5. If you have additional drivers in a folder, you can use the /Recurse option, which installs all the drivers from a folder and all its subfolders. To do this, type:

```
Dism /Image:C:\test\offline /Add-Driver /Driver:c:\drivers /Recurse
```

6. You can review the drivers in the Windows image by typing:

```
Dism /Image:C:\test\offline /Get-Drivers
```

In the list of drivers, notice that the added drivers have been renamed Oem*.inf. This ensures that all driver files in the driver store have unique names. For example, the New_Driver1.inf and New_Driver2.inf files are renamed Oem0.inf and Oem1.inf.

7. To complete the operation, commit the changes and unmount the image by typing:

```
Dism /Unmount-Image /MountDir:C:\test\offline /Commit
```

> **NEED MORE REVIEW?** **DISM**
>
> For a detailed reference for the DISM command-line options, you can visit TechNet at *https://technet.microsoft.com/library/hh825099.*

Manage driver packages with DISM

During the life of a Windows 10 installation, the system downloads and installs multiple versions of device driver packages over time. For devices with small hard-drive capacity, be aware of how to locate and delete outdated driver packages that the system retains.

You can use the built-in Disk Cleanup tool to remove device driver packages that have been kept after newer drivers are installed.

To clean up old device drivers by using the Disk Cleanup tool, perform these steps.

1. Click the Start button, type **Disk Cleanup,** and then select the Disk Cleanup app.
2. In the Drive Selection dialog box, select (C:) and click OK.
3. On the Disk Cleanup results screen, select Clean Up System Files.
4. In the Drive Selection dialog box, select (C:) and click OK.
5. On the Disk Cleanup results screen, select Device Driver Packages and click OK.
6. On the Are You Sure You Want To Permanently Delete These Files page, click Delete Files.

All driver packages that were installed during the Windows 10 setup process are stored in a directory called WinSxS, the side-by-side component store. This folder contains driver packages and operating system components so that you can add devices later without having to supply device drivers. If disk space is limited, you can purge the WinSxS directory contents, because it could occupy a significant amount of disk space.

To analyze the Windows Component Store for driver packages and other files that can be deleted, you can use the DISM command by using the following steps.

1. Right-click the Start button, select Command Prompt (Admin), and type the following.

```
DISM /Online /Cleanup-Image /AnalyzeComponentStore
```

The tool analyzes your system. Typical results are shown in Figure 3-17.

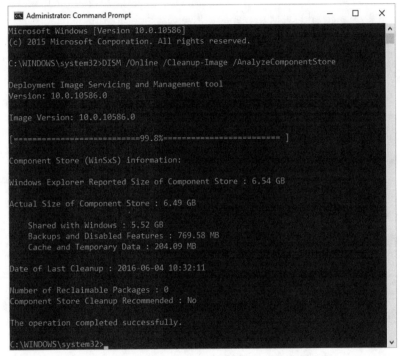

FIGURE 3-17 Analyzing the Component Store (WinSxS) with DISM

2. When the analysis is complete, you can initiate a cleanup of the Windows Component Store by typing the following command.

```
DISM /Online /Cleanup-Image /StartComponentCleanup /ResetBase
```

IMPORTANT   DO NOT DELETE THE WINSXS FOLDER

Do not manually delete the WinSxS directory or its contents to reclaim the space, because Windows creates many hard links from files in the WinSxS folder to locations in system folders.

Summary

- Device Manager is the primary tool for installing and managing devices.
- Device And Printers and Device Stage offer visual alternatives to Device Manager.
- Windows Update automatically updates device drivers.
- To install or pre-stage device drivers manually, use the PnPUtil command-line tool.
- Updated device drivers that are not stable can be rolled back to the previous version.
- You can use the File Signature Verification tool (Sigverif.exe) to check that all drivers are digitally signed and DISM to manage driver packages for offline images.
- Plug And Play is the feature that enables Windows to detect and install the correct device driver automatically for the attached hardware.
- Driver signing is enforced in Windows 10 and protects system security.
- The new Windows Imaging And Configuration Designer (ICD) generates provisioning packages with the .ppkg file extension, which can customize Windows 10.

Thought experiment

In this thought experiment, demonstrate your skills and knowledge of the topics covered in this chapter. You can find answers to this thought experiment in the next section.

Your organization has recently recruited 20 new members to the sales team, who will work across the United States. Your manager wants to issue them the following hardware, which will be shipped to the employee's home address directly from the online reseller.

- Surface Pro 4 tablet
- Bluetooth mouse
- Epson WF-3520 printer

The sales team members have standard user accounts, email accounts, and Internet access at home. You are required to ensure that the sales team members can operate the new equipment without delay and with minimal involvement of the company help desk. The organization holds its own certificate authority for creating certificates.

The company has commissioned a short introduction to Windows 10 and the functions of the Epson printer and mouse, which is available on the company intranet, by email, and offline. All users must view the training prior to using Windows 10.

Answer the following questions for your manager:

1. Where will you obtain the latest driver software for the mouse and printer drivers?
2. How will you provision the mouse and printer drivers on the Surface tablets?
3. Can you provision the mouse and printer drivers as one package or only separately?

4. How will you ensure that the users trust the provision of drivers?

5. How can you ensure that users are familiar with the operation of the Epson printer?

Thought experiment answers

This section contains the solutions to the thought experiment.

1. You would use the media and device driver supplied with the hardware equipment or download the latest version from the manufacturer's official website.

2. You would create a provisioning package with the Windows Imaging And Configuration Designer (ICD), export the .ppkg files, and deploy these to the users by email, postal mail, or an intranet site. The users could then run the provisioning packages on their devices. If they required further assistance, they could call the help desk.

3. You can use the ICD to create provisioning packages that deploy single or multiple customizations to Windows 10.

4. You would use only digitally signed device drivers and, additionally, digitally sign the provisioning package with the organizational certificate authority.

5. You should ask each member of the remote sales team to access the company intranet site and review the short introduction to Windows 10 and the functions of the Epson printer that will be available there. You could also ensure that they are aware of Device Stage for the Epson printer.

CHAPTER 4

Post-installation configuration

A fter you have installed Windows 10 and configured devices, you must configure the operating system to meet your users' specific needs. The nature of this post-installation configuration varies, but typically includes power settings, customization of the user interface, and, where necessary, configuration of accessibility options.

You might also configure some of the new features in Windows 10, such as Cortana and Microsoft Edge. The 70-698 Configuring Windows 10 exam also covers the configuration of the Client Hyper-V role and how to create, configure, and manage virtual machines.

Skills covered in this chapter:

- Configure and customize the user interface per device type
- Configure accessibility options
- Configure Cortana
- Configure Microsoft Edge
- Configure Microsoft Internet Explorer
- Configure Hyper-V
- Configure power settings

Skill: Configure and customize the user interface per device type

After you have activated Windows 10, you can customize the user interface. In some respects, the Windows 10 user interface is familiar to users of Windows 7. It has a Start menu, a desktop, and a taskbar; these things all appear in Windows 7. However, because Windows 10 is designed to work across a variety of device types, including phones, tablets, and traditional desktop computers, it provides additional ways for users to interact.

As an IT pro, it is important for you to understand how to customize the Windows 10 user interface, including Start, taskbar, desktop, and notification settings. This enables you to ensure that the operating system interface meets the needs of the users in your organization.

Customize the user interface

If you're a Windows 7 user, the most noticeable change in the user interface is the support for touch. As a consequence, much of the user interface has been redesigned to support touch actions, such as swipe and pinch. Because of these and other changes, the user interface is somewhat different from earlier versions of Windows, such as Windows 7.

Customize Start

These differences are nowhere more evident than in Start. The appearance of Start depends on your device type, for example, a tablet or desktop PC.

If you are using a tablet, then by default, Start appears full screen, as shown in Figure 4-1. This is easier to navigate when using a touch device.

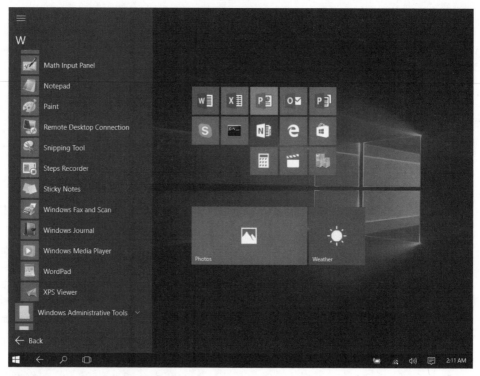

FIGURE 4-1 Start configured full screen

If you are using a non-touch device, then by default Windows 10 displays Start as a menu that is fairly similar to that in Windows 7, as shown in Figure 4-2. This is more easily navigable by using a mouse than by touch.

FIGURE 4-2 Start displayed partial screen

You can configure the Start menu behavior from Settings. Click Personalization and then click the Start tab. You can then select the option to Use Start Full screen, as shown in Figure 4-3.

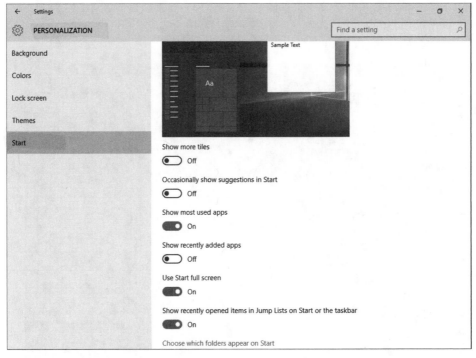

FIGURE 4-3 Start menu settings

Other Start customizations shown in Figure 4-3 include:

- **Show More Tiles**   This setting enables you to display more tiles when Start is config-ured for partial-screen mode.

- **Occasionally Show Suggestions In Start**   This setting enables or disables app sug-gestions in Start.

- **Show Most Used Apps**   Windows 10 tracks your app usage and lists your most fre-quently used apps in a Most Used Apps list in Start.

- **Show Recently Added Apps**   Any recently installed apps are marked as new in Start.

- **Show Recently Opened Items In Jump Lists On Start Or The Taskbar**   This setting enables Windows 10 to remember recently opened files and list those in the context menu of apps appearing in Start or on the taskbar.

- **Choose Which Folders Appear On Start**   This setting enables you to set shortcuts for the following folders on Start: File Explorer, Settings, Documents, Downloads, Music, Pictures, Videos, HomeGroup, Network, and Personal folder.

CONVERTIBLE DEVICES

Some devices, including the Microsoft Surface Pro 4, can switch in and out of Tablet mode with the removal and reattachment of the keyboard, or by reorienting the device. When a device switches like this, you can choose whether Windows switches to full-screen Start (tablet mode), as shown in Figure 4-4.

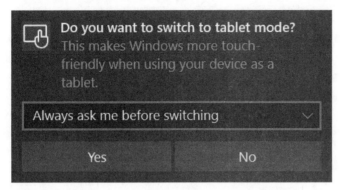

FIGURE 4-4 The tablet mode prompt on a convertible laptop

You can configure the default behavior through the Settings app. Click System and then click the Tablet Mode tab. As shown in Figure 4-5, you can then configure the following options.

- When I Sign In:
  - Automatically Switch To Tablet Mode.
  - Go To The Desktop.
  - Remember What I Used Last.
- When This Device Automatically Switches Tablet Mode On Or Off:
  - Don't Ask Me And Don't Switch.
  - Always Ask Me Before Switching.
  - Don't Ask Me And Always Switch.

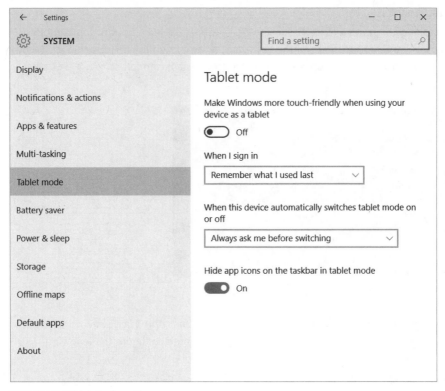

FIGURE 4-5 Tablet mode options

NOTE **TABLET MODE**

Tablet mode also changes applications so that they run full screen.

CONFIGURING TILES

In addition to enabling or disabling Start full-screen behavior, you can also customize the application tiles that appear on Start and how those tiles look and behave. From Start, click All Apps and then right-click the appropriate app, as shown in Figure 4-6. Click Pin To Start.

When a tile is pinned to Start, you can configure it. Right-click the tile and, from the context menu, you can:

- Unpin from Start.
- Resize.   Choose from Small, Medium, Large, and Wide, depending on the app.

- More:
  - If the app is a Windows Store app, choose from Turn Live Tile Off, Pin To Taskbar, Rate And Review, and Share.
  - If the app is a desktop app, choose from Pin To Taskbar, Run As Administrator, and Open File Location.
- Uninstall.

NOTE **UNINSTALLING DESKTOP APPS FROM START**

If the app you select to uninstall is a desktop app, Programs And Features opens in Control Panel. You must now manually remove the desktop app.

FIGURE 4-6 Customizing the presence and appearance of tiles on Start with a mouse

If your device is touch-enabled, the procedure is slightly different than when using a mouse to configure tiles. Rather than right-clicking a tile from Start, you must touch and hold a tile. Then you can unpin the tile by using the unpin icon. Use the ellipse button to access the context menu, as shown in Figure 4-7.

FIGURE 4-7 Customizing the presence and appearance of tiles on Start with touch

GROUPING TILES

After you have added the required tiles to Start, you might want to group the tiles. You can perform the following actions on groups.

- To create a new group of tiles, simply drag a tile to an area of unused space on Start.
- To name a group, hover your mouse or tap the screen immediately above the group of tiles and then type the name for your group in the text box that appears.
- To move tiles between groups, drag the required tile to the new group.

CONFIGURING START WITH GROUP POLICY OBJECTS

Although you can manually drag and resize tiles on Start for each computer in your organization, it is time-consuming. In an AD DS environment, you can control Start layout by using Group Policy Objects (GPOs). Figure 4-8 shows the named components that make up Start, including the section that is customizable known as *Start Layout*.

To use GPOs to control Start layout, first create an XML layout file and store the file in an accessible location such as a shared folder. The easiest way to do this is to use the following procedure.

1. Configure a test computer and establish the layout for Start that you want to propagate throughout your organization.
2. Open Windows PowerShell.
3. Run **the export-StartLayout filename.xml** cmdlet.
4. Copy the exported file to a shared folder.

Next, you must modify the following GPO path: User Configuration\Policies\Administrative Templates\Start Menu and Taskbar\Start Layout. To do this, complete the following procedure.

1. Open Group Policy Management on a domain controller.
2. Navigate to the appropriate AD DS container, such as your domain.

3. Open an existing GPO for editing or create a new GPO, link it to your chosen container, and open it for editing.

4. Navigate to the User Configuration\Policies\Administrative Templates\Start Menu And Taskbar folder and open the Start Layout value.

5. Enable the value and, in the Start Layout File text box, type the full UNC path name to your XML file, for example, \\LON-SVR1\Marketing\Marketing.XML.

6. Click OK and close Group Policy Management.

For the policy to be effective, users must sign out and sign back in. Alternatively, you can issue a **Gpupdate.exe /force** command from an elevated command prompt to force GPO propagation.

> **NEED MORE REVIEW?** **CUSTOMIZE WINDOWS 10 START WITH GROUP POLICY**
>
> For more information about customizing Start with GPOs, visit the Microsoft TechNet website at *https://technet.microsoft.com/library/mt431718(v=vs.85).aspx*.

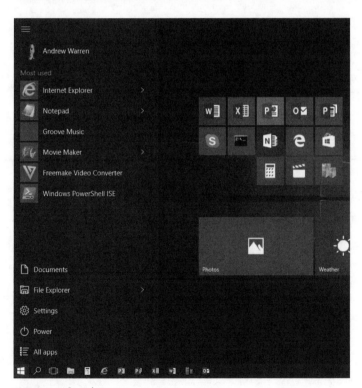

FIGURE 4-8 Start layout components

In addition to the Start layout, you can control other aspects of Start with GPOs. Figure 4-8 shows the controllable elements of Start, and Table 4-1 shows the elements that you can control with GPOs and the respective values to use within GPOs. Unless otherwise noted, the path for these GPO settings is User Configuration\Policies\Administrative Templates\Start Menu And Taskbar.

TABLE 4-1 Using GPOs to configure Start

Start element	Policy
User tile	Remove Logoff on the Start menu
Most Used	Remove frequent programs from the Start menu
Suggestions	Computer Configuration\Policies\Administrative Templates\Windows Components \Cloud Content\Turn Off Microsoft Consumer Experiences
Power	Remove And Prevent Access To The Shut Down, Restart, Sleep, And Hibernate Commands
All Apps	Remove All Programs List From The Start Menu
Jump lists	Do Not Keep History Of Recently Opened Documents
Start size	Force Start To Be Either Full Screen Size Or Menu Size
All Settings	Prevent Changes To Taskbar And Start Menu Settings

Customize the desktop

In addition to customizing Start to your requirements, you can configure Desktop and related settings. To configure Desktop, from Start, click Settings and then click Personalization.

From the Personalization settings app, you can configure the following settings.

- **Background**   You can select and configure a desktop background image or color.
- **Colors**   On the Color tab, you can choose a color scheme and optionally configure the following options.
  - Show Color On Start, Taskbar, Action Center, And Title Bar.
  - Make Start, Taskbar And Action Center Transparent.
  - Access the High contrast settings.
- **Lock screen**   From the Lock screen tab, as shown in Figure 4-9, you can select and configure a background image to display when your Windows 10 device is locked. In addition, you can:
  - Choose An App To Show Detailed Status, for example, Calendar.
  - Choose Apps To Show Quick Status, for example, Facebook, Mail, Calendar, Alarms & Clock.
  - Show Windows Background Picture On The Sign-In Screen.
  - Configure screen timeout settings and screen saver settings.

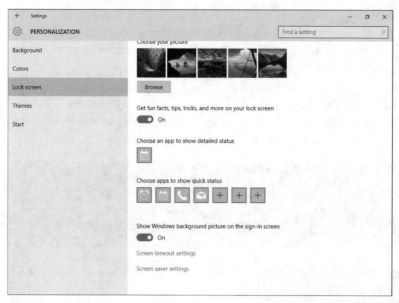

FIGURE 4-9 Customizing Lock Screen

- **Themes** This setting enables you to access Theme settings in Control Panel. You can also configure Desktop Icon settings, as shown in Figure 4-10.

- **Start** You can also configure Start settings, as previously discussed.

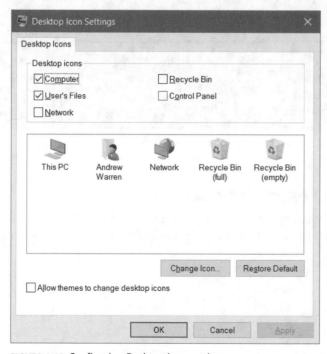

FIGURE 4-10 Configuring Desktop icon settings

MULTIPLE DESKTOPS

Windows 10 provides support for multiple desktops. This provides a simplistic multitasking view. Rather than running apps in multiple windows on the same desktop, you can add desktops for groups of apps or individual apps.

To add a new desktop, click the Task View button on the taskbar and then click New Desktop in the lower right of the display. A new desktop is created. To switch between desktops, click the Task View button and select the appropriate desktop as shown in Figure 4-11. Note that the desktop is only present until you sign out or restart your computer.

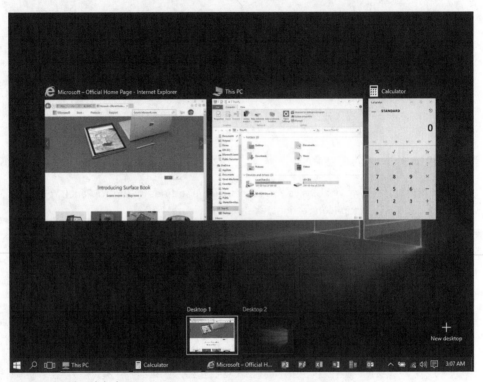

FIGURE 4-11 Virtual desktops

Configure Action Center and taskbar

In Windows 10, Microsoft introduces an improved Action Center, shown in Figure 4-12. This is accessible by swiping from the right or by clicking the Notifications icon in the system tray.

FIGURE 4-12 Windows 10 Action Center

Action Center includes the following elements.

- The Quick Action tiles, shown at the bottom of Figure 4-12. These are configurable.

- The notifications area, currently showing No New Notifications in Figure 4-12. You can configure how Windows notifies you of events.

Configure Quick Action tiles

The Quick Action tiles are commonly used features of the Windows 10 operating system. When the expanded view is selected, a larger number of tiles are visible. The tiles that appear in the expanded view shown in Figure 4-12 depend on your device type and orientation. For example, if your computer is not a tablet, and is not capable of converting into a tablet, the Tablet Mode tile is not available. By default, in the expanded view, the following tiles are available.

- **Tablet Mode**   Enables you to switch between tablet and desktop modes.
- **Rotation Lock**   Enables or disables the rotation lock. Normally, the display orients itself based on the orientation of your Windows 10 device, switching between landscape and portrait modes. Use this option to lock the orientation irrespective of physical orientation.

- **Flight Mode**   Disables all internal radios in the device, including Wi-Fi and Bluetooth. This is convenient when you want to save battery in addition to when you travel on an aircraft.
- **All Settings**   Provides a convenient shortcut to Settings.
- **Connect**   Enables you to find and connect to media servers. This includes Xbox and other devices running Windows that are sharing their media files. It can also include devices such as TV set-top boxes.
- **Project**   Enables you to link your device to an external monitor or wireless display.
- **Battery Saver**   Only available when your device is running on battery alone; helps reduce power consumption. You can configure Power Options and Battery Saver in Settings.
- **VPN**   Switches to the VPN tab in the Network & Internet settings app. From there, you can set up, configure, or connect to a VPN.
- **Bluetooth**   Enable or disables the Bluetooth radio.
- **Brightness**   Enables you to control display brightness. Click this tile to step through brightness levels in increments of 25 percent.
- **Note**   Opens Microsoft OneNote and displays your default note.
- **Wi-Fi**   Enables or disables the Wi-Fi connection.
- **Quiet Hours**   Toggles into quiet hours mode. This setting reduces the notifications you receive. You can configure Quiet Hours in Settings.
- **Location**   Enables or disables location services. Many services use location to customize services, such as mapping apps, for your device.

If you want to configure which tiles appear in the collapsed view, shown in Figure 4-13, from Quick Actions, click All Settings, choose System, and then click the Notifications & Actions tab.

FIGURE 4-13 Windows 10 Action Center with Quick Actions in collapsed view

You can then use the buttons under Choose Your Quick Actions to determine which tiles appear in the collapsed view, as shown in Figure 4-14.

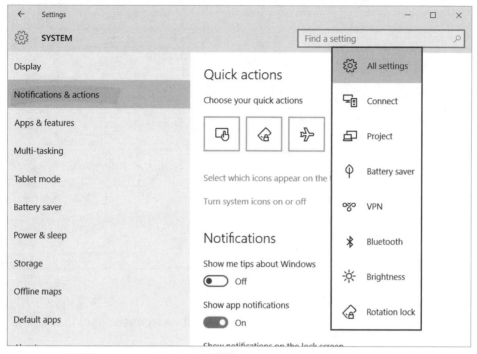

FIGURE 4-14 Windows 10 Quick Actions settings

Configure notifications

When Windows 10 wants to inform you about something, it raises a notification. You can see and act on the notifications in a list shown in Action Center. To respond to a notification, click it. You can remove notifications by clicking Clear All at the top of the page.

Windows notifies you about a variety of operating system events and situations, including the need to obtain updates or perform an antivirus scan, and Windows also prompts about which actions you want to take when a new device, such as a USB memory stick, has been detected.

As shown in Figure 4-15, you can configure which notifications you receive by opening Settings. Click System and then click Notifications & Actions. Under Notifications, you can configure the following options.

- Show Me Tips About Windows.

- Show App Notifications.

- Show Notifications On The Lock Screen.

- Show Alarms, Reminders And Incoming VoIP Calls On The Lock Screen.

- Hide Notifications When Presenting.

You can also configure individual apps and how they will notify you. Under Show Notifications From These Apps, enable or disable notifications for each listed app.

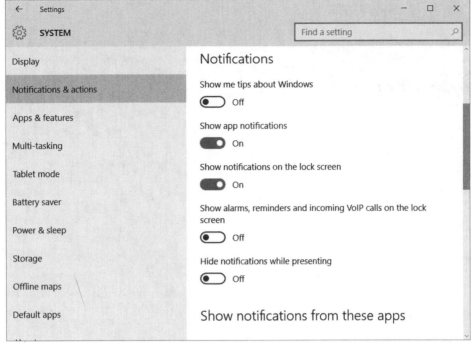

FIGURE 4-15 Configuring Windows 10 notifications

EXAM TIP

You can use GPOs to disable notifications in Windows 10 Pro, Windows 10 Enterprise, and Windows 10 Education editions. Use the User Configuration\Policies\Administrative Templates\Start Menu And Taskbar node and enable the Remove Notifications And Action Center value.

Configure the taskbar

You can configure the taskbar to suit your users' requirements. Right-click the taskbar, and then you can specify the following options, as shown in Figure 4-16.

- **Toolbars** Define which toolbars are accessible from the taskbar. Options for which toolbars are available, based on system configuration, but include Address, Links, and Desktop.
- **Search** Choose between Search and Hidden.
- **Show Touch Keyboard Button**
- **Lock The Taskbar**

FIGURE 4-16 Configuring the taskbar

For more configuration options, right-click the taskbar and then click Properties. As shown in Figure 4-17, you can then configure the following options.

- Lock The Taskbar
- Auto-Hide The Taskbar
- Use Small Taskbar Buttons
- Taskbar Location On Screen: Bottom; Left; Right; or Top
- Taskbar Buttons: Always Combine, Hide Labels; Combine When Taskbar Is Full; Never Combine
- Use Peek To Preview The Desktop When You Move Your Mouse To The Show Desktop Button At The End Of The Taskbar
- Show Taskbar On All Displays:
  - Show Taskbar Buttons On All Displays: All Taskbars; Main Taskbar And Taskbar Where Window Is Open; Taskbar Where Window Is Open
  - Buttons On Other Taskbars: Always Combine, Hide Labels; Combine When Taskbar Is Full; Never Combine

The Show Taskbar On All Displays options are only available if your computer has multiple displays.

FIGURE 4-17 Configuring the taskbar

As shown in Figure 4-14, you can also configure taskbar options from Settings. On the Notifications & Actions tab in System, under Quick Actions, you can use two options to control taskbar settings.

- Select Which Icons Appear On The Taskbar. Settings include:
  - Always Show All Icons In The Notification Area
  - Windows Explorer
  - Skype
  - Volume
  - Network
  - Power
  - Microsoft OneDrive
  - Location Notification
- Turn System Icons On Or Off. Settings include:
  - Clock
  - Volume
  - Network
  - Power
  - Location
  - Action Center

Skill: Configure accessibility options

The ability to interact easily with a computer is important for all users. Windows 10 provides a number of accessibility features to help ensure that your computer or tablet device is easy and comfortable to use, whatever your needs.

Configure and enable Ease Of Access settings

Windows 10 enables you to access and configure a number of accessibility settings by using the Ease Of Access Center. To open the Ease Of Access settings, from Start, click Settings and then click Ease Of Access.

As shown in Figure 4-18, there are seven groups of accessibility-related settings.

- **Narrator**   A screen reader that reads all screen elements, including text and buttons. After you enable this setting, you are prompted to choose a voice and then specify the individual sounds that you want to hear, for example: Read Hints For Controls And Buttons, Characters You Type, Words You Type, and so on.

- **Magnifier**   Makes things larger on the screen. When you enable this setting, you can optionally choose to invert colors, start Magnifier automatically, and enable tracking.

- **High Contrast**   This setting can make the display easier to read. Choose a High Contrast theme from the list.

- **Closed Captions**   Enables you to configure how closed captions appear in Windows apps, such as the Videos app.

- **Keyboard**   Settings that enable you to control how Windows responds to inadvertent key presses or overlong key presses.

- **Mouse**   Options that enable you to reconfigure the mouse pointer to be more clearly visible. You can also enable mouse buttons so that users can navigate with the cursor keys.

- **Other Options**   You can configure whether Windows plays animations and whether the desktop background is displayed. In addition, you can enable touch feedback so that Windows tells you when you touch the screen.

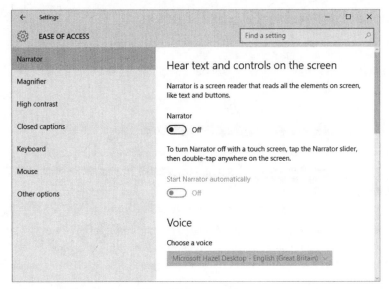

FIGURE 4-18 The Windows 10 Ease Of Access settings

Skill: Configure Cortana

Cortana is a new, voice-activated digital assistant in Windows 10 that can help you manage your computer and its content. For example, Cortana can remind you about events, manage appointments in your calendar, respond to voice search requests, and more.

Cortana is enabled by default when you sign in to Windows 10 on your computer or phone. However, if it has been disabled and you want to enable it, click the Search icon on the taskbar and then click the Cortana symbol on the bottom left of the pop-up list, as shown in Figure 4-19. Click Use Cortana. You might be asked to enable Location services. If so, click Settings and enable Location in the Privacy Settings app.

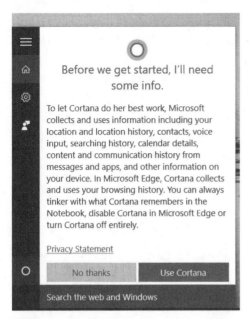

FIGURE 4-19 Enabling Cortana

After you enable Cortana, you can configure it. Click the Cortana search icon on the task-bar, click the Notebook icon, and then click Settings, as shown in Figure 4-20.

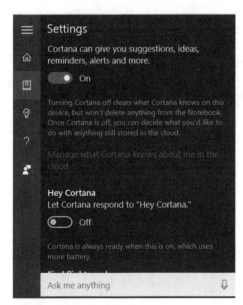

FIGURE 4-20 Configuring Cortana

From this Settings list, you can configure the following options.

- **Cortana Can Give You Suggestions, Ideas, Reminders, Alerts And More**   If you turn off this setting, Cortana is disabled.

- **Hey Cortana**   If enabled, Cortana responds to the "Hey Cortana" verbal command. Because this means that Cortana is always running, it does consume power.

- **Find Flights And More**   Cortana detects tracking information, such as flights, in messages on your device.

- **Taskbar Titbits**   Cortana can make suggestions in the Search box on the taskbar.

- **Missed Call Notifications**   On Windows 10 Mobile, Cortana notifies you of missed calls.

- **Device Search History**   Cortana can use your local device search history to optimize search results performed on local content.

- **Web Search History**   Cortana can use your web search history to optimize search results performed on web content.

> *NOTE* **CORTANA REQUIREMENTS**
>
> Because Cortana is an audio-based assistant, your computer must be equipped with sound, including a microphone.

Skill: Configure Microsoft Edge

Microsoft Edge, shown in Figure 4-21, is a new web browser that provides a consistent interface across device types, such as Windows 10–based tablets, laptops, and mobile phones. The interface is simple and touch-centric, making it the ideal browser for devices running Windows 10.

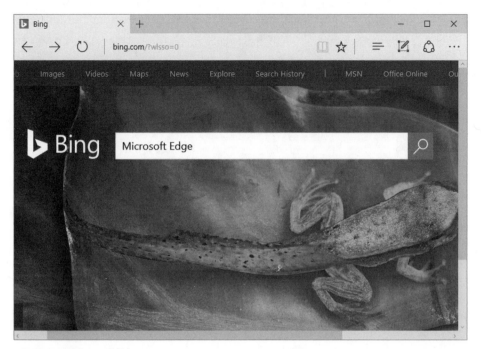

FIGURE 4-21 Microsoft Edge

Microsoft Edge includes a number of new features not available in Internet Explorer. These are:

- Reading mode, which enables you to view webpages in a simplified layout.
- The Hub, a feature that consolidates several items, including:
  - Browser History
  - Downloads
  - Favorites
  - Reading List
- Web Notes, which enable you to use tools to make notes, draw, write, and highlight webpages.

It is important to know how to configure Microsoft Edge, including how to migrate Favorites to this new browser, to support your organization's users.

Microsoft Edge has streamlined settings that you can easily configure from the More Actions link in the browser, as shown in Figure 4-22.

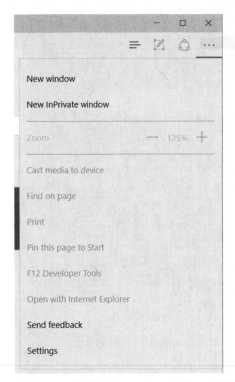

FIGURE 4-22 Configuring settings in Microsoft Edge

From this window, you can configure the following options.

- **Open a New InPrivate Window**   Provides the same privacy options enabled by InPrivate browsing in Internet Explorer
- **Zoom**   Enables you to zoom in or out on a webpage
- **Cast Media To Device**   Enables you to send content, such as a video, to wireless media devices
- **Find On Page**   Searches for content on the current webpage
- **Print**   Enables you to print the webpage
- **Pin This Page To Start**   Enables you to pin frequently accessed webpages directly to your Start page
- **Open With Internet Explorer**   Opens the current webpage in Internet Explorer. This is sometimes necessary when a webpage uses ActiveX controls.

- **Settings** This provides access to:
  - *Choose A Theme* Enables you to choose between light and dark themes. The dark theme might display better in low-light situations.
  - *Open With* Enables you to specify what you see when you open Microsoft Edge, such as a specific webpage or multiple tabbed webpages.
  - *Open New Tabs With* Enables you to set how new tabs are displayed. You can configure it to match the Open With setting, or you can define another value.
  - *Favorites Settings* You can enable a list of the sites on your Favorites bar or import your favorites from another web browser, such as Internet Explorer.
  - *Clear Browsing Data* Enables you to delete browsing history. You can be specific about what you want to delete.
  - *Sync Your Content* Enables you to sync your Microsoft Edge settings to your other devices to provide a consistent browsing experience.
  - *Reading* Enables you to configure a view style (light, medium, or dark) and the font size.
  - *Advanced Settings* Includes several options, with the defaults shown in parenthesis:
    - Show The Home Button (Off).
    - Block Pop-Ups (On).
    - Use Adobe Flash Player (On).
    - Proxy Set-Up (Automatically Detect Settings).
    - Offer To Save Passwords (On).
    - Manage My Saved Passwords.
    - Save Form Entries (On).
    - Send Do Not Track Requests (Off).
    - Get Cortana To Assist Me In Microsoft Edge (Off).
    - Search In The Address Bar With (Bing).
    - Show Search And Site Suggestions As I Type (On).
    - Cookies (Don't Block Cookies).
    - Let Sites Save Protected Media Licenses On My Device (On).

- Use Page Prediction To Speed Up Browsing, Improve Reading, And Make My Overall Experience Better (On).

- Help Protect Me From Malicious Sites And Downloads With Smartscreen Filter (On).

Enterprise Mode

Enterprise Mode enables you to use Microsoft Edge as your default browser but automatically switch to Internet Explorer 11 when sites requiring it are accessed. To enable and configure Enterprise Mode for Microsoft Edge, use the following procedure.

1. Download and install the Enterprise Mode Site List Manager tool for Windows 10 from *https://www.microsoft.com/download/confirmation.aspx?id=49974*.

2. Open the Enterprise Mode Site List Manager tool and add the URLs of any websites that are demonstrating compatibility issues with Microsoft Edge.

3. Click the option to open in Internet Explorer 11 for each of these sites.

4. Save the file to a network share.

5. Open the Group Policy Management console on a domain controller.

6. Locate and open the desired GPO to edit it.

7. Navigate to Computer Configuration\Policies\Administrative Templates\Windows Components\Microsoft Edge.

8. Enable the Configure The Enterprise Mode Site List policy and then, in the Type The Location (URL) Of Your Enterprise Mode IE Website dialog box, type the location of the XML file you saved. For example, type http://localhost:8080/sites.xml.

9. Click OK.

> *NEED MORE REVIEW?* **USE ENTERPRISE MODE TO IMPROVE COMPATIBILITY**
>
> **To review more about using and configuring Enterprise Mode, go to the Microsoft TechNet website article at** *https://technet.microsoft.com/library /mt270205.aspx?f=255&MSPPError=-2147217396*.

Skill: Configure Internet Explorer

Although Microsoft Edge is suitable for most users in most situations, Internet Explorer provides backward compatibility for websites that require features currently not supported in Microsoft Edge. Because your users might use both browsers, it is important to know how to configure both Microsoft Edge and Internet Explorer.

Internet Explorer contains a number of security and privacy features that can help make browsing safer. Specifically, the InPrivate Browsing and InPrivate Filtering features help maintain user privacy, whereas SmartScreen Filter helps guard against malicious websites and malware. To help your users get the best from Internet Explorer, it is important to know how to configure these and other settings.

To access Internet Explorer settings, from Internet Explorer, click the Tools menu, as shown in Figure 4-23.

FIGURE 4-23 Internet Explorer

You can then choose from among the following options.

- **Manage Add-Ons**   Add-ons enable enhancements to some websites, including by providing multimedia support and enhanced content. Use this option to enable and disable add-ons.

- **Compatibility View Settings**   Most websites render well in Internet Explorer 11, but some are designed for earlier versions of Internet Explorer. If you encounter websites that do not render correctly, you can use Compatibility View settings to render the website as if using an earlier version of Internet Explorer. To render a website using an earlier version of Internet Explorer, from the Compatibility View Settings dialog box, enter the name of the website and click Add.

EXAM TIP

You can display all intranet sites in Compatibility View by selecting the Display intranet Sites In Compatibility View check box in the Compatibility View Settings dialog box.

- **Internet Options**   To configure additional settings, click Internet Options. This opens the dialog box shown in Figure 4-24.

FIGURE 4-24 Configuring settings in Internet Explorer

The Internet Options dialog box has the following tabs.

- **General** Available options are:
  - Home Page
  - Start-Up Behavior
  - Change How Webpages Are Displayed In Tabs
  - Browsing History, Including Options To Delete Elements Of Browsing History
  - Colors, Languages, Fonts, And Accessibility Options
- **Security** Available options are:
  - You can configure the four security zones' settings. The zones are Internet, Local intranet, Trusted Sites, and Restricted Sites. You can add or remove websites from these zones and configure the security settings for each zone.
  - Enable Protected Mode. Protected mode makes it more difficult for malware to be downloaded, thereby helping to protect your computer from malicious software. It is enabled by default.
- **Privacy** Available options are:
  - Sites enables you to define cookie handling on a per-site basis.
  - Advanced enables you to define whether to accept, block, or prompt for first-party and third-party cookies.
  - Never Allow Websites To Request Your Physical Location.

- Turn On Pop-up Blocker. This is enabled by default. The Settings button enables you to configure per-website settings for pop-up handling.

- Disable Toolbars And Extensions When In Private Browsing Starts.

- **Content** Available options are:

  - Certificates enables you to view your certificates and trusted publishers.

  - Autocomplete enables you to define autocomplete options for the address bar, forms, and usernames and passwords. You can also delete autocomplete history here.

  - Feeds And Web Slices enables you to define when feeds and web slices from online content are updated.

- **Connections** Available options are:

  - Dial-Up and Virtual Private Network settings for connecting to the Internet.

  - LAN settings, including web proxy and script settings.

- **Programs** Available options are:

  - Define How Internet Explorer Opens.

  - Manage Add-Ons.

  - Configure HTML Editing.

  - Manage File Associations.

- **Advanced** Many options are available, enabling you to fine-tune Internet Explorer configuration and behavior.

Although you can manually configure these settings in Internet Explorer on each computer, you can also use GPOs in an AD DS domain environment to configure the settings for many computers. To configure the relevant GPO settings for Internet Explorer, open Group Policy Management and locate the appropriate GPO. Open the GPO for editing and navigate to Computer Configuration\Policies\Administrative Templates\Windows Components\Internet Explorer. You can then configure the appropriate values in the 11 child nodes, including values that control privacy, compatibility view, and security features. You can configure the same settings on the User Configuration node if you prefer.

NEED MORE REVIEW? **GROUP POLICY AND INTERNET EXPLORER 11**

To review further details about the GPO settings for Internet Explorer 11, refer to the Microsoft TechNet website at *https://technet.microsoft.com/itpro/internet-explorer/ie11 -deploy-guide/group-policy-and-ie11.*

Skill: Configure Hyper-V

Client Hyper-V enables you to run virtual machines on your Windows 10–based computer. There are a number of reasons for wanting to do this, including:

- Wanting to run multiple operating systems on a single computer.
- Supporting older applications that do not work properly when running natively on Windows 10.
- Creating a test or training environment that will not affect your production machine.

This section covers how to:

- Determine whether your computer can run Client Hyper-V
- Install the Client Hyper-V role
- Create and manage virtual machines in Client Hyper-V

Verifying Hyper-V prerequisites

To implement Client Hyper V in Windows 10, your computer must meet the following requirements.

- **Operating system edition**   You can only enable the Client Hyper-V feature on 64-bit versions of Windows 10 Pro, Windows 10 Enterprise, or Windows 10 Education.
- **Processor**   Your Windows 10–based computer must have a x64 processor with support for the following features.
  - Hardware-assisted virtualization.
  - Data Execution Prevention (DEP).
  - Second-level address translation (SLAT).
- **Memory**   Your Windows 10–based host computer must have at least 4 gigabytes (GB) of physical memory to support Client Hyper-V. In addition, you should have sufficient additional memory to support the virtual machines you plan to run.
- **Storage**   Hyper-V is disk intensive. Therefore, to optimize performance, or at least to reduce bottlenecks, you must ensure that your storage subsystem is fast. Consider using solid-state drives (SSD) for storing virtual machines.

Installing the Client Hyper-V role

If your computer meets the prerequisites, install the Client Hyper-V role. Open Control Panel, click Programs And Features, and then click Turn Windows Features On Or Off.

Then, as shown in Figure 4-25, select the Hyper-V check box and click OK. Files are copied. You must restart your computer before you can manage the virtual machine.

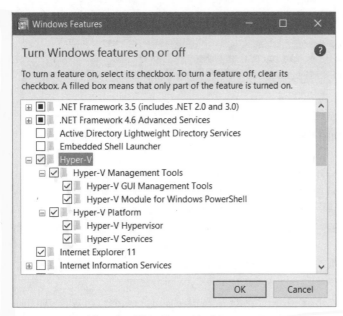

FIGURE 4-25 Enabling the Client Hyper-V role

Creating and managing virtual machines

Before you can create a virtual machine, you must be familiar with the core components that comprise it. These are:

- **Virtual switches** Virtual switches enable you to connect your virtual machines to networks. These networks can be:

  - Private, enabling only virtual machines connected to the same virtual switch to communicate.

  - Internal, so that only the virtual machines and the local host can communicate.

  - External, in which the virtual machines are connected to a physical network adapter in the host, potentially enabling communications with other physical or virtual devices elsewhere on your network.

- **Virtual hard disks** You must configure one or more virtual hard disks to represent the storage that your virtual machine will use. You can select from a number of virtual hard disk formats and disk types.

Creating a virtual machine

To create a virtual machine on your Windows 10–based computer, open the Hyper-V Manager console and then, in the Action pane, click New and then click Virtual Machine. The New Virtual Machine Wizard loads. Specify the following information to create your virtual machine.

- **Name** Enter a meaningful name for your virtual machine.
- **Storage Location** Define the location of the configuration files for your virtual machine.
- **Define The Generation Of The Virtual Machine** Generation 1 virtual machines support 32-bit and 64-bit guest operating systems. Generation 2 virtual machines only support 64-bit virtual machines but also support newer hardware features, including UEFI-based firmware. You cannot change the generation setting after you have created your virtual machine.
- **Specify The Memory** Configure the amount of memory you will assign to your virtual machine, and whether you want to enable dynamic memory.
- **Configure A Network Connection** Select from previously created network switches.
- **Define The Hard Disks** Configure a virtual hard disk type, size, and location.
- **Define Installation Options** Configure how you will install an operating system by connecting a physical DVD or ISO image that contains an installable operating system to your virtual machine.

Configuring settings

After you have created your virtual machine, you can configure additional settings or revise the settings you configured during the virtual machine creation, as shown in Figure 4-26. Configurable options include:

- **Add Hardware** You can add additional hardware, including SCSI controllers, network adapters, and video controllers.
- **BIOS** This enables you to define the startup order for your virtual machine.
- **Memory** You can revise your virtual machine's memory settings.
- **Processor** Add additional processors to your virtual machine.
- **IDE Controllers** This setting enables you to configure the attached virtual devices, such as disks and DVD drives.
- **Network Adapter** You can change the network adapter to a different virtual switch.

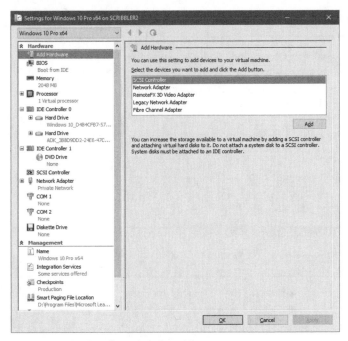

FIGURE 4-26 Settings for a virtual machine

Running virtual machines

To run a virtual machine, from the Hyper-V Manager, right-click the virtual machine that you want to start and then click Start. After it starts, you can connect to the virtual machine and interact with it just as you would a physical computer.

Managing checkpoints

One of the most useful things about Hyper-V virtual machines is the ability to create checkpoints of them; checkpoints are snapshots of a virtual machine at a point in time. You can use these to capture a configuration state. To create a checkpoint, right-click the appropriate virtual machine in Hyper-V Manager and then click Checkpoint.

After creating the checkpoint, you can operate the virtual machine as normal. When you want to return to that snapshot, right-click the virtual machine and then click Revert.

> *NEED MORE REVIEW?* **HYPER-V OVERVIEW**
>
> To review further details about using Hyper-V, refer to the Microsoft TechNet website at *https://technet.microsoft.com/library/hh831531.aspx*.

Skill: Configure power settings

A priority for many users of mobile devices, such as Windows 10–based tablets and laptops, is to be able to conserve battery life so that extended device use is possible. It is importwant to know how to configure power settings in Windows 10 to meet your users' needs.

> **This section covers how to:**
> - Configure basic power options
> - Configure power plans

Configuring basic power options

You can control Windows 10 power settings in several ways. You can configure basic power options by using the Power & Sleep tab in the System settings app, as shown in Figure 4-27.

On the Power & Sleep tab, you can configure the following options.

- Screen
  - On Battery Power, Turn Off After   Select a value or choose Never.
  - When Plugged In, Turn Off After   Select a value or choose Never.
- Sleep
  - On Battery Power, PC Goes To Sleep After   Select a value or choose Never.
  - When Plugged In, PC Goes To Sleep After   Select a value or choose Never.

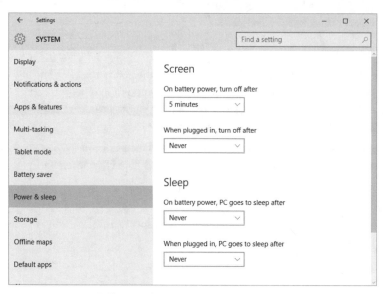

FIGURE 4-27 Power & Sleep options

You can configure additional power options by clicking the Battery Saver tab, as shown in Figure 4-28, and set the following options.

- **Battery Use**   View battery usage over the preceding 24 hours, 48 hours, or one week. You can also:

  - **Change Background App Settings**   Decide which apps can continue functioning in the background.

  - **Change Battery Saver Settings**   Determine the level of battery power at which battery saver is turned on. In addition, you can configure:

    - Allow Push Notifications From Any App While In Battery Saver.

    - Lower Screen Brightness While In Battery Saver.

    - Always Allowed   A list of apps that can still run in background mode even when the battery saver is on.

- **Battery Saver Settings**   Configure settings as previously described, but access the app from the main screen.

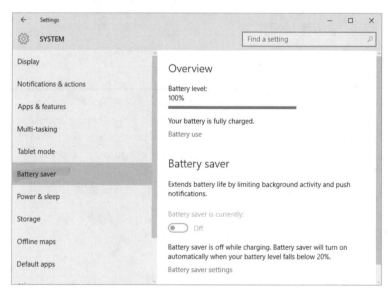

FIGURE 4-28 Battery saver options

Configuring power plans

In addition to these basic settings, Windows 10 provides a number of preconfigured power plans, as shown in Table 4-2. You can access these power plans from Settings by clicking System, Power & Sleep, and then Additional Power Settings.

> **NOTE POWER PLAN NAMES**
>
> The exact names of the power plans might vary depending on the configuration of your device.

TABLE 4-2 Power plans

Plan	Power consumption	Screen	System activity
Power Saver	Low	By default, the display is powered off after five minutes of inactivity.	Saves energy by reducing system performance whenever possible.
Balanced	Medium	You can configure the plan to turn off the display after a specified amount of time.	Measures computer activity and continues to use full power to all system components currently in use.
High Performance	High	This sets the screen to 100% brightness.	Keeps the computer's drives, memory, and processors continuously supplied with power.

You can select from among existing power plans by clicking the desired power plan or create a new power plan by clicking Create A Power Plan. Also, you can configure basic options such as whether your device will prompt you for a password when it wakes up, and what the power buttons and lid does on your computer. To reconfigure a plan, click Change Plan Settings. You can also choose Change Advanced Power Settings to configure detailed plan settings.

EXAM TIP

Windows 10 Mobile does not support power plans.

Summary

- Customize the Start menu, desktop, taskbar, and notification settings individually or by using XML templates and GPOs.
- The Ease Of Access Center contains a variety of tools and settings that you can use to ensure that Windows 10 is easy and comfortable for all your users to use.
- Cortana can be customized to provide specific digital assistance for your users.

- Microsoft Edge is a cross-platform web browser for Windows 10 that supports touch devices better.

- On 64-bit versions of Windows 10 Pro, Enterprise, and Education, you can enable the Client Hyper-V feature to create and run virtual machines.

- Windows 10 provides several ways to manage power settings, thereby extending the battery life of your users' devices.

Thought experiment

In this thought experiment, demonstrate your skills and knowledge of the topics covered in this chapter. You can find answers to this thought experiment in the following section.

The A. Datum Corporation has 3,000 workstations that were recently upgraded from Windows 7 and Windows 8.1. Most of the computer hardware is of a similar specification. Sixty-four-bit versions of Windows 10 Enterprise are deployed throughout the organization. All computers are part of the Adatum.com AD DS domain. A number of organizational units (OUs) exist within AD DS to represent the departments within the organization, such as Sales, Marketing, and Research.

Some of your users want a standardized Start layout. These users are all in the Marketing department, and their computers and user accounts all exist in the Marketing OU in the Adatum.com AD DS domain.

Users in the Research department run an older application that won't run properly on Windows 10. You envisage using the Client Hyper-V feature to run these applications.

As a consultant for A. Datum, answer the following questions.

1. Which services must be present on your network to support your plan?
2. How might you easily configure these users' Start layouts?
3. What are the requirements for Client Hyper-V?
4. Because the applications communicate with physical servers on the network, what type of network switch might you use?

Thought experiment answer

This section contains the solutions to the thought experiment.

1. The Volume Activation Services server role must be installed, together with either the KMS role service or the Active Directory–based activation role service.
2. To create a standard layout for Start, create a test workstation and configure Start as required. Export the Start layout by using the export-StartLayout Windows PowerShell cmdlet. Save the XML layout file to a shared folder. Configure a GPO linked to the Marketing OU to identify the location of the XML layout file by editing the User

Configuration\Administrative Templates\Start Menu and Taskbar\Start Layout setting in the GPO.

3. Client Hyper-V has the following requirements: The computer must be running a 64-bit version of Windows 10 Pro, Windows 10 Enterprise, or Windows 10 Education. The computer must have at least 4 GB of physical memory and support hardware-assisted virtualization, DEP, and SLAT.

4. Use an external network switch when the virtual machines need to communicate with computers elsewhere on the physical network.

CHAPTER 5

Implement Windows in an enterprise environment

The IT infrastructure requirements of large organizations differ from those of small organizations, and so do the required skills. These differences include the way Windows is deployed, activated, secured, and managed.

This means that if you work in an enterprise-level organization, you must be familiar with some of the technologies designed to make the deployment and management of Windows 10 easier.

Skills covered in this chapter:

- Provision with Windows Imaging and Configuration Designer (ICD) tool
- Implement activation
- Configure and optimize User Account Control (UAC)
- Configure Active Directory, including Group Policy

Skill: Provision with Windows Imaging and Configuration Designer tool

Although you can choose from among a number of methods to create and deploy installation media, the Windows Assessment And Deployment Kit (Windows ADK) provides a new tool for Windows 10, Windows Imaging and Configuration Designer (Windows ICD), shown in Figure 5-1. Windows ICD is part of Windows ADK.

Prepare installation media with ICD

You can use Windows ICD to:

- View settings and policies in a Windows 10 image or provisioning package.
- Create and manage Windows provisioning answer files.
- Define applications and drivers in an answer file.

- Build and flash a Windows image.
- Build provisioning packages to modify existing Windows installations.

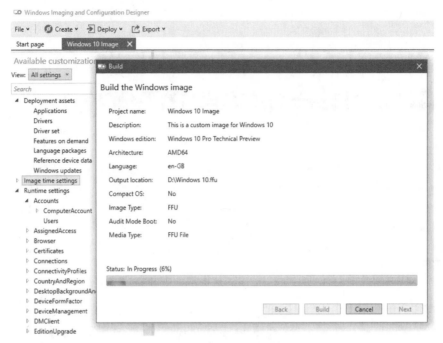

FIGURE 5-1 Building a deployment image with Windows ICD

To install Windows ICD, download and install Windows ADK. After you have installed Windows ICD, use the following procedure to create Windows 10 media.

1. In Windows Imaging and Configuration Designer, on the File menu, click New Project.

2. Enter a project name and description and click Next.

3. On the Select Project Workflow page, click Imaging and click Next.

4. On the Select Imaging Source Format page, select The Windows Image Is Based On A Windows Image (WIM) File and click Next.

5. On the Select Image page, click Browse and locate your Windows Image (WIM) file. Click OK. Because most images contain multiple operating system editions, click the relevant edition in the available images list and then click Next.

6. On the Import A Provisioning Package (Optional) page, click Finish.

You can now configure your image or deploy your image. To configure the image, choose from among the three tabs in the navigation pane.

- **Deployment Assets** Under Deployment Assets, you can add applications and drivers to your image, specify available features and language packs, and configure and deploy updates.
- **Image Time Settings** These settings include controlling the behavior of operating system components, including audio settings, BitLocker, devices such as Bluetooth and cameras, power settings, and much more. These settings are configured during image build while the image is offline.
- **Runtime Settings** You can use these settings to apply customizations to the operating system after the image is applied. Settings include regional settings, certificates, user accounts, desktop personalization settings, and many more.

When you have configured the customizations for your image, you can then create and deploy your image. Use the following procedure to deploy your image.

1. In Windows Imaging and Configuration Designer, on the Create menu, click Production Media.
2. On the Select The Image Format To Build page, click FFU and click Next.
3. On the Select Imaging Options page, click Next.
4. On the Configure Audit Mode Boot page, click Next.
5. Specify a location for your FFU file and click Next.
6. Click Build.

After you have built the image, you can deploy it. One option is to deploy it to an attached USB memory stick. When the image is deployed, you can distribute the USB memory stick to installers who can complete the installation process on your new computers.

> **NEED MORE REVIEW? GETTING STARTED WITH WINDOWS ICD**
>
> To find out more about using Windows ICD, visit the Microsoft MSDN website at *https://msdn.microsoft.com/library/windows/hardware/dn916112(v=vs.85).aspx*.

Skill: Implement activation

Activation is a very important part of configuring and managing Microsoft products, but IT pros often overlook it. This section explores Windows 10 activation options and procedures.

Like most Microsoft products, Windows 10 requires activation. Activation verifies that your copy of Windows 10 is legitimate and that the product key you used to license your copy is valid and not currently in use on another product. Figure 5-2 shows the current activation status of a computer running Windows 10.

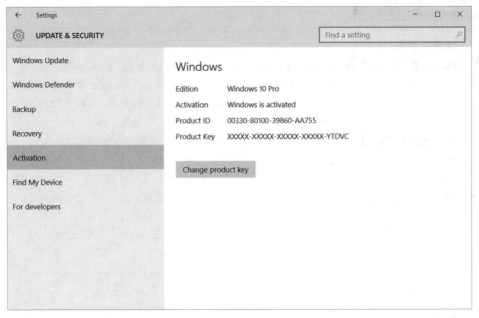

FIGURE 5-2 Viewing the Activation status of Windows 10

You can activate Windows 10 in a number of ways, by using an Internet-accessible service at Microsoft, by telephone, and by using bulk activation methods such as Key Management Service (KMS) and Active Directory Domain Services (AD DS)–based activation. This section explores activation and methods you can use to manage your organization's product activation.

> **This section covers how to:**
> - Select an activation method
> - Implement volume activation
> - Activate Windows 10

Select an activation method

To activate Windows 10, you might need a *product key*, a 25-character code. However, not all Windows 10 installations require the use of a product key to activate, relying instead on a *digital entitlement*. A digital entitlement is a process that automates the use of an existing product key.

You must use a product key for activation when:

- You purchase Windows 10 from a retail store or authorized reseller, either as a physical product or as a digital download.
- Your organization has a Microsoft volume licensing agreement for Windows 10.
- You purchased a new device on which Windows 10 is preinstalled.

You do not need a product key for activation and can rely on digital entitlement when:

- You upgrade to Windows 10 from a supported device running a legitimate copy of Windows 7 or Windows 8.1.
- You purchase Windows 10 from the Windows Store.
- You purchase Windows 10 Pro upgrade from the Windows Store.

The method you use to activate Windows 10 is determined by a number of factors, including how you obtained Windows 10 and whether your organization has a volume license agreement in place with Microsoft. The following scenarios determine how you activate Windows 10.

- **Retail** If you purchase Windows 10 from a retail store, it comes with a unique product key. You can enter the key during or after installation to activate your copy of Windows 10.
- **OEM** If you purchase a new computer on which Windows 10 is preinstalled, it comes with a unique product key, often on a sticker attached to the computer. You can activate Windows by using this preinstalled product key.
- **Microsoft volume licensing** Microsoft offers a number of volume licensing programs to suit different organizational sizes and needs. These programs support both Active Directory–based activation and KMS.

EXAM TIP

Retail versions of Windows 10 cannot be activated using volume licensing methods.

Implement volume activation

For large organizations with many hundreds or even thousands of devices, using manual product key entry and activation is impractical; it is both error prone and time-consuming. For these reasons, Microsoft provides three methods for volume activation. These are:

- **KMS** You can use this Windows Server role service to activate Windows 10 in your organization's network. Client computers connect to the KMS server to activate, thereby negating the need to connect to Microsoft for activation. It is not necessary to dedicate a server computer to perform activation through the KMS role.

EXAM TIP

KMS is designed for organizations with either 25 (physical or virtual) client devices persistently connected to a network or organizations with five or more (physical or virtual) servers.

- **Active Directory–based activation** Any device running Windows 10 that is connected to your organization's domain network and is using a generic volume license key (VLK) can use Active Directory–based activation. Periodically, the client must reconnect to the AD DS licensing service. Therefore, for the activation to remain valid, the client device must remain part of your organization's domain. As with KMS, you do not need to dedicate a server to the Active Directory–based activation role.

EXAM TIP

You cannot use Active Directory–based activation to activate computers running Windows 10 that are not members of your AD DS domain.

- **Multiple Activation Key** Multiple Activation Key (MAK) uses special VLKs that can activate a specific number of devices to run Windows 10. You can distribute MAKs as part of your organization's Windows 10 operating system image. This method is ideal for isolated client computers.

Volume Activation Services

To use either KMS or Active Directory–based activation to manage your volume activations, first install the Volume Activation Services server role on Windows Server 2012 R2. When it's installed, you can then use either KMS or Active Directory–based activation by installing one or both of the following, depending on your needs.

- Active Directory–based activation role service
- KMS role service

After you install the required roles, activate the roles with Microsoft. This involves entering and validating a KMS host key with Microsoft, either online or by telephone.

Volume Activation Management Tool

After you have installed the necessary server roles, you can use the Volume Activation Management Tool (VAMT) to manage your organization's volume activations centrally. Figure 5-3 shows the main console of the VAMT.

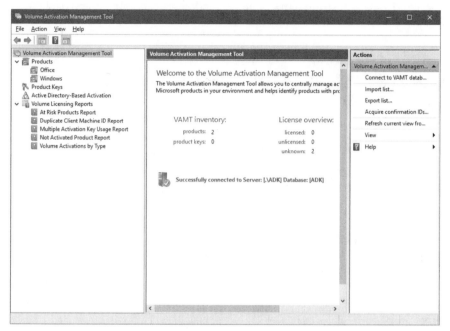

FIGURE 5-3 Volume Activation Management Tool

NOTE DOWNLOAD AND INSTALL VAMT

VAMT is one of the tools in the Windows Assessment And Deployment Kit (Windows ADK). To download the Windows ADK from the Microsoft website, go to *http://go.microsoft.com /fwlink/p/?LinkId=526740.*

This includes activations not only for Windows 10 but also for Windows Server and Microsoft Office. You can use VAMT to control activations for groups of computers running Windows 10 based on domain membership, workgroup name, IPv4 configuration, or computer names. After you have installed VAMT, you can use it to perform the following activation-related tasks.

- **Verify the KMS host key**   This enables you to set up your host for volume activations.

- **Discover computers and products**   You can discover computers and licensable products on your organization's network.

- **Monitor status** Collect licensing data from installed products and devices, including license state and last five characters of the product code.
- **Manage product keys** Determine the number of activations remaining for your MAKs and install these MAKs on remote devices.
- **Manage and view activation data** View and, if desired, export activation data for reporting purposes.

> **NOTE   VAMT ACTIVATION DATA**
>
> VAMT stores its activation data in an SQL Server database. You can see the connected database indicated in Figure 5-3.

> **NEED MORE REVIEW?   VOLUME ACTIVATION OVERVIEW**
>
> To review further details about volume activations, refer to the article on the Microsoft TechNet website at *https://technet.microsoft.com/library/hh831612.*

Activate Windows 10

If you are using one of the volume activation methods, you do not need to perform any task on your Windows 10–based devices. However, if you are manually managing activation on Windows 10–based devices, following installation, you must complete the following procedure.

1. Click Start and then click Settings.
2. Click Update & Security.
3. Click Activation.

    Figure 5-4 shows that the computer is not activated.

FIGURE 5-4 Dialog box showing that Windows is not activated

4. Click Change Product Key.

5. In the Enter A Product Key dialog box, type your 25-character product key.

Figure 5-5 shows the Enter A Product Key dialog box.

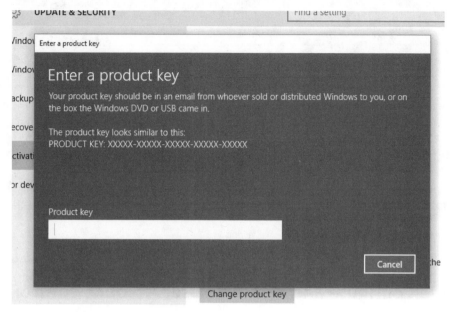

FIGURE 5-5 Entering a product key

6. On the Activate Windows page, click Next.

7. When prompted, click Close.

After you have activated Windows 10, you can view the activation status from Settings on the Activation tab of the Update & Security app, or you can view and manage the activation status of your Windows 10–based product by using the Slmgr.vbs command. For example, Figure 5-6 shows the result of typing the Slmgr.vbs -dli command. You can see that Windows 10 Pro is licensed properly.

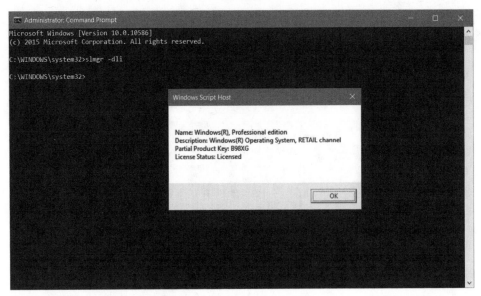

FIGURE 5-6 Checking the activation status of Windows 10

Skill: Configure and optimize User Account Control

After you are signed in, it is important to ensure that your user account operates as a standard user account and is only elevated to an administrative level when needed. User Account Control (UAC) can help you control administrative privilege elevation in Windows 10.

Configure User Account Control

In earlier versions of Windows, it was necessary to sign in using an administrative account to perform administrative tasks. This often led to users signing in with administrative accounts at all times, even when performing standard user tasks, such as running apps or browsing Internet websites.

However, being signed in with administrative privilege at all times poses a security risk because it offers the possibility for malicious software to exploit administrative access to files and other resources. Windows 10 provides UAC to help mitigate this threat.

When you sign in using an administrative account, UAC limits the account's access to that of a standard user, only elevating the account's privileges to administrative level when required, and only after prompting the user for permissions to do so. In addition, if a user signs in with a standard user account and attempts to perform a task requiring administrative privileges, UAC can prompt the user for administrative credentials.

Standard users can perform the following tasks without requiring elevation.

- Change their user account passwords.
- Configure accessibility options.
- Configure power options.
- Install updates by using Windows Update.
- Install device drivers included in the operating system or by using Windows Update.
- View Windows 10 settings.
- Pair Bluetooth devices.
- Establish network connections, reset network adapters, and perform network diagnostics and repair.

However, the following tasks require elevation.

- Install or remove apps.
- Install a device driver not included in Windows or Windows Update.
- Modify UAC settings.
- Open Windows Firewall in Control Panel.
- Add or remove user accounts.
- Restore system backups.
- Configure Windows Update settings.

EXAM TIP

This is not an exhaustive list of tasks but, merely, an indication of the types of tasks requiring or not requiring elevation.

When a user performs a task requiring elevation, depending on settings, UAC can prompt the user in two ways for elevation.

- **Prompt for consent**   This prompt appears to administrators in Admin Approval Mode when they attempt to perform an administrative task. It requests approval to continue from the user.
- **Prompt for credentials**   This prompt appears to standard users when they attempt to perform an administrative task.

In Admin Approval Mode, a user signed in with an administrative account operates in the context of a standard user until a task is attempted that requires administrative privilege. At that time, the user receives the configured prompt—by default, a prompt for consent.

UAC is enabled by default, but you can configure and, if necessary, disable UAC in Control Panel or use Group Policy Objects (GPOs) in an AD DS domain environment. To configure UAC in Control Panel, use the following procedure.

1. From Control Panel, click System and Security.

2. Click Change User Account Control settings.

As shown in Figure 5-7, you can use the slider bar in the Choose When To Be Notified About Changes To Your Computer dialog box to adjust the UAC settings.

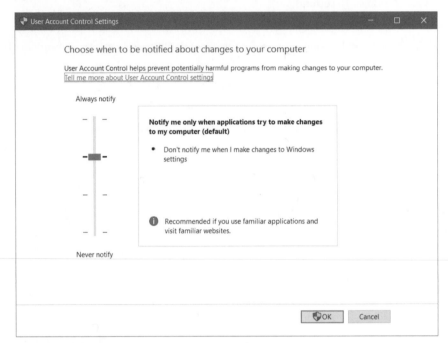

FIGURE 5-7 Configuring User Account Control prompts

The available settings are:

- **Never Notify Me When**   In this setting, UAC is disabled. Users signing in with standard accounts cannot perform administrative tasks because there is no means to prompt for credentials to perform those tasks. Users signing in with administrative accounts can perform any task requiring elevation, without a prompt for consent.

- **Notify Me Only When Applications Try To Make Changes To My Computer (Do Not Dim Desktop)**   In this mode, users are prompted, but Windows does not switch to Secure Desktop while awaiting user consent. This is less secure.

- **Notify Me Only When Applications Try To Make Changes To My Computer**   In this mode, users are prompted, and Windows switches to Secure Desktop while awaiting user consent. This is more secure.

- **Always Notify**   This is the most secure but most intrusive setting. Users are prompted not only for application installations but also any time they make Windows settings changes.

> **NEED MORE REVIEW?   HOW USER ACCOUNT CONTROL WORKS**
>
> To review further details about configuring UAC, refer to the Microsoft TechNet website at *https://technet.microsoft.com/itpro/windows/keep-secure/how-user-account-control-works*.

In addition to configuring UAC settings locally, you can also use GPOs in an AD DS environment to configure and manage the UAC settings for users in the domain. On a domain controller, open Group Policy Management and locate the appropriate GPO. Open the GPO for editing and navigate to Computer Configuration \ Policies \ Windows Settings \ Security Settings \ Local Policies \ Security Options and then locate the settings in the details pane that have the prefix User Account Control, as shown in Figure 5-8.

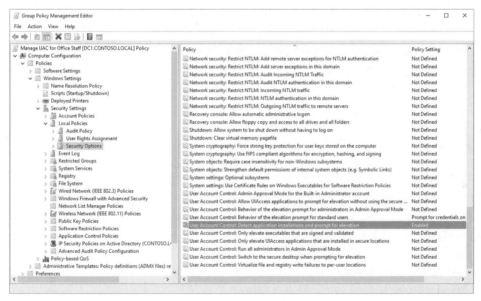

FIGURE 5-8 Configuring User Account Control with Group Policy

> **NEED MORE REVIEW?   UAC GROUP POLICY SETTINGS AND REGISTRY KEY SETTINGS**
>
> To review further details about configuring UAC by using GPOs, refer to the Microsoft TechNet website at *https://technet.microsoft.com/library/dd835564(v=ws.10).aspx*.

Skill: Configure Active Directory, including Group Policy

In this section, you review how Active Directory provides scalable management capabilities for larger organizations in relation to your domain resources. You also review how Active Directory stores computer and user objects in a secure distributed database containing containers such as organizational units (OUs). Finally, you practice installing the Active Directory server role.

Group Policy is a key technology designed to help manage and control how users use Windows 10–based computers. You know how to use local Group Policy to configure local settings on your computer, and this knowledge is valuable if you must apply the same type of settings to thousands of computers in a domain environment.

This section covers how to:

- Configure Active Directory
- Use Active Directory Administrative Center (ADAC)
- Configure Group Policy

Configure Active Directory

When users log on to a computer that is a member of a domain, their logon credentials are validated by a domain controller. The role of a domain controller is to maintain a copy of the Active Directory database securely for the domain that stores a vast amount of information, including details of user accounts in the form of objects.

In addition to user objects, you can also have objects for computers, printers, groups, and other logical entities in the organization. One of the roles of a domain controller is to maintain object replication so that all domain controllers have a complete, up-to-date database of objects in the directory. When running Windows 10, you must use Pro, Enterprise, or Education editions to join a computer to a domain.

Users with a domain account are managed and authenticated by a domain controller, which uses Active Directory to organize objects, settings, and permissions logically throughout the network. In some enterprise domains, there are millions of objects. You can view, modify, and configure objects by using the Active Directory Users And Computers console, the Active Directory Administrative Center, the command line, and the Active Directory module for Windows PowerShell.

Active Directory is organized in a hierarchical nature and partitioned into the following *logical* components.

- **Site** A group of TCP/IP subnets.
- **Forest** A security boundary providing a security scope of authority for administrators who share a common Active Directory Domain Services (AD DS) domain. The first domain created is referred to as the forest root domain.
- **Domain** Logical administrative, security, and replication boundary for users and computers that are stored in a common directory database.
- **Domain trees** Collection of domains that are grouped in hierarchical structures and share a common root domain.
- **Organizational units** Group objects for management, organization, and resources for easier administration, including delegation.

You should also understand the *physical* components that make up Active Directory.

- **Domain controllers** Servers that contain the Active Directory databases. A domain controller stores only the information about objects located in its domain. All domain controllers are kept in sync by using replication.
- **Global catalog servers** A domain controller that stores a full copy of all Active Directory objects in the host domain directory and a partial copy of all objects for all other domains in the forest. If you only have one domain controller, this is automatically a global catalog server also.
- **Operations masters** Specialized domain controllers that ensure that domain controllers synchronize properly.
- **Read-only domain controllers (RODC)** Specialized domain controllers that hold only a non-writable copy of Active Directory and are intended for use in branch offices and locations where servers are in a low physical security environment.

When you log on to a computer in a domain, your PC locates one of the domain controllers in your local site by using DNS (SRV resource records). The SRV record identifies computers that host specific services. You can use DNS Manager on your domain controller to verify that the SRV locator resource records for your domain controller are present and that the following SRV records have been created in the following folders, as shown in Figure 5-9.

- Forward Lookup Zones/_msdcs.Contoso.local/dc/_sites/Default-First-Site-Name/_tcp
- Forward Lookup Zones/_msdcs.Contoso.local/dc/_tcp

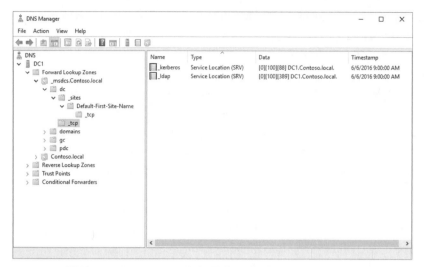

FIGURE 5-9 SRV locator resource records in DNS Manager

In these two locations, there should be an SRV record for each of the following services.

- _kerberos
- _ldap

To ensure that users can log on and access domain resources such as Group Policy, network file shares, and DNS, ensure that each site has two or more domain controllers for fault tolerance in case one fails.

To configure a server running Windows Server 2016 to become a domain controller, you must first install the AD DS server role and then run the Promote This Server To A Domain Controller Wizard from Server Manager. The wizard builds the Active Directory database, integrates it with DNS, and installs Active Directory tools, including the following.

- Active Directory Administrative Center (ADAC)
- AD DS snap-ins and command-line tools
- Active Directory module for Windows PowerShell
- Group Policy Management Console
- Active Directory Users And Computers
- Active Directory sites and services
- Active Directory domains and trusts

To install Active Directory on a server running Windows Server 2016 and promote it to become a domain controller, follow these steps.

1. Log on to the server as an administrator.
2. Open Server Manager.
3. On the menu, click Manage and then click Add Roles And Features.
4. In the Add Roles And Features Wizard, click Next three times.

5. On the Select Server Roles page, select the Active Directory Domain Services check box.

6. On the Add Features That Are Required For Active Directory Domain Services page, click Add Features and then click Next.

7. On the Select Features page, keep the default selection and click Next.

8. On the Active Directory Domain Services description page, click Next.

9. On the Confirm Installation Selections page, click Install.

10. When the installation of AD DS is finished, click Promote This Server To A Domain Controller.

11. On the Deployment Configuration page, select Add A New Forest, specify a Root Domain Name as Contoso.local, and click Next.

12. On the Domain Controller Options page, select the forest function and domain function level as "Windows Server Technical Preview," select the Domain Controller capabilities as DNS, enter a Directory Services Restore Mode password, and then click Next.

13. On the DNS Options page, click Next.

14. On the Additional Options page, verify the NetBIOS name as CONTOSO and then click Next.

15. On the Paths page, accept the default paths for the installation and click Next.

16. On the Review Options page, click Next.

17. On the Prerequisite Check page, confirm that All Prerequisites Checks Passed Successfully. Click Install.

   The installation should commence and take some time. The server reboots automatically when the installation is complete.

To appreciate fully that Active Directory is a database, open File Explorer on the domain controller and locate the files that relate to the Active Directory database. By default, the database file is located at C:\Windows\NTDS\Ntds.dit, and this is customizable during the installation of Active Directory. The folder should contain the following files and logs.

- **Ntds.nit**   The physical database file in which all Active Directory directory data is stored.

- **Edb.log**   Directory transaction log files are written prior to writing to the database. Maximum log file size is 10 MB for Active Directory.

- **Edb.chk**   File used to track which transactions in the log file have been committed to the database.

- **Res1.log and Res2.log files**   Provide temporary reserve space for additional log files if the edb.log becomes full.

- **Temp.edb**   A temporary scratch pad file for use during maintenance operations.

When Group Policy settings have been created, they are stored in the Policies subfolder in the C:\Windows\SYSVOL\sysvol directory, which is shared as SYSVOL across the network by the domain controller.

Use the Active Directory Administrative Center

The Active Directory Administrative Center (ADAC) is the primary GUI-based tool that you use for object-related tasks that need to be performed occasionally, typically for the administration of Active Directory in smaller environments. If you are responsible for a large environment, such as data centers, or enterprises with thousands of users, you would use the Active Directory module for Windows PowerShell, which enables you to script Active Directory administration tasks for automation purposes.

The ADAC can manage Active Directory objects, such as users, groups, computer accounts, OUs, and domains, and was designed to supersede the Active Directory Users And Computers MMC snap-in. The ADAC provides an enhanced management experience in the graphical user interface (GUI). You can still use the Active Directory Users And Computers MMC snap-in to perform common Active Directory tasks such as creating users, groups, and OUs, but for the exam, you should explore the new features in the ADAC.

Open the ADAC by using the Server Manager Tools menu, or by typing dsac.exe at the Start button, and familiarize yourself with the different user-interface features of the tool, as shown in Figure 5-10, including the following.

- **Breadcrumb bar**   Enables you to navigate to any container within Active Directory quickly by specifying the container's path
- **Navigation pane**   Enables you to browse for objects in Active Directory by using either the list or the tree view
- **Management list**   Displays the contents of the currently selected container
- **Preview pane**   Previews information about the object or container selected in the management list
- **Tasks pane**   Enables you to perform different actions on the selected items

You can perform the following tasks by using ADAC.

- Create new users.
- Create new groups.
- Create new organizational units (OUs).
- Create new computer accounts.
- Create new InetOrgPerson objects.
- Change the focus of the tool to another domain or domain controller.
- Raise the forest or domain functional level.
- Enable the Active Directory Recycle Bin.
- Configure fine-grained password policies.
- Configure Dynamic Access Control.

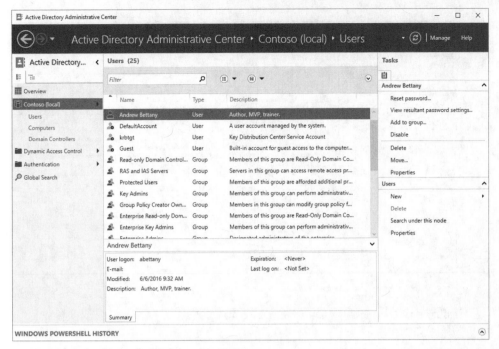

FIGURE 5-10 Active Directory Administrative Center

To create a new user account, follow these steps.

1. In the Active Directory Administrative Center, right-click the appropriate organizational unit, select New, and click User.

2. Complete the information on the Create User properties page.

3. Click OK to create the new user account, as shown in Figure 5-11.

To create a new OU called Remote Staff, using the Active Directory Administrative Center, follow these steps.

4. Open Server Manager, click Tools, and click Active Directory Administrative Center.

5. In the navigation pane, click Contoso (Local) and, in the Tasks pane, click New and then click Organizational Unit.

6. In the Create Organizational Unit dialog box, enter **Remote Staff** as the name and click OK.

7. Close the Active Directory Administrative Center.

The Active Directory Administrative Center offers a GUI interface that is very user friendly; for example, when completing data entry, the required information is indicated with a large red asterisk.

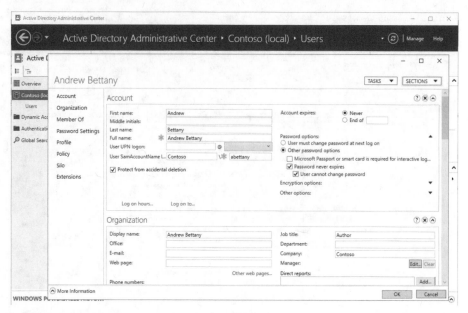

FIGURE 5-11 Creating a new user account using ADAC

Configure Group Policy

Group Policy provides you with a proven mechanism to create rules so that you can manage users' computers and other objects such as printers stored in Active Directory. Typically, Group Policy applies configuration settings that the organization declares are mandatory. These are pushed out to targeted groups of user accounts or computers. Standard users cannot modify a managed setting.

Group Policy in an Active Directory environment is typically managed using the Group Policy Management Console (GPMC) to create and manage policy settings, as shown in Figure 5-12.

Settings that apply to users and computers are stored in Group Policy Objects (GPOs). By using Group Policy, you can deploy settings on a per-computer or per-user basis, depending on which setting is configured and which objects the GPO is assigned to, using Group Policy Management.

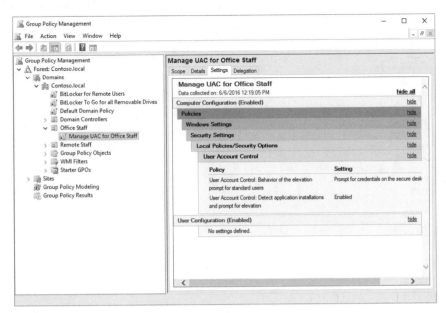

FIGURE 5-12 Group Policy Management console

A GPO is a collection of settings that, when applied, determine how a system functions. To apply the GPO to specific computers, users, or even for everyone in the domain, you associate the policy with Active Directory containers such as sites, domains, or organizational units.

There are more than 3000 policies, and new GPOs are added regularly as new features and functionality are added to the Windows client and server operating systems. For security reasons, you should not sign in locally to a domain controller to manage Group Policy. On a Windows 10–based computer that is a member of a domain, install the Remote Server Administration Tools (RSAT) for Windows 10. RSAT enables you to manage roles and features in Windows Server 2016 remotely, including Group Policy Management.

> **NOTE   REMOTE SERVER ADMINISTRATION TOOLS (RSAT) FOR WINDOWS 10**
>
> The Remote Server Administration Tools for Windows 10 enable you to open tools, including Server Manager, Microsoft Management Console (MMC) snap-ins, consoles, Windows PowerShell cmdlets and providers, and command-line tools for managing roles and features that run on Windows Server Technical Preview. To download the RSAT tools, go to *https://www.microsoft.com/download/details.aspx?id=45520*.

GPOs are separated into two sections: Computer Configuration and User Configuration, as shown in Figure 5-13.

The Computer Configuration section sets policies that are applied to the computer regardless of who logs on to it. The User Configuration is used to set policies that apply to users, regardless of which computer they log on to. By default, Computer Configuration settings are applied when the computer starts and before the user logs on. The User Configuration settings are applied when the user logs on.

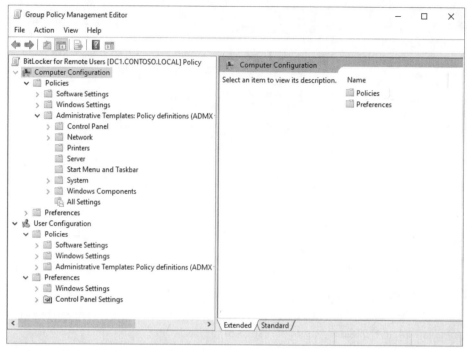

FIGURE 5-13 Group Policy Management Editor

On client machines, the Group Policy settings are automatically refreshed every 90 minutes with a random offset of 30 minutes (giving a random range between 90 minutes and 120 minutes). Settings that relate to Security settings have an immediate effect.

Examples of Group Policy settings that are commonly applied in enterprises include:

- **Folder Redirection**   This setting enables you to redirect the content of folders to a network location; for example, the Documents folder can be redirected to the user's home folder on a file server or to a removable SDHC card on the device.

- **Deploy Software**   You can distribute software packages and assign or publish them to a user or computer. Assigning makes the software available to install on demand by placing the app icon on the user's Start menu when the user next logs on. Publishing software to a user makes the app available in Control Panel Programs and is often used for nonessential apps.

- **Running a script**   Scripts are commands that can be run when you log on and log off or at startup and shutdown. They are useful for cleaning up desktops when users log off, such as deleting the contents of temporary directories, mapping drives and printers, and setting environment variables.

- **Deploying security templates** This is useful to implement consistent security settings quickly and efficiently to multiple computers based on a security template.
- **Group Policy preferences** These are unmanaged configuration settings that you do not consider mandatory but are recommended. These settings are pushed out to users and computers but can be modified by users if they want to do so. Group Policy preferences expand the range of settings in a Group Policy Object (GPO). Examples of Group Policy preferences include Folder Options, Drive Maps, Printers, Scheduled Tasks, Services, and Start menu, presented in an easy-to-use GUI interface.

EXAM TIP

In previous versions of Windows Server, you force a Group Policy refresh by restarting the client computer or running the gpupdate.exe command. Starting with Windows 2012 Server, you can refresh Group Policy directly from the Group Policy Management Console or by using the Invoke-Gpupdate cmdlet.

To create and apply a GPO to configure folder redirection, follow these steps.

1. Open Server Manager, click Tools, and click Group Policy Management.
2. In the Group Policy Management Console (GPMC), in the navigation pane, expand Forest: Contoso.local, expand Domains, and then expand Contoso.local.
3. In the navigation pane, right-click the Remote Staff OU and then click Create A GPO In This Domain And Link It Here.
4. In the Name text box, type **Folder Redirection** and then click OK.
5. In the GPMC, in the navigation pane, expand Remote Staff OU, right-click Folder Redirection, and then click Edit.

   The Group Policy Management Editor window opens.
6. In the Group Policy Management Editor window, under User Configuration in the navigation pane, expand Policies, expand Windows Settings, and then expand Folder Redirection.
7. Right-click Documents and then click Properties.
8. In the Document Properties dialog box, in the Setting drop-down menu, click Basic – Redirect Everyone's Folder To The Same Location.
9. In the Target folder location section, in the Root Path text box, type **\\DC1\Redirected** and then click OK.
10. In the Warning dialog box, click Yes.
11. Close the Group Policy Management Editor window.
12. In the Group Policy Management window, verify that the GPO has been created by viewing the contents of the Scope, Details, and Settings tabs.
13. Close Group Policy Management.

If you do not have access to a domain controller, you can still study GPOs. Local GPOs use the same settings found in the GPMC; however, these are used to configure individual computers, whereas the GPMC can manage GPOs for distribution across one, hundreds, or thousands of computers. To manage the local settings, you can use the Local Group Policy Editor by using the gpedit.msc.

Summary

- Build and deploy provisioning images with Windows ICD.
- Microsoft provides a number of ways to manage Windows 10 volume activation.
- User Account Control helps protect the operating system from unauthorized configuration changes and app installations.
- Active Directory is a sophisticated database that maintains details of objects such as users, groups, computers, and associated information within the enterprise.
- The Active Directory Administrative Center provides a user-friendly GUI tool for managing administrative tasks in smaller Active Directory environments.
- You can configure most Windows 10 settings by using GPOs in an AD DS environment.
- Group Policy preferences are useful for pushing out unmanaged configuration settings that users can modify if they choose.

Thought experiment

In this thought experiment, demonstrate your skills and knowledge of the topics covered in this chapter. You can find answers to this thought experiment in the next section.

You work in support at Contoso, Ltd. You are responsible for managing devices throughout the organization. Answer the following questions about enterprise management in the Contoso organization.

1. One of the remote users, Luke, uses a Bluetooth headset device when working from his home office. He is frustrated that each time he tries to pair the headset, User Account Control requires him to call the help desk to allow the pairing to complete. How can you help him while ensuring that Luke operates with the least privilege?

2. A number of remote users work away from home often. They have asked whether they can store personal photos, music, and videos on their SDHC cards on their Surface 4 Pro tablets. Management has agreed. How can you ensure that their personal media files are not stored on the company file servers?

3. You have made several changes to the Group Policy Object (GPO) that affects remote users only. Two of the remote users have not been affected by the GPO. What could be the issue?

Thought experiment answer

This section contains the solution to the thought experiment. Each answer explains why the answer choice is correct.

1. You need to review the UAC settings on Luke's computer. The default UAC setting enables a standard user to pair Bluetooth devices with the computer without receiving a UAC prompt. You suspect that the UAC has been set at the most restrictive level; it needs to be set at the default, Notify Me Only When Apps Try To Make Changes To My Computer (Default) setting.

2. You could create a folder redirection Group Policy that redirects remote users' music, photos, and videos folders to the local SDHC storage card. Each time a remote user browses to or saves to these locations, they are automatically redirected to the SDHC card.

3. Computers and users only receive the refreshed Group Policy every 90 minutes (plus 30 minutes random offset). You could wait a little longer to see whether the computers automatically receive the policy. If other computers have received the GPO setting, it is unlikely that the server side of the setting is the issue. You should instruct the users to log off and log back on to their computers, which should then apply the up-to-date GPO. If this does not trigger the updated policy, you should investigate network connectivity because the two computers might be using cached credentials to log on; they might not be connecting to the domain controller and receiving the GPO.

CHAPTER 6

Configure networking

The ability to connect devices running Windows 10 to both wired and wireless networks is important, whether this is a home network or your organization's network infrastructure. To configure networking settings correctly, understand fundamental IP settings and know how to configure name resolution. It is also important to understand network location profiles and how Windows Firewall uses these to define security settings on your Windows 10–based devices and facilitate network discovery. In addition, the 70-698 Installing and Configuring Windows 10 exam also covers network troubleshooting issues, and it is therefore important to know how to use Windows 10 networking tools to investigate and resolve network-related problems.

Skills covered in this chapter:

- Configure and support IPv4 and IPv6 network settings
- Configure name resolution
- Connect to a network
- Configure network locations
- Configure Windows Firewall, including Advanced Security and network discovery
- Configure Wi-Fi settings and Wi-Fi Direct
- Troubleshoot network issues

Skill: Configure and support IPv4 and IPv6 network settings

Before you can configure name resolution and firewall settings, you must have a grasp of the underlying fundamentals of networking and how to configure both Internet Protocol version 4 (IPv4) and Internet Protocol version 6 (IPv6) network settings.

Overview of IPv4

IPv4 is a mature networking protocol and is widely used on almost all Internet-connected client devices. Each client on an IPv4 network is assigned a unique IPv4 configuration that identifies that client device. This configuration is based on a number of elements.

- **An IPv4 address** IPv4 uses a 32-bit binary address, which is divided into four octets (or groups of eight digits), each of which is converted to a decimal number. Thus: 11000000101010000001000100000001 becomes 11000000.10101000.00010001.00000001 and converts to: 192.168.17.1.
- **A subnet mask** A subnet mask is also a 32-bit binary string, entered as four decimal digits, and is used to indicate the client's unique identity, known as the host ID, and the subnet where the client resides, known as the network ID.
- **A default gateway address** To facilitate communications between network segments, or subnets, each client device is assigned the IPv4 address of a router in the local network that is used to forward network traffic destined for devices in other subnets.
- **A Domain Name System (DNS) server address** DNS enables the client computer to resolve names into IPv4 or IPv6 addresses.

> **NEED MORE REVIEW? IPV4 ADDRESSING**
>
> To review further details about IPv4 addressing fundamentals, refer to the Microsoft TechNet website at *https://technet.microsoft.com/library/dd379547(v=ws.10).aspx*.

Subnets

A subnet is a network segment. One or more routers separate the subnet from other subnets. Each subnet on an Internet has a unique ID, just as each host within a subnet has a unique ID. You must use the 32 bits of an IPv4 address to define both the host's ID and the subnet ID in which that host resides.

Simple networks

Remember that each 32-bit IPv4 address is divided into four octets. In simple IPv4 subnetting, whole octets are reserved for defining the subnet portion of the IPv4 address, as shown in Figure 6-1; consequently, the remaining whole octets are available for defining the host portion of the address.

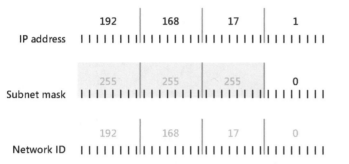

FIGURE 6-1 An IPv4 address using a simple Class C network addressing scheme

This simple subnetting is referred to as classful addressing, by which the address class, A, B, or C, defines the number of octets reserved for host and subnet IDs. Table 6-1 shows how this works.

TABLE 6-1 Characteristics of the default IPv4 address classes

Class	First octet	Default subnet mask	Number of networks	Number of hosts per network
A	1 to 127	255.0.0.0	126	16,777,214
B	128 to 191	255.255.0.0	16,384	65,534
C	192 to 223	255.255.255.0	2,097,152	254

> **NOTE OTHER ADDRESS CLASSES**
>
> There are also class D and class E addresses. Class D addresses are used for multicasting when a client device is part of a group. Class E addresses are reserved and are not used for hosts or subnets.

Complex networks

For some situations, using a classful addressing scheme can be ideal. But for many situations, it might be important to have more flexibility over the number of bits allocated to the subnet address portion of an IPv4 address. For example, instead of using 8, 16, or 24 bits for the subnet, you can use 12 or 18.

Bear in mind that the more bits you allocate to subnetting, the fewer bits remain for the host portion of the IPv4 address. That is, you can have more subnets, each containing fewer hosts, or you can have few subnets, each containing many hosts. Figure 6-2 shows how changing the subnet mask changes the subnet ID without changing the octets that define the whole IPv4 address. This scheme is often referred to as classless addressing, or Classless Interdomain Routing (CIDR).

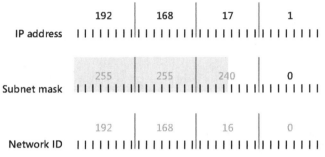

FIGURE 6-2 An IPv4 address using a classless network addressing scheme

In Figure 6-2, notice how changing the subnet mask from 255.255.255.0 to 255.255.240.0 shifts the device from subnet 192.168.17.0 to 192.168.16.0. In this case, by shifting the mask to the left, we have allocated more bits to describe hosts in each subnet, with correspondingly fewer subnets. You can see that to express a host's IPv4 configuration properly, not only must you state the IPv4 address, but you must also state the subnet mask. For example, in Figure 6-2, this host has an IPv4 configuration of 192.168.17.1/255.255.240.0.

EXAM TIP

You will often see devices with IPv4 configurations shown as 192.168.17.1/20. The number after the slash denotes the number of sequential binary 1s in the subnet mask (20 in this instance). If the mask were 255.255.248.0, that would be represented as /21.

NEED MORE REVIEW? IPV4 ROUTING

To review further details about IPv4 subnetting and routing, refer to the Microsoft TechNet website at *https://technet.microsoft.com/library/dd379495(v=ws.10).aspx*.

Public and private addressing

Devices that connect directly to the Internet require a unique public IPv4 configuration. However, due to the limitation of the 32-bit addressing scheme of IPv4, there is a limit to the number of hosts that can be connected to the Internet using a public configuration. To alleviate this potential but significant problem, many organizations use private IPv4 configurations for their network clients, only using public IPv4 configurations for Internet-facing devices, such as routers.

The Internet Assigned Numbers Authority (IANA) has defined the address ranges shown in Table 6-2 as being available for private use. A technology, such as network address translation (NAT), is used to enable devices using private IPv4 configurations to communicate with the Internet.

TABLE 6-2 Private IPv4 address ranges

Class	Mask	Range
A	10.0.0.0/8	10.0.0.0–10.255.255.255
B	172.16.0.0/12	172.16.0.0–172.31.255.255
C	192.168.0.0/16	192.168.0.0–192.168.255.255

Configuring an IPv4 connection

Devices running Windows 10 are configured to obtain an IPv4 configuration automatically by default, as shown in Figure 6-3.

FIGURE 6-3 The Internet Protocol Version 4 (TCP/IPv4) Properties dialog box

Typically, Windows 10–based devices obtain their IPv4 configurations from a Dynamic Host Configuration Protocol (DHCP) service, perhaps running on a Windows Server 2012 R2 server computer or provided as a service on a device such as a router or wireless access point (wireless AP).

EXAM TIP

If a Windows 10–based device fails to obtain an IPv4 configuration from a DHCP server, it reverts to using an Automatic Private IP Address (APIPA). If your computer has an IPv4 address that starts 169.254.*X.Y*, it is using an APIPA address. APIPA enables only local, subnet-based communications at best. You can override this behavior by opening the Alternative Configuration tab, shown in Figure 6-3, choosing User Configured, and specifying the IPv4 configuration to use when DHCP is unavailable.

To view or configure the IPv4 settings on your computer, perform the following procedure.

1. Right-click the network icon in the system tray and then click Open Network And Sharing Center.

2. Click Change Adapter Settings.

3. Right-click the appropriate network adapter and then click Properties.

4. Double-click Internet Protocol Version 4 (TCP/IPv4).

You can then configure the IPv4 settings. Click Use The Following IP Address and then specify the following: IP Address, Subnet Mask, Default Gateway, Preferred DNS Server, and Alternative DNS Server (Optional).

You can also configure a number of options from the Advanced TCP/IP Settings dialog box. From the Internet Protocol Version 4 (TCP/IPv4) Properties dialog box, click Advanced to open the dialog box, shown in Figure 6-4.

Configure the options on the following tabs.

- **IP Settings tab**   Enables you to configure additional IPv4 addresses and default gateways manually for this network interface.

- **DNS tab**   You can define additional DNS server addresses for name resolution and additional DNS suffix processing options.

- **WINS tab**   The Windows Internet Name Service (WINS) is an older name resolution service used by earlier versions of Windows and Windows Server. Generally, you do not need to configure anything here.

FIGURE 6-4 The IP Settings tab of the Advanced TCP/IP Settings dialog box

Configuring IPv4 from the command line and by using Windows PowerShell

In addition to configuring IPv4 settings from the user interface, you can also use the Netsh. exe command-line tool and Windows PowerShell cmdlets. You can use the Netsh.exe command-line tool to reconfigure many network-related settings. For example, the following command reconfigures the IPv4 settings.

```
Netsh interface ipv4 set address name="Ethernet" source=static addr=192.168.17.1
mask=255.255.240.0 gateway=192.168.31.254
```

There are numerous Windows PowerShell cmdlets that you can use to view and configure network settings, some of which are shown in Table 6-3. **TABLE 6-3** Windows PowerShell IPv4 networking-related cmdlets.

Cmdlet	Purpose
Get-NetIPAddress	Displays information about the IP address configuration
Get-NetIPv4Protocol	Displays information about the IPv4 protocol configuration
Set-NetIPAddress	Changes the IP address configuration
Set-NetIPv4Protocol	Changes the IPv4 protocol configuration

For example, to change the IPv4 configuration for a network connection with Windows PowerShell, use the following cmdlet.

```
Set-NetIPAddress –InterfaceAlias Ethernet –IPAddress 192.168.17.1
```

Overview of IPv6

It is still the case that almost all computers and other devices connect to the Internet by using an IPv4 configuration. However, some network services and devices do require an IPv6 configuration, so it is important to understand the IPv6 fundamentals, including how to configure IPv6. There are a number of reasons to consider IPv6. These include:

- **Some services require IPv6**   Services, such as DirectAccess, use IPv6 to facilitate remote connections.
- **Larger address space**   IPv6 uses a 128-bit address space, providing a vast increase in the availability of addresses for devices on the Internet.
- **Hierarchical addressing**   IPv6 uses a structured address space, which is more efficient for routers, helping to optimize network communications.
- **Support for stateless and stateful autoconfiguration**   You can configure your IPv6 devices to use DHCPv6 to obtain a stateful configuration, or you can rely on router discovery to use a stateless configuration, simplifying the process of enabling IPv6 on your network devices.

IPv6 addressing

As mentioned, IPv6 uses a 128-bit addressing scheme. This is usually written in hexadecimal.

The following is an example of an IPv6 address.

```
2001:CD8: 1F2D::2BB:FF:EF82:1C3B
```

IPv6 uses the following three address types.

- **Unicast addresses**   Packets are delivered to a single interface.
- **Multicast addresses**   Packets are delivered to multiple interfaces.
- **Anycast addresses**   Packet are delivered to multiple interfaces that are the closest in routing distance.

Unlike IPv4, IPv6 does not use broadcast messages. Instead, unicast and anycast addresses in IPv6 can have the following scopes.

- **Link-local**   IPv6 hosts on the same subnet
- **Site-local**   IPv6 hosts in the same organization, also known as private site addressing
- **Global**   IPv6 Internet addresses

EXAM TIP

Unicast site-local addresses are similar to IPv4 private addresses and have the FEC0::/64 prefix. Unicast link-local addresses are similar to IPv4 APIPA addresses and have the FE80::/64 prefix.

Configuring an IPv6 connection

Configuring IPv6 is almost identical to the process of configuring IPv4. By default, Windows 10 uses automatic IPv6 configuration. If a DHCPv6 server is available, it obtains its configuration from that service; otherwise, it will use stateless autoconfiguration. As with IPv4, you can use either the Windows user interface to configure IPv6, as shown in Figure 6-5, or you can use Netsh.exe or Windows PowerShell.

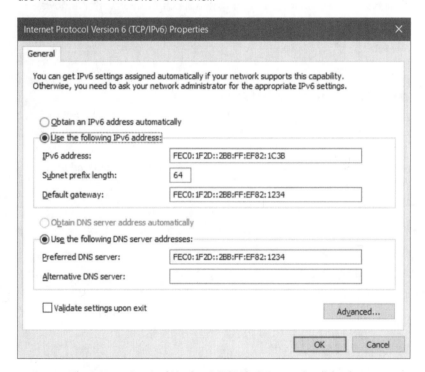

FIGURE 6-5 The Internet Protocol Version 6 (TCP/IPv6) Properties dialog box

To view or configure the IPv6 settings on your computer, perform the following procedure.

1.   Right-click the network icon in the system tray and then click Open Network And Sharing Center.

2.   Click Change Adapter Settings.

3.   Right-click the appropriate network adapter and then click Properties.

4. Double-click Internet Protocol Version 6 (TCP/IPv6).

There are numerous Windows PowerShell cmdlets that you can use to view and configure IPv6 network settings, some of which are shown in Table 6-4.

TABLE 6-4 Windows PowerShell IPv6 networking-related cmdlets

Cmdlet	Purpose
Get-NetIPAddress	Displays information about the IP address configuration
Get-NetIPv6Protocol	Displays information about the IPv4 protocol configuration
Set-NetIPAddress	Changes the IP address configuration
Set-NetIPv6Protocol	Changes the IPv4 protocol configuration

For example, to change the IPv6 configuration for a network connection with Windows PowerShell, use the following cmdlet.

```
Set-NetIPAddress -IPAddress 2001:CD8: 1F2D::2BB:FF:EF82:1C3B -PrefixLength 64
```

Skill: Configure name resolution

Devices running Windows 10 communicate over networks by using names rather than IPv4 or IPv6 network addresses. A service on the Windows 10–based device, known as a client re-solver, resolves names into IPv4 or IPv6 addresses. To configure Windows 10 networking, you must know how to configure name resolution.

> **This section covers how to:**
> - Describe name resolution
> - Configure DNS settings in Windows 10
> - Configure advanced DNS settings

Overview of name resolution

Although IP addressing is not especially complex, it is generally easier for users to work with host names rather than with the IPv4 or IPv6 addresses of hosts, such as websites, that they want to connect to. When an application, such as Microsoft Edge, references a website name, the name is converted to the underlying IP address by using a process known as name resolu-tion. Windows 10–based devices can use two types of name. These are:

- **Host names**   A host name, up to 255 characters in length, contains only alphanu-meric characters, periods, and hyphens. A host name is an alias combined with a fully qualified domain name (FQDN). For example, the alias *computer1* is prefixed to the domain name contoso.com to create the host name, or FQDN, of *computer1*.contoso.com.

- **NetBIOS names**   Less relevant today, NetBIOS names use a nonhierarchical structure based on a 16-character name. The sixteenth character identifies a particular service running on the computer named by the preceding 15 characters. Thus, LON-SVR1[20h] is the NetBIOS server service on the computer called LON-SVR1.

The way a client computer resolves names varies based on its configuration but is typically as shown in Figure 6-6.

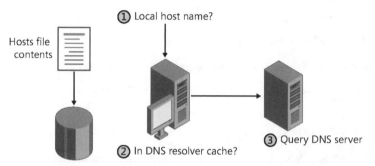

FIGURE 6-6 Typical stages of name resolution in a Windows 10 client

The following process identifies the typical stages of name resolution for Windows 10————based devices.

1. Determine whether the queried host name is the same as the local host name.

2. Search the local DNS resolver cache for the queried host name. The cache is updated when records are successfully resolved. In addition, the contents of the local Hosts file are added to the resolver cache.

3. Petition a DNS server for the required host name.

EXAM TIP

Windows 10 devices also use Link-Local Multicast Name Resolution for networks that do not provide DNS. You can find out more on the Microsoft Press Store website at *https://www.microsoftpressstore.com/articles/article.aspx?p=2217263&seqNum=8.*

NEED MORE REVIEW? IPV4 NAME RESOLUTION

To review further details about IPv4 name resolution, refer to the Microsoft TechNet web-site at *https://technet.microsoft.com/library/dd379505(v=ws.10).aspx.*

Configure DNS settings

To configure DNS settings for either IPv4 or IPv6, perform the following procedure.

1. Right-click the network icon in the system tray and then click Open Network And Sharing Center.

2. Click Change Adapter Settings.

3. Right-click the appropriate network adapter and then click Properties.

4. Double-click either Internet Protocol Version 4 (TCP/IPv4) or Internet Protocol Version 6 (TCP/IPv6).

5. Click Use The Following DNS Server Addresses and enter a valid IPv4 or IPv6 address for a DNS server that is accessible to the client.

You can also configure DNS settings by using Netsh.exe, as follows.

```
netsh interface ip set dns name="Ethernet" static 192.168.16.1
```

In addition, you can use Windows PowerShell to configure the DNS client settings.

```
Set-DNSClientServerAddress –interfaceIndex 12 –ServerAddresses ('192.168.16.1')
```

Configure advanced DNS settings

In addition to configuring the basic DNS client settings, you can configure advanced DNS settings, as shown in Figure 6-7. To configure these settings, from either the Internet Protocol Version 4 (TCP/IPv4) Properties dialog box or from the Internet Protocol Version 6 (TCP/IPv6) Properties dialog box, click Advanced and then click the DNS tab.

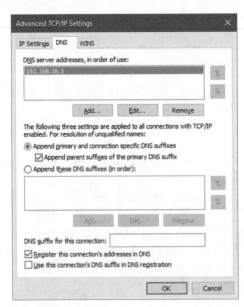

FIGURE 6-7 The DNS tab of the Advanced TCP/IP Settings dialog box

The advanced DNS settings are:

- **Append Primary And Connection Specific DNS Suffixes**   This option controls how the DNS resolver on the local client appends the DNS suffixes during queries. For example, if you query www, and your computer's primary suffix is contoso.com, the microsoft.com suffix is appended to your query to make www.contoso.com.

- **Append Parent Suffixes Of The Primary DNS Suffix**   In this example, the parent suffix of contoso.com is com. This option determines whether, after attempting www.contoso.com, the DNS resolver tries www.com.

- **Append These DNS Suffixes (In Order)**   This option enables you to define suffixes and order them for queries.

- **DNS suffix For This Connection**   You can define a DNS suffix for each network interface card installed in your device.

- **Register This Connection's Address In DNS**   Windows–based devices can register their IPv4 addresses with DNS servers that support dynamic updates of host records, such as the DNS server role service in Windows Server 2012 R2.

- **Use This Connection's DNS Suffix In DNS Registration**   This option determines whether the IP addresses and the connection-specific domain name of this connection are registered with DNS.

Skill: Connect to a network

It is important to know how to create and configure new network connections in Windows 10 in order to support your users' needs to connect with other computers, either at home or at their workplace. Windows 10 enables you to connect to a HomeGroup to share resources and peripherals and to your workplace by using a virtual private network (VPN) or by using DirectAccess.

This section covers how to:

- Connect to a HomeGroup
- Configure virtual private network connections
- Configure DirectAccess connections

Connect to a HomeGroup

HomeGroup enables you to join computers quickly and easily to create a simple file- and resource-sharing network. To create a homegroup, from the Network And Sharing Center, next to HomeGroup, click Ready To Create.

EXAM TIP

When your computer is joined to an Active Directory Domain Services (AD DS) domain, you cannot create or join a HomeGroup.

As shown in Figure 6-8, if a homegroup exists, you can join it. Otherwise, to create a homegroup, click Create A HomeGroup. Then, in the Create A Homegroup Wizard, specify what you want to share with other homegroup users. You can choose the following options.

- Pictures (Shared)
- Videos (Shared)
- Music (Shared)
- Documents (Not shared)
- Printers & Devices (Shared)

You are then provided with a password. Use this password when you want to access shared resources on other homegroup computers and devices.

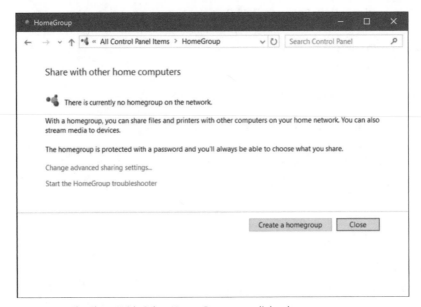

FIGURE 6-8 The Share With Other Home Computers dialog box

EXAM TIP

To create or join a homegroup, your network location profile must be set to private.

Configure VPN connections

You can use a VPN to connect to your workplace network over the Internet. A VPN provides for a secure connection through a public network by using authentication and encryption protocols. To create a VPN in Windows 10, from the Network And Sharing Center, under Change Your Network Settings, click Set Up A New Connection Or Network and then click Connect To A Workplace.

To configure your VPN connection, in the Connect To A Workplace Wizard, provide the following information.

- **How do you want to connect?**   You can connect by using an existing Internet connection or by dialing directly to your workplace.
- **Internet address**   This is the name or IP address of the computer that you connect to at your workplace, as shown in Figure 6-9. Typically, this is an FQDN, such as remote .adatum.com.
- **Destination name**   This is the name of this VPN connection.

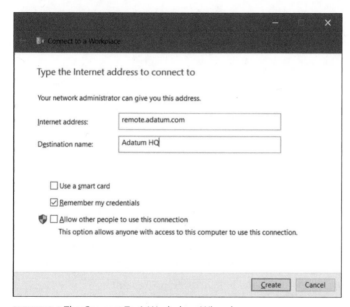

FIGURE 6-9 The Connect To A Workplace Wizard

After you have created the VPN connection, from the Network And Sharing Center, click Change Adapter Settings, right-click your VPN connection, and click Properties. As shown in Figure 6-10, you can then configure additional options as required by your organization's network infrastructure.

FIGURE 6-10 The Security tab of a VPN connection

These settings must match the remote access device that your device connects to, and includes the following options

- **Type Of VPN** Point-to-Point Tunneling Protocol (PPTP), Layer Two Tunneling Protocol with IPsec (L2TP/IPsec), Secure Socket Tunneling Protocol (SSTP), or Internet Key Exchange version 2 (IKEv2).
- **Data Encryption** None, Optional, Required, Maximum Strength

Under Authentication, you choose either Use Extensible Authentication Protocol (EAP) or Allow These Protocols. If you choose to use EAP, you then configure one of the following.

- Microsoft Secured Password (EAP-MSCHAP v2)(Encryption Enabled)
- Microsoft Smart Card Or Other Certificate (Encryption Enabled)
- Cisco: EAP-FAST (Encryption Enabled)
- Cisco: LEAP (Encryption Enabled)
- Cisco: PEAP (Encryption Enabled)

If you choose Allow These Protocols, you then configure the following options.

- Unencrypted Password (PAP)
- Challenge Handshake Authentication Protocol (CHAP)

- Microsoft CHAP Version 2 (MS-CHAP v2)
  - Automatically Use My Windows Log-on Name And Password (And Domain, If Any)
- Use Extensible Authentication Protocol (EAP), Including

EXAM TIP

You can use the Connection Manager Administration Kit (CMAK) to create and deploy VPN profiles for remote access. This kit can be installed as a Windows 10 feature from Control Panel. Find out more from the Microsoft TechNet website at *https://technet.microsoft.com /en-gb/library/cc726035.aspx.*

VPN profiles

Although manually configuring VPN connections is relatively simple, to complete the process on many computers, with the same or similar settings, is very time-consuming. In these circumstances, it makes sense to create a VPN profile and then distribute the profile to your users' computers.

When you use VPN profiles in Windows 10, you can take advantage of a number of advanced features. These are:

- **Always On**   You can configure the VPN profile so that the VPN initiates when the user signs in or when there has been a change in the network state, such as no longer being connected to the corporate Wi-Fi.
- **App-Triggered VPN**   You can configure the VPN profile to respond to a specific set of apps; if a defined app loads, then the VPN initiates.
- **Traffic Filters**   With traffic filters, your VPN profiles can be configured to initiate only when certain criteria, defined in policies, are met. For example, you can create app-based rules in which only traffic originating from defined apps can use the VPN. You can also create traffic-based rules that filter based on protocol, address, and port.
- **LockDown VPN**   You can configure LockDown to secure your user's device so that only the VPN can be used for network communications.

EXAM TIP

You can find out more about VPN profile options in Windows 10 from the Microsoft Tech-Net website at *https://technet.microsoft.com/itpro/windows/keep-secure/vpn-profile-options.*

You can create and distribute Windows 10 VPN profiles with these advanced settings by using Microsoft Intune and Configuration Manager.

NEED MORE REVIEW? **VPN CONNECTIONS IN MICROSOFT INTUNE**

To review further details about VPN connections in Microsoft Intune, refer to the Microsoft TechNet website *at https://docs.microsoft.com/intune/deploy-use/vpn-connections-in -microsoft-intune.*

NEED MORE REVIEW? **HOW TO CREATE VPN PROFILES IN CONFIGURATION MANAGER**

To review further details about creating VPN Profiles in Configuration Manager, refer to the Microsoft TechNet website at *https://technet.microsoft.com/library/dn261200.aspx.*

Configure DirectAccess connections

DirectAccess connections enable you to connect your Windows 10–based device to your organization's workplace without creating a VPN. Connections established with DirectAccess are not user-initiated, but are automatic.

You cannot initiate the configuration of DirectAccess solely on the client computer; rather, you must configure the server-side components. To configure DirectAccess on a Windows 10 client, you must use Group Policy Objects (GPOs) to deploy the required settings to your Windows 10–based devices. In addition, only Windows 10 Enterprise and Windows 10 Education support DirectAccess connections.

DirectAccess uses IPv6 and IPsec to facilitate connections to internal resources. Because most organizations do not have a native IPv6 network infrastructure, tunneling technology is used to enable communications, enabling the DirectAccess clients to use the IPv4-based Internet to communicate with your organization's servers. Protocols such as Intra-Site Automatic Tunnel Addressing Protocol (ISATAP), 6to4, Teredo, and IP-HTTPS are used to tunnel IPv4 communications.

The DirectAccess infrastructure consists of the following components.

- **DirectAccess server** This can be any server computer that is a member of an AD DS domain that is running Windows Server 2012 or later. This server establishes communication with intranet resources for remote DirectAccess clients.

- **DirectAccess clients** A DirectAccess client can be any domain-joined computer that is running the Enterprise edition of Windows 10, Windows 8.1, Windows 8, or Windows 7.

- **Network Location Server** DirectAccess clients use the Network Location Server (NLS) to determine their own location—that is, whether they are internal or external clients. If the client computer can securely connect to the NLS by using HTTPS, then the client computer assumes it is on the intranet (internal), and the organization's DirectAccess policies are not applied. If the client computer cannot reach the NLS, the client assumes it is on the Internet (external).

- **Internal resources** These are the server-based resources that users want to connect to, for example, file servers, web servers, and so on.
- **AD DS** You require an AD DS forest to implement DirectAccess.
- **Group Policy** DirectAccess is configured on client computers using GPOs. In addition, GPOs are used to centralize the administration and deployment of server DirectAccess settings.
- **Public key infrastructure (PKI)** In some more complex deployments, you require digital certificates for authentication.
- **DNS server** Name resolution based on DNS is required.

EXAM TIP

A DirectAccess client can be any domain-joined computer that is running the Enterprise edition of Windows 10, Windows 8.1, Windows 8, or Windows 7. Find out more about DirectAccess from the Microsoft TechNet website at *https://technet.microsoft.com/library /mt421256.aspx*.

Skill: Configure network locations

Windows manages network security settings based on how inherently secure a particular network connection is. For example, a Wi-Fi network that you connect to in a coffee shop is likely to be more at risk from potential security hazards than a wired network within your organization's head office. Network location profiles are a way for Windows to assign more or less rigorous network security settings. Understanding how to assign network location profiles and how to configure network security settings for those profiles enables you to support your users more effectively.

> **This section covers how to:**
> - Describe network location profiles
> - Configure a network location for a network connection

Overview of network location profiles

When you connect to a new network, whether a Wi-Fi or wired network, Windows prompts you to define the network location profile. Selecting a network location profile changes certain behaviors in Windows 10, including Windows Firewall settings, network discovery, and file- and print-sharing options, including HomeGroup settings. You can see the currently assigned network location profile in the Network And Sharing Center, as shown in Figure 6-11.

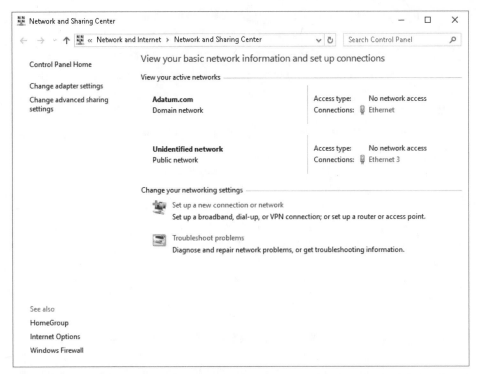

FIGURE 6-11 The Network And Sharing Center, showing the network connections and their assigned network location profiles.

Windows 10 provides three distinct types of network location.

- **Domain networks** These are networks that are connected to an AD DS domain. Assigning this option ensures proper communication with AD DS domain controllers. By default, network discovery is enabled.

- **Private networks** These are nondomain Work or Home networks, where you trust the people using the network and the devices connected to the network. Network discovery is enabled, and Windows 10–based devices on a home network can belong to a homegroup.

- **Guest Or Public networks** By selecting this network location profile, network discovery is disabled, helping to keep your computer from being visible to other computers on the network. HomeGroup is also not available.

EXAM TIP

The domain network location profile is assigned automatically to network connections that are connected to AD DS domains.

Configure network locations

As soon as you connect to a network, Windows 10 prompts you to define the network location, as shown in Figure 6-12. If you click Yes, the private network location is assigned. Selecting No results in Windows assigning the public network location profile.

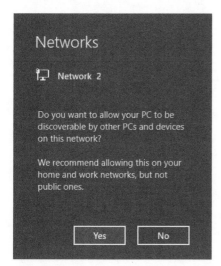

FIGURE 6-12 Network location assignment prompt

Changing your network location profile

If you want to change the network location in Windows 10, click Start, click Settings, and then click Network & Internet. Then, use the following procedure,

1. Select your network adapter. For a wired connection, click the Ethernet tab and then click the adapter you want to change. For a wireless connection, click the Wi-Fi tab and then click Advanced Options.

2. Under Make This PC Discoverable, change Allow Your PC To Be Discoverable By Other PCs And Devices On This Network. Enabling this option sets the network location profile to Private, and disabling it sets the network location profile to Public, as shown in Figure 6-13.

FIGURE 6-13 Changing your network location profile

Skill: Configure Windows Firewall, including Advanced Security and network discovery

After you connect a computer to a network, you might expose the computer to security risks. To mitigate these possible risks, you can implement a number of network security features in Windows 10, including Windows Firewall.

Windows Firewall blocks or allows network traffic based on the properties of that traffic. You can configure how Windows Firewall controls the flow of network traffic by using configurable rules. In addition to blocking or allowing network traffic, Windows Firewall can filter traffic and be used to implement authentication and apply encryption to this filtered traffic.

The way in which you configure Windows Firewall and your network location profiles can have a significant impact on file and printer sharing and can affect the discoverability of your device on connected networks.

> **This section covers how to:**
> - Configure Windows Firewall
> - Configure Windows Firewall with Advanced Security
> - Configure IPsec
> - Configure network discovery

Configure Windows Firewall

You can access the Windows Firewall settings by opening the Network And Sharing Center. Click Windows Firewall. As shown in Figure 6-14, for each network location profile, you can view and configure the following options.

- **Windows Firewall State**   Default: On. If you select Off, your device is unprotected by the Windows Firewall. You would normally only turn Windows Firewall off if using an alternative firewall product.

- **Incoming Connections**   Default: Block All Connections To Apps That Are Not On The List Of Allowed Apps.

- **Active Domain/Private/Public Networks**   Displays a list of current network connections assigned one or other of the network location profiles.

- **Notification State**   Default: Notify Me When Windows Firewall Blocks A New App.

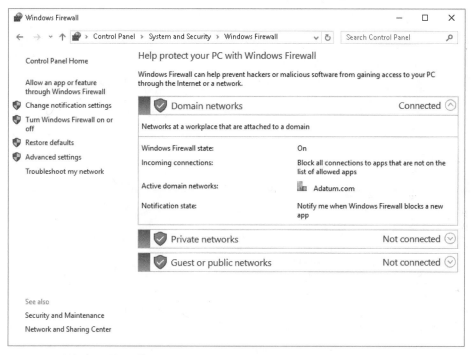

FIGURE 6-14 Windows Firewall

To change these values, click Change Notification Settings. For each network location profile, you can:

- Turn Windows Firewall on or off.
- Block all incoming connections, including those in the list of allowed apps.
- Turn off notifications.

Allowing apps through the firewall

If you want to allow an app through Windows Firewall, from Windows Firewall, click Allow An App Or Feature Through Windows Firewall. As shown in Figure 6-15, you can then choose which app to allow through the firewall by selecting the appropriate check box against the app's name.

If the app you want is not listed, click Allow Another App. You must then specify the path to the app and select which network profiles this app setting applies to.

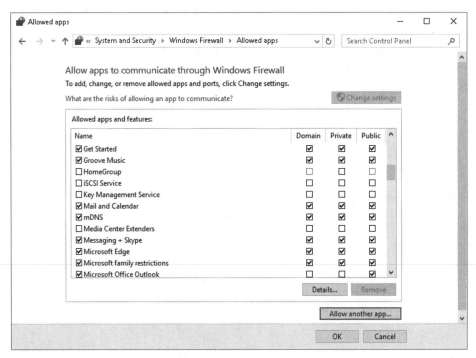

FIGURE 6-15 Windows Firewall Allowed apps window

You can also configure Windows Firewall by using either Netsh.exe or Windows PowerShell. For example, to configure an app exception in Windows Firewall with Netsh.exe, run the following command.

```
netsh firewall add allowedprogram C:\ Program Files (x86)\MyApp\MyApp.exe "My
Application" ENABLE
```

> **NEED MORE REVIEW?** **USING NETSH.EXE TO CONFIGURE WINDOWS FIREWALL**
>
> To find out more about controlling Windows Firewall with Netsh.exe, refer to the Microsoft Support website at *https://support.microsoft.com/ kb/947709*.

There are a significant number of Windows PowerShell cmdlets that you can use to configure and control Windows Firewall. For example, to allow a new app through the firewall, you
can use the following command.

```
New-NetFirewallRule -DisplayName "Allow MyApp" -Direction Inbound -Program "C:\Program
Files (x86)\MyApp\MyApp.exe" -RemoteAddress LocalSubnet -Action Allow
```

> **NEED MORE REVIEW?** **USING WINDOWS POWERSHELL TO CONFIGURE WINDOWS FIRE-
> WALL**
>
> To find out more about controlling Windows Firewall with Windows PowerShell, refer to
> the Microsoft Support website at *https://technet.microsoft.com/library/jj554906(v=wps.630)*
> *.aspx.*

Configure Windows Firewall With Advanced Security

You can perform more advanced Windows Firewall configurations by using the Windows
Firewall With Advanced Security management console snap-in, as shown in Figure 6-16. To
access the snap-in, from Windows Firewall, click Advanced Settings.

The Windows Firewall configuration is presented differently. Traffic flow is controlled by
rules, and there is a Monitoring node for viewing the current status and behavior of configured rules.

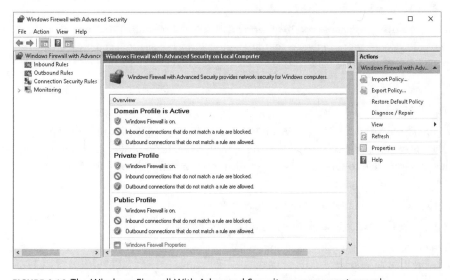

FIGURE 6-16 The Windows Firewall With Advanced Security management console

Windows Firewall With Advanced Security rules

Rules are criteria that define what network traffic is filtered and what action is taken on that filtered traffic. There are three types of rules.

- **Inbound rules**   Monitor inbound network traffic and allow or block inbound traffic that meets the criteria of the rule. You can configure the following types of inbound rules.

  - *Program rules*   Control connections that a specified app uses.

  - *Port rules*   Control connections that use a particular TCP or UDP port.

  - *Predefined rules*   Network-aware apps often create these types of rules so that you can enable or disable the app as a group setting.

  - *Custom rules*   These rules enable you to create very specific firewall settings based on one or several factors.

- **Outbound rules**   Monitor outbound network traffic and allow or block outbound traffic that meets the criteria of the rule. You can configure the following types of outbound rules: Program rules, Port rules, Predefined rules, and Custom rules.

- **Connection security rules**   Filter and secure network traffic by using IPsec. You use connection security rules to require authentication or encryption of connections between two computers.

> **NOTE   WHEN TO USE CONNECTION SECURITY RULES**
>
> Connection security rules enable you to determine when and how authentication occurs but do not allow connections between computers. To allow a connection, you must create an inbound or outbound rule.

Creating rules

To create a rule, from Windows Firewall With Advanced Security, right-click the appropriate node, click New Rule, and then complete the wizard to create your rule. For example, to create a new inbound rule to enable network traffic for a program, perform the following procedure.

1. Right-click Inbound Rules and then click New Rule.

2. On the Rule Type page, click Program and then click Next.

3. On the Program page, click This Program Path, browse and select the program executable, and then click Next.

4. On the Action page, choose Allow The Connection and click Next.

5. On the Profile page, select which network location profiles are affected by the rule and click Next.

6. Provide a name and description for your rule and click Finish.

In addition to using the Windows Firewall With Advanced Security management console, you can also use Windows PowerShell to configure and manage Windows Firewall With Advanced Security. You can use the following Windows PowerShell cmdlets to manage Windows Firewall rules.

- **Get-NetFirewallRule**   Displays a list of available firewall rules
- **Enable-NetFirewallRule**   Enables an existing firewall rule
- **Disable-NetFirewallRule**   Disables an existing firewall rule
- **New-NetFirewallRule**   Creates a new firewall rule
- **Set-NetFirewallRule**   Configures the properties of an existing firewall rule

> *NEED MORE REVIEW?* **USING WINDOWS POWERSHELL TO CONFIGURE WINDOWS FIREWALL WITH ADVANCED SECURITY**
>
> To find out more about controlling Windows Firewall With Advanced Security by using Windows PowerShell, refer to the Microsoft TechNet website at *https://technet.microsoft.com/library/hh831755.aspx*.

Configure IPsec

By default, Windows 10 does not encrypt or authenticate communications between computers. However, you can use Windows Firewall With Advanced Security connection security rules to apply authentication and encryption to network traffic in your organization.

Connection security rules are based on IPsec and help to ensure confidentiality, integrity, and authenticity of data in transit on your network. Connection security rules force authentication between two configured computers before communications are established and data are transmitted. You can also define encryption of data in transit by using connection security rules.

You can configure the following types of Connection Security rules.

- **Isolation rules**   Connections between computers are restricted based on authentication criteria. For example, membership of a domain can be used to isolate network traffic.
- **Authentication exemption rules**   You can define when authentication is not required between computers.

- **Server-to-server rules**   Use these rules to authenticate and secure communications between specific computers.

- **Tunnel rules**   These rules secure communications between two computers by using tunnel mode in IPsec instead of transport mode.

- **Custom rules**   These rules enable you to create specific connection security settings based on one or several factors.

NEED MORE REVIEW? **UNDERSTANDING CONNECTION SECURITY RULES**

To find out more about using and configuring Connection Security rules, refer to the Microsoft Support website at *https://technet.microsoft.com/library/e36be3e2-6cab-4b06 -984d-b5649e04eb66.aspx*.

Configure network discovery

Network discovery is the ability for your computer to locate devices and resources on the networks to which it is connected, and for other devices to discover your device and resources.

Network discovery is tightly linked to network location profiles and to Windows Firewall configuration. As we have seen, by default, network discovery is enabled for devices connecting to networks that are assigned the Domain or Private network location profile, but network discovery is disabled on public networks.

To change network discovery settings, from the Network And Sharing Center, click Change Advanced Sharing Settings. As shown in Figure 6-17, you can then configure network discovery for each network location profile.

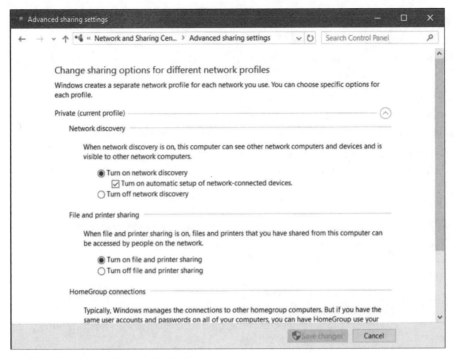

FIGURE 6-17 Advanced Sharing Settings

Skill: Configure Wi-Fi settings and Wi-Fi Direct

It is not uncommon these days for even laptop computers to be equipped only with a wireless network port but no RJ-45 connection. Consequently, with the increasing prevalence of wireless networking, it is more important than ever to know how to configure wireless settings in Windows 10.

> **This section covers how to:**
> - Describe wireless networking standards
> - Configure Wi-Fi and Wi-Fi Direct in Windows 10

Overview of wireless networking standards

You can configure wireless networks by using one of several modes to suit your requirements and using one of a number of standards to secure the network and achieve compatibility between your wireless devices.

Modes

Wireless networking can be configured in one of three modes.

- **Ad-hoc**   This setting enables you to configure wireless connection between devices in a peer-to-peer manner without requiring a wireless access point (AP).

- **Wi-Fi Direct**   This setting is a wireless networking standard that you can use to connect your wireless devices without a wireless AP. Similar to ad hoc wireless networking, it is typically used to connect to peripherals such as printers and media players.

- **Infrastructure**   Based on wireless APs, infrastructure networks consist of wireless local area networks to enable communications between wireless client devices.

Standards

To ensure compatibility between wireless networked devices, a number of standards have evolved. The 802.11x wireless standards are described in Table 6-5.

TABLE 6-5 802.11 wireless standards

Standard	Definition
802.11a	Provides up to 54 megabits per second (mbps) and uses the 5 gigahertz (GHz) range. Not compatible with 802.11b.
802.11b	Provides 11 mbps and uses the 2.4 GHz range.
802.11e	Defines Quality of Service and multimedia support.
802.11g	For use over short distances at speeds up to 54 mbps. Backwardcompatible with 802.11b and uses the 2.4 GHz range.
802.11n	Increases data throughput at speeds up to 100 mbps, and it uses both 2.4 GHz and 5 GHz ranges.
802.11ac	Builds on 802.11n to achieve data rates of 433 mbps. 802.11ac uses the 5 GHz frequency range.

Security

It is comparatively easy to gain access to a wireless network, so it is important to secure network traffic on your wireless network infrastructure. A number of wireless security standards exist that can help, as shown in Table 6-6. When choosing a security method, ensure that your wireless devices and infrastructure support that method.

TABLE 6-6 Wireless security standards

Standard	Explanation
Wired Equivalent Privacy (WEP)	WEP is an old wireless security standard, and a number of documented security issues surround it. Use WEP only if there is no choice.
Wi-Fi Protected Access (WPA)	WPA has two variations. WPA-Personal. Easier to implement than WPAEnterprise and, therefore, ideal for smaller networks. Authentication is based on a password. The password and the network Service Set Identifier (SSID) generate encryption keys for each wireless device. WPA-Enterprise. Designed for larger networks and requires the use of a Remote Authentication Dial-In User Service (RADIUS) server to provide for authentication.
WPA2	An improved version of WPA that is the de facto Wi-Fi security standard. It employs larger encryption key sizes than WPA.

Configure wireless settings

After you have selected the appropriate wireless infrastructure components and chosen your wireless security standard, you must set up and configure your wireless network in Windows 10.

Connect to a wireless network

To connect to a wireless network, in the system tray, click the network icon to see a list of available wireless networks. Click the appropriate network and then click Connect. Enter the required security information as shown in Figure 6-18 and click Next.

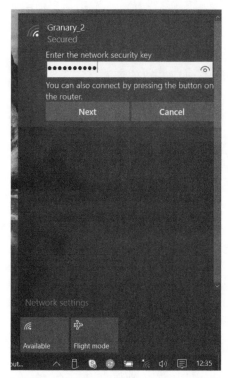

FIGURE 6-18 Connecting to a wireless network

Configure existing wireless networks

To review or edit your existing wireless networks, from Settings, click Network & Internet. On the Wi-Fi tab, click Manage Wi-Fi Settings, as shown in Figure 6-19, and then complete the following procedure.

1. Choose Options.

2. Connect To Suggested Open Hotspots.

3. Connect To Networks Shared By My Contacts.

4. Select how you will share your networks with your contacts. Choose from:

   - Outlook.com Contacts

   - Skype Contacts

   - Facebook Friends

5. At the bottom of the page, beneath Manage Known Networks, click the network you want to manage.

6. Click to Share or Forget the network.

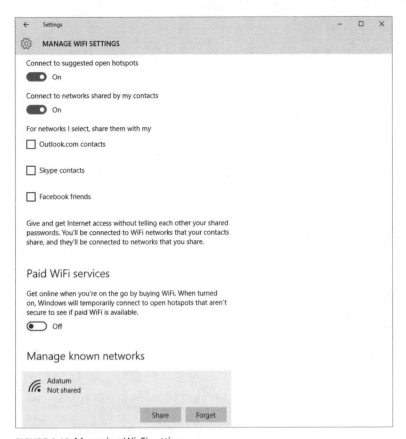

FIGURE 6-19 Managing Wi-Fi settings

Advanced settings

To configure advanced wireless settings, from the Network And Sharing Center, under View Your Active Networks, click the wireless network you want to configure, as shown in Figure 6-20. Then, in the Wi-Fi Status dialog box, click Wireless Properties. You can then view the security settings for your wireless network connection.

FIGURE 6-20 Managing advanced Wi-Fi settings

You can also manage wireless networks by using Netsh.exe. For example, to list the wireless network profiles on your computer, type:

```
Netsh wlan show profile
```

NEED MORE REVIEW? **USING NETSH.EXE TO MANAGE WIRELESS NETWORKS**

To find out more about managing Wi-Fi settings by using Netsh.exe, refer to the Microsoft TechNet website at *https://technet.microsoft.com/library/dd744890(WS.10).aspx.*

Configuring Wi-Fi Direct

Windows 10 supports Wi-Fi Direct, a means of connecting your Windows 10–based device to other devices and peripherals without requiring a wireless AP. Your users might want to use Wi-Fi Direct to transfer files between devices more quickly than is possible with Bluetooth, or to use media streaming to a compatible device for a presentation.

To set up Wi-Fi Direct in Windows 10, you need a compatible network adapter. Type **ipconfig /all** at the command line and verify that one of the network adapters listed returns the Description value Microsoft Wi-Fi Direct Virtual Adapter, as shown in Figure 6-21.

```
Wireless LAN adapter Local Area Connection* 2:

   Media State . . . . . . . . . . . : Media disconnected
   Connection-specific DNS Suffix . :
   Description . . . . . . . . . . . : Microsoft Wi-Fi Direct Virtual Adapter
   Physical Address. . . . . . . . . :
   DHCP Enabled. . . . . . . . . . . : Yes
   Autoconfiguration Enabled . . . . : Yes
```

FIGURE 6-21 Viewing available network adapters with Ipconfig

After you have checked that your wireless network adapter supports Wi-Fi Direct, use the Netsh.exe command-line tool to set up your Wi-Fi Direct network. You can use the following command to start the process of enabling Wi-Fi Direct.

```
netsh wlan set hostednetwork mode=allow ssid=wifidirect key=passphrase
```

Use the following command to start Wi-Fi Direct.

```
netsh wlan start hostednetwork
```

To stop the Wi-Fi Direct network, use:

```
netsh wlan stop hostednetwork
```

Skill: Troubleshoot network issues

Windows 10 is a reliable and robust operating system, and the networking technologies built into it are tried and tested. However, networking is an inherently complex area, and problems might occur on your network. When you are facing a networking problem, use an appropriate procedure for troubleshooting the issue. This procedure might include the following steps.

1. Determine the scope of the problem. Knowing how many users are affected can help you determine possible causes.
2. Determine the IP configuration. Verify that the network configuration of affected devices is correct.
3. Determine the network's hardware configuration. Determine whether there are problems with the networking hardware or device drivers for that hardware.
4. Test communications. Perform a series of tests that help you pinpoint the nature of the problem. Tests might include:
   - Verifying basic communications.
   - Checking the routing and firewall configuration of your network.
   - Testing name resolution.
   - Testing connectivity to specific applications on servers.

Know how to troubleshoot network-related problems that occur on your network to minimize disruption to your users.

This section covers:
- Network troubleshooting tools in Windows 10
- How to troubleshoot name resolution

Network troubleshooting tools

Windows 10 provides a number of tools that you can use to diagnose and resolve many network-related issues. These tools are identified in Table 6-7.

TABLE 6-7 Windows 10 network troubleshooting tools

Tool	Purpose
Event Viewer	Windows collects information about system activity into event logs. For example, the System log stores information about IP conflicts and network-related service failures.
Windows Network Diagnostics	You can use Diagnose Connection Problems to help you diagnose and repair a network issue. Windows Network Diagnostics presents possible descriptions of the issue and suggests a potential solution. You can access this tool by clicking Troubleshoot Problems In Network And Sharing Center.
IPConfig	Use this command-line tool to display the current TCP/IP configuration of your Windows 10–based device. You can use the command with the following switches. ipconfig /all View detailed configuration information. ipconfig /release Release the leased configuration back to the DHCP server. ipconfig /renew Renew the leased configuration. ipconfig /displaydns View the DNS resolver cache entries. ipconfig /flushdns Purge the DNS resolver cache. ipconfig /registerdns Register or update the client's host name with the DNS server.
Ping	This command-line tool can be used to verify connectivity to a target computer system by sending a series of network packets to that target system. Consider that many firewalls block the ICMP packets Ping uses, so you might receive false negatives. Type ping www.contoso.com.
Tracert	Use this tool to determine the path that packets take to a designated target computer system. This helps you diagnose routing-related problems.
NSLookup	Use this tool to troubleshoot name resolution.
Pathping	This traces a network route similar to how the Tracert tool works but provides more statistics on the hops through the network.
Windows PowerShell	In addition to the configuration cmdlets referred to earlier, there are also a number of Windows PowerShell cmdlets you can use to troubleshoot and test network connectivity. For example, the test-connection cmdlet behaves in a way similar to Ping. exe. Type test-connection www.contoso.com.

Troubleshoot name resolution

Many network failures can be caused by failure in name resolution, such as when the wrong server IP address is returned, or a service has not registered itself with a DNS server correctly or at all. When troubleshooting name resolution issues, use a suitable procedure, which might consist of the following steps.

1. Clear the DNS resolver cache.   Use the Ipconfig /flushdns command from an elevated command prompt. This ensures that all subsequent name resolution attempts are performed rather than being satisfied from DNS resolver cache. You can also use the Clear-DnsClientCache Windows PowerShell cmdlet to achieve the same thing.

2. **Attempt to verify basic connectivity by using an IP address.** Use the Ping command, or the test-connection Windows PowerShell cmdlet, to verify communications to an IP address; for example, type **test-connection 172.16.16.1**.

3. **Attempt to verify connectivity to a host name.** Using the same tools, check whether you can communicate with a host by using its name, for example, **test-connection LON-DC1**. If this is successful, it is likely that your problem is not related to name resolution.

4. **If the test is not successful, edit the hosts file.** Add the correct IP address and name to your hosts file. For example, add the line **172.16.16.1 LON-DC1.adatum.com** to C:\Windows\System32\Drivers\Etc\Hosts. Repeat the procedure to verify connectivity to a host name. Name resolution should now be successful.

5. **Display the resolver cache.** Use the Get-DnsClientCache cmdlet (or use IPConfig / displaydns) to verify that the entry appears in a resolved cache. You have proven that the problem is likely a name resolution issue. Remove the entry from the hosts file and clear the resolver cache.

6. **Test the name server.** Test the name server by performing a query against it by using the Resolve-dnsname lon-DC1.adatum.com. cmdlet. Alternatively, use the NSLookup. exe –d2 LON-cl1.adatum.com. command. You can see the partial output from the Resolve-dnsname cmdlet in Figure 6-22.

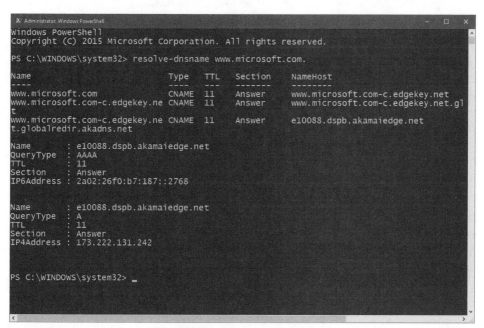

FIGURE 6-22 Using Resolve-dnsname to test name resolution

The information returned from the name server test shows IP addresses of the server you queried against. It also shows which name servers provided the response. It is important to know how to interpret this returned information to diagnose any failures or faults properly.

> **NEED MORE REVIEW? DIAGNOSING NAME RESOLUTION PROBLEMS**
>
> To find out more about troubleshooting name resolution, refer to the Microsoft TechNet website at *https://technet.microsoft.com/library/cc959340.aspx*.

Summary

- Each device on a network requires a unique IPv4 and, optionally, IPv6 configuration.
- Windows 10–based network devices use name resolution to change names in IP addresses for network communications.
- Network location profiles enable Windows 10 to determine appropriate security settings for designated network connections.
- Windows Firewall helps protect your Windows 10–based devices when connected to networks and verifies that settings in Windows Firewall and the selected network location profile determine whether network discovery is enabled.
- Windows 10 provides support for most Wi-Fi networking standards, including Wi-Fi Direct.
- Windows 10 provides a number of tools that you can use to help troubleshoot networking issues.

Thought experiment

In this thought experiment, demonstrate your skills and knowledge of the topics covered in this chapter. You can find answers to this thought experiment in the next section.

You have been hired to deploy Windows 10 at a new office for A. Datum Corporation. The office was a greenfield site with no computer infrastructure and has just had all the network cabling and wireless infrastructure installed by a contractor. You must help plan and implement networking services at the new location and verify that all equipment is working on the network.

As a consultant for A. Datum, answer the following questions about networking.

1. You connected a number of devices to the wireless APs in the new building. They seem to be connected, but you want to verify that they can communicate with each other. Is it true that the Test-Connection Windows PowerShell cmdlet is the equivalent of the Ping command-line tool?

2. You want to be able to view the current network configuration of the installed laptops in the new building. Which of the following commands enable you to do this?

   A. Ping

   B. Tracert

   C. NSlookup

   D. IPconfig

   E. Get-NetIPAddress

   F. Netsh

3. You are troubleshooting name resolution to the LON-DC1 domain controller. You suspect a problem might reside with the configured DNS server that was just installed at the site. If you create an entry for LON-DC1 in the local hosts file of a test computer running Windows 10, which is used first, the DNS server or the local resolver cache?

4. You have been asked to set up a VPN solution for some users who want to work from home. Which VPN tunneling protocols can you use with Windows 10?

5. You notice that one of your computers has an IPv4 address that starts 169.254. What could this mean?

Thought experiment answers

This section contains the solutions to the thought experiment.

1. Yes, the Test-Connection Windows PowerShell cmdlet is the equivalent of the Ping command-line tool.

2. The IPconfig, Get-NetIPAddress, and Netsh commands enable you to view the network configuration of computers running Windows 10.

3. The DNS resolver cache is checked before a DNS server is petitioned.

4. You can use the following VPN tunneling protocols: Point-to-Point Tunneling Protocol (PPTP), Layer Two Tunneling Protocol with IPsec (L2TP/IPsec), Secure Socket Tunneling Protocol (SSTP), or Internet Key Exchange version 2 (IKEv2).

5. It means that the device is configured to obtain an IPv4 address automatically and has been unable to obtain an IPv4 configuration from a DHCP server. This might be because the DHCP server is offline or because an insufficient number of addresses are available on the server.

CHAPTER 7

Configure storage

M ost devices shipped with Windows 10 are supplied with a single physical disk that is configured with one volume that holds the operating system and user data. If the device is a tablet or ultra-book, the hard drive will probably be of the solid-state drive (SSD) or smaller mSATA form factor drive type, which provides very high disk read/write performance and is often sealed in the device to reduce the size. Cloud technologies will continue to improve in terms of both speed and reliability, and more users will store less data on their devices and instead rely on Office 365, Microsoft OneDrive, and other cloud services. During this transition to the cloud, understand how to configure and manage the storage hardware and file systems available to you with Windows 10.

Skills covered in this chapter:

- Configure disks, volumes and file systems
- Create and configure virtual hard disks
- Configure removable devices
- Create and configure Storage Spaces
- Troubleshoot storage issues and removable devices

Skill: Configure disks, volumes, and file systems

Traditionally, desktop devices that you come across often have multiple hard drives. These drives offer huge storage capacity relatively cheaply, but they can be heavy and mechanical. When you have multiple drives to use, you can access alternative configurations such as multi-boot, boot to VHD, or RAID-enabled systems used for increased speed or data redundancy. Desktop sales are in decline, and it is expected that in the future the demand for desktop PCs will be driven by specialty audiences who have them custom made for specific purposes such as computer-aided design (CAD) or gaming.

This section reviews the essentials you need to know about disks, volumes, and file systems and outlines new features Windows 10 offers you.

Although the exam might focus on newer technologies such as OneDrive or Storage Spaces, you should still understand how to create and manage simple, spanned, and striped volumes in Windows 10. This chapter introduces you to the new Resilient File System (ReFS) file format and describes how ReFS compares to and complements the NTFS file format, which has been part of Windows for more than 20 years.

> **This section covers how to:**
> - Configure disks
> - Configure volumes
> - Configure file systems
> - Use disk management tools

Configure disks

Before you can store data or applications on a drive, you must first partition it by using the master boot record (MBR) or the GUID partition table (GPT) partitioning scheme. To help you decide which scheme is more appropriate, review the comparison in Table 7-1.

TABLE 7-1   MBR and GPT disk partitioning schemes

Disk Partitioning Scheme	Description & Features
Master boot record	Contains the partition table for a disk and the master boot code. The MBR is created during the initial partitioning; it is located on the first sector of the hard disk and allows four-partition entries in a table that records the size and location of disk partitions. Windows platforms require an MBR-partitioned system disk to boot to. MBR is compatible with BIOS or the newer Unified Extensible Firmware Interface (UEFI). No partition can be larger than 2 terabytes (TB). MBR disks offer no redundancy. If the MBR or associated startup files become corrupted, the drive and operating system might not start.
GUID partition table	GPT disks contain a more robust array of partition entries that record the start and end logical block addressing (LBA) fields of each partition on a disk. GPT is compatible with BIOS or UEFI. Windows cannot start from a GPT disk by using BIOS. Windows Vista and later versions (64-bit only) support boot from GPT when running on UEFI-based computers. Supports up to 128 partitions per disk. GPT definition supports 18-exabyte volume sizes (although disks are not currently available in that size, and Windows file systems are limited to 256 TB). Not available for removable media. GPT offers cyclic redundancy check (CRC32) integrity protection and automatic GUID entry backup.

During the startup process, the MBR is examined to determine which partition is set as active, and the operating system startup files, including the boot sector and Windows Boot Manager found on this partition, are loaded.

Because of the limited number of partitions that MBR supports, one can be configured as an extended partition with multiple logical volumes inside.

Both MBR and GPT disks support basic and dynamic disks, which will be discussed later. Basic disks support only primary partitions, extended partitions, and logical drives.

The majority of older disks are configured as MBR, whereas modern systems that use x64-bit operating systems and UEFI-based hardware are increasingly using the newer GPT partitioning scheme.

Configure volumes

Volumes are used to arrange areas on disks. A simple volume is a contiguous, unallocated area of a physical hard disk that you format with one of the supported file systems: NTFS, ReFS, exFat, FAT32, or FAT.

After a volume is formatted, you can then assign a drive letter to it, elect not to provide a drive letter, or mount the drive in an existing volume by using a volume mount point.

Windows 10 supports either simple or dynamic disk volume types. Simple volumes are available on basic disks, whereas mirrored, spanned, or striped volumes are available only if you convert a basic disk to the dynamic disk type.

Simple volumes reside on a single disk, either in a contiguous block or in multiple regions of the same disk that link together. They are not themselves fault-tolerant, and the volume I/O performance is comparable to the disk I/O performance. Most business user scenarios create a basic disk with a single basic volume for storage. This offers simple configuration, simplicity, and ease of use for the user.

It is best practice to store the operating system on a different volume, separate from business data, so that if the operating system becomes unstable, the user can reset the operating system or reinstall it without affecting the business data. The data can be stored in OneDrive or in OneDrive for Business, but businesses might create a basic disk with two or more simple volumes. The operating system will be stored on the first volume, and the second volume will be used to store data.

All volume types, except simple volumes, require dynamic disks and are only available to Windows operating systems. They can offer specialty volume types, which can provide increased performance, fault tolerance, or advanced features. They use a database to record information about the dynamic disk and dynamic volume status. Windows 10 can repair a corrupted database on one dynamic disk by copying the replicated database stored on another dynamic disk.

Mirrored volumes

A mirrored volume uses two disks and presents them to Windows 10 as a single logical volume. The data on each disk is an identical copy of the other and, therefore, provides redundancy and fault tolerance if one disk fails. Mirrored volumes are also referred to as RAID-1 (redundant array of independent disks) volumes and offer a slight performance boost for read operations because you can read from both disks simultaneously, but they are slightly slower for write operations.

To create a mirrored volume, you must use equal-sized areas of unallocated space from two disks and, after you establish the mirror, you cannot modify or resize the mirrored volume. If one of the mirrored drives fails and is replaced, you must repair the mirrored volume, which then re-creates the data on the new drive and reestablishes data redundancy.

Spanned volume

A spanned volume creates a join across unallocated spaces on at least two and, at most, 32 disks and presents this to the operating system as a single logical disk. Because Windows 10 manages the spanned volume, you must be able to boot to the operating system to access the data on the drive. Spanned volumes provide no protection against a disk failure; all data will be unavailable from the remaining disk and will need to be recovered from a backup. There is no performance benefit to using spanned volumes; they are predominately used to provide volume expansion capacity, such as when replacement of the drive with a larger unit is not possible.

Striping

Historically, a user could stripe data between two volumes on separate hard drives to achieve improved write performance by writing data in stripes cyclically across the disks. This is referred to as a RAID-0 volume and is created from equal-sized areas of unallocated space from multiple disks. After you create one, you can delete a striped volume, but you cannot extend or shrink the striped volume.

The performance characteristics of SSDs, with their extremely fast data transfer rates compared to traditional magnetic hard disk drives, are challenging the need to choose disk striping. A striped volume requires two or more disks. Because striped volumes offer no protection against disk failures, use striping for its I/O performance characteristics only when redundancy is not required, such as for paging file isolation or gaming rigs.

> **NOTE RAID-5**
>
> RAID-5 requires at least three disks and provides striped volumes with fault tolerance by adding parity information to each volume. It is not possible to create software-based RAID-5 with Windows 10. If you require RAID-5 type functionality, consider using the new Storage Spaces feature, discussed later in this chapter.

Configure file systems

Windows 10 supports dozens of file systems, and this book focuses on the most common and new file systems. You can view a complete list of which file systems Windows 10 supports, as shown in Figure 7-1, by launching the System Information tool and following these steps.

1. Click Start and type **Msinfo32**.

2. In the left pane, select Software Environment.

3. Select System Drivers.

4. In the results pane, click the Type column to sort the list of drivers.

   The file system drivers have the attribute of File System Driver.

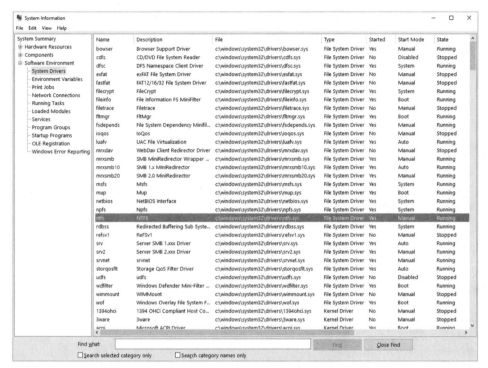

FIGURE 7-1 Windows file system drivers in System Information

Windows 10 supports the most common file systems, including NTFS, ReFS, exFat, FAT32, and FAT, which are described in Table 7-2. The most commonly used formats are NTFS and exFat, with the new ReFS becoming popular for servers and storage applications.

TABLE 7-2 File formats commonly used with Windows 10

File System	Description
NTFS	NTFS Enterprise-class file system, used by Windows for more than 20 years.
ReFS	Maximum file size of 16 exabytes (EB) Maximum volume size of 1 yottabyte Built-in resilience Compatibility with existing APIs and technologies Does not support NTFS compression or Encrypting File System (EFS) Cannot boot Windows 10 from an ReFS volume Currently, ReFS not a replacement for NTFS

File System	Description
exFat	ReFS (Resilient File System) Designed by Microsoft for flash storage devices Extended file allocation table Supported on Windows since Vista SP1 Volume size limit of 256 terabytes (TB) File size up to 16 EB Supports more than 1,000 files per directory
FAT32	Supported by Windows 95 SP2 and later versions; extended FAT16 to allow larger number of files per partition File size limit of 4 GB Volume size limit of 32 GB
FAT	Sometimes referred to as FAT16 Introduced in 1981 and supported by DOS, OS/2, Linux, Windows 3.x, and later versions Volume size limit of 4 GB

NOTE **FAT FILE SYSTEM**

FAT is a simple file system and offers no native file-level encryption, compression, or local security for FAT or FAT32. Anyone with access to the file can read, change, or delete any file stored on a FAT partition.

NTFS

NTFS is the native file system Windows 10 uses and is widely used across most Windows operating systems; it offers you the ability to protect and secure files. NTFS offers the following characteristics.

- File-level compression
- Per-user volume quotas
- Symbolic links and junction points
- Volume sizes up to 256 TB
- Up to 2^{32}-1 files per volume
- Maximum file size of 16 TB
- File names and total path size limited to 255 characters
- Enterprise-level file and folder encryption
- Metadata transactional logging to ensure that file structure can be repaired
- Limited self-healing capabilities

ReFS

Windows 10 includes support for the new file system called Resilient File System (ReFS), which was introduced with Windows Server 2012 and Windows 8.1 and has been designed to respond to the increased scale, access speed, and distributed nature of storage currently available. At present, ReFS is not intended to replace NTFS but offers benefits to users such as storage stability, flexibility, scalability, and availability. ReFS offers enhanced data integrity and self-healing capabilities with the intention that repairs can be made while the operating system remains online.

Storage Spaces uses ReFS and is covered later in the chapter. When Storage Spaces is configured to use ReFS, it can automatically repair corrupt data to ensure that data is always available and resilient during drive failures.

Some ReFS characteristics are:

- **Transactional write model** Offers protection against power failures
- **Proactive repairing/self-healing** Corruption detection, automatic repairs
- **Data integrity** Reduces disk corruption through check-sums employed on metadata
- **Improved availability** Repairs ReFS volumes while still online
- **Scalability** Works with extremely large data sets, in excess of PB

ReFS supports Long File Names and File Path, with the total path size limited to 32,768 characters.

Using disk management tools

You can use various tools and methods to manage Windows 10 disks and create volumes or partitions on them, including:

- Disk Management.
- Windows PowerShell.
- DiskPart.

Disk management

This is the traditional GUI tool used for performing most configuration and management tasks relating to disks and volumes. The GUI uses the familiar Microsoft Management Console (MMC) that most administrative tools use.

You can connect to the disks on a local or remote computer and perform tasks on both basic and dynamic disks and virtual hard disks. Remote disk management can be used only on domain-joined computers.

Examples of the types of disk management tasks that you can perform using the GUI include:

- Partition creation, including creating a basic, spanned, or striped partition.
- Disk conversion between basic disks to dynamic disks. (To convert a dynamic disk to a basic disk, you must first delete all present volumes.)
- Extending and shrinking partitions.
- Viewing information relating to disk and volumes, such as volume name, layout, type, file system, status, capacity, free space, and percentage of disk free for each volume.

To open Disk Management, follow these steps.

1. Right-click Start and select Disk Management or type **diskmgmt.msc** in the search box and then click diskmgmt.

2. Wait for Disk Management MMC to open and load the disk configuration information as shown in Figure 7-2.

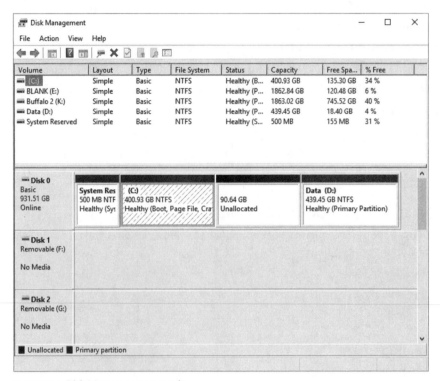

FIGURE 7-2 Disk Management console

You can use the Disk Management console to convert a basic disk to a dynamic disk by right-clicking the disk you want to convert and then selecting Convert To Dynamic Disk.

Windows PowerShell

Windows PowerShell offers many disk-related tasks from the command line; it can be used locally or remotely and can be scripted. Windows PowerShell now natively enables you to manage disks, volumes, and partitions and perform a range of tasks that cannot be performed using DiskPart or Disk Management.

Table 7-3 details some of the most common Windows PowerShell cmdlets that you should become familiar with.

TABLE 7-3 Common disk-related Windows PowerShell cmdlets

Command	Description	Additional parameters
Get-Disk	Return one or more disks visible to the operating system.	-FriendlyName -Number
Clear-Disk	Cleans a disk by removing all partition information and placing it in an un-initialized state. Erases all data on the disk.	-Number –RemoveData -FriendlyName
Initialize-Disk	Initializes a RAW disk for first time use, enabling the disk to be formatted and used to store data.	-FriendlyName -PartitionStyle -VirtualDisk
Set-Disk	Updates the physical disk on the system with attributes.	-PartitionStyle -IsOffline -IsReadonly
Get-Volume	Gets the specified volume object or all volume objects if no filter is provided.	-DriveLetter -DiskImage -FileSystemLabel -Partition
Format-Volume	Formats one or more existing volumes or a new volume on an existing partition. Acceptable file formats include NTFS, ReFS, exFat, FAT32, and FAT.	-DriveLetter -FileSystem -FileSystemLabel
Get-Partition	Returns a list of all partition objects visible on all disks or, optionally, a filtered list using specified parameters.	-Disk -DriveLetter -PartitionNumber -Volume

> **NEED MORE REVIEW?**   **STORAGE CMDLETS IN WINDOWS POWERSHELL**
>
> You can review all storage cmdlets for Windows PowerShell and syntax explanations and examples at *https://technet.microsoft.com/library/hh848705(v=wps.630).aspx*.

To shrink a partition in Windows PowerShell, type the following command.

```
Resize-Partition –DiskNumber 0 –PartitionNumber 2 –Size 50GB
```

To create simple volumes in Windows PowerShell, open it and type the following commands.

```
Get-Disk –Number 0
```

```
New-Partition –UseMaximumSize –DiskNumber 0 | Format-Volume –Confirm:$false –FileSystem
NTFS –NewFileSystemLabel Simple2
```

```
Get-Partition –DiskNumber 0
```

Make a note of the partition number you just created to use in the next step.

```
Set-Partition –DiskNumber 0 –PartitionNumber <partition number> –NewDriveLetter G
```

Windows PowerShell is the preferred command-line method for disk operations. The Windows PowerShell storage cmdlets do not recognize dynamic disks, so it is recommended to use Storage Spaces rather than dynamic disks.

DiskPart

DiskPart is a built-in command-line tool that offers you all the functionality of Disk Management plus some advanced features that can also be scripted into .bat files to automate disk-related tasks. One limitation of DiskPart is that it only runs locally.

> **NOTE   ABBREVIATING COMMANDS**
>
> When you use DiskPart, some of the commands can be abbreviated, such as using SEL instead of SELECT and PART instead of PARTITION, and VOL instead of VOLUME.

To open DiskPart, follow these steps.

1. Right-click Start and select Command Prompt (Admin); accept UAC.
2. Type **DiskPart** and press Enter.

    DiskPart launches in the command line.
3. For a list of all DiskPart commands, type **help** or **commands,** or type **?**.
4. When you have finished using DiskPart, you can leave the interface by typing **Exit** and pressing Enter.

EXAM TIP

The following list shows several DiskPart commands whose functions you should understand.

- Active   Marks the selected partition as the active partition
- Add   Enables you to add a mirror to a simple volume
- Assign   Enables you to assign a drive letter to a selected volume
- Convert   Converts between basic and dynamic disks
- Create   Enables you to create a volume, partition, or virtual disk
- Extend   Extends the size of a volume
- Shrink   Reduces the size of a volume
- Format   Used to format the volume or partition (for example, FORMAT FS=NTFS LABEL="New Volume" QUICK COMPRESS)

If you want to create a USB bootable drive manually that contains the Windows installation files, you can use DiskPart commands to create, partition, and mark the USB drive as active.

Skill: Create and configure virtual hard disks

You saw in Chapter 1, "Prepare for installation requirements," and 4, "Post-installation configuration," that Hyper-V is included in most editions of Windows 10 and provides virtualization technologies that can be used from the client operating system. Virtual hard disks (VHD) provide the portable, self-contained storage medium that you can use with Hyper-V but also natively with all versions of Windows 10.

Virtualization is still a relatively new technology, especially if compared to disks, volumes, and file systems, and your exposure to the virtual alternatives of the older technology will likely increase. This is a significant growth area in IT, and you should familiarize yourself with the terminology and concepts that surround this topic.

You learned the concepts of disks, volumes, and file systems, and these can now be adapted directly to the virtual space.

This section covers how to:

- Work with VHDs
- Create VHDs with Hyper-V Manager
- Use Disk Management to create a VHDs
- Create VHDs by using Windows PowerShell
- Link to differencing disks

Work with VHDs

A VHD can be thought of as a container object that holds files, folders, and volumes. The container, or VHD, is a single file with the VHD or VHDX file extension. You can think of a VHD file being similar in concept to a ZIP file. Analogous container types could include ISO, RAR, and WIM; they are all objects that contain files and folders inside them.

Because a VHD is just a file, it is portable and can be saved and transported on a USB drive or copied over a network. Be aware, however, that VHDs can grow very large, and the original open file format of VHD, which had a maximum size of 2048 GB, was soon changed to the VHDX format that allowed up to a 64 TB file size. A VHD can contain data or, as you learned in Chapter 2, "Install Windows 10," can also install and boot to an operating system inside the VHD. Windows 7 and later support booting to VHD.

Wherever possible because of the disk-intensive nature of VHD, consider using an SSD to host the VHDs. This is especially applicable if you use a single drive on your Windows 10–based computer and use virtual machines and VHD as the disk I/O; performance is likely to degrade quickly because of the increased disk read/write times and disk activity.

You can continue to use either the VHD or VHDX specification for your hard drives, but you should know the main differences between the two formats. VHD offers users ease of use and backward compatibility, whereas the VHDX format offers improvements in both scale and functionality. You can compare the two choices in Table 7-4.

TABLE 7-4 Virtual hard disk format

Type	Features
VHD	Original format. Up to 2048 GB (about 2 TB) in size. Compatible with virtualization technologies, including Virtual PC and Virtual Server. Useful when you are working with older operating systems and require backward compatibility. Can convert VHDX files to VHD by using Windows PowerShell.
VHDX	Introduced with Windows 8 and Windows Server 2012. Up to 64 TB in file size. Not compatible with operating systems older than Windows Server 2012 or Windows 8. Uses a 4 KB logical sector size to improve performance compared with VHD files. Offers protection against data corruption related to power failures by continuously keeping track of file updates in the metadata. Larger block sizes for dynamic and differencing disks. Can convert VHD files to VHDX by using Windows PowerShell or in the Hyper-V Manager. VHDX file format supports the shared virtual hard disk feature first available with Windows Server 2012 R2 and available in Windows Server 2016. Newer generation-2 virtual machines that are hypervisor-aware require VHDX file format. Shared VHDX allows guest clustering within Windows Server 2012 R2 and Windows Server 2016. VHDX format is not supported in Microsoft Azure.
VHD Set (VHDS)	Introduced with Windows 10 and Windows Server 2016. Same technical features as the VHDX format. Used as a shared virtual hard disk. Allows online resize. Supports host-based backup. Not supported in operating systems earlier than Windows 10.

There are multiple ways to create a virtual hard disk:

- Client Hyper-V Manager
- Disk Management
- Windows PowerShell

You can also use the DiskPart command-line tool, but this is becoming deprecated in favor of Windows PowerShell, which offers more extensive functionality and support.

Create VHDs with Hyper-V Manager

The client Hyper-V feature can be added to Windows 10 if the computer is running the Windows 10 Pro or Enterprise edition and has hardware that supports virtualization.

To create a virtual hard disk within Hyper-V Manager, complete the following steps.

1. Launch Hyper-V Manager.
2. In the Action pane, click New and then click Hard Disk.
3. Select the format for the disk as VHD, VHDX, or VHD Set, as shown in Figure 7-3, and click Next.

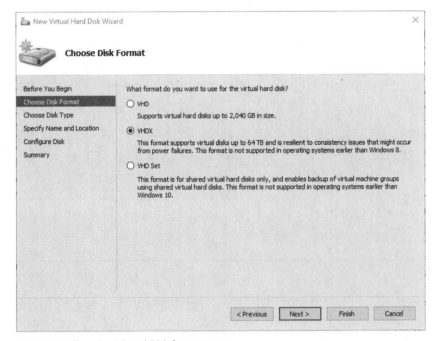

FIGURE 7-3 Choosing Virtual Disk format type

4. Select the Disk Type (Fixed, Dynamically expanding, or Differencing) and click Next.
5. Provide the virtual disk with a name and storage location and click Next.
6. Configure the disk; the default settings are normally used and will create a new blank VHD with 127 GB. Click Next and then click Finish.

Use Disk Management to create VHDs

The Disk Management MMC includes a wizard that enables you to create a VHD that you can then mount and use. Not all of the VHD options are available in the Disk Management console, such as the ability to create VHD Sets or differencing disks; you should use Windows PowerShell or Hyper-V Manager if these tasks are required.

To create a simple VHD file, complete the following steps.

1. Right-click the Start button and select Disk Management.

2. Click Action on the menu bar and then select Create VHD.

    The Create And Attach Virtual Hard Disk wizard appears, as shown in Figure 7-4.

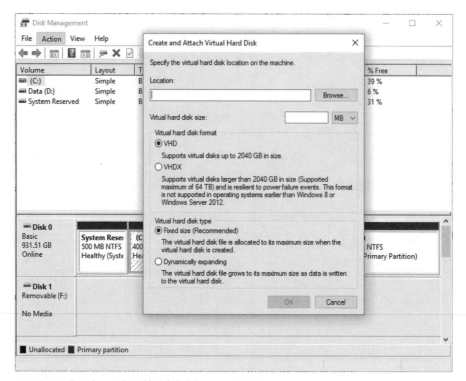

FIGURE 7-4 Creating a virtual hard disk by using Disk Management

3. Select the location where you want to store your VHD.

4. Configure the VHD format and VHD type and click OK.

    The new disk will appear in the lower pane of the screen and display the following characteristics.

    -   Unknown Status

    -   Not Initialized

    -   Disk icon is cyan blue with downward-pointing red arrow

5. To use the disk, initialize it by right-clicking the downward-pointing red arrow on the disk icon and selecting Initialize Disk.

6. In the Initialize Disk dialog box, ensure that the disk you want to initialize is selected and choose MBR (Default) or GPT partition style and click OK.

    The disk is marked with the status of Basic and you can now create a partition, allocate a driver letter, and format the drive with a file system just like a normal disk.

Apart from the icon color in Disk Management, there is no other visual indicator in File Explorer or Disk Management to indicate that the disk is virtual. After you have finished using the VHD, you can detach the disk by right-clicking the disk icon in the lower pane of Disk Management and selecting Detach VHD. After you have detached the VHD, the VHD file is no longer locked to Windows 10 and becomes a portable hard drive.

Create VHDs by using Windows PowerShell

Disk Management offers the ability to create basic VHDs in a GUI environment, but if you need to create more complicated VHDs, such as differencing disks, or if you need to create 20 VHDs for a team of developers to work with, it would be easier and quicker to build Windows PowerShell scripts to do so. This section focuses on virtual hard disks.

You can manage every aspect of virtual disks with Windows PowerShell in both production and lab environments. Windows PowerShell enables you to configure, provision, and subsequently maintain all of your virtual estate rapidly. Windows PowerShell can be used to build a full virtual environment, including virtual disks, virtual machines, and virtual networks and switches.

More than 50 cmdlets are available in Windows PowerShell in Windows 10 that enable you to manage virtual and physical disks. This number will expand as new functionality is added. Table 7-5 outlines some of the common Windows PowerShell cmdlets that enable you to manage disks natively. After a VHD disk has been created, it is managed in the same way as a physical disk.

TABLE 7-5 Common native Windows PowerShell VHD and disk cmdlets

Command	Description	Additional parameters
New-VHD	Creates one or more new virtual hard disks	–SizeBytes sets the size, such as 10GB. Set the VHD type by using the following parameters: -Fixed -Differencing -Dynamic
Get-Disk	Provides information on all disks	-FriendlyName provides information about disks that have the specified friendly name. -Number provides information about a specific disk.
Convert-VHD	Converts the format, version type, and block size of a virtual hard disk file	Specify the name of the new VHD as .vhdx or .vhd, and the cmdlet will use this format. –VHDType <VHDType> allows the specification of the VHD type such as -Differencing or –Fixed.
Clear-Disk	Cleans a disk by removing all partition information	-ZeroOutEntireDisk writes zeroes to all sectors of a disk, effectively wiping it clear.
Initialize-Disk	Prepares a disk for use by the operating system. Default is to create a GPT partition.	-PartitionStyle<PartitionStyle> specifies the type of partition, either MBR or GPT.

Command	Description	Additional parameters
Optimize-VHD	Optimizes the allocation of space in a non-fixed VHD/X. Used with the Compact operation to optimize the files. Reclaims unused space and rearranges blocks, normally reducing the size of a virtual hard disk file.	–Mode Full (Default for VHD) Scans for zero blocks and reclaims unused blocks. –Mode Retrim Retrims the drive without scanning for zero blocks or reclaiming unused blocks. –Mode Quick (Default for VHDX) Reclaims unused blocks but does not scan for zero blocks.
Set-Disk	Updates a disk with the specified attributes	-PartitionStyle<PartitionStyle> specifies the type of partition, either MBR or GPT. You can use this cmdlet to convert a disk to another type of partition style.
Get-Volume	Returns information on all volumes	-DriveLetter<Char> gets information about the volume with the specified drive letter. -FileSystemLabel<String> returns information on NTFS file systems or Resilient File System (ReFS) volumes.

There are two new cmdlets that relate to the new virtual hard disk (VHD) set files, which can be used with Windows Server 2016 Technical Preview and Windows 10. These cmdlets are:

- **Get-VHDSet**   Obtains information about a virtual hard disk (VHD) set file such as a list of all checkpoints that the set contains.

- **Optimze-VHDSet**   Optimizes the allocation of space that virtual hard disk (VHD) set files use, when used with the compact operation to optimize the files. Reclaims unused space and rearranges blocks, normally reducing the size of a virtual hard disk file.

To create a VHD, you use the New-VHD cmdlet, which was introduced in Windows 8.1. You must specify the path to the VHD, the name for the newly created VHD, VHD type, the size of the disk, and format type, as shown.

```
New-VHD -Path D:\VHD\MyDynamicDisk.vhdx -SizeBytes 100GB -Dynamic
```

The New-VHD cmdlet executes and creates the VHD. As with Disk Management, the newly created VHD will not be mounted, initiated, or formatted without further action. You see how to do this by adding these instructions to the end of the New-VHD script next.

Within Windows 10 is a scripting interface called PowerShell ISE, which enables you to create, execute, and save Windows PowerShell scripts. Type **PowerShell ISE** into the Start search to launch Windows PowerShell ISE. After it launches, locate the right pane that shows all available commands in the GUI. If you type a cmdlet or wild card such as **vhd** in the name box, the filter function returns all available commands related to .vhd management. Highlight a cmdlet, such as New-VHD, and then click the blue help icon to view a very useful and detailed help relating to the cmdlet, as shown in Figure 7-5.

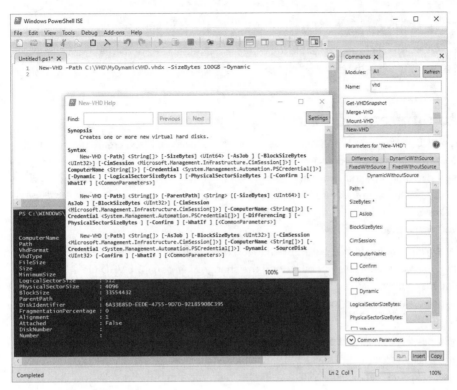

FIGURE 7-5 Windows PowerShell ISE Help

Windows PowerShell enables you to string instructions together and then execute them as a single action. The following example builds on your initial script and creates a new, dynamically expanding, 127 GB virtual hard disk with the .vhdx extension, mounts it, initializes it, and then formats the drive, using NTFS so it is ready to use.

1. Click the Start button, type **powershell**, right-click Windows PowerShell, and then select Run As Administrator. Click Yes in the UAC dialog box.

2. Type the following PowerShell commands all into one line without pressing Enter:

```
New-VHD -Path "D:\VHDs\Test.vhdx" -Dynamic –SizeBytes 127GB | Mount-VHD –Passthru
|Initialize-Disk -Passthru |New-Partition -AssignDriveLetter
-UseMaximumSize |Format-Volume -FileSystem NTFS -Confirm:$false -Force
```

3. Press Enter.

Link to differencing disks

Creating a VHD is easy, and the VHDs are very versatile. However, if you create many virtual disks, you can soon find they consume a huge amount of disk space. This is why you will most often use a dynamically expanding disk. Even when using dynamically expanding disks, you might still find that you quickly use hundreds of GB for your VHD storage. One special type of virtual disk is a differencing disk, which can be useful in reducing the amount of space VHDs use on your host drive.

A *differencing disk* is a virtual hard disk that you can use to hold changes to a virtual hard disk or the guest operating system by storing the changes in a separate VHD file. A differencing disk needs to be associated with another virtual hard disk, which is marked as read-only. The read-only disk is referred to as the parent (or fixed) disk, and the differencing disk is the child disk.

An example scenario would be if you had three virtual machines running Windows Server 2016 with different roles installed. Each VM would have its own separate VHDs. A large proportion of the virtual machines or VHDs would be identical, and only the roles installed would reflect the differences. Assume that the used space in each VHD was 20 GB each, totaling 60 GB. In this example, building a solution that uses differencing disks instead would have the following:

- 1 x parent virtual hard disk containing the installed Windows Server 2016 (17 GB)
- 3 x child differencing disks linked to the parent disk (3 GB each)

After the parent disk has been created and the default Windows Server 2016 installed, this system would be shut down and marked as read only; the read-only status is not mandatory but is highly recommended.

The differencing disks are then created, linked to the parent, and they expand dynamically as data is written to them. When you first start and connect to the virtual machine in this example, you find the default Windows Server 2016 installation that is present on the parent disk but view it seamlessly through the differencing disk. The user and system will not be aware of the infrastructure. As you make changes, install roles, and configure the operating system, these changes are saved only in the differencing disk, which will grow in size.

You can see in this small-scale scenario that you could save 34 GB in hard-drive space on the host system, a 50 percent reduction by using differencing disks.

The disk configuration criteria in Table 7-6 provide some further examples of VHDs and their different applications.

TABLE 7-6 Example VHD configurations

Disk Format	Disk Type	Size	Application
VHD	Dynamically Expanding	127 GB	Default type and size VHD. Useful general purpose disk and backward compatible. If using the Disk Management tool, the Fixed type is the default VHD format.
VHDX	Dynamically Expanding	127 GB	Default format, type, and size virtual disk.
VHDX	Fixed	50 GB	Size on disk matches VHDX size. Suitable for hosting an operating system; fastest disk type and format.

Skill: Create and configure Storage Spaces

Storage Spaces was introduced with Windows 8 and Windows Server 2012. It is a technology that is useful for desktop or server devices that have multiple hard disks that can be combined to provide storage redundancy by pooling separate disks and allowing Storage Spaces to manage their administration effectively.

This section covers how to:

- Use Storage Spaces and storage pools
- Configure Storage Spaces
- Manage Storage Spaces by using Windows PowerShell

Use Storage Spaces and storage pools

Storage Spaces uses NTFS and the new ReFS file format to configure volumes, which provides greater file resilience through ReFS self-healing capabilities. The redundancy aspects are derived by distributing data across several disk drives and using virtual disk arrays in a RAID configuration or as mirror sets. The operating system maintains the logical disks and presents the virtualized disk as a logical unit number (LUN), which the system can then access. You might have seen the LUN terminology before; it is a term used with Storage Area Network protocols such as Fibre Channel or iSCSI.

The requirements for creating a virtual disk with Storage Spaces are shown in Table 7-7.

TABLE 7-7 Creating virtual disks with Storage Spaces

Requirement	Description
Physical disk	Any size physical disks, such as Serial ATA (SATA), Serially Attached SCSI (SAS), or USB connected disks, can be used. You need a minimum of one physical disk to create a storage pool and more if you require mirrored disks. Disks must not be initialized or formatted.
Storage pool	A collection of one or more physical disks that you use to create virtual disks. All unformatted physical disks can be added to a storage pool.
Storage space	A logical disk created from one or more physical disks. It allows thin provisioning or just-in-time (JIT) disk allocations and can offer resiliency to physical disk failures through built-in functionality such as mirroring.
Disk drive	The drive letter allocated to the logical virtual disk and accessed through File Explorer.

A storage space is created from a storage pool. As you add additional disks, you can create redundant storage spaces. Four types of storage layouts are available to you with Storage Spaces, as shown in Table 7-8.

TABLE 7-8 Storage Space storage layouts

Storage option	Description	Redundancy
Simple	A simple space has data written across all disks in a logically sequential way that offers increased performance. With multiple disks, automatic data striping enables read/write operations to multiple segments of data concurrently.	Simple spaces provide no failover capabilities. If a disk that is storing the data fails, the data will be lost.
Two-way or three-way mirrors	Mirrored spaces maintain multiple copies of the data by way of data duplication to ensure that all data is redundant. Two-way mirrors maintain two data copies, and three data copies are maintained for three-way mirrors. Data is also striped across the multiple physical drives, which offers the speed enhancements (greater data throughput and lower access latency) of striped disks without the data-loss risk of a simple space.	Data is mirrored so that if a single disk is lost, the data is available on another of the mirrored disks in the space. A resilient, two-way mirror requires a minimum of two physical disks and can tolerate a single drive failure. This requires a minimum of at least five physical disks for three-way mirroring and can tolerate two drive failures. The ReFS file format automatically maintains data integrity and can only be selected when using mirrored drives.
Parity	Parity is similar to RAID 5, which stores data, along with parity information across multiple physical drives. The parity writes are rotated across the available disks, which ensures an even distribution and drive optimization. A minimum of three physical drives is required for parity spaces.	Parity spaces have increased resiliency through disk read/write journaling so that if a drive is lost or corrupted, the missing data can be retrieved from the journal. The journal is stored across the remaining multiple disks.

A further feature that is available with Storage Spaces is how you provision the virtual disk spaces for use. Storage Spaces offers you two schemes.

- **Thin provisioning** Enables you to allocate an intended storage that has greater capacity than is physically present at the time of creation. If you over-specify the amount of capacity compared to the data you currently have, the storage space engine disregards the extra storage capacity until data sets grow to require the storage. At this point, the extra storage is allocated. At any point, you increase the maximum size of an existing storage space and add drives as they are required at a later date. Thin provisioning is more economical and efficient because it allows organizations to deploy physical storage only when needed, thereby saving on operating costs, such as data center rack space costs associated with storing unused drives in situ.

- **Fixed provisioning** Similar to traditional fixed storage allocation methods, by which you specify that the spaces will not increase beyond the initial storage capacity allocated at the same time as storage space creation. With fixed provisioning, you specify the hard limit for the size of the storage pool.

Configure Storage Spaces

When you have connected your physical drives to your computer, you can configure Storage Spaces by using the following steps.

1. Click Start and type Storage Spaces and then open Storage Spaces.
2. Select Create A New Pool And Storage Space.
3. If requested, accept the UAC prompt.
4. Select the drives you want to add, as shown in Figure 7-6.

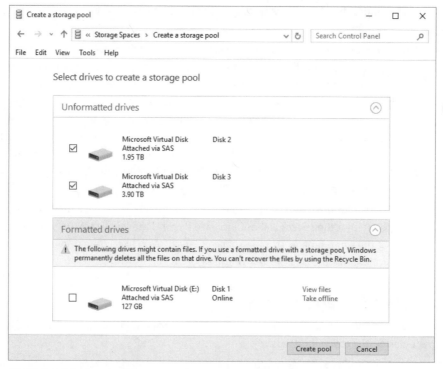

FIGURE 7-6 Selecting the drives to create a storage pool

All drives that are offline are automatically selected. Storage Spaces automatically identifies available drives to create the storage pool.

5. Click Create Pool.

6. When the create pool operation completes, provide a name for the storage space and select the drive letter you want to use.

7. Select the type of resiliency you require. (This will depend on how many drives you have added to the storage space.)

8. Select either the NTFS or ReFS file system. (Only if you choose a mirrored resiliency type can you format the storage space by using either the NTFS or ReFS file system.)

9. Set the Size (Maximum) of the storage space. The size can be larger than the current capacity of the storage pool, as indicated in the note at the bottom of the dialog box.

10. Click Create Storage Space to create your storage pool in the storage space.

After the storage pool has been created, the Manage Storage Spaces console manages and maintains it within Control Panel, where you can add, rename, or delete drives. If a physical disk is removed permanently from the pool, it must be reformatted before it can be used in another PC. Just like with mirrored or RAID disk sets, if you need to move the pooled disks to another computer, always move them as a unit so that their integrity is maintained.

As part of your exam preparation, create a storage space, provision a storage pool, and simulate a drive failure. You can see in Figure 7-7 that one of the physical drives used to create the storage space has been disconnected from the computer. Even with only one drive, the H drive continues to be available within File Explorer, and applications and users will be unaware of the failure until they review the notification in the Action Center as shown in Figure 7-7.

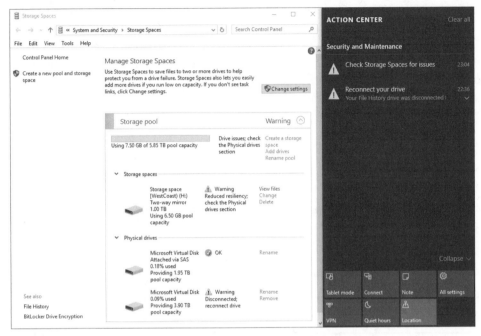

FIGURE 7-7 Reduced storage pool resiliency

If the removed physical drive is replaced, the storage pool checks the integrity of the pool and makes the necessary repairs. When it's repaired and full operational resiliency is restored, the icon changes from a warning symbol to the check mark indicating that everything is OK, as was originally shown before the disruption.

Storage Spaces can use the new ReFS file system for mirrored resilient spaces, offering built-in automatic file repair. This helps prevent data loss and can be carried out while the disks are online and do not require a system reboot to check and repair errors. ReFS and Storage Spaces therefore provide enhanced resiliency in the event of storage device failure.

EXAM TIP

Because ReFS is a new file system available in Windows 10, be aware of the self-healing capabilities ReFS offers, which are used for mirrored storage spaces. Remember that ReFS cannot be used for simple or parity resiliency types.

Windows 10 includes several enhancements to the Storage Spaces feature. You can now optimize the drive usage and remove drives from a pool without reducing the effectiveness of the protection against drive failure.

The new optimization features are not available in previous versions of Windows, although you can upgrade an older pool to benefit from the new features in Windows 10. After you have added a new drive to the storage pool, a new action item becomes available, called Optimize Drive Usage.

Optimizing drive usage after adding new drives to an existing pool is beneficial because it redistributes data across all the drives and makes best use of the pool's new capacity and increased resiliency. This takes place organically by default, but optimizing forces the process to start immediately. The rebalancing process only works on simple and mirrored spaces and is not supported for parity spaces.

When you remove a drive from a pool, the data stored on the removed drive is reallocated to other drives in the pool. Because this is a planned removal (as opposed to a failed drive scenario), this operation can take several hours, depending on the amount of data that has been stored on the drive. To remove a drive, perform the following steps.

1. Click Start, type **Storage Spaces**, and then open Manage Storage Spaces.
2. Select Change Settings.
3. If requested, accept the UAC prompt.
4. Expand Physical Drives to see the drives in your pool.
5. Find the drive you want to remove and select Prepare For Removal.
6. Leave your computer switched on until the drive is ready to be removed.
7. When the drive shows Ready To Remove, select Remove and then click Remove Drive.
8. You can now safely disconnect the drive from your PC and re-purpose it.

> **NOTE SPEED UP DRIVE PREPARATION**
>
> Storage Spaces prepares drives for use, optimizes them, and moves data off a drive when you plan to remove it as a background task. When your computer is powered on, you can temporally modify your power and sleep settings to ensure that your computer does not sleep.

Manage Storage Spaces by using Windows PowerShell

You can script the creation, repair, and administration of Storage Spaces by using Windows PowerShell. There are many more storage management–specific cmdlets that relate to storage operations. Some of the Storage Spaces–specific cmdlets that can be used are shown in Table 7-9.

TABLE 7-9 Storage cmdlets in Windows PowerShell

Storage Cmdlets	Description
New-StoragePool	Creates a new storage pool, using a group of physical disks
Add-PhysicalDisk	Adds a physical disk to a storage pool for the creation of one or more VirtualDisk objects
Get-StoragePool	Gets a specific storage pool or a set of StoragePool objects that are available
Set-StoragePool	Modifies the properties of the specified storage pool
Set-PhysicalDisk	Sets the attributes on a specific physical disk
Get-VirtualDisk	Returns a list of VirtualDisk objects that are available
New-VirtualDisk	Creates a new virtual disk in the specified storage pool
Repair-VirtualDisk	Deletes an existing virtual disk and reclaims the space for use by other virtual disks in the same storage pool
Optimize-StoragePool	Rebalances a storage space configured as simple or mirrored, optimizing files based on disk space, disk size, and file size
Update-StoragePool	Upgrades the storage pool metadata to enable new features and functionality on pre–Windows 10 storage pools
RemovePhysicalDisk	Removes a physical disk from a specified storage pool
Remove-StoragePool	Deletes a storage pool and associated VirtualDisk objects

To list all the cmdlets that are available, use the Get-Command –Module Storage cmdlet.

> **NEED MORE REVIEW?   STORAGE CMDLETS IN WINDOWS POWERSHELL**
>
> You can review the documentation relating to Storage Spaces Windows PowerShell cmd-lets on MSDN at *https://technet.microsoft.com/library/jj851254(v=wps.630).aspx*.

Skill: Configure removable devices

Removable devices such as USB flash drives and Secure Digital High-Capacity (SDHC) memory cards are common and can offer portability benefits but also pose a potential threat to data security and loss. In this section, you learn how to prepare removable devices for use, protect the data if the drive is lost or stolen, and restrict access to portable drives.

> **This section covers how to:**
> - Format removable devices
> - Secure removable devices
> - Restrict access to removable devices

Format removable devices

You can format removable devices in the same way as you can configure hard drives. All drives without a file format, or that have one that Windows 10 doesn't understand, are considered RAW. To use the drive, first format the drive. If you insert an unformatted drive in your USB port, Windows prompts you to format the drive. Depending on the size of your drive, you can format the drive using the FAT, FAT32 (default), NTFS, or exFat file format, using the format wizard. Be mindful when formatting a USB drive because, when you perform a quick format, the drive is not checked for errors. Although this is quicker, the system won't mark bad sectors on the drive, and this can lead to data integrity problems later on.

For drives larger than 32 GB, the exFat is a good general-purpose format; it handles files larger than 4 GB and optimizes the drive space well. For smaller drives, the FAT32 is best because it is compatible with virtually all operating systems and is fast.

You should format using NTFS if you are seeking advanced functionality such as file compression, permissions on individual files and folders, and file encryption using EFS.

> **NOTE RAW**
>
> A drive listed with RAW as the file system type can still contain data. If the drive has been formatted with a file format Windows 10 doesn't use, the operating system automatically assigns the RAW file system driver to the volume and displays a dialog box for you to format the drive. Label thumb drives, especially when they are used with various devices.

Secure removable devices

Data stored on USB flash drives is inherently insecure and should be protected. This can be achieved by using NTFS permissions, encrypted using EFS, or by using BitLocker encryption. The most appropriate of these methods in an enterprise scenario is likely to be using BitLocker To Go because users understand it easily, and you can manage and configure the feature by using Group Policy.

BitLocker To Go is not designed to replace EFS or NTFS permissions; it adds an additional layer of security and protection on removable drives, including SDHC cards, USB flash drives, and external hard disk drives. BitLocker To Go is available in the Pro, Enterprise, and Education editions of Windows 10 only.

When encrypting removable media with BitLocker To Go, you have two options.

- **Encrypt used disk space only**   Encrypts only the part of the drive that currently has data stored on it. This is quicker and appropriate in most cases.

- **Encrypt entire drive**   Encrypts the full volume, including areas that contain no data, which takes longer to complete.

To enable BitLocker Drive Encryption on a removable drive, perform the following steps.

1. Insert a USB drive into your computer.

2. Open File Explorer and right-click the USB drive in the left pane.

3. Select Turn On BitLocker from the context menu.

   The Starting BitLocker Wizard appears and initializes the drive.

4. On the Choose How You Want To Unlock This Drive page, choose Use A Password To Unlock The Drive.

5. In the Enter Your Password and Reenter Your Password boxes, type a password and click Next.

6. On the How Do You Want To Back Up Your Recovery Key page, click Save To A File.

7. In the Save BitLocker Recovery Key As dialog box, select This PC\Documents.

8. In the Save BitLocker Recovery Key As dialog box, click Save and then click Next.

9. On the Choose How Much Of Your Drive To Encrypt page, click Encrypt Used Disk Space Only (Faster And Best For New PCs And Drives) and then click Next.

10. On the Choose Which Encryption Mode To Use page, click Compatible Mode (best for drives that can be moved from this device) and click Next.

11. In the Are You Ready To Encrypt This Drive page, click Start Encrypting.

    During the encryption process, the BitLocker Drive Encryption Wizard shows the encryption progress on the taskbar. The process can take some time to complete and can be paused at any time by clicking the Pause button on the BitLocker Drive Encryption dialog box, as shown in Figure 7-8.

FIGURE 7-8 BitLocker Drive Encryption

When the encryption has completed, BitLocker is fully enabled on the removable drive. If you eject the USB drive and then insert the drive back into your PC or another computer, Windows 10 prompts you to enter the password to unlock the drive.

Restrict access to removable devices

The abundance and increasing capacity of USB flash drives enables users to store huge quantities of data and travel around with it. The drives are small and extremely portable and can easily be lost. It is essential for organizations to restrict access to removable drives for several reasons, including:

- Risk of data loss or theft.
- Spread of malware.
- Document version control.

Risk of data loss/theft

With technologies such as BitLocker To Go, it is possible to ensure that all data stored on removable drives is encrypted, which helps prevent against data theft by an external user accessing the data contained on the removable drive. Because of their size and low value, removable drives are lost on a regular basis both inside the office or home and off premises. If an unauthorized person finds the drive and can access sensitive data, they could publish, sell, or use it illegally. It is therefore advantageous (and in some instances a legal requirement) for data to be inaccessible to unauthorized users.

You can configure Group Policy to help prevent users from saving or copying data to any removable drives that are not encrypted by BitLocker. There are three policy settings located at Computer Configuration\Administrative Templates\Windows Components\BitLocker Drive Encryption\Removable Data Drives, and they are described in Table 7-10. These settings are useful when you need to enforce the use of BitLocker encryption on USB storage devices.

TABLE 7-10 GPO settings for securing removable devices

Group Policy Setting	Policy description
Deny Write Access To Removable Drives Not Protected By Bitlocker	You can configure whether BitLocker protection is required for a computer to write data to a removable data drive.
Control Use Of Bitlocker On Removable Drives	Control the use of BitLocker on removable data drives, including whether users can apply BitLocker protection to their removable drives.
Enforce Drive Encryption Type On Removable Data Drives	With this policy setting, you can configure the encryption type that BitLocker uses on removable drives, either full encryption or used-space-only encryption.

EXAM TIP

Combining BitLocker protection and write access to removable drives with your knowledge of Group Policy are skills likely to be tested in the exam.

In most organizations, there are groups of users without any reason to read or write to removable drives. For these groups of users, you can remove their right to such devices. You can effect this setting at the user or group level or for all users on a PC. To restrict access to removable devices, configure the access policies by following these steps.

1. Click Start, type **gpedit.msc,** and open the Group Policy Editor.

2. Navigate to Computer Configuration\Administrative Templates\System\Removable Storage Access.

   You can deny read and write access to many types of storage, including CD, DVD, floppy drives, removable drives, tape drives, or media players (or all removable storage), as shown in Figure 7-9.

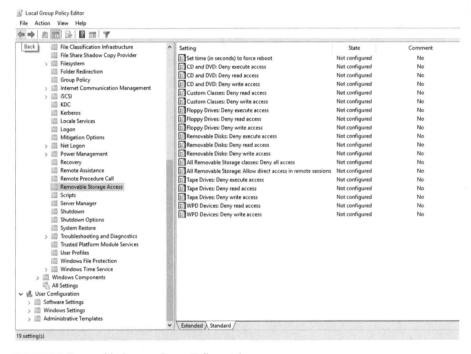

FIGURE 7-9 Removable Storage Group Policy settings

3. If a setting is appropriate for your requirements, select the setting and set it to Enabled.

4. Close Group Policy Editor.

Spread of malware

Allowing users to access USB flash drives in an unrestricted way can become a path for viruses to spread. A significant volume of malware finding its way to office computers originates with home users who might frequently download files, such as music or software, from the Internet. They also receive emails containing viruses. If a USB flash drive is used at home and then later at the workplace, on a work laptop, or at a client site, the risk of cross infection is high.

If you evaluate which users in your organization pose the highest risks and find that some high-risk users need access to removable drives, consider granting them access to specific USB storage devices only. IT departments can issue employees with USB flash drives, perhaps adorned with corporate branding, and these flash drives can be tightly controlled using Group Policy so that only these devices can be used on your enterprise computers.

Two other GPO settings are useful to restrict access to removable devices.

- Prevent Installation Of Removable Devices.

- Allow Installation Of Devices That Match Any Of These Device IDs.

The first policy prevents users from installing removable devices. A device is considered removable if the device driver used when the device is connected declares the hardware as removable.

The second policy enables you to add a list of allowed devices to the policy and include the specific hardware ID for your USB flash drive, as shown in Figure 7-10. Hardware IDs are found in Device Manager by selecting the device and viewing the Details tab for the device. When you review the information on the Details tab, the following abbreviations might be useful.

- HID = Human Interface Device, such as keyboards and mice.

- VID = Vendor ID.

- PID = Product ID.

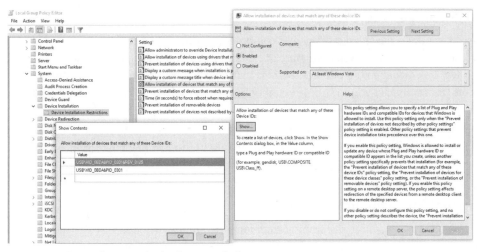

FIGURE 7-10 Preventing unauthorized storage device usage

Document version control

When you save documents to removable drives, you can create issues regarding document version control. It becomes difficult to synchronize documents that are taken outside of the shared repositories such as OneDrive For Business or shared folders on the network.

When this scenario causes you problems, consider enforcing Group Policy settings to prevent the use of removable drives for your users. By ensuring that users only access and modify corporate data through controllable and accountable channels, you help prevent issues with data duplication, versioning conflicts, and data access.

Skill: Troubleshoot storage issues and removable devices

You have reviewed how to manage and configure storage, using traditional tools, including File Explorer, Disk Management, DiskPart, Windows PowerShell, and Storage Spaces in Windows 10. In this section, you review what can go wrong with storage devices, how to troubleshoot issues, and, if possible, how to recover from them.

> **This section covers how to:**
> - Initialize a basic disk
> - Import foreign disks
> - Recover from hard drive failure
> - Replace failed disks

Initialize a basic disk

When you install a new hard disk on your computer, Windows 10 does not recognize it because it won't contain a valid signature. When you open Disk Management after installing the drive, Disk Management displays a wizard that provides a list of the new disks Windows 10 detects and enables you to choose whether to initialize the disk by using a master boot record or GUID partition table.

After it is initialized, the disk status in the left pane of Disk Management changes to Online and is ready to use. If you cancel the wizard, the disk status remains Not Initialized, and you won't be able to create partitions on the disk.

Import foreign disks

If you need to move a disk drive from one computer to another, Windows 10 will not automatically mount the drive or assign drive letters by default. In Disk Management, a warning icon appears in the left pane next to the disk displaying the Foreign status.

Dynamic disks appear as Foreign when they are added to the system, and you must first import the Foreign disks to change their status to Online. To add a Foreign disk to your system, right-click the disk and then click Import Foreign Disks. All existing volumes on the foreign disk become visible and accessible after you import the disk.

> **NOTE** **DO NOT MOUNT REMOVABLE MEDIA DEVICES**
>
> Windows 10 automatically mounts removable media devices and optical disks.

Hard drive failure

Hardware performance and reliability continue to improve. With new innovations such as the ReFS self-healing file system and the emergence of SSD drives that have no moving parts, your systems are less susceptible to failure than in the past. Although this is true, your systems will continue to have vulnerabilities that you need to be aware of.

Hard drives of all varieties are generally rated based on their mean time between failures (MTBF), which is the predicted elapsed time between inherent failures of a system while in operation, usually expressed in thousands or tens of thousands of hours. Most drives have a quoted MTBF of somewhere between 100,000 and 1 million hours, which is between 11 and 110 years.

With a removable drive such as a USB flash drive, it might not be possible or economically viable to repair the drive. System and data drives can often be repaired and data recovered, but this depends largely on the type and severity of the failure. Hard disk drives fail for many reasons, including:

- **Logical failure** Including corruption of errors recorded in the file allocation table (FAT) or master file table (MFT) on system volumes. In some cases, Windows RE can automatically repair corrupted file tables; otherwise, you need specialized software tools to fix the problem.

- **Mechanical failure** Disks with rotating, magnetically coated disk platters can fail when the read/write heads of the hard disk come in contact with the hard disk platters. This is often caused by physical damage or shock, computer movement, static electricity, or power surges. Drive motor failure causes the drive to stop working, but the data might still be intact.

- **Electronic failure** The hard disk's electronic circuit controller board can fail with age or become damaged by electrical power surges. You might be able to recover data because the disk platters and other mechanical components might be undamaged.

- **Firmware failure** If the hard disk firmware code is corrupt or unreadable, your computer will be unable communicate with the drive. You could attempt to re-flash the firmware or reset it to factory defaults; check the manufacturer's website for the procedure.

- **Bad sectors** These can be either logical or physical sectors on the disk. Where a disk is damaged through shock or vibration, the hard disk drive firmware monitoring the drive automatically mark bad sectors. If the damage is minor, often no data is lost. If the number of physical bad sectors becomes too high, it would be worthwhile to replace the drive before data loss becomes likely.

> *NOTE* **HARD DISK DRIVE MONITORING SOFTWARE**
>
> Some motherboards and hard disks include self-monitoring, analysis, and reporting technology (SMART) software. SMART monitors the hard disk proactively, checking for reliability issues and marking bad areas on the drive as they are detected. By preventing the drive from storing data in bad sectors, they can reduce data loss.

SSDs are gaining in popularity and reliability. SSDs have always been very fast when compared to mechanical drives, but the early SSDs did not exhibit the levels of reliability that traditional hard drives offer. Reliability has improved significantly, and speed continues to increase. When comparing SSDs, look at factors other than speed alone, such as warranties, MTBF, and cost.

Although there are no moving parts, the memory cells that store data inside an SSD drive can wear out after extensive write operations, which results in errors or even drive failure. The MTBF for SSDs is now comparable to mechanical drives and will continue to improve as the technology and error checking software evolves.

Replacing failed disks

Hard drives can fail, and they should be viewed as a system vulnerability, which is the primary reason for maintaining regular backups. If you experience a failed local disk drive, the data is no longer available, and you need to replace the drive and recover the data from your backup or recovery drive.

The benefit of using a redundant storage solution such as mirrored volumes using Disk Management or using Storage Spaces in Windows 10 is that, when a disk drive fails, the data in storage is still accessible. When you replace the failed disk, full redundancy is reestablished automatically.

If you suffer a single disk failure in a mirrored volume, you can recover your system by using these steps.

1. Shut down your computer if necessary.
2. Connect a replacement disk that is the same size or larger to the computer and restart.
3. Right-click Start and select Disk Management; accept UAC.
4. Right-click the mirror on the Missing or Offline disk and then click Remove Mirror.
5. Right-click the volume to be re-mirrored and click Add Mirror, which includes an operational disk from the previous mirror, and then add a new disk by using the Add Mirror Wizard in Disk Management.

   The mirror creation process commences, which re-synchronizes both volumes to restore redundancy.

If you are using Storage Spaces, you can use parity or a two-way or three-way mirror storage space. If you experience a drive failure, you can restore full redundancy by performing these steps.

1. Shut down your computer if necessary.
2. Connect a replacement disk that is the same size or larger to the computer and restart.
3. Right-click Start, type **Storage Spaces**, and click Manage Storage Spaces.
4. Click the Change Settings button and accept UAC.
5. Add a new disk to the storage pool.

   Storage spaces repairs the mirror automatically.
6. After you've added a new drive to your pool, you can click Remove next to your failed drive to delete it from the storage pool.
7. The mirror is rebuilt as a background task, and you can close Storage Spaces.

With Storage Spaces, avoid allowing it to become completely full, because the storage space will unmount. When storage spaces are over 70 percent full, consider adding additional storage.

Rebalancing the data stored on the disks in a storage pool can improve performance. You can run the Optimize-StoragePool Windows PowerShell cmdlet to ensure that the data is distributed evenly between the various disks in the storage pool.

Older storage spaces created in Windows 8 or 8.1 should be updated to allow the data to be rebalanced, using the Update-StoragePool Windows PowerShell cmdlet. Updated storage pools can be then optimized.

Summary

- A disk can use the MBR or GPT disk partitioning scheme, and Windows 10 (x64) can boot from a GPT disk if it is using a UEFI-enabled motherboard.
- Disks can support either simple or dynamic volumes. Dynamic volumes can offer enhanced volume features, including mirrored, spanned, and striped volumes.
- Updated device drivers that are not stable can be rolled back to the previous version.
- The most common file systems Windows 10 supports include NTFS, ReFS, exFat, FAT32, and FAT. ReFS is a new file system used with Storage Spaces in Windows 10; it offers self-healing and repairing capabilities.
- Windows PowerShell is the preferred method to manage disks, but you can also use Disk Management and DiskPart.
- You must initialize foreign disks before they can be used by Windows 10.
- Windows 10 supports VHD and the newer VHDX format natively.
- Storage Spaces enables you to combine redundant storage into a new, managed storage pool in which virtual disks are created, providing data redundancy and increased resilience at low cost.
- BitLocker To Go can be used to secure removable hard drives and thumb drives with BitLocker encryption.

Thought experiment

In this thought experiment, demonstrate your skills and knowledge of the topics covered in this chapter. You can find answers to this thought experiment in the next section.

Your organization has a central head office and five remote branch offices located across the United States. Operational data is cloud-based, using OneDrive for Business. There is a business requirement for full computer backups for each of the staff members at the five branches, and currently this is being performed locally to a second drive partition on each device. Your manager wants to ensure that each office has local file storage redundancy for the backups and has asked you to recommend a solution. During the past 2 months, you have upgraded many of the desktop computers and installed new 128 GB SSD drives. You have 50 spare drives of various sizes as follows.

- 32 x 1 TB SATA drives (2 years old)
- 18 x 320 SATA drives (4 years old)

Each branch office currently uses a Windows 10–based computer, which is used as a printer server. The printer is connected directly to it and shared across the network. Your solution should use the equipment currently available and not incur additional cost.

Answer the following questions for your manager.

1. What feature will you recommend to be used?
2. How will you use the spare drives?
3. If the print server can only fit a maximum of four drives per computer, how would this affect your proposal?
4. If you have any drives left over, how would you use these?
5. What user-level training will be required at the branch office?

Thought experiment answer

This section contains the solution to the thought experiment.

1. You would suggest using Storage Spaces on the Windows 10 print server computer.
2. Answers might vary, but you would only use the 1 TB drives because they offer larger capacity, and they are quite new. Allocate five drives to each print server computer as a three-way mirror. Alternatively, five drives could be configured as a parity drive array. After the storage pool has been created, a new drive letter should be made available and shared on the network to the members of staff for the backup storage.
3. With only four drive bays available, you would use three of the 1 TB drives in a parity drive array; the currently installed Windows 10 operating system would use the other drive bay.
4. These drives could be labeled as storage space drive spares and distributed to each site to be used if the branch experiences a drive failure.
5. Users should not need significant training; all users should direct their current backup application to the new drive letter available on the print server computer.

CHAPTER 8

Configure data access and usage

Being able to access your data from anywhere is a key feature of Windows 10, whether at home using a HomeGroup, at work across a LAN, or when mobile using the Internet. This chapter discusses multiple methods of configuring sharing and setting access permissions on the share so that you are in control of who can see or edit the data. You review how to troubleshoot data access issues and stay informed of your usage status when using a metered connection.

Skills covered in this chapter:

- Configure file and printer sharing
- Configure HomeGroup connections
- Configure folder shares
- Configure public folders
- Configure OneDrive
- Configure File System permissions
- Configure OneDrive usage
- Troubleshoot data access and usage

Skill: Configure file and printer sharing

Data is often shared in an organization, perhaps within a team for project work or between you and your boss. You must know how this can be achieved in Windows 10 within a networked environment, whether that is at home or in a larger workplace network. You must be able to manage shared files and printers.

File and printer sharing is disabled by default, and it is automatically turned on when you share the first folder on a Windows 10 device. If you want to configure this setting manually, you can do so in the advanced sharing settings in the Network And Sharing Center in Control Panel.

Another consideration is that when sharing is enabled, the Windows Firewall is automatically configured to allow users to access shares on a computer in the network. This is a potential security risk. Although the firewall settings are configured automatically when you first share a folder, they are not returned to their default status even if you remove all shared folders.

> **This section covers how to:**
> - Understand Server Message Block and Network Discovery
> - Share files by using a sharing wizard
> - Share a printer

Server Message Block and Network Discovery

Shares are provided by the Server Message Block (SMB) application-layer network protocol and not by NTFS. You can see what version of SMB your Windows 10 system is using by following these steps.

1. Log on to your computer by using an administrative user account.
2. Open File Explorer and navigate to a shared or mapped folder on the network so that the shared files are visible in the right navigation pane.
3. On the File Explorer menu, click File and then click Open Windows PowerShell As Administrator.
4. Accept UAC if prompted.
5. Type the Windows PowerShell cmdlet **Get-SmbConnection**.

   Windows PowerShell should report the current SMB version (dialect) in use, as shown in Figure 8-1.

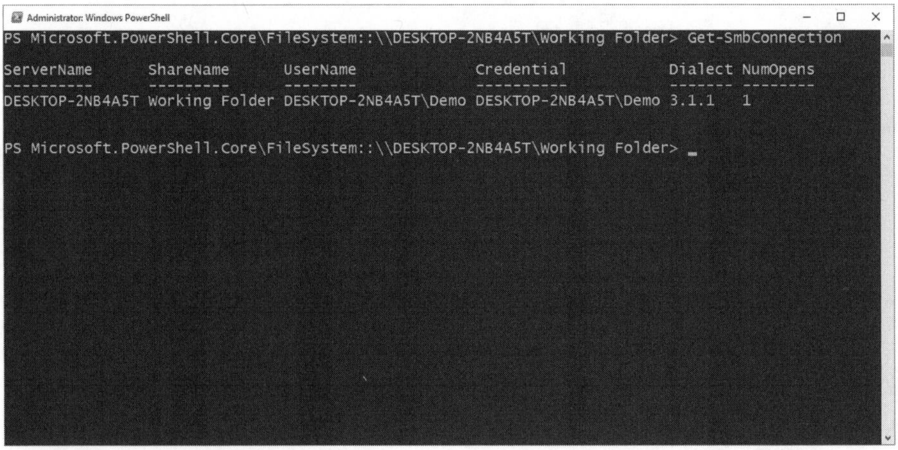

FIGURE 8-1 Windows 10 SMB version

Windows automatically negotiates between the client and server (or client and client) to ensure that both parties use the latest SMB version. Using the latest version (version 3.0 and later in Windows 10 and Server 2012 R2) offers many new benefits such as scalability, failover, and performance enhancements.

> **NEED MORE REVIEW?** SMB 3.0 OVERVIEW
>
> This TechNet resource, although focused on Windows Server 2012 and SMB 3.0, is useful to obtain more information relating to the benefits of using the latest version of SMB compared to previous versions. Visit *https://technet.microsoft.com/library /hh831795%28v=ws.11%29.aspx?f=255&MSPPError=-2147217396*.

The network discovery feature was introduced in Windows Vista and uses a new layer 2–level protocol called Link Layer Topology Discovery (LLTD). It allows Windows to identify other devices present on the local subnet and, when possible, establish the quality of service (QoS) bandwidth capabilities of the network.

Knowing what is on the network increases the communication between devices. One downside of this increased awareness capability is that the firewall security settings are slightly relaxed. This means that not only does your computer see other network computers and devices, it also becomes discoverable on the network by other Windows clients. To maintain security, the network discovery feature is disabled by default.

EXAM TIP

Administrators working in a domain environment can manage the settings of the two network discovery settings, LLTD Mapper (LLTDIO) and Responder (RSPNDR), in Group Policy settings, which can be found here: Computer Configuration\Policies \Administrative Templates\Network\Link Layer Topology Discovery.

Sharing files by using a sharing wizard

The Share tab in File Explorer enables you to launch the File Sharing Wizard and provides the same functionality as the Share With shortcut menu. Next to this is Advanced Security, which enables you to fine-tune the sharing beyond the limitations of the File Sharing Wizard.

Files typically cannot be shared without first sharing the parent folder. In Windows 10, files that reside in the user profile, such as Documents, Downloads, and Pictures folders, can be shared. To do this, follow these steps.

1. Log on to your computer, using an administrative user account.
2. Open File Explorer and navigate to the user profile.
3. Right-click the files, such as pictures, in the user's profile.
4. Select Share With, Specific People, as shown in Figure 8-2.

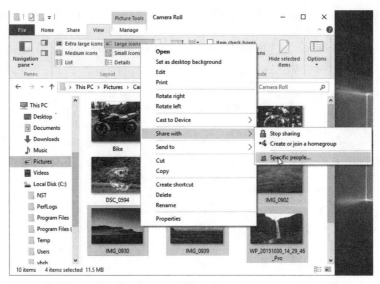

FIGURE 8-2 Share, using the sharing wizard

5. In the Choose People To Share With dialog box, select a user or group and click Add.

6. Set Permission Level to Read or Read/Write and click Share.

   Note that you are sharing. The File Sharing Wizard completes, and the files are shared.

7. Optionally, you can use the links in the File Sharing Wizard to send someone the links to the shares.

8. Click Done.

When you configure basic sharing permissions, you have one of two simplified options.

- **Read** Users and groups can open but cannot modify or delete files.

- **Read/Write** Users and groups can open, modify, or delete a file and modify permissions.

After you create a share, all users see the share name over the network. Only users who have at least the Read permission can view its content.

> **NOTE   ADMINISTRATORS CAN SHARE FILES AND FOLDERS**
>
> To share a file or folder across the network in Windows 10, you must be a member of the Administrators group or provide UAC credentials for an administrator.

Later in the chapter, you see in more detail how to configure shared folders by using advanced security.

Share a printer

Windows 10 enables you to share an installed print device and manage it directly through the Print Management tool. In this section, you review how to share a printer and how to administer printers and print servers.

When you add a new printer, Plug and Play normally installs it automatically. Sometimes the terminology relating to printers can be confusing, so review the following list of terms to ensure that you are clear.

- **Printing device** The physical printer or device is connected locally or through the network.

- **Printer port** Modern printers connect by Wi-Fi or Bluetooth, whereas older devices connected by USB, serial, or parallel ports. Plug and Play should auto-configure the correct port settings for Windows 10 to communicate directly with the print device.

- **Print job** This is the computer representation of the document that needs to be printed.

- **Print job output** This is the printed document.

- **Printer** This is the Windows 10 representation of a physical printing device, such as the printer icon.

- **Printer driver** The printing device needs to be given instructions on how to render print jobs from Windows 10, such as size, color, and number of copies. The print device also communicates with Windows 10 with information such as print status, ink levels, and paper jams. These communications are enabled through the printer driver.

- **Page-description language (PDL)** The driver uses the PDL to convert a print job to the print language used to print the document, such as PostScript, Printer Control Language (PCL), Portable Document Format (PDF), and XML Paper Specification (XPS).

Type 4 print class drivers

To protect the system from rogue drivers and to aid simplified sharing, Windows 10 uses the new Type 4 Print Class Driver for each printer device model; this was first introduced with Windows 8. Unlike the older Type 3 printer drivers, an administrator only needs to install a Type 4 printer driver rather than multiple drivers, such as 32-bit and 64-bit drivers, to support both types of client architecture. Type 4 drivers can support multiple printer models and often install faster than the older Type 3 drivers.

The security of Windows 10 is enhanced because Type 4 printer drivers can only be updated by using Windows Update or Windows Software Update Services (WSUS).

> **NEED MORE REVIEW? WINDOWS 10 PRINT AND DOCUMENT SERVICES ARCHITECTURE**
>
> This TechNet resource is useful to obtain more information relating to the Type 4 Printer Class Drivers. Visit *https://technet.microsoft.com/library/jj134171.aspx.*

The printer GUI, produced by the original equipment manufacturer (OEM) and found in Windows 10, for example, in Control Panel or Device Stage, is typically installed independently rather than with the Type 4 driver; it's designed to provide information to the user and interacts with the printer device through the printer driver.

Adding and sharing a printer

In addition to sharing a printer, you can also modify the printer security to ensure that only authorized users can print to the device. Complete the following steps to add and share a local printer.

1. Click the Start button and type **printer.**

2. Click Devices And Printers.

3. In Devices And Printers, click Add A Printer.

4. On the Add A Device page, click The Printer That I Want Isn't Listed.

5. On the Find A Printer By Other Options page, select Add A Local Printer Or Network Printer With Manual Settings and click Next.

6. On the Choose A Printer Port page, verify that Use An Existing Port is selected and click Next.

7. On the Install The Printer Driver page, in the Manufacturer list, select Microsoft. In the Printers list, select Microsoft PCL6 Class Driver and click Next.

8. On the Type A Printer Name Page, in the Printer Name box, type **Reception Printer** and click Next.

9. On the Printer Sharing page, click Next.

10. Verify that the printer is set as the default printer and click Finish.

Setting printer security permissions

To modify the printer's security to allow only members of the Users group to print, complete the following steps.

1. Click the Start button and type **printer.**

2. Click Devices And Printers.

3. In Devices And Printers, right-click Reception Printer, select Printer Properties, and then select the Security tab.

4. In the Reception Printer Properties dialog box, verify that Everyone is selected and then click Remove.

5. Click Add. In the Enter The Object Names To Select (Examples) box, enter **Users** and click OK.

6. In the Permissions For Users section, add the Manage Documents Allow permission, verify that the Allow Print permission is selected, and click OK.

The default security settings for a shared printer allow the Everyone group to print, and members of the Administrators group can print, manage the printer, and manage documents, as shown in Figure 8-3.

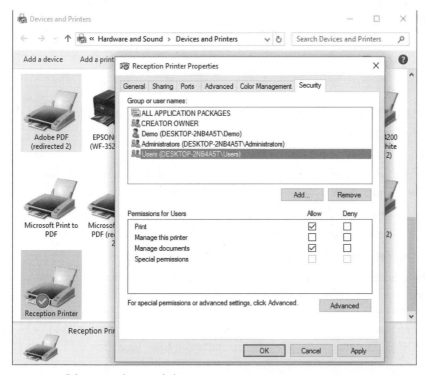

FIGURE 8-3 Printer security permissions

> *NOTE* **RESTART PRINTER SPOOLER**
>
> Although members of the Everyone group can print to a printer, only administrators can cancel print jobs. Rather than cancel a print job, sometimes restarting the Print Spooler service can resolve a stalled printer.

Skill: Configure HomeGroup connections

Introduced in Windows 7, the HomeGroups feature aims to provide a simplified process of sharing files and printers on small networks such as in small offices or homes, where Active Directory Domain Services (AD DS) is not used. Computers running Windows 7 or newer can connect to HomeGroups.

Although HomeGroups are created automatically by using the Create A HomeGroup Wizard, they are password protected by a system-generated password. By protecting access to this password, a HomeGroup owner has control over who can connect to their HomeGroup.

> **This section covers how to:**
> - Create a new HomeGroup
> - Join a HomeGroup

Create a new HomeGroup

To simplify creation for home and small office staff, the process of creating a HomeGroup is wizard-based.

If a HomeGroup has not been created on your device, you can create a new one. Launch the Create A HomeGroup Wizard in one of several ways, as follows.

- Click the Create A HomeGroup button in the HomeGroup node in File Explorer.
- Click the Create A HomeGroup button in the HomeGroup node in Control Panel.
- Click the HomeGroup link in the Network And Internet Settings app.

You must have Administrator privileges to enable the HomeGroup feature, but anyone can join one with the correct password. After you have joined a HomeGroup, you can choose which of your folders you want to share with the HomeGroup. For other users to access files and folders shared in a HomeGroup, the computer that hosts the resources must be turned on and connected to the network, but the user does not need to be logged on.

Follow these steps to configure a HomeGroup.

1. Click the Create A HomeGroup button in the HomeGroup node in File Explorer.
2. On the Create A HomeGroup page, click Next.
3. On the Share With Other HomeGroup Members page, select the files and devices that you want to share, set permission levels, and click Next.
4. When the wizard generates a HomeGroup password, make a note of it or print it and then click Finish.

   The Change HomeGroup Settings page appears, and other members can now join your HomeGroup.

After you have created a HomeGroup, review the options available on the Change HomeGroup Settings page because this enables you to modify settings, including:

- Viewing or printing the HomeGroup password.
- Changing HomeGroup password.
- Modifying the items that you are sharing.
- Allowing devices on your network to have access to streaming media content.
- Leaving an existing HomeGroup.

- Starting the HomeGroup troubleshooter.
- Modifying advanced sharing settings.

In addition to allowing users and computers access to files and folders in your HomeGroup, you can also allow devices on your network to have access to streaming media content such as music, games, and videos from your HomeGroup, as shown in Figure 8-4.

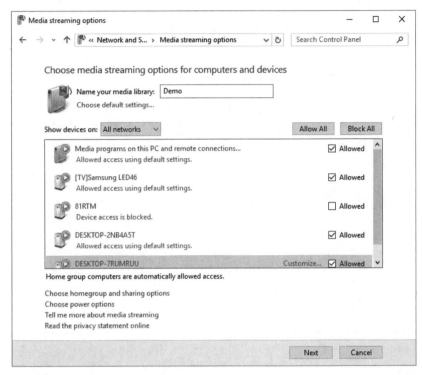

FIGURE 8-4 Media streaming with HomeGroup

Join a HomeGroup

If a HomeGroup has already been created on the network, the details are displayed when you open the HomeGroup item in the Network And Sharing Center. To join the HomeGroup on your network, perform the following steps.

1. Open the HomeGroup item in the Network And Sharing Center.

2. Any existing HomeGroups should be automatically detected, and the name of the user and computer with the HomeGroup appears.

3. Click Join Now.

4. On the Join A HomeGroup page, click Next.

5. On the Share With Other HomeGroup Members page, select the files and devices that you want to share, set permission levels, and click Next.

6. Enter the HomeGroup password that has been provided to you from the person who created the HomeGroup.

   If the password is correct, the wizard completes, and you have joined the HomeGroup.

7. Click Finish.

If you want to leave the HomeGroup and stop sharing your files and folders, open the HomeGroup item in the Network And Sharing Center and then click Leave. If you want to re-join the HomeGroup, run the Join A HomeGroup Wizard again.

Skill: Configure folder shares

When you share a folder, other users can connect to the shared folder and its contents across the network. Shared folders available on the network are no different from normal folders, and they can contain applications, corporate data, or private data. Be careful when creating a network share, to ensure that you do not accidentally provide access to a user or group of users who should not have access. By default, everyone on the network is given read access to the share, although you can change this setting.

Normally, a shared folder is located on a file server, but in a small network environment, the sharing can be located on a Windows 10–based computer or network-attached storage (NAS) device. When choosing the device or server, the resources should be available whenever the users need them and, often, this means the server is always on.

By providing a central location for shared folders to reside on, you enable the following features.

- Simplification of management
- User familiarity
- Ease in backing up data
- Consistent location and availability

When a user tries to use resources accessed on a shared folder, the access permissions are determined by taking into consideration both the share permission and the NTFS security permissions. The most restrictive set of permissions prevail to the user.

Ensure that you do not create shared folders where the share permissions (SMB) become the primary access security mechanism. They are more restrictive than the NTFS permissions because users gaining access to the resource locally or by logging on through Remote Desktop would completely bypass SMB permissions. It is therefore essential for NTFS permissions to be configured independently to protect the resource.

This section covers how to:

- Create a share
- Shared folders permissions

Create a share

To allow access to a locally stored folder across a network, first share the folder. Files contained in folders are also shared, but files cannot be specifically shared independently, except from within a user profile.

There are a number of ways you can create a share, for example:

- Shared Folders snap-in
- File Explorer
- Command prompt
- Windows PowerShell cmdlets

Create a share by using the Shared Folders snap-In

You can create and manage file shares centrally on your computer by using the Shared Folders snap-in, which can be loaded into an empty Microsoft Management Console (MMC), or the snap-in found in Computer Management.

When you create a new share in the Shared Folders snap-in, the Create A Shared Folder Wizard appears and guides you through specifying the folder path, share name, description, and other settings, as shown in Figure 8-5.

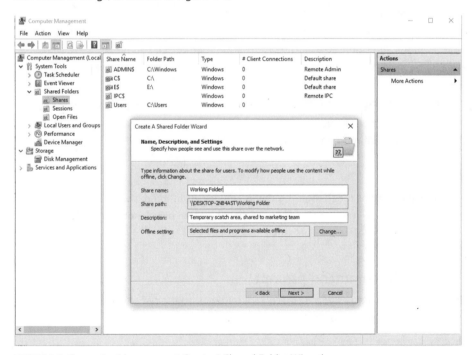

FIGURE 8-5 Computer Management Create A Shared Folder Wizard

By default, the share name will be the same as the folder name, and permissions for the share are set at read-only access for the Everyone group, but you can choose other options or full customization by completing the underlying Share Permissions discretionary access control list (DACL) page.

The Shared Folders snap-in enables you to view existing shares and modify their properties, including settings such as offline file status, share permissions, and even the NTFS security permissions.

EXAM TIP

To launch the Create A Shared Folder Wizard directly from a command prompt, use Shrpubw.exe.

Sharing folders by using File Explorer

There are three methods of sharing a folder in File Explorer.

- Use the Share With option, found on the Share tab on the ribbon bar (also called Network File And Folder Sharing).
- Select Advanced Security from the Share tab on the ribbon bar.
- Use the Sharing tab in the Properties dialog box.

All the methods present you with slightly different GUIs and wizards from which to choose the sharing options. Although they all result in sharing folders that can be accessed across the network, the main difference between each method is the speed and simplicity that some offer the novice.

In practice, most home users and small businesses prefer to use the sharing wizards found on the ribbon bar, but more experienced users seek the advanced level of control that can be gained through the Sharing tab in the Properties dialog box.

EXAM TIP

Review the three options for configuring shares and pay attention to the limitations of the wizard-based methods. The wizards configure the file system permissions automatically, based on the limited choices they present.

Sharing from the command prompt

The command prompt enables you to share a folder by using the net share command. To create a simple share, you would use the following example.

```
net share MyShareName=c:\Temp\Data /remark:"Temp Workarea"
```

This command shares the c:\Temp\Data folder with the share name MyShareName and includes a description of Temp Workarea.

You must have administrative privileges to create a shared folder by using Net Share.

Review the additional command-line options that you can use with Net Share, as shown in Table 8-1.

TABLE 8-1 Net Share command-line options

Option	Description
/Grant:user permission	Enables you to specify Read, Change, or Full Share permissions for the specified user
/Users:number	Enables you to limit the number of users who can connect to the share concurrently (default and maximum for Windows 10 is 20 users)
/Remark:"text"	Enables you to add a description to the share
/Cache:option	Enables you to specify the offline files caching options for the share
sharename /Delete	Enables you to remove an existing share

> **NOTE SHARING CAUTION**
>
> **The Net Share command will not create a folder and share it. You can only share folders that already exist on the computer.**

Sharing by using Windows PowerShell

If you need to script the creation of shares, Windows PowerShell is the most appropriate choice and provides several cmdlets that enable you to manage shares in Windows 10. Windows PowerShell offers more in both scope and functionality than Net Share and will continue to expand in the future.

An example command for creating a share is:

```
New-SmbShare –Name MyShareName –Path c:\Temp\Data
```

Other Windows PowerShell cmdlets used in the administration of shares are shown in Table 8-2.

TABLE 8-2 Windows PowerShell Share cmdlets

Cmdlet	Description
Get-SmbShare	Lists the existing shares on the computer
Get-SmbShareAccess	Lists the access control list of the SMB share
New-SmbShare	Creates a new SMB share
Set-SmbShare	Modifies the properties for an existing share
Remove-SmbShare	Deletes an existing share
Grant-SmbShareAccess	Sets the share permissions on an existing share
Get-SmbShareAccess	Lists the current share permissions for a share

Shared folders permissions

Permissions that are set on the share determine the level of access a user has to the files in the share. They can be set on FAT or later file systems. When you use the NTFS file system, be careful not to restrict access at the share level, because this might affect the effective permissions. You can configure the permissions when you share a folder and set a level that the user or group will have when they connect to the folder through the share across the network.

Sharing permissions have three options.

- **Read**   Users and groups can view the files, but they cannot modify or delete them.
- **Change**   Users and groups can open, modify, delete, and create content, but they cannot modify file or folder permissions; the Change permission incorporates all Read permissions.
- **Full**   Users and groups can perform all actions, including modifying the permissions; the Full permission incorporates all Change permissions.

Unlike in earlier versions of Windows, there is no longer a visual icon or indicator in File Explorer to distinguish whether a folder is shared. All shared folders on your device appear in the Shared Folders node of the Computer Management console. You can also view the shared folders that exist on your device by using the Get-SmbShare Windows PowerShell cmdlet or typing **net view \\localhost /all** at the command prompt.

After a user has found the share in File Explorer, they can access the files directly. Another common way that users can connect to a shared folder over the network is by using the shares Universal Naming Convention (UNC) address. UNC addresses contain two backward slashes (\\) followed by the name of the computer that is sharing the folder and the shared folder name; for example, the UNC name for the Marketing shared folder on the LON-DC1 computer in the Fabrikam.com domain would be:

```
\\LON-CL1.Fabrikam.com\Marketing
```

Configure public folders

Windows 10 continues to provide support for public folder sharing, which can offer a simplified way to make files that you copy into a public folder immediately available to other users on your computer or network.

Public folder sharing is not enabled by default in Windows 10, but when it is turned on, anyone with a user account on your computer, or any Windows device on your network, can access the contents of the public folders, and the default permissions for public folders enable members of the Everyone group to read, write, change, and delete any public files.

By default, Windows 10 provides the following public folders.

- Public Documents
- Public Downloads
- Public Music
- Public Pictures
- Public Videos

To share something publicly with your friends or colleagues, copy or move it into one of the public folders. You can navigate to these folders directly in File Explorer from the %systemdrive%\Users\Public folder.

To turn on the Public folder-sharing feature, follow these steps.

1. Open Network And Sharing Center.
2. Click Change Advanced Sharing Settings.
3. Expand the All Networks profile section.
4. In the Public Folder Sharing section, select Turn On Sharing So Anyone With Network Access Can Read And Write Files In The Public Folders.
5. Click Save Changes.
6. Accept the UAC if prompted.

To turn off public folder sharing, select Turn Off Public Folder Sharing in the Network And Sharing Center.

Public folder sharing does not allow you to fine-tune sharing permissions, but it does provide a simple and user-friendly way for users to make their files available to others.

When you enable public folder sharing, the Everyone system group is granted full control permissions for the share and underlying folder permissions.

Skill: Configure OneDrive

OneDrive is a cloud-based service designed for storing files and synchronizing settings aimed at the consumer market. Microsoft gives each user 5 gigabytes (GB) of free cloud storage. To access the service, the user must use a Microsoft account, and the service can be accessed natively from a computer or smartphone.

A business-oriented service called OneDrive For Business is based on Microsoft SharePoint technologies; it stores data in a specialized library in the cloud. OneDrive For Business is part of an Office 365 subscription and provides 1 terabyte (TB) of free space per user.

OneDrive desktop app

OneDrive is integrated with Windows 10, using the OneDrive app, and when you sign in to Windows with a Microsoft account, a OneDrive folder is created in File Explorer at C:\Users \Username\OneDrive.

To protect against data loss, you are advised to use OneDrive as your preferred location for all your data. When you add, modify, or delete files stored in the OneDrive favorite, your changes are replicated to OneDrive as long as you are online.

If you are using an operating system other than Windows 10, you might still be able to use the OneDrive desktop app; it is supported on the following operating systems.

- Windows 10
- Windows 8.1
- Windows 8
- Windows 7
- Windows Vista with Service Pack 2 (SP2)
- Windows Server 2008 R2
- Windows Server 2008 SP2
- Mac OS X 10.7 (Lion)
- Mac OS X Mountain Lion

The OneDrive app, located in the taskbar notification area, enables you to modify synchro-nization settings. You can choose to synchronize all or selected files and folders from your cloud storage account to your device.

Review the settings available in the desktop app and implement file synchronization.

OneDrive web portal

Although integration is tight between the Windows 10 OneDrive app and the online version of OneDrive, the online version currently has slightly more functionality, although it can be slower to manipulate your files, depending on available bandwidth.

In the portal, users can:

- Manage all their files stored on OneDrive.
- Access previous versions of files.

- Access the OneDrive Recycle Bin.
- Buy more storage (subscription-based).
- Configure advanced sharing options for files and folders.
- Create Microsoft Excel surveys.

Users of mobile phones can also allow the automatic upload of all photos to their private OneDrive photos folder. With photos consuming some of your free 5 GB cloud storage each time you take a picture, you may be surprised at how quickly the quota is used up, but adding additional storage is relatively inexpensive. If you subscribe to Office 365, OneDrive comes with 1 TB of storage and the ability to install Office applications locally on your PC, Mac, or iPad.

In OneDrive, you can access Microsoft Office Online, which enables you to create Word, Excel, Microsoft PowerPoint, and Microsoft OneNote files. After you create an Office online file, you can share the documents online, collaborate with other users, and edit documents at the same time. In addition, you can create text documents and Excel surveys. The surveys are simple; others can fill them out just by opening the link to the survey. You then see everyone's response compiled in the online spreadsheet.

Privacy is a significant concern for many users, especially when discussing personal data. Although OneDrive is aimed at consumers and is therefore not suitable for enterprise data, Microsoft has upgraded the level of security and encryption to protect data held on the OneDrive service. Data is now protected with Perfect Forward Secrecy (PFS) encryption when you access OneDrive through the web portal, *onedrive.live.com*, mobile OneDrive application, and OneDrive sync clients.

Fetch files on your PC

Another unique feature in the OneDrive desktop app is the ability to retrieve any file remotely from the computer with the app installed, from any web browser. To enable this setting, follow these steps.

1. Log on to Windows 10 with a Microsoft account.
2. Right-click the OneDrive app in the taskbar notification area.
3. Click Settings.
4. Select the Settings tab.
5. Select Let Me Use OneDrive and click OK, as shown in Figure 8-6.

FIGURE 8-6 OneDrive desktop app settings

6. Restart the OneDrive app to complete the process.

7. Ensure that the device you want to connect to is powered on and connected to the Internet.

8. Open OneDrive in your browser. From the list of devices in the left pane, select the PC that you want to retrieve files from.

Although Mac users can use OneDrive and download the OneDrive app, they can't fetch files from a Mac.

EXAM TIP

The Fetch Files On Your PC setting is a hidden feature and is likely to be included in the exam. Be sure you know how to enable it. Visit the Office support resource at *http://aka.ms /fetch-files-on-your-PC* **to obtain some additional information about the setting.**

Skill: Configure File System permissions

Most users are familiar with using the File Explorer tool to view and manage files and folders. When administrating shared files and folders over a network, this is still the primary tool to configure file- and folder-level permissions. Although permissions have been part of NTFS and earlier versions of Windows, ensure that you are familiar with the changes offered in Windows 10.

Use File Explorer to manage files and folders

The most common tool used is File Explorer, which is located on the taskbar and the Start screen. Typical functions provided through File Explorer include:

- Creating new folders and files.
- Viewing and accessing files and folders.
- Searching for files and information contained in files.
- Managing properties of files and folders.
- Previewing contents or thumbnails of files and folders.

The quick access area is new in Windows 10 and appears at the uppermost left area of the File Explorer navigation pane; it includes pinned shorts for the Desktop, Downloads, Documents, Pictures, and Music. As you browse and access files in other folders on your computer, folder shortcuts for these items appear in the right navigation pane under Frequent Folders or Recent Files. You can modify the behavior of Quick Access by right-clicking Quick Access and selecting Options, as shown in Figure 8-7.

On a shared computer, you might want to clear the check boxes for Show Recently Used Files In Quick Access and Show Frequently Used Folders In Quick Access.

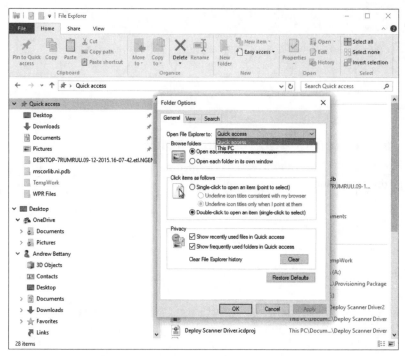

FIGURE 8-7 File Explorer Quick Access

Set file and folder permissions

Volumes formatted using either NTFS or the newer ReFS enable you to configure file and folder permissions. NTFS is robust, reliable, and effective and enables you to configure granular permissions on both files and folders that determine how individual users and groups can use the objects.

The creator of the resource, such as a file or folder, is automatically assigned the special status of creator-owner, and they can grant or deny permissions to it. Administrators and anyone given the Full Control permission also can modify permissions for that file or folder.

To modify permissions to a file or folder, access the Security tab in the object's properties, as shown in Figure 8-8.

FIGURE 8-8 Security permissions for a file

If a user leaves the organization or the account is deleted, an Administrator can take ownership of the files and folders to modify permissions by changing the Owner principal in the Advanced settings in Properties.

If you have the permission to modify the security settings in the access control list (ACL), you can add or remove users or groups and then grant or deny a specific permission level. In organizations, you assign permissions to groups rather than to multiple users because this minimizes administrative effort.

Review the acronyms relating to objects that you might use when applying security permissions, as shown in Table 8-3.

TABLE 8-3 Security Permission acronyms

Name	Acronym	Description
Access control list	ACL	A list of users and groups with permissions on the object
Access control entry	ACE	Identifies specific permissions granted to a user or group
Discretionary access control list	DACL	Specifies which user has access to the object
System access control list	SACL	Specifies which operations can be performed by specific users

When assigning permissions to several groups, remember that the security settings have a cumulative effect; you should review the effective permissions obtained for the user by following these steps.

1. Open Windows Explorer.

2. Navigate to the file or folder whose effective permissions you want to view.

3. Right-click the file or folder, click Properties, and click the Security tab.

4. Click Advanced and then click the Effective Access tab.

5. Next to the User/Group, click Select A User.

6. On the Select User Or Group dialog box, click in the Enter The Object Name To Select (Examples) box, enter the name of a user or group, and then click OK.

7. Click View Effective Access.

   You should now see the detailed effective permissions of the user or group for that file or folder.

When configuring permissions for files and folders, you can configure basic or advanced permissions. Unless you are seeking a very fine degree of control to a resource, you typically work with basic permissions and assign them to groups and users, as shown in Table 8-4.

TABLE 8-4 Basic file and folder permissions for NTFS and ReFS

File permission	Description
Full Control	Complete authority and control of all file or folder permissions.
Modify	Ability to read a file, write changes to it, and modify permissions.
Read & Execute	Ability to see folder content, read files and attributes, and start programs.
Read	Ability to read a file but not make any changes to it.
Write	Ability to change folder or file content and create new files.
Special Permissions	Indication of whether additional advanced permissions have been configured for the file or folder.

> **NOTE BASIC AND ADVANCED PERMISSIONS**
>
> If you are familiar with older versions of Windows, you might notice that Windows 10 uses the modern naming for permissions as follows: Standard Permissions has been changed to Basic Permissions, and Special Permissions has been changed to Advanced Permissions.

Basic permissions are easier to manage and document. Under the hood, a basic permission is made from a combination of individual advanced special permissions. Consider that permissions for folders can have a different effect on files, as described in Table 8-5.

TABLE 8-5 Basic NTFS file and folder permissions

Basic Permission	Description: When Applied to a Folder	Description: When Applied to a File
Full Control	Permits reading, writing, changing, and deletion of files and subfolders. Allows the modification of permissions on folders.	Permits reading, writing, changing, and deletion of the file. Allows modification of permissions on files.
Modify	Permits reading, writing, changing, and deletion of files and subfolders. Does not allow changes to permissions on folders.	Permits reading, writing, changing, and deletion of the file. Does not allow changes to the permissions on files.
Read & Execute	Allows the content of the folder to be accessed and executed.	Allows the file to be accessed and executed (run).
List Folder Contents	Allows the contents of the folder to be viewed.	Does not apply to files.
Read	Allows content to be read.	Allows access to the contents. Does not allow files to be executed.
Write	Allows addition of files and subfolders to the folder.	Allows a user to modify but not delete a file.

Behind the basic permissions is a matrix of 13 advanced permissions that can also be applied to files and folders. Each basic permission is a collection of one or more advanced permissions, as shown in Table 8-6.

TABLE 8-6 Basic and advanced permissions

Advanced Permission	Full Control	Modify	Read & Execute	List Folder Contents	Read	Write
Traverse Folder/ Execute File	X	X	X	X		
List Folder/Read Data	X	X	X	X	X	
Read Attributes	X	X	X	X	X	
Read Extended Attributes	X	X	X	X	X	
Create Files/Write Data	X	X				X
Create Folders/ Append Data	X	X				X
Write Attributes	X	X				X
Write Extended Attributes	X	X				X
Delete Subfolders And Files	X					
Delete	X	X				
Read Permissions	X	X	X	X	X	X
Change Permissions	X					
Take Ownership	X					

It is recommended to use basic permissions unless there is a clear requirement for setting advanced permissions; otherwise, they can become complex and difficult to troubleshoot. If you do use the advanced permissions, it is best practice to document any modifications so that you can review the configuration and, if necessary, reverse the settings.

Many inexperienced users who configure NTFS permissions can complicate the settings on files by setting advanced permissions, frequently using deny permissions, and setting for individual users instead of for groups. There is a strict canonical order or hierarchy of how Deny and Allow permissions can interoperate, and the general rule is that a Deny setting prevents an Allow setting.

EXAM TIP

Remember the principle of least administration when applying NTFS or ReFS permissions. If you want to prevent a user or group from having any access to a resource, you could set no permissions. If neither Allow nor Deny permission is explicitly configured or inherited on a resource, users are prevented from accessing the file or folder.

Review Table 8-7 to understand the relationship between Deny and Allow settings and how the behavior changes, depending on how the setting is applied.

TABLE 8-7 Allow and Deny NTFS permissions

Permission Type	Description	Check box status
Explicit Deny	The user is denied the permission on the file or folder.	Check box is selected.
Explicit Allow	The user is allowed the permission on the file or folder.	Check box is selected.
Inherited Deny	Deny permission is applied to the file or subfolder by virtue of permissions given to the parent folder.	Check box is dimmed but selected.
Not configured	When no permissions are assigned, the user has no permission to access the file or folder.	Check box is cleared.
Inherited Allow	Allow permission is applied to the file or subfolder by virtue of permissions given to the parent folder.	Check box is dimmed but selected.

NOTE **WHEN ALLOW OVERRIDES DENY**

When applying permissions to groups and allowing inheritance, sometimes one group has an explicit Allow setting, and another group has an inherited Deny setting. If a user is a member of both groups, the Allow setting will override the implicit Deny.

Although the majority of administrators will use File Explorer to set individual ACLs for files and folders, you can also use Windows PowerShell or the ICACLS command-line utility.

Windows PowerShell offers two cmdlets that you can use to manage file and folder permissions: Get-Acl and Set-Acl. For additional information and examples of how to use these cmdlets, type **Get-Help Get-Acl**, or **Get-Help Set-Acl**.

ICACLS enables you to configure and view permissions on files and folders on a local computer. Some of the most common ICACLS parameters and permission masks are shown in Table 8-8.

TABLE 8-8 Common ICACLS parameters and permission masks

Parameter/ Permission Mask	Description
/grant	Grants specific user access rights. Permissions replace previously granted explicit permissions.
/deny	Explicitly denies specified user access rights. An explicit Deny ACE is added for the stated permissions, and the same permissions in any explicit grant are removed.
/reset	Replaces ACLs with default inherited ACLs for all matching files.
F	Full access.
M	Modify access.
RX	Read and execute access.
R	Read-only access.
W	Write-only access.
(OI)	Object inherit.
(NP)	Do not propagate inherit.

To grant a permission, use the /grant switch, as the following example on an existing folder named C:\Temp\Working Folder shows.

1. Open File Explorer.

2. Navigate to the folder on which you want to set permissions.

3. Click File and then click Open Command Prompt.

4. Type the following command.

   ```
   Icacls.exe "C:\Temp\Working Folder"\ /grant Demo:(OI)M
   ```

5. Type **Icacls.exe "C:\Temp\Working Folder"** to view the permissions.

NEED MORE REVIEW? **TECHNET ICACLS**

This TechNet resource provides additional information for you to review relating to ICACLS. Visit *https://technet.microsoft.com/library /cc753525%28v=ws.11%29.aspx?f=255&MSPPError=-2147217396.*

Understand NTFS inheritance

Setting NTFS permissions on hundreds of files and folders would take a long time, especially if each setting were configured manually. Fortunately, you don't need to because by default NTFS and ReFS security permissions are inherited from their parent folder.

You can review the inheritance status of a file or folder in File Explorer by following these steps.

1. Open File Explorer.
2. Navigate to the folder whose inheritance settings you want to review.
3. Right-click the file or folder, choose Properties, and click Advanced.
4. On the Permissions tab, review the permission entries and notice the Inherited From column, as shown in Figure 8-9.

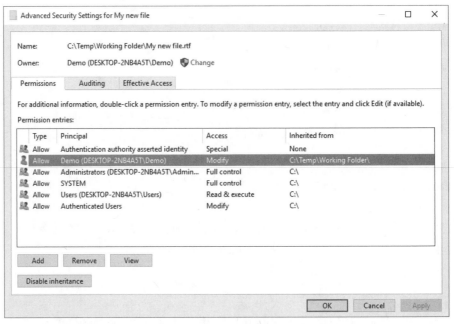

FIGURE 8-9 NTFS inheritance

Figure 8-9 shows a Disable Inheritance button. If you select this button, you are presented with the following choices.

- Convert Inherited Permissions Into Explicit Permissions On This Object
- Remove All Inherited Permissions From This Object

The option to convert inherited permissions to explicit permissions on this object stops inheritance from flowing from the parent folders and changes the permissions on all child items from implicit permissions to explicit permissions. You can then modify the permissions.

If you choose the second option, Remove All Inherited Permissions From This Object, you completely remove all permissions. This provides you with a folder structure with no permissions at all.

Both of these options are powerful. Best practice recommends employing inheritance wherever possible, to ease administration. You should also document and test your outline folder structure before it becomes too large. A big change on a small structure is simple to put in place, whereas modifying a large, established file structure could be cumbersome.

Skill: Configure OneDrive usage

After it is configured, OneDrive can provide you with a reliable and robust service that is very economical to use. Across the world, millions of users access OneDrive, and for many users this is their first experience of the cloud. Users can use the web portal interface or the OneDrive app and work seamlessly between both.

As a cloud service, OneDrive might become unavailable, but this is rare. The underlying backend infrastructure is designed to withstand multiple levels of failure and resiliency; often, any connection glitches will be local to the user rather than at the data center.

This section reviews how to perform some tasks in OneDrive to ensure that you can access your files and share them easily.

> **This section covers how to:**
> - Share files with OneDrive
> - Recover files from OneDrive
> - Block access to OneDrive

Share files with OneDrive

By default, three folders are created on a newly configured OneDrive account: Documents, Pictures, and Public. For the Documents and Pictures folders, sharing is turned off by default, and you are the only one who can access the content. To share a file or folder, you configure the share permissions so that they become publicly accessible. This can be easily achieved by moving, copying, or creating files or folders in the Public folder. The Public folder has the default share permissions of View for Everyone, which means anybody can see the contents, but they cannot edit any documents in that folder.

When you create a new file or folder in OneDrive, you can choose how you want to share it; the default share permission is Can Edit. If you right-click the folder, or select it and click Share, you can generate a URL link to send to someone, or OneDrive can email them the link for you, as shown in Figure 8-10. You can modify the share permission and include a personal message to accompany the shared link.

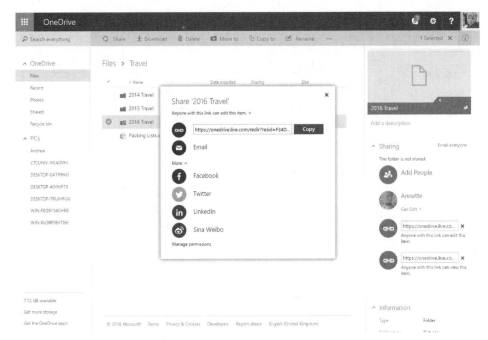

FIGURE 8-10 OneDrive file and folder sharing

If you click the Manage Permissions link, the right pane appears, and you can use this to add descriptions to your resources, invite individuals or groups, and modify share permissions.

Sharing is limited to granting view (read-only) permission or edit permission. You remain the owner of your files and can control who has access to your files.

For files that you want to share with a larger audience, for example, an Excel survey, you can also publish a link to an item directly to social media, such as Facebook, Twitter, LinkedIn, or Sina Weibo.

To stop sharing or modify permissions, select the shared item and, in the right pane, click the drop-down Can Edit button under the user account and then click Stop Sharing.

Recover files from OneDrive

From File Explorer, you can use the Recycle Bin to recover deleted files. OneDrive offers the same functionality and because the OneDrive service is synchronized through the OneDrive app, you can continue to use Recycle Bin in File Explorer; your deleted OneDrive files will be waiting to be recovered.

If you realize immediately that a file or folder has been deleted accidently when you are online, you can use the Undo feature from the OneDrive web portal.

The Undo feature works in a fashion similar to the one in an Office document in that if you delete an object in OneDrive by selecting Delete on the context menu, you see an option to Undo the operation. Click the Undo button to restore the deleted file immediately.

Recycle Bin offers similar functionality to that found in File Explorer. Click Recycle Bin in OneDrive and you see that files that have been deleted are listed in alphabetical order. You can sort the Recycle Bin items by name, original location, date deleted, and size. Select the items you want to restore and then click the Restore button, as shown in Figure 8-11. If all the files in Recycle Bin require restoring, you can use Restore All Items.

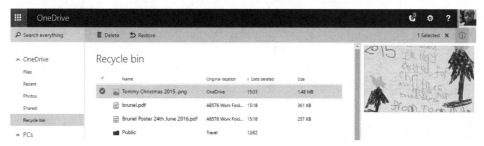

FIGURE 8-11 Restoring from the OneDrive recycle bin

If you click Delete while you have selected files or folders in the Recycle Bin, the items will be permanently deleted.

OneDrive and Windows 10 synchronize the Recycle Bin entries that relate to the OneDrive folder on the PC and deletions online. Recycle Bin stores items for a minimum of three days and up to a maximum of 90 days, with the default capacity of the Recycle Bin set to 10 percent of the total storage limit.

When the online Recycle Bin becomes full, old files that are less than 90 days old are also deleted to make room for new items.

Block access to OneDrive

In an enterprise environment, you might want to prevent your users from accessing OneDrive from domain-enrolled devices. Because you cannot implement policies to restrict or control what data is copied to or from OneDrive, a possible solution is to block all OneDrive access. This can be accomplished by using Group Policy and can be implemented at the domain level or on individual devices as follows.

1. Type **gpedit.msc** to open the Local Group Policy Editor.

2. Navigate to the Computer Configuration\Policies\Administrative Templates \Windows Components\OneDrive node.

3. Enable the Prevent The Usage Of OneDrive For File Storage policy setting.

When applied, this Group Policy setting prevents the user from starting the OneDrive app, and they receive a notification that the use of OneDrive has been blocked. In addition to blocking the app, consider also restricting access to the OneDrive web portal by adding the *https://onedrive.live.com* URL to the block list on your organizational firewall. This would also prevent access from all devices, including users' personal devices.

OneDrive synchronization

The OneDrive synchronization client provided with Windows 10 enables OneDrive users to choose specific folders to sync to the desktop. In this way, you can select only the content that you want to be available on specific devices instead of syncing an entire library of files.

One feature that was available with Windows 8.1 and early preview releases of Windows 10 is called File Placeholders. This feature enables File Explorer to display the full contents of a OneDrive data store without actually syncing all those files. That feature was removed from Windows 10 in a preview release in late 2014; Microsoft explained that the feature caused too many problems in usability and reliability. The OneDrive development team says this capability (or its equivalent) will return in a future release of the sync client.

Skill: Troubleshoot data access and usage

It can be frustrating when you use a system and something goes wrong. Understanding common areas that can pose problems and their resolutions can often reduce frustration and prevent data loss. Often, the only time you think about troubleshooting and recovery is at the very time a computer fails. Often, this is too late to help. Windows 10 introduces some new features and offers several strong data recovery and restoration tools, which you will review in troubleshooting scenarios.

This section covers how to:

- Troubleshoot data access
- Troubleshoot share and NTFS permissions
- Troubleshoot dynamic access control
- Troubleshoot data recovery
- Recover BitLocker encrypted drives

Troubleshoot data access

Access Denied is not a helpful message, even for experienced administrators. The message tells you that you do not have the necessary level of privilege to access the resource. This can relate to the following.

- User rights assignments

- Security options and permissions

A user rights assignment might mean that you are not allowed to carry out a task, such as accessing the system remotely over the network, or you are not allowed to shut down a system or take ownership of a file. These rights are configured as part of Group Policy, and you can familiarize yourself with the types of circumstances that can be managed by using user rights assignments in Computer Configuration\Windows Settings\Security Settings \Local Policies\User Rights Assignment, as shown in Figure 8-12.

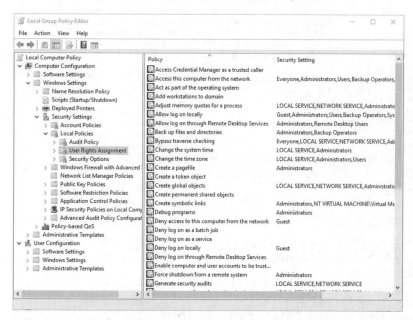

FIGURE 8-12 User rights assignment

If you see that user rights are affecting users, you can modify the group membership that relates to the setting or, if the policy has been set in error, you can disable the setting.

Security options often relate to object permissions (such as devices, resources, shares). They can permit or deny the ability of the user to perform a task, such as to log on using a Microsoft account; influence how UAC affects users with administrative accounts; prevent anonymous access to shares; or deny access to a device outside of normal office hours.

These permissions are normally configured in a domain environment, but you can also familiarize yourself with them through local Group Policy to see the types of security policies that can be managed using Security Options, which you can find in Computer Configuration \Windows Settings\Security Settings\Local Policies\Security Options, as shown in Figure 8-13.

Reviewing the settings and establishing which, if any, are being applied through Group Policy can give you a better understanding of whether users are being affected by these access policies.

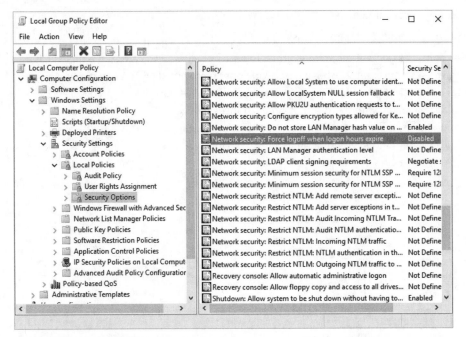

FIGURE 8-13 Security Options

If you use the HomeGroup feature, there is a useful troubleshooting wizard that can resolve connection issues with HomeGroup resources over the network. To launch the HomeGroup troubleshooter, type **HomeGroup** in Search and select Find And Fix Problems With HomeGroup.

Troubleshoot share and NTFS permissions

It can be easy when combining share and NTFS permissions to restrict access to resources across the network. By accepting the default share permissions, you provide standard users with only read access even if NTFS permissions are less restrictive.

Unfortunately, there is no wizard to diagnose which restrictions are in effect, but you can use the Effective Permissions feature in NTFS to determine the permissions being applied to a specific user or group (Principal).

NTFS is all about rules, and they are applied thoroughly by the file system. Wrongly applied settings, often combined with default inheritance, can spread a wrongly configured setting across hundreds of files instantly. Unlike most operations, there is no undo option.

If you simply cannot decipher which NTFS settings are creating the problems, or if the problems are too complex or widespread, you could try to reset the file and folder permissions by using the ICACLs command-line utility.

This is especially useful if you get locked out of files and folders due to incorrect or deleted NTFS permissions.

To reset permissions using ICACLS, follow these steps.

1. Log on to your computer, using an administrator user account.
2. Open File Explorer and navigate to the folder that is giving you the problems.
3. On the File Explorer menu, click File and then click Open Windows PowerShell As Administrator.
4. Accept UAC if prompted.
5. Type **icacls * /RESET /T /C /Q**.

The process of resetting files and folders to their default settings is very quick. After the original operating system defaults have been applied, you can configure the desired settings.

Troubleshoot dynamic access control

If you use an Active Directory domain-based environment, your administrator might have deployed dynamic access control (DAC), a new way to implement a very robust method of applying data governance across resources stored in AD DS file servers.

DAC helps organizations control and audit data access by enabling you to set access controls on files and folders, based on conditions that are retrieved from Active Directory. If DAC is enabled, you see the condition statements being applied in the permission entry dialog box relating to the file or folder under review.

> *NEED MORE REVIEW?* **INTRODUCING DYNAMIC ACCESS CONTROL**
>
> **To read more information about the steps required to enable DAC in a domain-based environment, visit TechNet at** *http://social.technet.microsoft.com/wiki/contents/articles/14269 .introducing-dynamic-access-control.aspx.*

Troubleshoot data recovery

When data is deleted or lost due to hardware failure, you will often look to the current backup and restore from disk or from the cloud. Both of these solutions are slow (though often much quicker than the older method, which involved magnetic tape drives). It can take less than a second to delete a thousand files, and yet to restore them from the traditional methods can take a great deal longer. For the recovery of data from Windows 7 backups, Windows 10 retains the traditional Backup And Restore (Windows 7) tool.

In a fast-paced, mobile world, users require a more agile and self-service model of recovering files that might become corrupt.

Consider using tools such as the Previous Versions feature, which enables you to restore files to a previous state instantly and empowers users to recover files without calling the help desk.

Another restorative tool that works particularly well when a system becomes corrupted or infected with a virus or malware is to use System Restore, located on the System Protection tab of System Properties in Control Panel. The System Restore feature is disabled by default and cannot repair or restore corrupted files and folders or NTFS permissions, only the system state and registry.

Some of the advancements developed for the data center have also migrated to Windows 10. You can now employ features such as Storage Spaces, which allow for local data resilience, and the new ReFS, which offers file healing and protection features.

A trend that is likely to continue is to use the cloud to decouple data from a device and place it in the data center, where it should be more secure and significantly more resilient to hardware failures. OneDrive enables you to do this at a user level and to synchronize changes made to resources in the cloud.

Recover BitLocker encrypted drives

If you encrypt your device or hard drive by using BitLocker and use a Microsoft account, you can specify that BitLocker saves a recovery key to your Microsoft account that is located in your OneDrive. If you become locked out of your device, perhaps because you moved the hard drive to another computer, and you need to obtain your saved BitLocker recovery key, follow these steps.

1. Open an Internet browser.

2. Navigate to *https://onedrive.live.com/recoverykey* and sign in with your Microsoft account.

    The Recovery keys for all your BitLocker-protected drives will be available.

EXAM TIP

Remember the URL for locating the BitLocker recovery key, *https://onedrive.live.com /recoverykey*. **In an enterprise environment, you can use Active Directory or the Microsoft BitLocker Administration And Monitoring (MBAM) tool to help you administer and manage BitLocker deployment and key recovery in enterprise environments.**

Summary

- SMB facilitates shares over the network by using SMB v 3.11.
- Share permissions are effective through shares and NTFS and are applicable to files and folders locally and when shared.
- Public folders, HomeGroups, and simple folder sharing are useful for home-user and small networks to enable file sharing.
- Windows 10 supports Type 4 printer-class drivers, which are more secure and easier to share and maintain. OEMs can install device management software in Device Stage.

- OneDrive is a free, cloud-based, consumer-oriented file storage service that is built into Windows 10 and used by many other operating systems through the OneDrive app.

- OneDrive Fetch Files On Your PC enables you to access locally stored files from the OneDrive web portal.

- Effective Permissions is useful to determine the permissions a particular user would have through NTFS permissions.

- The OneDrive Recycle Bin and Undo Delete feature enable you to recover deleted files.

- User Rights assignments affect what users can do to a system, and Security Permissions affects which access permissions a user has.

- For home and small-business users, BitLocker recovery keys are stored in their Microsoft account at *https://onedrive.live.com/recoverykey*.

Thought experiment

In this thought experiment, demonstrate your skills and knowledge of the topics covered in this chapter. You can find answers to this thought experiment in the next section.

You are helping a small consulting business configure its file and folder strategy. Eleven employees work from a single office, which also acts as a technology center, home to a showcase demonstration area and meeting rooms. The company is still in the startup growth phase, and financial resources are restricted. It currently does not use a domain environment, but its location has excellent Internet access and uses the cloud extensively for email, Dropbox, and OneDrive. All devices use Windows 10 Pro with Microsoft accounts, and no dedicated IT support is available.

You need to ensure that the company can share files and folders in a cost-effective way.

Answer the following questions on behalf of the company.

1. The staff members have personal experience using OneDrive. How could they use OneDrive in the small company?

2. Employees need to have access to their data resources when not connected to the Internet. How would OneDrive help them?

3. In the demonstration area, a Windows tablet is used as a media playback device. It is configured to play a slideshow of all media files within a specified directory on the local drive. How would you ensure that this device has the latest media content available at all times?

4. The owner has concerns about using OneDrive for storing business resources and the long-term viability of using OneDrive. Should he be concerned?

Thought experiment answer

This section contains the solution to the thought experiment.

1. Each employee could continue to use OneDrive and create a folder to contain their work files, which could then be shared among the employees as required. Alternatively, the owner/manager could create folders in the company OneDrive and then share the folders (with edit permissions) with the staff to create, store, and synchronize resources.

2. The employees could configure the OneDrive app settings to synchronize their local devices with the files and folders they use. They could then work on these files; the files would then synchronize automatically when the users were connected to the Internet.

3. Answers might vary. You could use OneDrive. Create a shared folder stored on OneDrive to contain the media. Employees can then add new content to this media folder in OneDrive. Configure the media playback device to synchronize only with this folder.

4. Answers might vary. OneDrive is aimed at the consumer audience. The data stored in OneDrive is encrypted and therefore secure from unauthorized access. Employees should be granted access to only the shared resources they require. The default amount of space per OneDrive account is 5 GB, which is likely to be exhausted quickly, but this can be increased for a small monthly fee. As the company increases in size, the complexity of managing resource permissions on OneDrive could become onerous. The company should then consider using Office 365 or OneDrive For Business.

CHAPTER 9

Implement Apps

Without apps, a computer is merely an electronic device of little practical use. However, after you install apps, the computer becomes almost infinitely useful. It is therefore important to know how to install, configure, and maintain apps on devices running Windows 10.

Windows 10 supports both desktop apps and Windows Store Apps. These two types of apps are installed and managed differently. Desktop apps tend to be large and complex, multipurpose software programs and are typically designed for desktop computers and laptop computers.

Windows Store Apps are designed to be used across multiple platforms, including on desktops and laptops and, more significantly, on smaller touch devices such as phones and tablets. Many of these Windows Store Apps are small and focused, designed to perform a single or small subset of tasks.

As an IT professional, you will be expected to implement and configure both desktop and Windows Store Apps for your users across all their devices. You will also be required to know how to configure Windows features and manage application startup behavior in Windows 10.

Skills covered in this chapter:

- Configure desktop apps
- Configure app startup options
- Configure Windows features
- Implement Windows Store Apps
- Create and deploy provisioning packages

Skill: Configure desktop apps

Most users are very familiar with desktop apps, such as Microsoft Office 2016, and might have many years' experience using them. Desktop apps are designed to run on more traditional computers, such as desktop and laptop computers, and might have fairly significant requirements in terms of the computer's memory, processor, and, possibly, graphics subsystem.

> **This section covers how to:**
> - Install desktop apps
> - Uninstall or change a desktop app

Install desktop apps

There are a number of ways to install desktop apps. These include:

- Installing the app interactively by using the .exe or .msi installer file that is provided on the product media, for example, a vendor-supplied DVD.

- Using automatic app deployment methods such as the Microsoft Deployment Toolkit (MDT) or System Center 2012 R2 Configuration Manager.

- Implementing an Active Directory Domain Services (AD DS) Group Policy Object (GPO)–based deployment method.

- Building the required apps into a desktop computer image for deployment, enabling you to deploy the required apps at the same time that you deploy Windows 10.

The method you choose depends largely on the number of computers you must deploy the app to.

Install desktop apps interactively

To perform an interactive desktop app installation, insert the product DVD into your Windows 10–based computer and, typically, Windows prompts you for the next step by raising the Choose What To Do With This Disc dialog box, as shown in Figure 9-1. Normally, you would click Run Setup.exe and then follow the on-screen instructions the vendor provided. It is also possible to copy the installation files from a product DVD and place them in a shared folder on a Windows Server and then, from a Windows 10–based client computer, map a network drive and run Setup.exe.

FIGURE 9-1 The Choose What To Do With This Disc dialog box, after inserting the Microsoft Office 2013 product DVD.

If your app is packaged as an .msi installer file rather than as an .exe file, the Windows Installer service manages the app installation and configuration. You can use .msi installer packages to install apps locally, but you can also use automatic deployment methods to add, repair, or uninstall an app by using the installer package. In addition, .msi installer packages generally provide superior app removal to those that use an .exe installer.

> **NOTE** **SILENT INSTALLATION**
>
> You can often silently install apps that use an .msi installer. This means that little or no user input is required to complete installation.

You can use the Msiexec.exe command from an elevated command prompt to perform desktop app installations. For example, the following command installs an app from the \\LON-SVR1\Apps shared folder.

```
Msiexec.exe /i \\LON-SVR1\Apps\desktop-app.msi
```

> **NEED MORE REVIEW?** **MSIEXEC.EXE (COMMAND-LINE OPTIONS)**
>
> To review further details about using Msiexec.exe, refer to the Microsoft TechNet website at *https://technet.microsoft.com/library/cc759262(v=ws.10).aspx*.

Install desktop apps automatically

If you have many computers to configure, performing interactive installations of desktop apps quickly becomes infeasible. In these situations, consider using an automated method to deploy your desktop apps. You can choose from a number of automated deployment methods, based on your IT infrastructure and your organizational needs.

USING GPOS TO DEPLOY APPS

Using GPOs to deploy apps offers a relatively simple method for automating desktop app deployment. However, there are a number of requirements. These are that:

- The target computers must be members of an AD DS domain.
- Your apps must be available as .msi installer packages.

When you use GPOs to deploy your apps, you can target the app deployment to container objects in your AD DS environment: site, domain, or organizational unit (OU). By using GPO filtering, you can also deploy apps to specific users or computers, perhaps by creating Windows Management Instrumentation (WMI) filters that target specific computers based on their hardware or software characteristics.

There are two deployment types that you can use when considering GPOs. These are:

- **Assign** Assigned apps are automatically installed. If you assign an app to a user, the app is installed when the user signs in. If you assign the app to that computer, it is installed when the computer starts.

- **Publish** Published apps can be installed by the user from Control Panel in Programs And Features. You can only publish apps to users, not to computers.

However, GPO deployment has a number of potential drawbacks, such as:

- **No scheduling capability** Your apps deploy the next time a GPO refresh occurs.

- **No reporting function** It is not easy to verify successful deployment of or updates to your apps.

If you have a very large number of computers, or a range of device types and users' needs, GPO-based deployment can be difficult to target correctly, and it is harder to maintain apps by using GPOs in these more complex organizations.

> *NEED MORE REVIEW?* **GROUP POLICY SOFTWARE INSTALLATION OVERVIEW**
>
> To review further details about using GPOs to deploy apps, refer to the Microsoft TechNet website at *https://technet.microsoft.com/library/cc738858(v=ws.10).aspx.*

USING MDT TO DEPLOY APPS

One alternative to using GPOs is to use MDT to deploy your apps. MDT uses a lite-touch installation (LTI) process to enable you to deploy Windows 10 and associated apps. Using MDT requires more specialized technical skills that using GPOs, but it is not overly complex.

> *NOTE:* **ZERO-TOUCH INSTALLATION**
>
> You can use MDT in conjunction with Configuration Manager to perform zero-touch installation (ZTI) of Windows 10 and associated apps in your organization.

To perform LTI deployments of apps using MDT, you need a management computer on which to install the MDT components and associated images. You also need a reference computer; this computer provides a source image that is used during the deployment process. To create your reference computer:

1. Create an MDT task sequence (a set of MDT instructions) and a boot image for the reference computer.

   This boot image contains the required elements of MDT, including the task sequence and related files.

2. Start the reference computer.

 The required elements are transferred to the reference computer.

3. Deploy Windows 10 and the required desktop apps to the reference computer.

4. Capture an image of the reference computer.

You now have a source image built from your reference computer, based on Windows 10 and including your organization's apps. Complete the following procedure to deploy the image to your target computers.

1. Copy the captured image to the management computer (with MDT installed).

2. Use MDT to create a new boot image and task sequence for the target computers.

3. Start the target computers.

 The required elements are transferred to the target computer.

4. Run the Windows Deployment Wizard to deploy the previously captured image.

> ***NEED MORE REVIEW?*** **DEPLOY WINDOWS 10 WITH THE MICROSOFT DEPLOYMENT TOOLKIT**
>
> **To review further details about using the MDT to deploy Windows 10 and desktop apps, refer to the Microsoft TechNet website at** *https://technet.microsoft.com/itpro/windows /deploy/deploy-windows-10-with-the-microsoft-deployment-toolkit.*

USING CONFIGURATION MANAGER TO DEPLOY APPS

For very large organizations, or those with complex and diverse operating system and app deployment requirements, consider using Configuration Manager to deploy apps. You can use Configuration Manager to target deployments to groups of users or computers. You can also schedule your deployments.

To use Configuration Manager, first install the Configuration Manager client on your computers. Using Configuration Manager provides a number of advantages over previous automated deployment methods, as shown in Table 9-1.

TABLE 9-1 Benefits of using Configuration Manager to deploy apps

Feature	Benefits
Collections	These consist of manually created groups of users or computers, or the results of queries of user or computer properties. This enables you to target your deployments very specifically.
Multiple deployment methods	Configure a single app deployment but provide for multiple deployment methods, depending on configured conditions. This enables you to configure an app to install locally if a user is logged on to his or her primary device but, otherwise, to stream as an App-V app if the user is logged on to a secondary device. You can also use this feature to target 32-bit and 64-bit variants of apps to the appropriate platform.

Feature	Benefits
Reporting	This enables you to verify how successful an app deployment was after it has finished. You can also perform app deployment simulations to see what the implication of a planned deployment might be.
Wake on LAN	To minimize interruptions to users, you can schedule deployments to operate during nonbusiness hours and then have the target devices woken prior to deployment.
Inventory	This enables you to gather and maintain a software inventory of your organization's deployed apps.

Using Configuration Manager does require more IT infrastructure and more specialized IT skills for personnel involved in planning and performing app deployment.

> **NEED MORE REVIEW? HOW TO DEPLOY APPLICATIONS IN CONFIGURATION MANAGER**
>
> To review further details about deploying apps with Configuration Manager, refer to the Microsoft TechNet website at *https://technet.microsoft.com/library/gg682082.aspx*.

> **NOTE PLAN FOR APP DEPLOYMENT IN MICROSOFT INTUNE**
>
> You can also use Microsoft Intune to automate deployment of your desktop app deployments. However, to use Microsoft Intune, you must first deploy the Microsoft Intune client to your organization's computers. For further information, refer to the Microsoft TechNet website at *https://technet.microsoft.com/library/dn646955.aspx*.

Uninstall or change a desktop app

To uninstall a desktop app, change components in an app, or repair an app, open Control Panel and then click Programs And Features, as shown in Figure 9-2. You can then locate the appropriate app, right-click it, and choose from the available options. These typically include Uninstall, Change, and, sometimes, Repair. The available options vary according to the installation method used to deploy the apps.

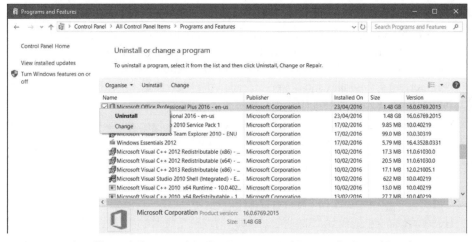

FIGURE 9-2 Uninstalling a desktop app by using Programs And Features in Control Panel

> **NOTE** **REMOVING APPS DEPLOYED WITH GPOS**
>
> If you deployed apps using GPOs, you can also remove or even upgrade them by using the same GPOs. For further information, refer to the Microsoft TechNet website at *https://technet.microsoft.com/library/cc728016(v=ws.10).aspx*.

Skill: Configure app startup options

The ability to start a computer quickly is important to most users. Windows 10 has a number of features designed to help the operating system start more quickly than some earlier versions of Windows. It is important to know how to manage these startup settings to optimize Windows startup times.

Many apps have additional components that run in the background to perform automatic updates or provide user notifications of app-related events. These components initialize during startup and, in addition to consuming system resources, they can have an impact on how fast Windows 10 can start. It is therefore important to know how to manage these components.

> **This section covers how to:**
>
> - Control Windows 10 Fast Startup
> - Configure app startup behavior

Control Windows 10 Fast Startup

Fast Startup is a Windows 10 feature that enables Windows 10 to start more quickly. The feature achieves this by combining some of the features of Windows 10 hibernation with standard shutdown features. In essence, a hybrid hibernate/shutdown is achieved, with elements of important system files and drivers stored in the Hiberfil.sys file and used to initiate the computer more quickly during startup.

To control Windows 10 startup properly, it might be necessary to access your computer's UEFI firmware settings. In Windows 10, this is fairly straightforward. Use the following procedure.

1. Click Start and then click Settings.

2. Click Update & Security and then click Recovery.

3. Under Advanced Start-Up, click Restart Now.

4. Your computer starts in recovery mode. Click Troubleshoot when prompted.

5. Click Advanced Options, click UEFI Firmware Settings, and then click Restart.

6. The procedure now varies according to the hardware vendor of your computer, but in the UEFI settings, look for and, if necessary, enable Fast Boot or Fast Startup. Save your UEFI settings and then exit; restart your computer.

After you have verified that Fast Startup is enabled in your computer hardware, you can then configure the setting in Windows 10. To do this, complete the following procedure.

1. From Settings, click System and then click Power & Sleep.

2. On the Power & Sleep tab, click Additional Power Settings.

3. In the Power Options dialog box, click Choose What The Power Buttons Do.

4. In the System Settings dialog box, click Change Settings That Are Currently Unavailable.

5. Under Shut-Down Settings, select the Turn On Fast Start-Up (Recommended) check box, as shown in Figure 9-3, and then click Save Changes.

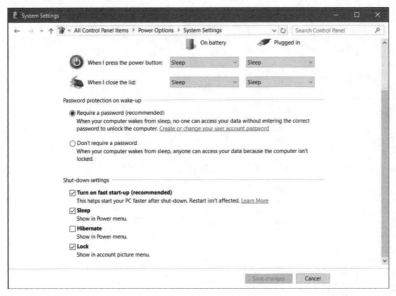

FIGURE 9-3 Configuring Fast Startup in System Settings in Power Options

NEED MORE REVIEW? **HOW TO DEPLOY APPLICATIONS IN CONFIGURATION MANAGER**

You can also use GPOs to configure Fast Startup in Windows 10. To review further details about using GPOs to configure Fast Startup, refer to the Microsoft TechNet website at *https://blogs.technet.microsoft.com/keithmayer/2012/11/05/supporting-windows-8-fast -startup-with-group-policy/.*

Configure app startup behavior

In addition to controlling Fast Start-up, you can also improve system startup time by controlling the apps that load during startup. A simple way to view and edit app startup behavior is to use Task Manager, as shown in Figure 9-4.

On the Start-up tab, you can see that each background app running is assessed for its impact on startup. This impact is reported as None, Low, Medium, or High. If you decide that an app's impact is too high, you can right-click the app and then click Disable. This prevents the app from running at startup.

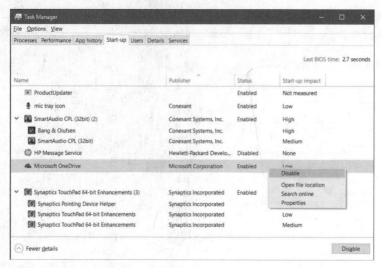

FIGURE 9-4 The Start-up tab in Task Manager

You can also view the startup information for apps in the system registry. Open the Registry Editor (Regedit.exe) and navigate to the following two registry keys.

- HKEY_CURRENT_USER\SOFTWARE\Microsoft\Windows\CurrentVersion\Run   contains the apps configured to start for a particular signed-in user.

- HKEY_LOCAL_MACHINE\SOFTWARE\Microsoft\Windows\CurrentVersion\Run, as shown in Figure 9-5, contains the apps configured to start for any signed-in user.

From each of these keys, in the results pane, you can delete the listed values to prevent the associated app from running at startup. However, you should exercise caution when editing the registry unless you are comfortable with the attendant risks of making a mistake.

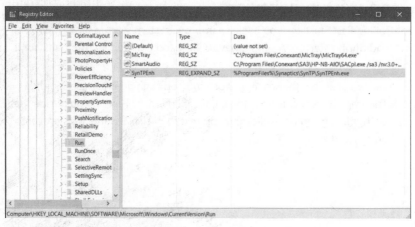

FIGURE 9-5 The Run key in the Registry

Skill: Configure Windows features

Windows 10 provides many features and components, not all of which are enabled by default. For example, the Client Hyper-V feature and related components are disabled by default. You can use the Settings app, Control Panel, or command-line tools to add to and remove features and components from Windows 10.

To add or remove features in Windows 10, from Settings, click System and then click the Apps & Features tab. You can see a list of installed apps, but at the bottom of this list, click the link for Programs And Features. The Control Panel Programs And Features app loads.

In Programs And Features, click Turn Windows Features On Or Off. The Turn Windows Features On Or Off dialog box appears. As shown in Figure 9-6, you can select which optional components you want to install by clicking the appropriate component. When you have finished your selection, click OK. The components and features you selected are installed.

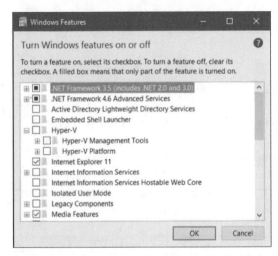

FIGURE 9-6 Adding components to Windows 10 with the Turn Windows Features On Or Off dialog box

In addition to using the Settings app, you can also enable and disable Windows features by using either Windows PowerShell or the Dism.exe command-line tool. For example, to install the Client Hyper-V components on your computer, from the Windows PowerShell Admin prompt, type the following cmdlet and press Enter.

```
Enable-WindowsOptionalFeature -Online -FeatureName Microsoft-Hyper-V -All
```

To remove features, use the Disable-WindowsOptionalFeature cmdlet.

> **NEED MORE REVIEW? ENABLE-WINDOWSOPTIONALFEATURE**
>
> To review further details about using Windows PowerShell to manage Windows features, refer to the Microsoft TechNet website at *https://technet.microsoft.com/library/hh852172 .aspx*.

To use the Dism.exe command-line tool, from an elevated command prompt, run the following command.

```
DISM /Online /Enable-Feature /All /FeatureName:Microsoft-Hyper-V
```

> **NEED MORE REVIEW? DEPLOYMENT IMAGE SERVICING AND MANAGEMENT TECHNI-CAL REFERENCE FOR WINDOWS**
>
> To review further details about using Dism.exe, refer to the Microsoft TechNet website at *https://technet.microsoft.com/library/hh824822.aspx*.

Skill: Implement Windows Store Apps

Windows Store Apps are designed to be more focused on one or a small subset of tasks and are usually optimized for a specific device type, tablet, phone, or desktop computer, for example. The recent proliferation of these small, task-focused apps, and of the app stores used to deliver them, raises challenges for IT support staff. Because your users want to be able to use these apps across all their devices, it is important to know how to configure your Windows 10–based devices to support the use of these new apps properly.

> **This section covers how to:**
> - Manage Windows Store Apps
> - Configure Windows Store App settings
> - Sideload apps
> - Distribute apps by using Windows Store for Business

Manage Windows Store Apps

The Windows Store provides a single point of access for your users to browse, download, and install their apps, including both kinds of desktop apps, such as Office and Windows Store Apps.

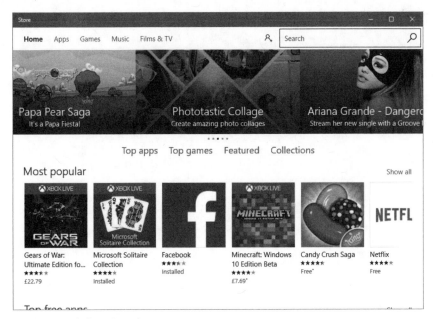

FIGURE 9-7 Windows Store home page

Install apps

When users access the Windows Store, they land on the home page, as shown in Figure 9-7. Installing apps is simple. A user clicks a desired app and then clicks a button to install the app. The button might be labeled Free or Trial or appear with a price if the app is not free. When the app is installed, a tile appears in the All Apps list on Start.

EXAM TIP

In Windows 8.1, users' apps synchronized across their devices without action on their part. In Windows 10, users must manually install their apps across their devices.

Update apps

By default, Windows 10 checks for app updates daily. Again, by default, Windows 10 automatically updates any apps for which updates are available. If you do not want Windows 10 to update Windows Store Apps automatically, complete the following procedure.

1. Open the Windows Store.

2. Near the Search box at the top of the window, click the account symbol and then click Settings.

3. As shown in Figure 9-8, under App Updates, turn off Update Apps Automatically.

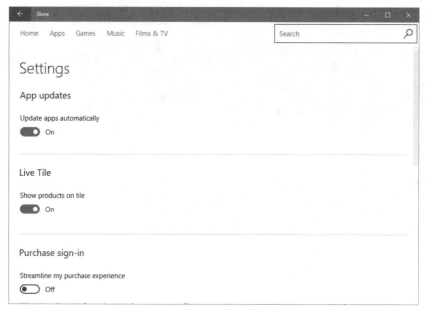

FIGURE 9-8 Disabling Windows Store automatic app updates

After you have disabled automatic app updates, you might want to update apps manually. To do this, perform the following procedure.

1. In the Windows Store, near the Search box at the top of the window, click the account symbol and then click Downloads And Updates.

2. All apps with pending updates appear. You can tap or click Update All. Alternatively, you can select which apps to update manually.

EXAM TIP

Although users do not need a Microsoft account to access the Windows Store, they must sign in with their Microsoft account to download and install apps.

Configure Windows Store App settings

There is a number of settings you can use to customize Windows Store App settings. The first of these controls is where Windows 10 saves Windows Store Apps.

To configure the default file save location for Windows Store Apps, from Settings, click System. On the Storage tab, in the results pane, under New Apps Will Save To, click the appropriate storage location, as shown in Figure 9-9.

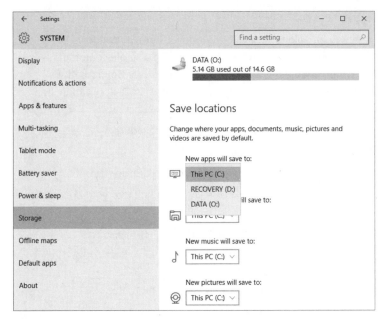

FIGURE 9-9 Configuring the Storage location for new Windows Store Apps

If you want to move existing Windows Store Apps to a new storage location, in the System settings app, click the Apps & Features tab and then locate and click the appropriate Windows Store App. As shown in Figure 9-10, click Move to specify a new location for the app.

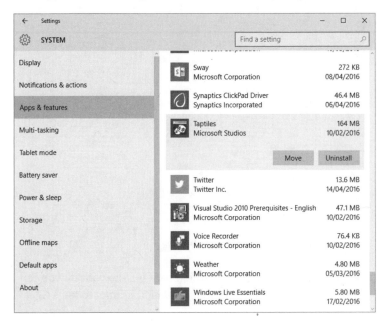

FIGURE 9-10 Changing the Storage location for an existing Windows Store app

Block the Windows Store App

If you do not want your users to be able to access the Windows Store, in Windows 10 Enterprise, you can use GPOs to block the Windows Store App. On a single computer, using the Local Group Policy Editor, enable the following GPO value: User Configuration\Administrative Templates\Windows Components\Store\Turn off the Store application, as shown in Figure 9-11.

To do this in a domain environment, complete the following procedure.

1. Open Group Policy Management on a domain controller.

2. Navigate to the appropriate AD DS container, for example, your domain.

3. Open an existing GPO for editing or create a new GPO and link it to your chosen container and open for editing.

4. Navigate to the User Configuration\Policies\Administrative Templates \Windows Components\Store folder and open the Turn Off The Store Application value.

5. Enable the value, click OK, and close Group Policy Management.

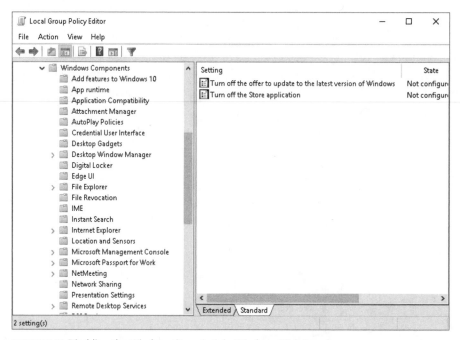

FIGURE 9-11 Disabling the Windows Store App in Windows 10 Enterprise

For the policy to be effective, users must sign out and sign back in. Alternatively, you can issue the Gpupdate.exe /force command from an elevated command prompt to force GPO propagation.

Sideload apps

Many organizations now develop and use Windows Store Apps. One way to make these apps available to your users is to sideload them. *Sideloading* is a technique by which the app is installed without requiring access to the Windows Store.

When you sideload an app, you must have an .appx installer file for your app.

EXAM TIP

Windows Store Apps must be digitally signed by a certificate authority that your users' computers trust. This includes apps that you internally develop and deploy.

After you have created and packaged your app, you can use either the Dism.exe tool or Windows PowerShell to sideload and manage your custom apps. To sideload an app, use the following procedure.

1. Open Settings and click Update & Security.

2. On the For Developers tab, select Sideload Apps, as shown in Figure 9-12.

3. In the Use Developer Features dialog box, click Yes.

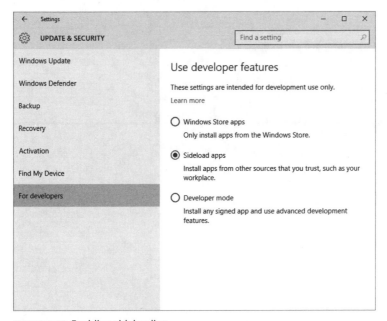

FIGURE 9-12 Enabling sideloading

4. After you have enabled sideloading, open Windows PowerShell.

5. Run the add-appxpackage PATH\your_app.appx cmdlet, where *PATH\your_app.appx* is replaced with the specific path and file name for your app.

Distribute apps by using Windows Store for Business

Although sideloading apps is relatively straightforward, it is perhaps not the best way to distribute custom or line-of-business (LOB) apps in your organization. Consequently, Microsoft has introduced the Windows Store for Business.

The Windows Store for Business provides you with a means to distribute your LOB apps more easily and consistently to users' devices within your organization. This enables you to manage and maintain these custom apps in the same way as you do commercially available apps from the Windows Store.

As shown in Figure 9-13, you can also create a private store so that users in your organization can easily view, download, and install your LOB apps.

FIGURE 9-13 Using a private store in the Windows Store for Business

> **NEED MORE REVIEW?** **WINDOWS STORE FOR BUSINESS**
>
> To review further details about Windows Store for Business, refer to the Microsoft TechNet website at *https://technet.microsoft.com/itpro/windows/manage/windows-store-for-business*.

Skill: Create and deploy provisioning packages

Although you can use the manual procedures outlined earlier in this chapter to deploy apps, for large numbers of target devices, it makes sense to try to deploy apps by using packaging and deployment tools. Windows 10 includes the ability to create and use provisioning packages.

Using provisioning packages offers benefits enabling you to:

- Configure devices quickly without needing new deployment images.
- Configure user-owned devices without needing to implement Multiple Device Management (MDM).
- Configure multiple devices simultaneously.
- Configure devices that are not connected to the corporate network.

You can use provisioning packages to perform a number of management tasks, including the following.

- **Deploy apps**   You can deploy both Windows apps and line-of-business apps.
- **Enroll devices into MDM**   You can enroll devices in Microsoft Intune or a non-Microsoft MDM service.
- **Distribute certificates**   You can distribute a root CA certificate or client certificates your organization requires.
- **Configure and deploy connectivity profiles**   You can distribute Wi-Fi, email, and VPN profiles.
- **Apply device policies**   Your policies might include settings for controlling device lock, password restrictions, encryption settings, and update settings.

> **This section covers how to:**
> - Create provisioning packages
> - Apply provisioning packages

Create provisioning packages

To create provisioning packages, you can use the Windows Imaging And Configuration Designer (ICD) tool. To use this tool, you must first install the Windows Assessment And Deployment Kit (Windows ADK).

> **NOTE   DOWNLOAD WINDOWS ADK**
>
> **You can download the Windows ADK from the Microsoft website at** *http://go.microsoft.com /fwlink/p/?LinkId=526740*.

After downloading the Windows ADK, run the setup program (ADKsetup.exe) and choose the following components.

- Deployment tools
- Windows Preinstallation Environment (Windows PE)
- Windows Imaging And Configuration Designer (ICD)
- Windows User State Migration Tool (USMT)

Complete the installation process, and then you are ready to create and deploy your provisioning packages. Start by opening Windows ICD. On the Start page, shown in Figure 9-14, click New Provisioning Package.

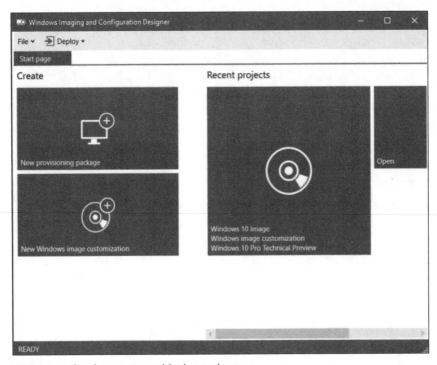

FIGURE 9-14 Creating a new provisioning package

Use the following procedure to create your provisioning package.

1. In the New Project Wizard, on the Enter Project Details page, in the Name box, type the name for your provisioning package and a meaningful description. For example, type **Desktop apps** and then click Next.

2. On the Choose Which Settings To View And Configure page, choose whether the package is applicable to all Windows editions, only to desktop editions, only to mobile editions, or to IoT editions and then click Next.

3. On the Import A Provisioning Package (Optional) page, click Finish.

On the Available Customizations page, shown in Figure 9-15, expand Deployment Assets and Runtime Settings.

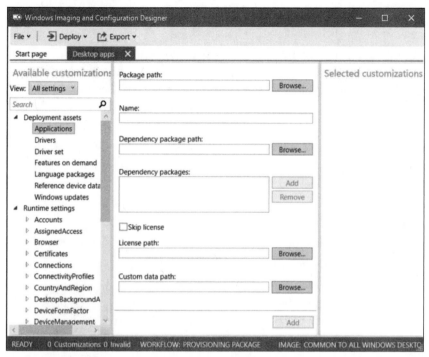

FIGURE 9-15 Available customizations for your package

You can now choose which customizations you want to make from those available in the navigation pane. To create an application provisioning package, use the following procedure.

1. In Windows ICD, on the Available Customizations page, in the navigation pane, expand Deployment Assets and then click Applications.

2. Next to Package Path, click Browse and locate the .appx or .appxbundle package that you want to deploy.

3. In the Name box, type a meaningful name for your package.

4. If your app requires dependencies, specify those by locating the path to the .appx or .appxbundle dependency packages.

5. If you don't have or do not want a license file for your app, select the Skip License check box; otherwise, use License Path to define the location for your license file.

6. When you are ready, click Add.

You have created a customization for your app. You are now ready to deploy this customization by applying the provisioning package.

Apply provisioning packages

To apply a provisioning package, you must start by exporting the package. To export your provisioning package, in the Windows ICD, use the following procedure.

1. Click Export and then click Provisioning Package.

2. In the Build Wizard, on the Describe The Provisioning Package page, the Name box is already complete with the name you specified earlier. You can now specify version numbers and vendor information. Complete this information and then click Next.

3. On the Select Security Details For The Provisioning Package page, choose whether you want to encrypt or sign your package, or both, and then click Next. To sign your package, you must have an appropriate digital certificate that users of your package trust.

4. On the Select Where To Save The Provisioning Package page, specify where you want to store the package and then click Next.

5. On the Build The Provisioning Package page, click Build. Your provisioning package is exported to your specified location.

6. The All Done page appears, showing you where the package is located. Click Finish.

You can now apply the package in one of two ways.

- **Deployment time** You can apply any provisioning packages as part of a Windows image. You can then distribute the image to target devices. In this way, you deploy apps at the same time as Windows 10. Refer to Chapter 1, "Prepare for installation requirements," for further information on how to use Windows ICD to create Windows 10 images.

- **Runtime** Use this option to distribute the package to devices already running Windows 10. Make the package file available and then instruct users to run the package file. For example, distribute the package file by email or place the package file in a shared folder.

> *NEED MORE REVIEW?* **BUILD AND APPLY A PROVISIONING PACKAGE**
>
> To review further details about provisioning packages, refer to the Microsoft MSDN website at *https://msdn.microsoft.com/library/windows/hardware/dn916107(v=vs.85).aspx*.

Summary

- Although you can install desktop apps manually by using product DVDs, you can choose between several methods and technologies to deploy the apps to multiple computers.

- Windows 10 is optimized to start quickly, but you can enable Fast Startup and configure the startup behavior of apps to improve startup times further.

- You can add and remove Windows features by using the Settings app and by using either Windows PowerShell or the Dism.exe command-line tool.

- You have extensive control over the configuration of Windows Store Apps and can use sideloading or the Windows Store for Business to manage your organization's LOB apps.

- You can deploy apps by using provisioning packages, either as part of a Windows 10 deployment image or subsequently to deployed Windows 10 devices.

Thought experiment

In this thought experiment, demonstrate your skills and knowledge of the topics covered in this chapter. You can find answers to this thought experiment in the next section.

Windows 10 is about to be deployed throughout your organization. You must now consider strategies for how best to implement apps for your users. Users require access to a number of desktop apps, including Microsoft Office 2016. Many users also want to be able to download and install Windows Store Apps for their Windows 10–based devices. Finally, your IT manager has been discussing the feasibility of making the sales-tracking app available to your users. Only the sales team uses this small, task-focused app.

As a consultant for A. Datum Corporation, answer the following questions about the app deployment within the A. Datum organization.

1. You have 1,000 Windows 10–based desktop computers that require Microsoft Office 2016. How will you deal with this?

2. You want to deploy a subset of A. Datum's required apps to several hundred computers after Windows 10 has been deployed. What technologies could you use to assist in this?

3. How might you make the Sales app available to your users?

4. After deploying the required apps to your users' devices and computers, you begin to receive complaints about slow startup times. What can you do to improve startup times?

5. You have a line-of-business app that users in your Sales department need to access. How might you achieve that without using the Windows Store for Business?

Thought experiment answer

This section contains the solution to the thought experiment.

1. Ideally, the Windows 10 desktop image used to deploy Windows 10 can be customized to include all the required desktop apps. Then, deployment of both Windows 10 and the desktop apps can be performed in a single step.

2. You could consider using either MDT or Configuration Manager to deploy your apps to the target group of computers. Although you could use GPOs to target this

deployment, it is not the most efficient way to deploy and maintain apps in a large enterprise network.

3. Assuming that the Sales app is a Windows Store App, you could sideload the app onto the required computers. You could also consider signing up for the Windows Store for Business and creating a private store for the distribution of this type of LOB app.

4. You could verify that all devices are configured through their UEFI firmware to enable Fast Boot/Fast Startup. After that, verify that Fast Startup is enabled in the appropriate Windows 10 power plan. Finally, if the previous actions do not resolve the startup time issues, consider checking whether any apps that initialize during startup have an excessive effect on startup time. Use the Task Manager Start-up tab for this solution.

5. Consider using a provisioning package that contains the customization for your line-of-business app. Then, you could export the provisioning package and distribute the resultant package by using a GPO to your Sales users' devices.

CHAPTER 10

Configure remote management

When you have a large number of computers to manage, or a workforce that uses their devices in a number of locations, it is important to be able to manage those computers by using remote management tools.

As a result, the 70-698 Configuring Windows exam includes objectives on choosing the appropriate remote management tools and knowing how to use those tools to manage your organization's devices and computers.

Skills covered in this chapter:

- Choosing the appropriate remote management tools
- Configuring remote management settings
- Configuring Remote Assistance
- Configuring Remote Desktop
- Configuring Windows PowerShell remoting
- Modifying settings, using Microsoft Management Console or Windows PowerShell

Skill: Choose the appropriate remote management tools

Windows 10 provides a number of tools that you can use to manage your organization's computers remotely. These include Remote Assistance, Remote Desktop, Windows PowerShell remoting, and many management console snap-ins. Knowing which tools to use to support a given situation helps you address your users' needs more quickly.

> ### This section covers how to:
> - Determine the available remote management tools in Windows 10
> - Select the appropriate remote management tool for a given situation

Remote management tools in Windows 10

You can use a variety of tools to manage Windows 10 devices remotely. Table 10-1 shows the available remote management tools in Windows 10.

TABLE 10-1 Windows 10 remote management tools

Tool	Purpose
Remote Assistance	A built-in tool that provides for interaction with the remote user. By using Remote Assistance, you can view or take remote control of the user's computer and perform remote management of it. You can also use a text-based chat facility to interact with the user.
Remote Desktop	A built-in tool that you can use to access a computer remotely over the Remote Desktop Protocol (RDP). In the past, users often accessed their computers from other locations by using Remote Desktop. Security concerns and the adoption of mobile devices have made this a less common use of this tool. However, you can also use Remote Desktop to manage a remote computer. It does not provide for user interaction and requires the user of the computer to sign out before you can access the computer remotely.
Windows PowerShell	Windows PowerShell is a powerful command-line management tool and scripting environment. You can use it to perform virtually any management function in Windows 10. You can also use Windows PowerShell to manage remote computers. This is known as Windows PowerShell remoting.
Microsoft Management Console	Microsoft Management Console (MMC) is an extensible interface for management applications in both Windows clients and Windows Server. To perform management by using MMC, a specific tool for the management task, known as a snap-in, is loaded into the console. For example, to perform management of disks and attached storage, you add the Disk Management snap-in to MMC. You can use MMC snap-ins to manage Windows 10 devices remotely by targeting the remote computer from the MMC interface.

Selecting the appropriate remote management tool

Given that a variety of tools is available, it is important to know which one to use in a given situation. When considering the appropriate tool, use the guidance in Table 10-2 to help you make your choice.

TABLE 10-2 Selecting the appropriate Windows 10 remote management tool

Scenario	Tool
User requires help and guidance. For example, you must help the user perform a specific task in an application such as printing, using the appropriate settings.	Remote Assistance
You must perform a single remote management task on a single computer and require no user interaction.	Remote Desktop or MMC
You must perform the same management task on several or many remote computers.	Windows PowerShell
You must perform a remote management task that you have performed many times in the past and expect to perform again in the future.	Windows PowerShell

Scenario	Tool
You are unsure of the nature of a problem a user is experiencing on her computer and wish to investigate computer settings.	Remote Desktop
You want to be able to perform the same management task, using the same management tool on any computer.	MMC

You can see from Table 10-2 that you can sometimes use several methods to address a specific remote management scenario. It is therefore a question of choosing the most appropriate method. Generally, if you know you will be required to perform the same management task again, on the same or a different computer, it is worth considering Windows PowerShell remoting. If you need to provide user interaction, choose Remote Assistance. After that, it's probably a personal preference of whether you use an MMC snap-in remotely or Remote Desktop.

Skill: Configure remote management settings

Depending on the remote management tool you have decided to use, it is almost certain that you must configure the target computer (the one you wish to manage) and possibly the local management computer (the one you are using) to enable the selected remote management tool. For example, it is common to have to enable the appropriate feature through Windows Firewall to allow for management of a remote Windows 10–based device.

> **This section covers how to:**
> - Configure Windows Firewall to enable remote management
> - Enable remote management through System Properties

Configuring Windows Firewall to enable remote management

To enable remote management through Windows Firewall on a target computer, open Control Panel and complete the following procedure.

1. In Control Panel, click System And Security and then click Windows Firewall.
2. In Windows Firewall, click Allow An App Of Feature Through Windows Firewall.
3. In Allowed Applications, click Change Settings.
4. In the Allowed Apps And Features list, scroll down and select the appropriate management feature.

   For example, as shown in Figure 10-1, select Remote Assistance. This enables the selected management feature on the Private network location profile. If you also wish to allow the remote management feature on Public networks, select the Public check box.

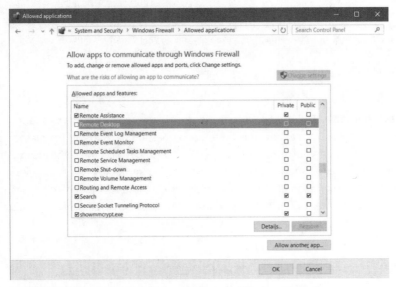

FIGURE 10-1 Allowing Remote Assistance through Windows Firewall

5. Click OK. The available remote management features are:

- Remote Assistance.
- Remote Desktop.
- Remote Event Log Management.
- Remote Event Monitor.
- Remote Scheduled Tasks Management.
- Remote Service Management.
- Remote Shut-down.
- Remote Volume Management.
- Virtual Machine Monitoring.
- Windows Firewall Remote Management.
- Windows Management Instrumentation (WMI).
- Windows Remote Management.
- Windows Remote Management (Compatibility).

It is not always feasible, or especially desirable, to reconfigure these settings manually on each computer to enable the appropriate remote management feature. Instead, in an Active Directory Domain Services (AD DS) environment, you can use Group Policy Objects (GPOs) to configure the desired firewall settings.

Enabling remote management through System Properties

Both Remote Assistance and Remote Desktop can be enabled through the System Properties dialog box, as shown in Figure 10-2. To access these settings, from the Settings app:

1. Click System and then click About.

2. In the details pane, under Related Settings, click System Info.

3. In the System Properties dialog box, click the Remote tab.

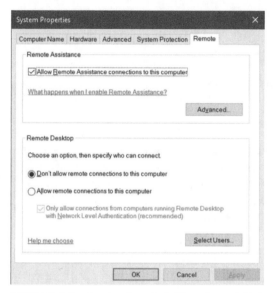

FIGURE 10-2 Configuring Remote Settings through System Properties

Enabling Remote Assistance

To enable Remote Assistance, on the Remote tab of the System Properties dialog box, select the Allow Remote Assistance Connections To This Computer check box. Then, optionally, click Advanced. As shown in Figure 10-3, you can then configure the following additional settings.

- **Allow This Computer To Be Controlled Remotely** This setting enables you to determine whether the person providing remote support can take remote control of the computer or only view the computer desktop. This setting is enabled by default when Remote Assistance is enabled.

- **Set The Maximum Amount Of Time Invitations Can Remain Open** One way of initiating a Remote Assistance session is for the user to invite the support person to connect. This setting defines the validity period of the invitations. The default is 6 hours.

- **Create Invitations That Can Only Be Used From Computers Running Windows Vista Or Later** Windows Vista and later versions of Windows use a superior method of encrypting Remote Assistance network traffic. It is advised to select this option if you are using Windows Vista and later on all support computers.

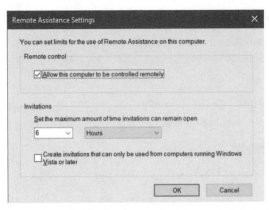

FIGURE 10-3 Configuring Remote Assistance advanced settings

Enabling Remote Desktop

To enable Remote Desktop, on the Remote tab of the System Properties dialog box, select the Allow Remote Connections To This Computer check box. Then, optionally, select Only Allow Connections From Computers Running Remote Desktop With Network Level Authentication (Recommended). This setting improves security of the Remote Desktop network traffic between the management computer and the target computer.

Click Select Users. As shown in Figure 10-4, you can then add the users or groups that you want to have remote access to this computer by using Remote Desktop.

FIGURE 10-4 Configuring Remote Desktop users

EXAM TIP

When you enable Remote Assistance or Remote Desktop by using these methods, the corresponding Windows Firewall setting is automatically configured to allow the selected app.

Skill: Configure Remote Assistance

After you have enabled Remote Assistance, you can configure and use this tool to help your users to administer and manage their computers remotely. There are two fundamental ways of initiating a Remote Assistance session: one is for the user to request assistance, and the other is for the support person to offer it.

This section covers how to:

- Request help with Remote Assistance
- Offer help with Remote Assistance
- Use GPOs to configure Remote Assistance settings
- Use Remote Assistance to manage a computer remotely

Requesting help using Remote Assistance

If a user is experiencing problems with their computer, they can request assistance from support personnel by using the Request Assistance feature of Remote Assistance. This is known as solicited remote assistance. To request assistance, the user must open Control Panel, select System And Security, and then click Launch Remote Assistance.

As shown in Figure 10-5, you can then choose between:

- **Invite Someone You Trust To Help You**   Choose this option if you require assistance.
- **Help Someone Who Has Invited You**   Choose this option if you can provide assistance.

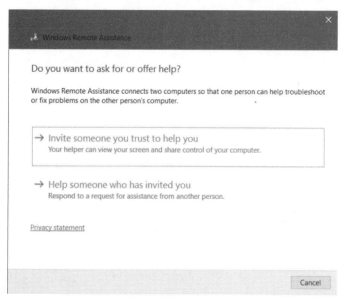

FIGURE 10-5 Requesting Windows Remote Assistance

To request help, click Invite Someone You Trust To Help You. You can then choose from among three options, as shown in Figure 10-6. These are:

- **Save This Invitation As A File**   Choose this option to create an RA Invitations file. These have a .msrclIncident file extension. You are prompted to save the request file. Store this file in a location that is accessible to the user you are requesting help from. Typically, this location will be a file server shared folder. After you have defined a save location, a dialog box appears with the password for the remote assistance session. Share this password with your helper. When your helper double-clicks the file you saved, they are prompted for the password, and then the Remote Assistance session begins.

- **Use Email To Send An Invitation**   If you choose this option, your default email program is opened by Remote Assistance, and the invitation file is automatically attached to an email message. You must enter the email address of the person you want to invite. When you send the message, the same dialog box appears containing the session password. Again, share this password with your helper. When your helper double-clicks the attached file in the email you sent, they are prompted for the password, and then the Remote Assistance session begins.

- **Use Easy Connect**   Easy Connect enables you to establish a Remote Assistance session without the need to use an invitation file. After you have established an Easy Connect session, you can save the name of the helper for future use, enabling you to receive remote assistance without the need to exchange a password.

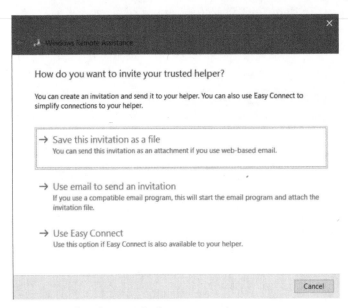

FIGURE 10-6 Choosing a method to request assistance

EXAM TIP

Easy Connect only works if both computers are running Windows 7 or later and if both computers have access to the global peer-to-peer network. This network can sometimes be inaccessible to users of computers that are placed behind network routers than do not support the Peer Name Resolution Protocol. This protocol is used to transfer Remote Assistance invitations over the Internet.

EXAM TIP

You can open the Windows Remote Assistance tool by running Msra.exe from the command line or the Windows Run dialog box.

Offering help with Remote Assistance

A user might not be in a position to request assistance. In these circumstances, an administrator can offer assistance. This is known as unsolicited remote assistance. To offer remote assistance, run Msra.exe and choose Help Someone Who Has Invited You. Then, on the Choose A Way To Connect To The Other Person's Computer page, click Advanced Connection Option For The Help Desk, as shown in Figure 10-7.

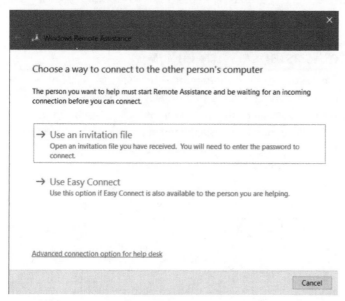

FIGURE 10-7 Offering Remote Assistance

On the Who Do You Want To Help page, in the Type A Computer Name Or IP Address box, as shown in Figure 10-8, type the relevant computer name or IP address of the computer that you want to send the offer of help to and then click Next.

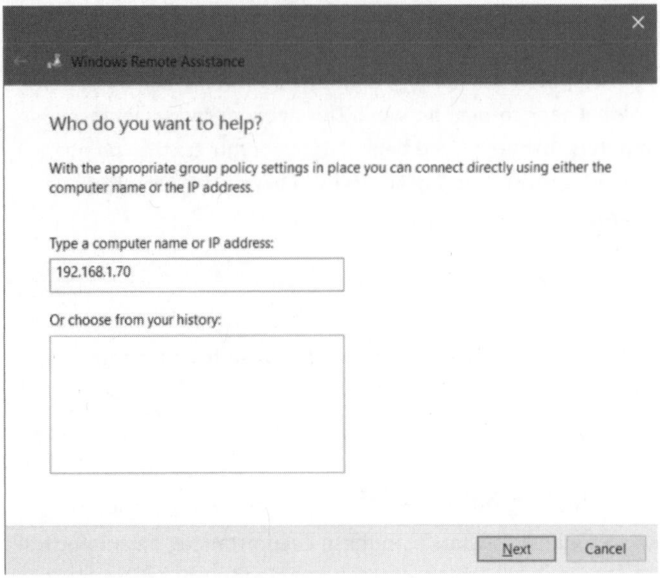

FIGURE 10-8 Offering Remote Assistance

The user on the target computer must accept your offer, and then the remote assistance session is initiated. This is often a useful way to start a remote assistance session, especially when you are attempting to support novice users.

Configuring Remote Assistance with GPOs

Although you can configure the necessary settings for Remote Assistance manually on each computer, in an AD DS domain environment, it is easier to use GPOs to distribute the required settings. Table 10-3 shows the settings you can configure for Remote Assistance by using GPOs. To configure these settings, open Group Policy Management and locate the appropriate GPO. Open the GPO for editing and navigate to Computer Configuration > Policies > Administrative Templates > System > Remote Assistance.

TABLE 10-3 Configuring Remote Assistance with GPOs

Policy Setting	Explanation
Allow Only Windows Vista Or Newer Connections	Enables Remote Assistance to generate invitations with more secure encryption. This setting does not affect Remote Assistance connections initiated by unsolicited offers or Remote Assistance.
Turn On Session Logging	Enables session logging. Logs are stored in the user's Documents folder in the Remote Assistance folder.
Turn On Bandwidth Optimization	Provides performance improvements in low-bandwidth situations. Adjust from No Optimization through Full Optimization.

Policy Setting	Explanation
Configure Solicited Remote Assistance	Enables solicited Remote Assistance on a computer. If you disable this setting, it prevents users from asking for Remote Assistance. You also can use this setting to configure invitation time limits and whether to allow remote control.
Configure Offer Remote Assistance	Enables unsolicited Remote Assistance on this computer.

Using Remote Assistance to manage a computer remotely

After you have configured the desired settings and established a Remote Assistance session, you can perform the following tasks.

- **Request Control**   Enables you to ask the remote user for permission to take remote control of their computer. They must allow you to do this. Remember also that the ability to gain remote control is a configurable option.

- **Chat**   Enables you to open a chat window to communicate with the remote user. You can use this to explain what you are doing, or the remote user can use chat to discuss the details of their computer problem.

Skill: Configure Remote Desktop

After Remote Desktop is enabled on a computer, you can use the Remote Desktop Connection program to connect to the computer. When connected, you can use the computer as if locally signed in and perform all management tasks that your user account has the rights to perform. This makes using Remote Desktop particularly useful.

This section covers how to:

- Create and edit Remote Desktop connections
- Configure Remote Desktop with GPOs

Creating and editing Remote Desktop connections

To create a Remote Desktop connection, from Start, click All Apps, click Windows Accessories, and then click Remote Desktop Connection. As shown in Figure 10-9, you must then specify the computer that you want to connect to. Use either a computer name or an IP address. You can configure additional connection properties by using the options discussed in Table 10-4.

TABLE 10-4 Configurable Remote Desktop Connection options

Tab	Settings
General	<ul><li>Logon settings:<ul><li>Computer</li><li>Username</li><li>Allow Me To Save Credentials</li></ul></li><li>Connection settings:<ul><li>Save</li><li>Save As</li><li>Open</li></ul></li></ul>
Display	<ul><li>Display configuration:<ul><li>Small >> Large</li><li>Use All My Monitors For The Remote Session</li></ul></li><li>Colors:<ul><li>Choose The Color Depth Of The Remote Session</li></ul></li><li>Display The Connection Bar When I Use Full Screen</li></ul>
Local Resources	<ul><li>Remote audio:<ul><li>Remote audio playback:<ul><li>Play On This Computer</li><li>Do Not Play</li><li>Play On Remote Computer</li></ul></li><li>Remote audio recording:<ul><li>Record From This Computer</li><li>Do Not Record</li></ul></li></ul></li><li>Keyboard, apply Windows key combinations:<ul><li>Only When Using The Full Screen</li><li>On This Computer</li><li>On The Remote Computer</li></ul></li><li>Local Devices And Resources:<ul><li>Printers</li><li>Clipboard</li><li>Smart Cards</li><li>Ports</li><li>Drives</li><li>Other Supported Plug And Play (Pnp) Devices</li></ul></li></ul>
Experience	<ul><li>Performance:<ul><li>Modem (56 kbps)</li><li>Low-Speed Broadband (256 Kbps – 2 Mbps)</li><li>Satellite (2 Mbps – 16 Mbps With High Latency)</li><li>High-Speed Broadband (2Mbps – 10 Mbps)</li><li>WAN (10 Mpbs Or Higher)</li><li>Detect Connection Quality Automatically</li></ul></li><li>Persistent Bitmap Caching</li><li>Reconnect If The Connection Is Dropped</li></ul>

Tab	Settings
Advanced	■ Server authentication, If Server Authentication Fails:
	• Connect And Don't Warn Me
	• Warn Me
	• Do Not Connect
	■ Connect From Anywhere:
	• Connection Settings:
	◦ Automatically Detect RD Gateway Server Settings
	◦ Use These RD Gateway Server Settings
	◦ Do Not Use An RD Gateway Server
	• Log-on Settings:
	◦ Username
	◦ Use My RD Gateway Credentials For The Remote Computer

FIGURE 10-9 Creating a Remote Desktop connection

When you have finished configuring the connection, from the General tab, click Connect. You can also choose to save your configuration to a .rdp file for subsequent use.

EXAM TIP

You can open the Remote Desktop Connection app by running Mstsc.exe from the command line or the Windows Run dialog box.

Configuring Remote Desktop with GPOs

Just as with Remote Assistance, although you can configure Remote Desktop settings manually on each computer, in an AD DS domain environment, it makes sense to configure these settings with GPOs. Table 10-5 contains the configurable GPO settings for Remote Desktop. To configure these settings, open Group Policy Management and locate the appropriate GPO. Open the GPO for editing and navigate to Computer Configuration > Policies > Administrative Templates > Windows Components > Remote Desktop Services.

TABLE 10-5 Configuring Remote Desktop with GPOs

Policy Setting	Explanation
Remote Desktop Connection Client \Do Not Allow Passwords To Be Saved	Determines whether users can save passwords on this computer from Remote Desktop Services clients.
Remote Desktop Connection Client \Prompt For Credentials On Client Computer	If enabled, a user is prompted to provide credentials for a remote connection to a Remote Desktop server on their client computer rather than on the Remote Desktop server.
Remote Desktop Session Host\Connections \Allow Users To Connect Remotely By Using Remote Desktop Services	If enabled, users that belong to the Remote Desktop Users group on the target computer can connect remotely to the target computer, using Remote Desktop Services.
Remote Desktop Session Host \Device And Resource Redirection	You use these settings to specify whether to allow or prevent data redirection from local devices (such as audio and clipboard) to the remote client in a Remote Desktop Services session.
Remote Desktop Session Host\Security \Set Client Connection Encryption Level	If enabled, all communications between clients and Remote Desktop servers is encrypted, using the encryption method specified. By default, the encryption level is set to High.
Remote Desktop Session Host \Session Time Limits	These policies control session time limits for disconnected, idle, and active sessions and whether to terminate sessions when specified limits are reached.

Skill: Configure Windows PowerShell remoting

Although using Windows PowerShell cmdlets can sometimes seem daunting, they do offer a convenient and quick way of configuring many machines more quickly than by using a graphical tool. In addition, through the use of scripting, you can use Windows PowerShell to complete frequently performed management tasks.

Using Windows PowerShell to manage remote computers is referred to as *Windows PowerShell remoting*, but before you can use Windows PowerShell remoting, you must know how to enable and configure it.

Windows PowerShell is ubiquitous across the Windows platform, appearing in both Windows 10 and Windows Server. Therefore, using Windows PowerShell to perform management tasks on both local and remote computers makes sense because you can transfer those skills to other management and administration situations.

Many cmdlets in Windows PowerShell can be used with a -ComputerName parameter, making the use of the command remotely no more complex than specifying the name of the computer you want to run the command against. For example, to determine the IP configuration of a computer, you can run the following command.

```
Get-NetIPConfiguration -computername LON-CL1
```

However, not all cmdlets accept the -ComputerName parameter, and for these, you must enable and configure Windows PowerShell remoting. The function of Windows PowerShell remoting is to enable you to connect to one or several remote computers and execute one or more cmdlets or scripts on those remote computers and return the results to your local computer.

Although Windows PowerShell remoting is enabled by default on Windows Server 2012 R2, you must manually enable it on Windows 10. To do this, complete the following procedure.

1. If necessary, start the Windows Remote Management service. You must also enable Windows Remote Management through the Windows Firewall. As shown in Figure 10-10, you can do this by running the **winrm quickconfig** command at an elevated command prompt. When prompted, press Y and Enter twice.

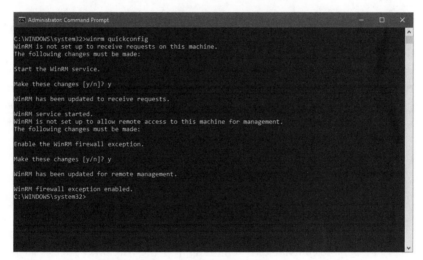

FIGURE 10-10 Enabling Windows Remote Management

2. To enable Windows PowerShell remoting, you must run the **enable-PSremoting -force** cmdlet from a Windows PowerShell (Admin) window.

Skill: Modify settings, using Microsoft Management Console or Windows PowerShell

With both Remote Desktop and Remote Assistance, you use RDP to connect to a remote computer. After you establish a connection, you can perform any management task interactively just as if you were sitting at the remote computer. This is not the case with either MMC or Windows PowerShell remoting.

With MMC, you must enable the necessary remote management feature that you wish to exploit by modifying the Windows Firewall configuration. Then you can use the appropriate management console snap-in and target the desired remote machine.

In Windows PowerShell, you enable remote management by enabling the Windows Remote Management service and then enabling Windows PowerShell remoting. Thereafter, you connect to the remote computer and run the appropriate Windows PowerShell cmdlets or scripts.

> **This section covers how to:**
> - Use MMC to manage remote computers
> - Use Windows PowerShell to manage remote computers

Using MMC to manage remote computers

It is very easy to use MMC snap-ins to manage remote computers. Some management snap-ins enable you to specify additional computers to connect to from the console. As shown in Figure 10-11, you can right-click the uppermost node in the navigation pane and then click Connect To Another Computer.

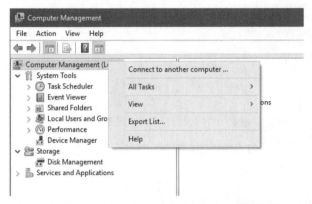

FIGURE 10-11 Connecting to another computer with MMC

If the management snap-in you want to use does not enable you to connect to additional computers, you can create a new management console by running **mmc.exe** and adding the appropriate snap-in to the empty console. When prompted, specify Another Computer, as shown in Figure 10-12.

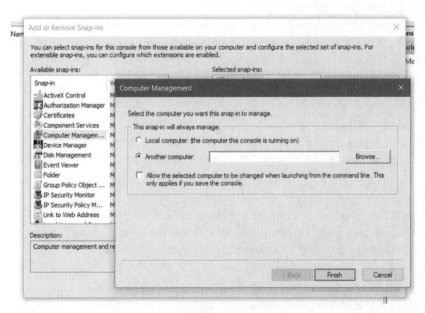

FIGURE 10-12 Connecting remotely with MMC

It is important to realize that the remote computer must recognize you. This means that you must authenticate your connection by using a username and password that have the necessary management rights on the target computer. This is simple in an AD DS domain environment because you can use domain admin credentials. However, in workgroup environments, this is trickier. Generally, you must be able to provide credentials of a member of the target computer's local Administrators group.

In addition to authentication, the necessary Windows Firewall feature must be enabled. The available remote management features are:

- Remote Assistance.
- Remote Desktop.
- Remote Event Log Management.
- Remote Event Monitor.
- Remote Scheduled Tasks Management.
- Remote Service Management.
- Remote Shut-down.
- Remote Volume Management.
- Virtual Machine Monitoring.
- Windows Firewall Remote Management.
- Windows Management Instrumentation (WMI).
- Windows Remote Management.
- Windows Remote Management (Compatibility).

After you have enabled the required remote management feature in Windows Firewall, and modified your MMC to connect to a remote computer using appropriate credentials, performing remote management is no different from performing local management.

Using Windows PowerShell to manage remote computers

After you have enabled Windows PowerShell remoting, you can use Windows PowerShell cmdlets and scripts to manage the remote computer in virtually the same way that you manage local computers. However, you must first establish a connection with the remote computer.

After you have established a connection, you can run any cmdlets or scripts against the remote machine. When you connect to the remote computer and run a remote command against it, the command is transmitted across the network and run on the remote computer. The results are sent back to your local computer and displayed in your Windows PowerShell window.

One way to establish a remote connection and run a command is to use the invoke-command cmdlet. You can also use the Invoke-command cmdlet to establish a temporary remote connection. For example, the following command retrieves the contents of the system event log from the remote computer LON-CL1.

```
Invoke-Command -ComputerName LON-CL1 -ScriptBlock {Get-EventLog -log system}
```

If you intend to run several cmdlets, or to run more complex scripts, it is useful to establish a persistent connection to the remote computer. Use the New-PSWorkflowSession cmdlet to do this. For example:

```
$s = New-PSWorkflowSession -ComputerName LON-CL1
```

You can now use the Enter-PSSession command to establish the persistent connection.

```
Enter-PSSession $s
```

You will now have a Windows PowerShell prompt that looks like this.

```
[LON-CL1]: PS C:\>
```

Any commands that you run in this session run on the LON-CL1 computer. The session remains active until you close with the exit-PSSession command.

You can also use these commands to establish remote connections with multiple computers. For example, to connect simultaneously to computers called LON-CL1 and LON-CL2, use the following command.

```
$s = New-PSSession -ComputerName LON-CL1, LON-CL2
```

Next, run the remote Windows PowerShell cmdlets against the new session.

```
Invoke-Command -Session $s -ScriptBlock { Get-EventLog -log system }
```

You can run any Windows PowerShell command remotely in this way.

> **NEED MORE REVIEW?** **AN INTRODUCTION TO POWERSHELL REMOTING: PART ONE**
>
> To review further details about using Windows PowerShell remoting, refer to the Microsoft TechNet website at *https://blogs.technet.microsoft.com/heyscriptingguy/2012/07/23 /an-introduction-to-powershell-remoting-part-one/*.

Summary

- You can choose from a number of management tools to perform remote management.
- To configure and enable remote management settings, you must first modify the Windows Firewall configuration.
- Remote Assistance can be used to view or take remote control of a remote user's computer.
- Both Remote Desktop and Remote Assistance can be configured manually or by using GPOs.

- Windows PowerShell remoting enables you to perform remote management of any Windows 10–based computer with Windows PowerShell.
- Management console snap-ins support both local and remote connections.

Thought experiment

In this thought experiment, demonstrate your skills and knowledge of the topics covered in this chapter. You can find answers to this thought experiment in the next section.

You work in support at A. Datum Corporation. Many of your users work in small branch offices. Some work from home, using work laptops. It is important for you to be able to manage these users' computers remotely. As a consultant for A. Datum, answer the following questions about remote management in the A. Datum organization.

1. One of your users telephones the help desk, requiring assistance with an application. They need to know how to perform a grammar check with Microsoft Word 2016. They are not very experienced and, despite your best efforts and explanation of how the process works, they are still confused. What remote management tool might you consider using in this situation?

2. Another user calls the help desk. They've lost a file and need you to locate it. They're due to leave the office for a conference this afternoon, and they tell you that's the best time for you to resolve the issue. What remote management tool would you use?

3. You try to connect to this user's computer later that afternoon, but despite knowing that the necessary Windows Firewall settings are configured, you cannot connect. Why?

4. You want to use Windows PowerShell remoting. You try to connect to a remote machine but are unsuccessful. What steps must you perform on the remote machine before Windows PowerShell remoting can work?

Thought experiment answer

This section contains the solution to the thought experiment. Each answer explains why the answer choice is correct.

1. Using Remote Assistance would enable you to demonstrate how to perform the grammar check. You could take remote control of the user's computer and show them the procedure.

2. Remote Desktop is the most suitable tool. Remote Assistance requires the interaction of the user to accept your connection request—and, initially, to invite you to help. Remote Desktop requires no invitations and does not require the remote user to assist you in connecting.

3. The most likely reason you can't connect is that Remote Desktop users must be granted access in addition to the Windows Firewall configuration changes being made.

4. You must start the Windows Remote Management service and reconfigure the Windows Firewall, and then Windows PowerShell remoting must be enabled. You can perform these steps by running **winrm quickconfig** and then **enable-PSremoting**.

CHAPTER 11

Configure updates

Keeping computers safe and protected from external threats such as malware and hackers is a big challenge. In earlier versions of Windows, you could decide whether the operating system is automatically updated with the latest features, security updates, and fixes through the Windows Update feature. Many users chose to disable automatic updates, and these computers were then vulnerable. With over a billion Windows devices worldwide, even if this number was a small percentage of the total, it could mean millions of users were unprotected.

Windows 10 is the latest version of Windows, and it will continually benefit from new feature upgrades rolled out through Windows Update. To enhance the security protection delivered in Windows 10, the consumer can no longer turn off security updates or upgrades. Enterprise users can still choose to test updates and deliver them internally, using Windows Server Update Service (WSUS) or other management tools to keep their devices updated. For organizations that require deployment of a static installation of Windows 10 that will not have upgrades, Microsoft ships a special build of Windows 10.

Skills covered in this chapter:

- Configure Windows Update options
- Implement Insider Preview
- Current Branch (CB) and Current Branch for Business (CBB)
- Long Term Servicing Branch (LTSB) scenarios
- Manage update history
- Roll back updates
- Update Windows Store apps

Skill: Configure Windows Update options

With Windows as a service, Windows 10 will receive security updates as they are required in addition to a regular schedule of rollup updates and feature upgrades. The process of continually bringing your computer up to date is known as *servicing*. It is expected that new features will appear two to three times a year. During the year, several milestone builds will be available to volume licensing, system builders, and MSDN customers; such milestone builds will include all updates and upgrades built in and serve as the latest start point for a new installation or upgrade.

It is important to distinguish the different types of Windows 10 updates.

- **Servicing updates**   Regular security updates and software updates
- **Feature upgrades**   New features and functionality

Both types will be cumulative and contain all previous updates, which reduces the likelihood of a hacker or malware attack through a missing update.

Feature upgrades are mandatory and must be applied within one year for the following versions of Windows 10.

- Windows 10 Home
- Windows 10 Pro
- Windows 10 Enterprise
- Windows 10 Education

Upgrades are delivered to devices running Windows 10 Home when Microsoft releases them. When downloaded to the device, the upgrades are installed immediately.

Enterprise editions of Windows 10 (Windows 10 Pro, Windows 10 Enterprise, and Windows 10 Education) are configured for immediate installation of feature upgrades by default, but you can configure the device to defer the installation in the Settings app. Typically, this defers the upgrades four to six months after they are provided to consumer devices. Through Group Policy, you can defer upgrades for up to one year.

A new special build of Windows 10, available only to enterprise customers, called the Long Term Servicing Branch (LTSB), will be available and won't force feature upgrades.

> **This section covers how to:**
> - Configure Windows Update settings
> - Use Group Policy to configure Windows Update
> - Troubleshoot Windows Update

Configure Windows Update settings

As with earlier versions of Windows, security updates will continue to be distributed on the second Tuesday of each month by Windows Update, and additional reliability improvements, hardware driver updates, and ad hoc security updates will be pushed out through Windows Update.

New Windows features will be delivered in update packages that behave just like complete in-place upgrades. This might alarm some users, especially those who never allowed updates on earlier versions of Windows. You can choose how updates are applied to your computers. This can be through the Settings app or by Group Policy.

To configure Windows Update settings on a computer, follow these steps.

1. Click the Start button and open Settings.

2. Click Update & Security, Windows Update.

   The Windows Update page opens.

3. Review the date and time Windows last checked for updates.

4. Click Check For Updates.

5. To configure and control Windows Update in more detail, click Advanced Options.

   The Choose How Updates Are Installed dialog box opens, as shown in Figure 11-1.

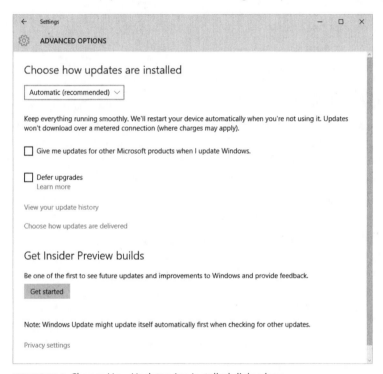

FIGURE 11-1 Choose How Updates Are Installed dialog box

On the Advanced Options page, choose one of the following options to configure how updates are installed.

- **Automatic (Recommended)** Windows 10 downloads and applies updates and, if necessary, your computer restarts automatically when it is not in use.

- **Notify To Schedule Restart** Windows 10 downloads and applies updates and, if it needs to restart, you can schedule a restart time to apply the updates.

The check boxes enable you configure the following options.

- **Give Me Updates For Other Microsoft Products When I Update Windows**   This enables Windows Update to keep other Microsoft products, such as Microsoft Office, up to date at the same time as Windows 10.

- **Defer Upgrades**   Enterprise editions of Windows 10 (Windows 10 Pro, Windows 10 Enterprise, and Windows 10 Education) enable you to defer upgrades to your computer. Windows 10 does not download or install new Windows 10 features immediately when they are available; they can be delayed for several months.

> *IMPORTANT* **DEFERRING UPGRADES**
>
> **Deferring upgrades will not defer security updates.**

The following two options offer additional update information.

- View Your Update History
- Choose How Updates Are Delivered

View Your Update History

The View Your Update History page shows you the updates that have been applied and those that failed to be applied. Each update contains a unique name and reference number and a summary of the effect the update will have on the system. A detailed description of each update is available online by clicking More Info in each update.

You can also select Uninstall Updates, which opens Installed Updates in Control Panel. You remove any update by selecting it and clicking Uninstall on the menu bar.

If you have installed the preview build of Windows 10 on your device, you can also uninstall this by clicking Uninstall Latest Preview Build. This option opens the Recovery page in the Update And Security Settings app and enables you to reset your PC.

Choose How Updates Are Delivered

Windows 10 includes a new feature that enables you to choose how updates are delivered and enables Windows Update to obtain updates through peer-to-peer file sharing.

To review and configure this option, use the following steps.

1. Click the Start button and open Settings.
2. Click Update & Security, Windows Update.
3. On the Windows Update page, click Advanced Options.
4. Select the Choose How Updates Are Delivered link.

   The Choose How Updates Are Delivered dialog box, shown in Figure 11-2, is where you can configure how updates are delivered.

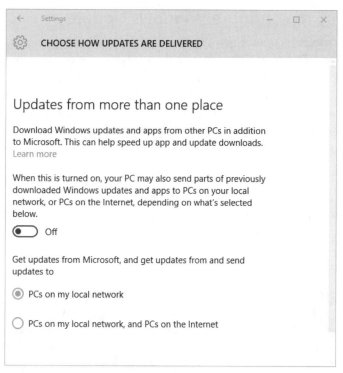

FIGURE 11-2 Choose how updates are installed

5. Move the toggle to On.

6. Configure the additional peer-to-peer sources as either:

   - PCs On My Local Network (Default).

   - PCs On My Local Network, And PCs On The Internet.

7. Exit the Settings app.

After you choose to receive updates from more than one place, Windows obtains updates from Microsoft and from computers on the local network and, optionally, from PCs on the Internet. By allowing Windows to obtain the update files from additional sources, the settings can be applied more quickly. This can be especially useful when using a reduced bandwidth or metered connection because after one device has been updated, it can share the update file fragments peer-to-peer with other devices locally without needing to download them from Microsoft.

If you disable the Updates From More Than One Place setting, Windows Update obtains updates directly from the Microsoft update servers.

Use Group Policy to configure Windows Update

You can use Group Policy to configure the new Windows Update settings and then use Active Directory Domain Services (AD DS) to distribute the settings to the devices across the network.

Although there are many Group Policy Objects (GPOs) that relate to Windows Update for earlier versions of Windows, three nodes in Group Policy contain Windows Update settings for Windows 10. They are found in the Computer Configuration/Administrative Templates /Windows Components/ area with the following node names.

- Windows Update
- Data Collection And Preview Builds
- Delivery Optimization

Windows Update

The Windows Update node contains several settings, including:

- Configure Automatic Updates

  Specifies whether the computer will receive security updates and other important downloads through the Windows automatic updating service. This setting enables you to specify whether to enable automatic updates on your computer. If this service is enabled, you must select one of the four options in the Group Policy setting.

  - 2 = Notify before downloading and installing any updates

  When Windows finds updates that apply to your computer, you are notified in the notification area by an icon, with a message that updates are ready for download. When they are downloaded, the icon appears again to notify you that the updates are ready for installation. If you click the notification, you can then select which updates to install.

  - 3 = Automatically download and notify for install

  When Windows finds updates that apply to your computer, it automatically downloads them in the background. When the download is complete, a notification area icon appears, advising that the updates are ready for installation. Click the icon or notification to select which updates should be installed.

  - 4 = Automatically download and install them on the schedule specified below

  Specify the install schedule by using the options in the Group Policy setting. If you do not specify a schedule, all installations will be every day at 3:00 A.M. If updates require a restart to complete the installation, Windows restarts the computer automatically. If a user is signed in to the computer when Windows is ready to restart, it notifies the user and offers an option to delay the restart.

    - 5 = Allow local administrators to select the configuration mode that Automatic Updates should notify and install updates

With this option, local administrators can use the Windows Update Control Panel to select a configuration option, such as to choose the scheduled installation time. Local administrators cannot disable Automatic Updates configuration. If you set a GPO to Enabled, Windows searches Windows Update for updates that apply to your computer whenever the computer is online. With the status set to Disabled, all updates must be manually triggered for download and installation. If the status is Not Configured, the Group Policy is not used to configure Automatic Updates, and the computer uses the Automatic Updates in Control Panel or the Settings app.

■ Defer Upgrades And Updates

This policy enables you to defer upgrades for up to eight months and delay updates for up to four weeks, as shown in Figure 11-3. The policy is not configured by default. If you do not delay updates, your PC installs security updates as they become available. An option to Pause Upgrades And Updates is available if an issue arises with an update or upgrade. This setting delays updates and upgrades until the next monthly update or upgrade becomes available. This setting will not affect Windows Defender antimalware definition updates.

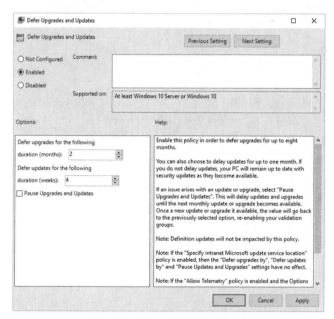

FIGURE 11-3 Deferring upgrades and updates in Group Policy

Data collection and preview builds

The Data Collection And Preview Builds node contains four settings.

- Toggle User Control Over Insider Builds

  This policy setting determines whether users can access the Insider build controls in Advanced Options for Windows Update. If you enable or do not configure this policy setting, users can download and install Windows preview software on their devices. If you disable this policy setting, Get Insider Builds will not be available.

- Allow Telemetry

  This policy setting determines the amount of diagnostic and usage data related to Microsoft software that is reported to Microsoft. The policy offers four choices.

  - **Security**   No telemetry data is reported to Microsoft except security data such as Windows Defender data.

  - **Basic**   Reports a limited amount of diagnostic and usage data.

  - **Enhanced**   Sends enhanced diagnostic and usage data.

  - **Full**   Sends the same data as the Basic setting plus additional diagnostics data, such as the system state at the time of a system halt or crash, and the files and content that might have caused the problem.

  If you disable or do not configure this policy setting, users can configure the Telemetry level in the Settings app.

- Disable Pre-release Features Or Settings

  Use this policy setting to configure the level to which Microsoft can experiment with Windows 10 to study your preferences or device behavior. There are two settings.

  - **Device Setting Only**   Permits Microsoft to configure device settings only

  - **Full Experimentations**   Enables Microsoft to conduct full experimentations and study user preferences

- Do Not Show Feedback Notifications

  - This policy setting enables an organization to prevent its devices from showing feedback questions from Microsoft through the Windows Feedback app.

Delivery optimization

The Delivery Optimization node contains the following five settings.

- Download Mode

  Use this setting to configure the use of Windows Update Delivery Optimization in downloads of Windows apps and updates. These settings offer slightly more granularity in the Settings app, allowing the device to receive updates from more than one place. There are four options, as follows.

  - **None**   Disable the feature

  - **Group**   Peers on same NAT only

- **LAN**   Local Network/Private Peering (PCs in the same domain by default)
- **Internet**   Internet Peering only
- Group ID

  Set this policy to specify an arbitrary group ID to which the device belongs by using a globally unique identifier (GUID) as the group ID. This segments the devices when using the Group option in the Download Mode setting.
- Max Cache Age

  Use this to define the maximum time the Delivery Optimization cache can hold each file.
- Max Cache Size

  This option limits the maximum cache size Delivery Optimization can use as a percentage of the internal disk size.
- Max Upload Bandwidth

  This policy defines a limit for the upload bandwidth that a device uses for all concurrent upload activity by Delivery Optimization (kilobytes per second).

EXAM TIP

Review the new GPOs that relate to the new Windows Update functionality found in Windows 10.

Troubleshoot Windows Update

If a machine is not receiving updates and you have checked the Settings app and Group Policy settings, verify that the two services in Windows relating to Windows Update are running.

The first is the Windows Update service, which checks which updates have been installed locally and what is available on the update servers. The Windows Update service also handles the download, installation, and reporting of the state of updates.

Background Intelligent Transfer Service (BITS) is a supplemental service that handles the transfer of update files in the most efficient manner.

Both services need to be running for Windows Update to function correctly.

Skill: Implement Insider Preview

With Windows 10, rollouts of new upgrades are made available to different sets of users, depending on the update settings you have configured in Windows 10. With the continual development of Windows 10, Microsoft has created a process to support the incremental build process that Windows 10 uses.

Microsoft internally implements a new version of Windows 10 on a regular basis, such as daily and weekly, and initial user issues such as bugs or improvement feedback is relayed immediately back to the development team rapidly. These versions are deemed too early for widespread public release, but when they have experienced a level of acceptance and reliability, they are ready for the next group of users to field test.

The first publicly available version of Windows 10 was made available to a growing volunteer user base called *Windows Insider*. Initially, this group of IT pros and consumers were invited to download and review the Windows 10 Technical Preview (in 2014). Nowadays, the program has grown to over 7 million members. These insiders sign up to receive early feature upgrades to their Windows 10 devices and receive a dedicated newsletter to keep them informed from the program manager at Microsoft. You must be registered as a Windows Insider and use a Microsoft account.

NEED MORE REVIEW? **WINDOWS INSIDER**

For additional information and to sign up as a member of the Windows Insider Preview Program, visit *https://insider.windows.com/*.

Most of the content that is previewed in the Windows 10 Insider Preview will eventually be implemented in the mainstream version of Windows 10, so it can be useful if you are interested in testing new feature upgrades early in the process. You should be cautious, however, because the Insider builds can contain incomplete or unstable code. For this reason, do not use Windows Insider builds in a production environment.

Each new Windows 10 build proceeds through progressive branches on its way to the general public users and enterprise users. Figure 11-4 shows a diagram of how the build and branch development process works. The guideline dates define how long each branch remains in the testing and bug-fixing period before the build moves on to the next branch on the right.

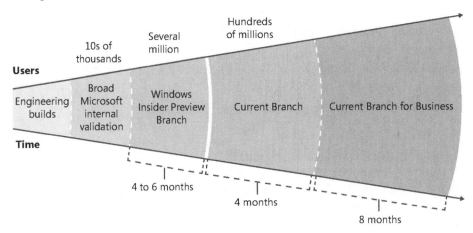

FIGURE 11-4 Windows 10 upgrade timeline and build branches

In the Windows Insider program are two levels of adoption of preview builds that participants can currently choose. These two update speeds are referred to as rings. The Fast ring makes new builds available as soon as Microsoft releases them; the second option, the Slow ring, delays the availability of the build until it has been exposed to the Fast ring members and most if not all the bugs have been addressed by interim incremental updates.

If the Windows Insider Program proves to be too volatile or risky, members can change from Fast to Slow or leave the program at any time. Consider using a virtual machine to keep abreast of the evolution of Windows 10.

Each version that progresses to the Current Branch stage is assigned a version number with the version numbering scheme corresponding to the release date and the year and month in *yydd* format, such as 1511 or 1607.

To enable the Insider Preview builds on your Windows 10 device, follow these steps.

1. Sign up to be part of the Windows Insider Program at *https://insider.windows.com/*.

2. Sign in to your PC with the Microsoft account you used in step 1.

3. Open the Settings app.

4. Select Update & Security and then Advanced Options.

5. Click Get Started under Get Insider Builds.

6. Read the warning message shown in Figure 11-5 and click Next to continue.

FIGURE 11-5 Windows Insider build warning

7. Restart your PC.

8. Sign back in to your PC with the Microsoft account you used in step 1.

9. Open the Settings app.

10. Select Update & Security and then Advanced Options.

11. Under Get Insider Builds, you can choose either the Slow or Fast ring.

After you have configured your test computer for Insider builds, you can also consider volunteering to give Microsoft feedback. When you encounter problems or crashes in Windows 10 Insider builds, Windows automatically reports information back to Microsoft. When evaluating Windows 10, you can use the Feedback Hub, which enables you to communicate with Microsoft and view suggestions, give feedback, and vote on issues from other Insiders.

You can also participate in Quests, which are short tutorials that guide you through how to use new features, as shown in Figure 11-6. Each Quest provides you with an overview and then a series of steps that you should perform. If the quest is not achievable, you can provide feedback to Microsoft on the issue and, in addition, review other feedback in this area.

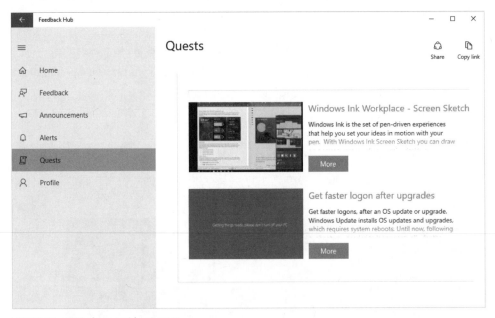

FIGURE 11-6 Windows Insider Quests

To launch the Insider Hub app, click Start and type **Hub**. If the app is not yet installed in the build that you are using, you can install it by using the following steps.

1. Sign in to your PC with the Microsoft account used for the Insider Program.

2. Open the Settings app.

3. Select System.

4. Click Apps & Features.

5. Select Manage Optional Features. Scroll down, locate the Insider Hub in the list, select it, and click Install.

    After it is installed, the Insider Hub app appears in your All Apps list.

If the pace of change is too fast, you can swap from the Fast ring to the Slow ring, or you can easily stop getting insider builds on your computer. Visit the Advanced Options page in the Windows Update settings or the Windows Insider Program page in the Update And Security settings app and click Stop Insider Preview Builds.

When you click Stop Insider Preview Builds, Microsoft offers the option to pause Insider Preview builds for a while, and you can defer them for between one and five days. Alternatively, you can choose Need To Stop Getting Insider Builds Completely. Your computer must restart, and your Microsoft account remains as part of the Insider program.

Skill: Current Branch and Current Branch for Business

Enterprises require more control of their updates and could be concerned with the new rolling Windows 10 upgrade process. The progressive branches shown in Figure 11-4 show the time frame in which Microsoft plans to deliver feature updates to Windows 10 customers.

For the majority of business customers, two branch choices are available to choose from.

- Current Branch (CB)
- Current Branch for Business (CBB)

These two main servicing options are described in detail in this section.

This section covers how to:

- Use Current Branch
- Use Current Branch for Business
- Update mobile devices
- Implement continuous servicing

Use Current Branch

This servicing option ensures that devices are kept up to date with the latest Windows 10 features through the upgrades that are released two to three times a year. When Microsoft releases a new public build, all devices that have the default configuration begin downloading and installing the upgrade.

In the real world, the default configuration is most appropriate for early adopters; IT team members; and other, broader piloting groups who need to test the mainstream business build before full rollout with CBB. All versions of Windows 10 are on Current Branch unless they have been configured to defer upgrades, which moves them to CBB.

Windows 10 Home edition does not have a defer upgrades option and therefore will always be on CB and upgrade through Windows Update automatically.

Other Windows 10 editions can upgrade through Windows Update, WSUS, or other management systems such as System Center Configuration Manager. You can use the GUI interface, Group Policy, or a management tool to defer upgrade implementation for approximately four months before you are required to deploy the upgrade.

With each release of a Current Branch feature update, Microsoft produces new ISO images that volume licensing, system builders, and similar kinds of users can download from MSDN or similar websites. You can use these images to upgrade existing machines or use as a base image to create new custom images. Organizations using WSUS will be able to deploy these feature upgrades to devices already running Windows 10.

Use Current Branch for Business

This servicing option is for the majority of users within an organization. Businesses often prefer or require more time to test the feature upgrades prior to mainstream deployment. Only the Windows 10 Pro, Windows 10 Enterprise, and Windows 10 Education editions support Current Branch for Business by Windows Update, WSUS, or other management systems.

Microsoft re-releases the feature upgrade a second time, approximately four to six months after the initial release, and at this time, all devices using Current Branch for Business begin downloading and installing the upgrade. If the organization uses tools to control the update process, such as Group Policy or System Center Configuration Manager, an additional deferral of at least eight months is available. Throughout this time, monthly security updates will continue to be made available to all machines on CB or CBB.

When the maximum deferral period has expired, the upgrades will be automatically installed.

EXAM TIP

The CBB servicing option is not available for the Home edition of Windows 10.

To configure a PC for Current Branch for Business, the Defer Upgrades setting needs to be configured. This can be done in any of these ways.

- Manually using the Settings app
- Group Policy
- Mobile device management (MDM) such as Microsoft Intune or Windows Update for Business

NEED MORE REVIEW? **WINDOWS 10 RELEASE INFORMATION**

Microsoft has produced a webpage designed to help you determine whether your devices are up to date with the latest Windows 10 feature upgrades and servicing updates. Visit *https://technet.microsoft.com/windows/mt679505.aspx?OCID=WIP_r_14_Body_Win10Updates.*

The servicing approach is similar to the way Android and iOS devices receive updates. The change for many large organizations might have a significant impact because they will want to balance their desire to deliver the latest operating-system features, functionality, and security to their users with the need to provide predictable and stable devices.

Update mobile devices

One of the challenges with a highly mobile workforce is that those employees seldom connect to the corporate network, which makes it difficult to ensure that they are regularly updated.

Many new devices that run Windows 10 might not be part of the domain, perhaps because they are constantly mobile, do not belong to the organization, or are privately owned. These devices can be upgraded to an enterprise SKU such as Windows 10 Enterprise, using a provisioning package, and then managed using a mobile device management (MDM) service or Windows Update for Business to provide the same type of control provided today with WSUS or System Center Configuration Manager.

Implement continuous servicing

The servicing lifetime of Current Branch or Current Branch for Business is finite. Windows 10 will be continually upgraded itself. To continue receiving monthly security updates, you must ensure that new feature upgrades on machines running these branches are installed. For many organizations, this requires a change to the current deployment and image servicing methodology.

There are three stages to consider when deploying Windows 10 in an enterprise. These are:

- **Evaluate**   Use the Windows Insider Preview for this stage.
- **Pilot**   Deploy the Current Branch.
- **Deploy**   Use the Current Branch for Business for the main deployment.

The diagram shown in Figure 11-7 depicts the Current Branch release schedule, which is useful to overlap with your new deployment and image servicing methodology.

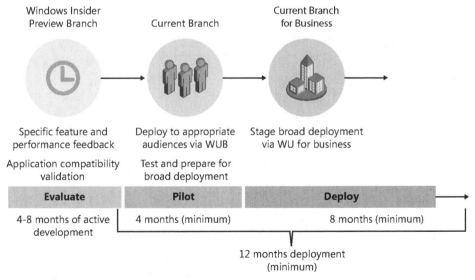

FIGURE 11-7 Current branch release schedule

Skill: Long-Term Servicing Branch scenarios

For some organizations, the concept of a continually changing and upgrading operating system would be a reason for not installing Windows 10. Microsoft has therefore created a specialized edition of Windows 10 Enterprise that only enterprise customers can obtain and install.

This special branch of Windows 10 is referred to as the Long-Term Servicing Branch (LTSB), and it is aimed at businesses that have computers that need to run in a known (and fixed) environment that does not change. Microsoft envisages that the maximum period an organization will use a particular build of LTSB is five years, but it will provide long-term support for 10 years.

There are key differences in the feature set between this edition and other Windows 10 editions. The following features and apps are not included in the LTSB:

- Microsoft Edge web browser
- Windows Store Client
- Cortana
- Microsoft Outlook Mail/Calendar, Microsoft OneNote, and Weather Windows universal apps

These apps or services are likely be frequently updated with new functionality, so their support cannot be maintained on PCs running the LTSB.

The LTSB receives security and other updates as they are released, but there will be no upgrades. It is recommended that each build version of LTSB have a normal life expectancy of five years.

Certain industries that use a base operating system to host line-of-business (LOB) or critical applications are likely to consider deploying LTSB. These scenarios include:

- Factory production, factory floor machinery.
- Manufacturing control systems.
- Hospital emergency room computers.
- Retail point-of-sale (POS) systems.
- Automated teller machines (ATM).
- Pharmaceutical firms that might have regulatory requirements for PCs used for the development of their products.
- Kiosk devices.

Where a device is running a dedicated app, such as in a kiosk or banking ATM, and does not allow users to log on, or have users interact with the operating system, the LTSB might be appropriate.

The Windows 10 Enterprise Long-Term Servicing Branch (LTSB) ISO images are made available on MSDN and sites such as the Volume Licensing Service Center, as shown in Figure 11-8.

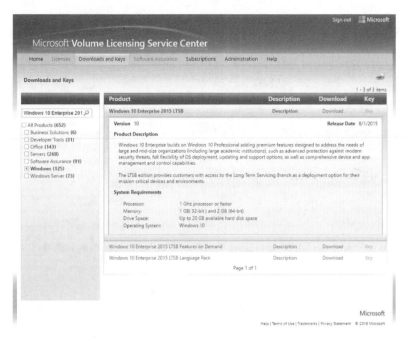

FIGURE 11-8 Microsoft Volume Licensing Service Center

The LTSB should not be viewed as an alternative to receiving the mandatory upgrades. There will be few, if any, scenarios in which an entire organization would justify using the Long-Term Servicing Branch for all users and PCs.

The release schedule for the LTSB is likely to be one release per year and is expected to be less often than CB and CBB releases. When they are released, each LTSB will be supported with security and reliability fixes for an extended period up to a maximum of 10 years.

At any stage during the lifetime of a device running LTSB, the device can be upgraded to a more recent version of the Windows 10 Enterprise LTSB, or the device can be upgraded to a later CB or CBB build. It is not possible to upgrade directly from CB or CBB to LTSB.

Skill: Manage update history

Updates are necessary to maintain the security and reliability of Windows 10. However, in rare cases, an update can actually create a problem for your system. In such cases, you need a mechanism to review installed updates and, if necessary, uninstall and block offending updates from being installed again. In Windows 10, you can uninstall the update or driver that is causing that instability.

Microsoft releases important updates every second Tuesday each month, known as "Patch Tuesday." Security and definition updates can be released at any time, and the Windows Update service automatically checks for new Windows Updates at the default time of 3:00 A.M. or the time you set in automatic maintenance.

This section covers how to:

- View update history
- Hide or show Windows Update in Windows 10

View update history

To view your update history and see which Windows updates failed or successfully installed on your Windows 10–based PC, follow these steps.

1. Open Settings and click Update & Security.

2. Click Windows Update and then click Advanced Options.

3. Click View Your Update History.

   A list of your installed Windows updates appears, similar to the list shown in Figure 11-9.

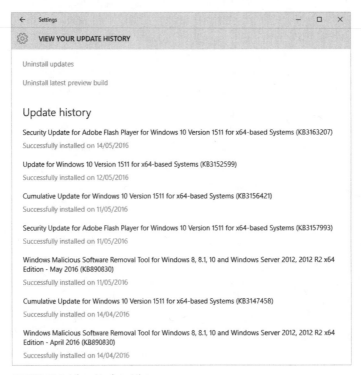

FIGURE 11-9 View Update History

4. Click one of the Successfully Installed On (date) links to see more details for that update.

5. Close Settings.

Each update contains a summary of the payload. If you click More Info at the bottom of the summary, you are directed to the detailed knowledge base description on the Microsoft support pages.

If you prefer to use Control Panel, you can see a list in Installed Updates in Control Panel by using these steps.

1. Right-click the Start button and select Control Panel.

2. Open Programs > Programs And Features.

3. Click View Installed Updates.

    The support link appears in the lower part of the screen.

4. Close Control Panel.

The Control Panel view is limited, and the support link does not open the support web-page when selected.

Hide or show Windows Updates in Windows 10

In an enterprise environment, you use tools, such as Windows Server Update Services (WSUS), to manage and approve each update before it is made available to a pilot group and then the main corporate population. On consumer devices, updates are automatically installed.

In rare cases, a specific driver or update might cause undesired results such as poor performance or instability. You can manually remove an update, but for consumers, the update will be reinstalled automatically the next time Windows Update checks whether updates are missing.

To assist with this problem, Microsoft has made available a utility for Windows 10 that you can install. The Show or Hide Updates troubleshooter enables you to view updates and mark individual drivers or updates to prevent it from being reinstalled. You can download the utility from *https://support.microsoft.com/kb/3073930*. To hide updates, follow these steps.

1. Sign in to Windows 10 with an account that has administrative privileges.

2. Open the wushowhide.diagcab file to launch the wizard.

3. Click Advanced.

4. Select the Apply Repairs Automatically check box and then click Next.

    The tool detects problem updates and searches for updates.

5. Click Hide Updates.

6. Select the check box for each of the updates you want to hide, as shown in Figure 11-10, and then click Next.

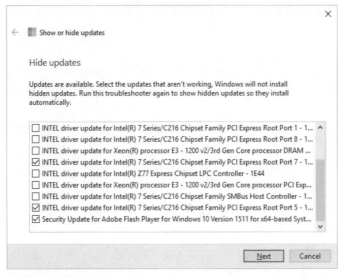

FIGURE 11-10 Hide Updates

The selected updates are now hidden.

7. Click Close.

To show previously hidden updates, follow these steps.

1. Sign in to Windows 10 with an account that has administrative privileges.

2. Open the wushowhide.diagcab file to launch the wizard.

3. Click Advanced.

4. Select the Apply Repairs Automatically check box and then click Next.

5. Click Show Hidden Updates.

6. Select the check box for each of the hidden updates you want to show in Windows Update again and then click Next.

The selected hidden updates are now no longer hidden.

7. Click Close.

NEED MORE REVIEW? **WINDOWS 10 UPDATE HISTORY**

Microsoft has published the Windows 10 update history that accompanies the periodic software updates. View this list at *http://windows.microsoft.com/en-us/windows-10/update-history-windows-10*.

Skill: Roll back updates

With the rhythm of regular updates becoming the method of keeping devices secure and up to date, there might be instances when an update causes problems and you need to consider removing the update completely by rolling it back. You might have experience with driver rollbacks; the same concept is used for rolling back Windows updates.

Sometimes you need to remove a single Windows update. You can perform this task in a number of ways, through Control Panel, the Settings app, or the command prompt.

> **This section covers how to:**
> - Uninstall a Windows update by using Control Panel
> - Uninstall a Windows update in Settings
> - Uninstall a Windows update by using the command prompt
> - Revert to a previous build of Windows 10

Uninstall a Windows update by using Control Panel

If you prefer to use Control Panel, you can see an Installed Updates list in Control Panel by following these steps

1. Right-click the Start button and select Control Panel.
2. Open Programs > Programs And Features.
3. Click View Installed Updates.
4. Select an update that you want to uninstall.

   If Windows allows you to uninstall it, Uninstall appears on the toolbar.
5. In the Uninstall An Update dialog box, click Yes to confirm.
6. Accept the UAC if prompted.

   A restart might be needed to complete the removal of the update.

Uninstall a Windows update in Settings

The Settings app ultimately opens the same Installed Updates list in Control Panel. Perform these steps if you prefer to use the Settings app.

1. Open Settings and click Update & Security.
2. Click Windows Update and then click Advanced Options.
3. Click View Your Update History.

   A list of your installed Windows Updates appears.
4. Click Uninstall Updates at the top of the screen.

The link opens the Control Panel > Programs> Programs and Features > Installed Updates page.

5. Select an update that you want to uninstall.

   If Windows allows you to uninstall it, Uninstall appears on the toolbar.

6. In the Uninstall An Update dialog box, click Yes to confirm.

7. Accept the UAC if prompted.

   A restart might be needed to complete the removal of the update.

Uninstall a Windows update by using the command prompt

Sometimes you will want to remove the same update from multiple devices. After you have tested the command-line tool on your test device, you can use the command prompt or Windows PowerShell to script the command and distribute it to multiple devices by using Group Policy or Windows PowerShell.

You can use the Windows Management Instrumentation command-line utility to generate a list of installed Windows Update packages on a Windows 10–based device, as shown in Figure 11-11.

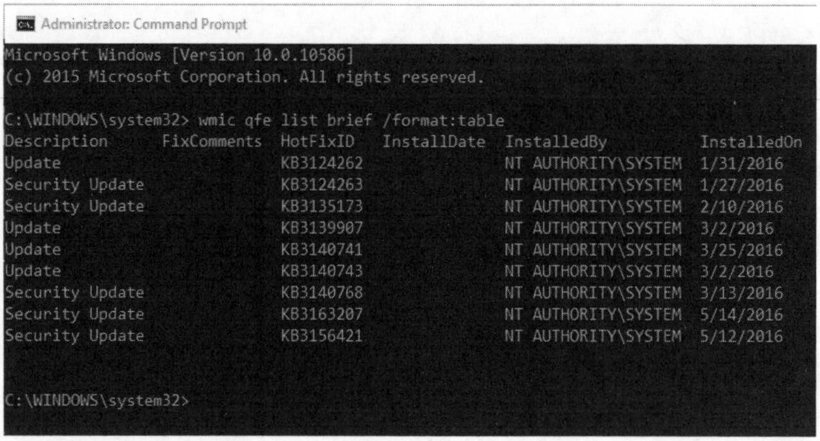

```
Administrator: Command Prompt
Microsoft Windows [Version 10.0.10586]
(c) 2015 Microsoft Corporation. All rights reserved.

C:\WINDOWS\system32> wmic qfe list brief /format:table
Description      FixComments  HotFixID   InstallDate  InstalledBy          InstalledOn
Update                        KB3124262               NT AUTHORITY\SYSTEM  1/31/2016
Security Update               KB3124263               NT AUTHORITY\SYSTEM  1/27/2016
Security Update               KB3135173               NT AUTHORITY\SYSTEM  2/10/2016
Update                        KB3139907               NT AUTHORITY\SYSTEM  3/2/2016
Update                        KB3140741               NT AUTHORITY\SYSTEM  3/25/2016
Update                        KB3140743               NT AUTHORITY\SYSTEM  3/2/2016
Security Update               KB3140768               NT AUTHORITY\SYSTEM  3/13/2016
Security Update               KB3163207               NT AUTHORITY\SYSTEM  5/14/2016
Security Update               KB3156421               NT AUTHORITY\SYSTEM  5/12/2016

C:\WINDOWS\system32>
```

FIGURE 11-11 Installed Windows Update packages

To generate the list of installed Windows Update packages on your device, open an elevated command prompt and type the following command.

```
wmic qfe list brief /format:table
```

When you have identified an update that you want to remove, you can use the Windows Update Stand-Alone Installer (Wusa.exe) command-line tool to uninstall updates by providing the package number (from the Microsoft Knowledge Base) of the update to be uninstalled. The syntax for the tool is as follows.

```
wusa.exe /uninstall /kb:<KB Number>
```

Substitute *<KB Number>* in the command with the actual KB number of the update you want to uninstall. The WMIC and WUSA commands work in either the command prompt or Windows PowerShell.

Revert to a previous build of Windows 10

Since Windows 8, you have had the option to remove an update completely and revert to the pre-update status. With Windows 10, this process has become more reliable and more refined.

With the Insider Preview of Windows 10, you have been able to remove the preview version and install the full version. If you upgraded from a previous version of Windows within the past 30 days, and things are not working out, you can simply roll back to your previous operating system installation, and your settings, apps, and any files, such as photos or documents, you've added during the past 30 days to your Windows 10 installation will be retained with the older version of Windows.

During any system upgrade—for example, upgrading from Windows 8.1 or implementing the Windows 10 1511 build upgrade—Windows creates a Windows.old folder on the system volume to retain a copy of your previous version of Windows. Because this file can be very large, 10 GB or larger, the file is automatically deleted after 30 days. You can preserve a copy of this file, or rename it, to prevent the deletion. You would need to replace and rename it back to the original Windows.old filename if you wanted to use it.

If you have recently upgraded to a newer build of Windows 10 and want to revert to the previous version, you can do so by using Recovery in the Settings app or the Go Back To Previous Windows From Windows 10 in the Advanced Startup options.

> **NOTE   PREVIEW BUILDS ARE EXPERIMENTAL**
>
> When using Insider Preview builds of Windows 10, there can be changes to menus, options, and processes. The steps to revert to a previous build might change when you carry out these steps. The steps shown in this book were used to revert Windows 10 build 14332 to Windows 10 build 10240.

To use Recovery in the Settings app, use these steps.

1. Search for the word "recovery" and select Recovery Options in the System settings.
2. On the Recovery page, shown in Figure 11-12, select Get Started.

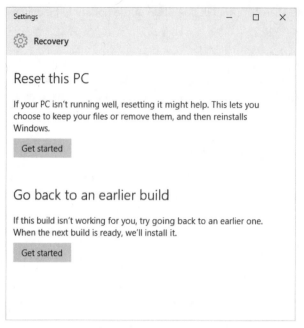

FIGURE 11-12 Go Back To An Earlier Build of Windows 10

The Getting Things Ready dialog box appears, and Windows checks whether the Windows.old file is present.

3. Answer the short questionnaire to provide feedback to Microsoft about why you are going back and then click Next.

4. On the Check For Updates page, click No, Thanks.

5. On the What You Need To Know page, click Next.

6. On the Don't Get Locked Out page, click Next.

7. On the Thanks For Trying Windows 10 page, click Go Back To Earlier Build.

Your computer restarts, and the earlier build of Windows now starts restoring.

To use the Go Back To Previous Windows From Windows 10 in Advanced Startup, use these steps.

1. Boot to advanced startup options.

2. In the Choose An Option dialog box, click Troubleshoot.

3. On the Troubleshoot page, click Advanced Options.

4. On the Advanced Options page, if you don't see Go Back To The Previous Build, click See More Recovery Options if displayed.

5. Click Go Back To The Previous Build.

6. On the Go Back To The Previous Build page, select an administrator account and enter the password for this administrator account.

7. Click Continue.

8. On the Go Back To The Previous Build page, click Go Back To Previous.

   Your computer restarts, and the earlier build of Windows now starts restoring.

> **NOTE   WE'RE SORRY, BUT YOU CAN'T GO BACK**
>
> If the Windows.old file is not found, Windows 10 recovery will not be able to take you back to a previous version of Windows.

You can check which version of Windows 10 your device is currently running by using these steps.

1. Click the Start button and then click Settings.

2. Click System and then select About.

   The details of your Windows 10 operating system appears, as shown in Figure 11-13.

FIGURE 11-13   Windows 10 Version and OS Build

3. Alternatively, you can click the Start button and type **WinVer**.

From the About screen shown in Figure 11-13, you can determine whether you should upgrade your system. If you are using version 10.0 (Build 10240), this is the initial release version of Windows 10 (RTM), and you should install a later Windows 10 update. The version used at the time of writing is version 1511 (OS Build 10565.xxx), which is the first published Current Branch version.

Skill: Update Windows Store apps

Windows 10 supports the Windows Store apps introduced in Windows 8. Windows Store apps are different from traditional desktop apps, such as Office apps. However, in Windows 10, Microsoft introduced a new Universal Windows Platform (UWP), which provides a common app platform across every device that is capable of running Windows 10. Apps that are designed for the UWP can call both the traditional desktop apps (using the Win32 application program interfaces [APIs] and Microsoft .NET Framework) and the Windows Store apps. This means developers can now create a single app that can run across all devices.

In earlier versions of Windows, the system would check whether updates were available. If they were, the Store tile on the Start page would display an indication that updates are available.

Windows 10 automatically checks the Windows Store for updates to installed apps on a daily basis and displays a counter (downward pointing arrow along with a number) on the menu bar of the Windows Store app for how many apps you can update. When an update is available, Windows 10 by default automatically downloads the files and updates the installed apps. You can modify this behavior and manually select which apps you want to update by following these steps.

1. Sign in to Windows 10, using a Microsoft account.
2. Open the Windows Store.
3. Next to the Search box, click the account symbol and then click Settings.
4. Under App Updates, slide Update Apps Automatically to Off, as shown in Figure 11-14.

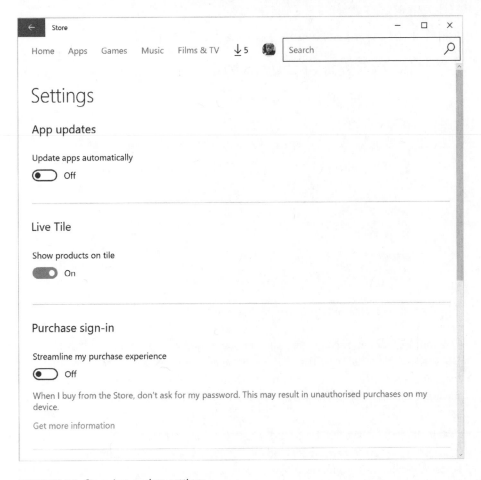

FIGURE 11-14 Store App update settings

To update apps manually, perform the following procedure.

1. Sign in to Windows 10, using a Microsoft account.
2. Open the Windows Store.
3. Next to the Search box, click the account symbol and then click Downloads And Updates.

   All apps with available updates appear.
4. You can click Update All or manually select individual apps to update by clicking the downward-pointing arrow, as shown in Figure 11-15.

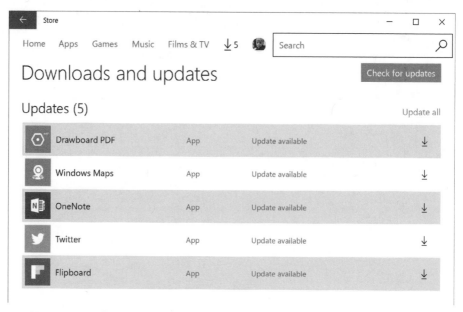

FIGURE 11-15 Manually downloading Store apps

Windows Store apps can be regularly updated by the developer and made available to the Store for you to install. Previous versions of the app can be automatically updated whenever the device is connected to the Internet. Because apps install and update in the background, the first indication that there was an update might be when a new or updated tile appears in Start.

Administrators have limited control over the installed Windows Store app updates, though it is possible to turn off automatic updates for apps at any time by configuring the App Updates setting in the Windows Store or changing Group Policy. You cannot control which specific updates are installed; the device downloads and receives all available updates or no updates.

Administrators can also block many features of the Store app completely by using the settings found in the Group Policy node: Computer Configuration\Administrative Templates \Windows Components\Store. The settings that are most appropriate for Windows 10 are listed in Table 11-1.

TABLE 11-1 Windows Store Group Policy settings

Group Policy Setting	Description
Turn off Automatic Download And Install of Updates	Enables or disables the automatic download and installation of app updates. If enabled, the automatic download and installation of app updates is turned off.
Disable All Apps From Windows Store	Disable turns off the launch of all apps from the Windows Store on the device. The Windows Store is also disabled.

Group Policy Setting	Description
Turn Off The Store Application	Denies or allows access to the Store application. If enabled, access to the Store app is denied, and apps cannot be updated.
Only Display The Private Store Within The Windows Store App	Denies access to the retail catalog in the Windows Store app but displays the Company app store.

Summary

- Windows 10 will be updated with ongoing servicing updates containing security, software updates, and feature upgrades, providing new features and functionality.
- Windows 10 Home users cannot disable updates or defer feature upgrades.
- Pro, Enterprise, and Education editions of Windows 10 can opt to use the current branch for business and defer upgrades by at least four months.
- A special build of Windows 10, Long-Term Servicing Branch (LTSB), is available, which won't force businesses to accept feature upgrades.
- Delivery Optimization enables Windows 10 to source Windows Update from local PCs and from devices on the Internet.
- The Windows Insider program enables members to gain access to the pre-release versions of Windows 10 and provide feedback directly to the development team.
- Windows updates can be rolled back individually and prevented from re-installing.
- You can remove a preview build completely and revert to the previous build of Windows without losing settings or data.
- Windows Store apps are automatically updated, but you can modify this setting and manually update each app.
- You can restrict access to the Windows Store, apps, and app updates by using Group Policy.

Thought experiment

In this thought experiment, demonstrate your skills and knowledge of the topics covered in this chapter. You can find answers to this thought experiment in the next section.

Your organization is considering upgrading the whole company to Windows 10 in the next six to nine months. You need to be able to recommend which version of Windows 10 the company requires as well as keep up to date with the continual development of the operating system. Your organization specializes in the health care industry and has approximately 2,000 members of office and mobile staff. The Research and Development team use a specialist LOB application that does not need access to the Internet or require any operating software updates.

Your team needs to understand the new Universal Windows Platform Store apps to see whether some current applications can use this format. Until this research is complete, you need to restrict the use of Store apps.

Answer the following questions for your manager.

1. How will you keep abreast of the latest development in Windows 10 and access the preview builds?

2. Which branch of Windows 10 will you recommend for the office and mobile staff and the Research and Development team?

3. How could you prevent users from installing apps from the Windows Store?

Thought experiment answer

This section contains the solution to the thought experiment.

1. You should sign up to be a Windows Insider at *https://insider.windows.com/*, build a virtual machine, and install an evaluation version of Windows 10 on it. Configure Windows 10 to be on the Fast ring of Insider builds. You will also receive a regular Insider newsletter.

2. As an enterprise customer, you would recommend the Current Branch of Windows 10 Enterprise for all staff users and the Long-Term Servicing Branch version for the devices that are required to run the Research and Development LOB application.

3. You could configure the Group Policy setting, Disable All Apps From Windows Store, which is found in the Computer Configuration/Administrative Templates/Windows Components/Store node. This prevents the launching of all apps from the Windows Store on all devices. The Windows Store will also be disabled. The Group Policy should be applied to all Windows 10–based devices.

CHAPTER 12

Monitor Windows

With the emergence of solid state drives, there are fewer moving parts in a modern computer, but the internal workings of a device and the operating system are still hugely complicated. To the majority of users, their device is a tool to facilitate their work and, in this regard, a computer system that performs poorly or slows them down either at home or at the workplace reduces their productivity and can increase their frustration.

Windows 10 has built-in, self-tuning mechanisms that maintain the system. If you need to review and diagnose potential causes of poor performance manually, you can use some of the many tools to resolve issues. In response to a major increase in system attacks, Microsoft keeps Windows secure from malware by enabling Windows Update to download new definitions for Windows Defender automatically. This chapter reviews numerous tools and focuses on the skills required to configure and monitor Windows 10 so that you can assess issues through logs and real-time data collection.

Skills covered in this chapter:

- Configure and analyze Event Viewer logs
- Configure event subscriptions
- Monitor performance using Task Manager
- Monitor performance using Resource Monitor
- Monitor performance using Performance Monitor and Data Collector Sets
- Monitor system resources
- Monitor and manage printers
- Configure indexing options
- Manage client security by using Windows Defender
- Evaluate system stability using Reliability Monitor
- Troubleshoot performance issues

Skill: Configure and analyze Event Viewer logs

A key built-in security tool in all Windows operating systems are event logs, which are accessed in the Windows Event Viewer and provide information regarding system events that occur. Event logs are generated as a background activity by the Event Log service and can include information, warning, and error messages about Windows components and installed applications and actions carried out on the system.

> **This section covers how to:**
> - Understand event logs
> - Create a custom view

Understand event logs

You can start Event Viewer, as shown in Figure 12-1, by typing **eventvwr.msc**.

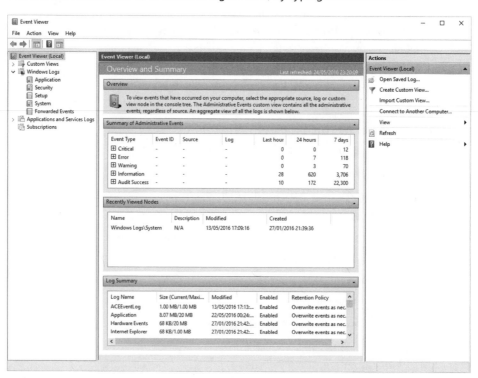

FIGURE 12-1 Event Viewer Overview And Summary

Upon opening, the console retrieves the events that have occurred on your computer and displays them. You can configure the Event Viewer to work with event logs from remote computers; you must enable remote management in your firewall.

There are two types of log files.

- **Windows logs**   Include Application, Security, Setup, System, and Forwarded Events
- **Applications and services logs**   Include other logs from applications and services to record application-specific or service-specific events

Because logs are created as part of the operating system, they can provide forensic-level metadata that can help you understand problems that are difficult to diagnose, using real-time analysis of the system.

The Windows logs are described in more detail in Table 12-1.

TABLE 12-1 Built-in Windows logs

Log	Description	LOG FILE Location	Default LOG Size
Application	Events logged by installed applications.	%SystemRoot%\System32\Winevt\Logs\Application.Evtx	20,480 KB
Setup	Records events logged by Windows during setup and installation.	%SystemRoot%\System32\Winevt\Logs\Setup.Evtx	1,028 KB
Security	Contains auditable events such as log-on, logoff, privilege use, and shutdown.	%SystemRoot%\System32\Winevt\Logs\Security.Evtx.	20,480 KB
System	Contains events logged by Windows 10. This is the main system log.	%SystemRoot%\System32\Winevt\Logs\System.Evtx	20,480 KB
Forwarded Events	Used when event forwarding is operational. This log records forwarded events from other computers.	%SystemRoot%\System32\Config\ForwardedEvents.Evtx	20,480 KB

The default Windows 10 event log maximum file size is 20 MB. If your system reaches this maximum size, new events will overwrite old events.

Open Event Viewer and take some time to familiarize yourself by reviewing some logs. There are several levels of events, with meanings as follows.

- **Information**   These logs provide information about changes related to a component or system process, usually a successful outcome.
- **Audit Success/Failure**   If you have enabled auditing, these log entries appear in the security log.
- **Error**   Error events warn you that a problem has occurred.
- **Warning**   These events are not critical, although they could lead to more serious problems and should be investigated.
- **Critical**   These events are the most severe and could lead to failure or loss of function. They are highly significant and indicate that a problem is occurring or has occurred.

In Event Viewer, select each of the Windows logs and look at the types of events that have been generated. The Actions pane on the right side provides tools and wizards to help you work with logs, including saving a log, clearing/deleting entries in a log, opening a previously saved log, and attaching a task to an event.

> **NOTE EVENT ID**
>
> The Event ID found in an event log provides an ID for the specific event type that occurred. You can find more detailed information about an Event ID in the Microsoft Knowledge Base.

Create a custom view

When you explore Event Viewer, you might find so many entries that it is hard to locate specific issues. You'll want to remove entries, but you should not clear a log on a production machine without first saving the log. A better method of removing log entries such as informational or warning log entries is to create a custom view that shows only specific events. This acts like a saved filter that you can invoke.

To create a custom view in Event Viewer that displays only Critical events in the System log, follow these steps.

1. Open Event Viewer.
2. On the Action menu, click Create Custom View.
3. On the Filter tab, select the Critical check box in Event Level.
4. In By Log, use the Down Arrow and expand Windows Logs; select only the System check box.
5. Click OK.
6. Type a name, such as System-Critical for the log name, and click OK.

   The custom view immediately refreshes and displays log entries that match the criteria.
7. Your custom view filter, in this case named System-Critical, is located in the left pane, under the Custom Views node.
8. Close Event Viewer.

With all events, you can double-click the event log entry to reveal its Properties dialog box. The Event Properties dialog box provides you with additional detailed information together with a Copy button so that you can copy the event data to the Clipboard and then work with the data or seek help. Event descriptions have become easier to understand than in previous versions of Windows. The experience of reading event log entries will also help build your understanding.

Skill: Configure event subscriptions

You can configure Event Viewer to view other computers' event logs. Manually connecting to other computers on a regular basis can be cumbersome. You can automate the collection of event logs from other computers by creating event subscriptions.

All computers participating in a subscription must be configured to allow remote administration. This is achieved by enabling the Windows Remote Management service on the source computer. On the collector computer, start the Windows Event Collector service, which enables the computer to collect events from remote devices. To configure the computers to collect and send events, perform the following two short procedures.

> **This section covers how to:**
> - View subscriptions
> - Create a subscription
> - Access event logs remotely

View subscriptions

To enable the collector computer to view subscriptions:

1. Open an elevated command prompt.
2. Type **wecutil qc** and press Enter.
3. Type **Y** and press Enter to start the service.

    Windows Event Collector service announces it was configured successfully.
4. Close the command prompt window.

To enable remote collection of events on the source computer:

1. Open an elevated command prompt.
2. Type **winrm quickconfig** and press Enter.
3. Type **Y** and press Enter; repeat when prompted.

    The WinRM firewall exception is now enabled.
4. Close the command prompt window.

EXAM TIP

The winrm quickconfig and wecutil qc commands are needed to create and allow subscriptions to be successfully collected. Make sure that you know which command is run on each participant for the exam.

You can create two kinds of subscriptions: collector initiated and source-computer initiated. The subscriptions are described in Table 12-2, with some of the key terms related to event subscriptions.

TABLE 12-2 Event subscription terms

Term	Description
Subscription	A group of events you configure based on specific criteria you create is called a subscription. Subscriptions enable you to receive events from other computers, called sources.
Source	The event source computer is the computer that provides you with events on your network. The source computer can be a PC or a server.
Collector	The event collector computer is the computer on which you view the collected events. The collector computer can be a PC or a server.
Collector-initiated subscription	In a collector-initiated subscription, the subscription must contain a list of all the event sources that need to be added one at a time. This is used on small networks because each must be configured manually.
Source computer–initiated subscription	The source computer transmits local events to the collector computer. This is a push type of arrangement, often configured using Group Policy.

Create a subscription

To create a collector-initiated subscription, follow these steps.

1. Open Event Viewer.
2. Click the Subscriptions node.
3. If the option to start the Windows Event Collection Service dialog box appears, click Yes.
4. In the Action pane, click Create Subscription.
5. Type a name and a description for the subscription, as shown in Figure 12-2.

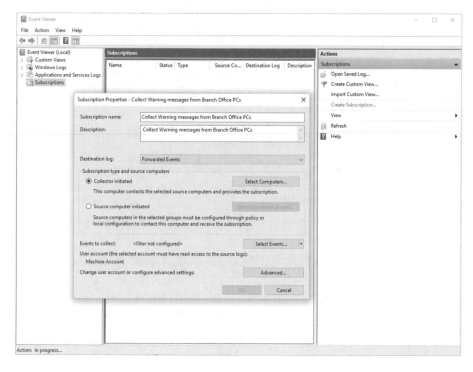

FIGURE 12-2 Creating an event subscription

6. Under Subscription Type And Source Computers, click Collector Initiated and click Select Computers.

7. In the Computers dialog box, click Add Domain Computers, select the computer to be polled for subscriptions, and click OK.

8. Under Events To Collect, click Select Events and define the event criteria, such as event levels, log type, and event source, that will be used to match and collect events. Click OK.

9. Click OK to save and make the subscription active.

   The new subscription is listed in the Subscriptions node main pane.

If you want to view events on other computers on your network, you can do so without creating a subscription. This is useful for ad hoc monitoring, for example, to see whether a particular event has occurred.

Access event logs remotely

To view event logs on a remote system, follow these steps.

1. Open Event Viewer.

2. Right-click Event Viewer (Local) in the left pane and choose Connect To Another Computer.

3. When the Select Computer dialog box opens, click Another Computer and enter the name, type the domain name or IP address of the computer, or click Browse to search for the computer on your network.

4. If you need to specify logon credentials, select the Connect As Another User check box. Click Set User and type the logon credentials for a local administrator or user on the remote device and then click OK.

> **NOTE VIEW EVENTS ON REMOTE COMPUTERS**
>
> You must have administrator privileges to view events on a remote computer. You must also configure Windows Firewall on all participants to allow traffic on TCP port 80 for HTTP or on TCP port 443 for HTTPS.

Skill: Monitor performance using Task Manager

If you have used an earlier version of Windows, you probably have used Task Manager. This is one of the most useful tools available in Windows for gaining an immediate insight into how a system is performing.

> **This section covers how to:**
> - Access Task Manager
> - Use the Task Manager tabs

Access Task Manager

The Task Manager built into Windows 10 shows you which processes (tasks) are running on your system and, importantly, shows the system resource usage that directly relates to performance. If a particular task or process is not responding, or continues to run after you have closed the application, you can use Task Manager to view this behavior and force the offending process to end.

When troubleshooting, you might find that some users are comfortable using Task Manager to review the system status and end problematic tasks.

If you are moving to Windows 10 from Windows 7 or earlier, notice that Task Manager has been redesigned extensively and is now much more user-friendly, informative, and colorful and slightly less technical.

To open Task Manager, right-click the Start button and then click Task Manager. There are several other ways to open Task Manager, including Ctrl+Shift+Esc or right-clicking the task-bar, Cortana, or the Task View button and then clicking Task Manager.

By default, the Task Manager opens to show only the running applications, as shown in Figure 12-3. While using this view, you can highlight any of the listed applications and click End Task to stop a running app.

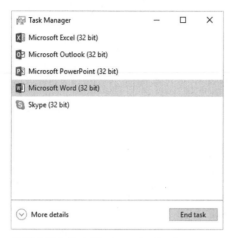

FIGURE 12-3 Task Manager simple view

If you click More Details, Task Manager reopens and displays seven tabs, which enable you to review specific areas of your computer activity. The tabs are described in Table 12-3.

TABLE 12-3 Task Manager tabs

Task Manager Tab	Description
Processes	Shows all running apps and background processes
Performance	Shows real-time statistics for CPU, memory, disk, Ethernet, Bluetooth, and Wi-Fi usage
App History	Shows historical data for universal and modern apps usage for the previous month
Startup	Lists the apps that start when the computer boots
Users	Lists all the users currently logged on to the computer locally and remotely
Details	Shows detailed statistics on all running and suspended processes
Services	Displays all running and stopped system services

Each tab offers you a different view of the system. Most users might be interested only in the simple view, whereas most IT professionals will only use the detailed version of Task Manager.

Processes tab

All running apps and background processes are grouped as shown in Figure 12-4, and within each process, there might also be more detail. Where an app or process has an arrow beside it, you can click the arrow to see the related processes. For example, if you are running Word and have two documents open, when you click the arrow next to the Word app, the display expands to show both instances of the app that are running. If you highlight an app instance or process and click End Task, Windows 10 attempts to close the activity.

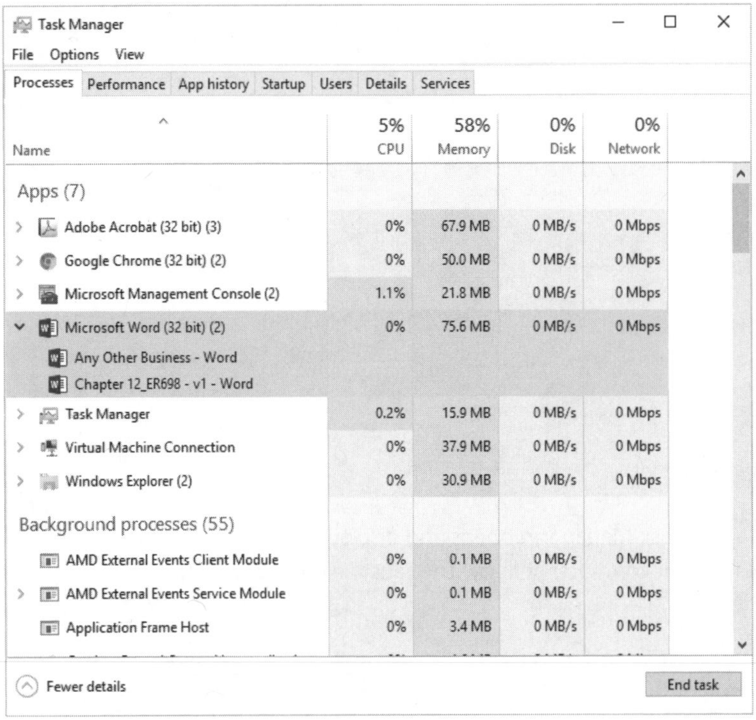

FIGURE 12-4 Task Manager simple view

The new visual appearance of the Processes tab contents is representative of a heat mapping of the data. This is designed to be easier for you to spot the high resource usage and problematic issues requiring attention or further investigation.

Each of the data columns on the heat map is sortable by clicking each heading, such as Memory or Disk. Notice that when you click a column heading, all apps and processes are listed together and are no longer grouped in the first column.

Performance tab

The Performance tab provides a graphical, real-time, statistical view for CPU, Memory, Disk, and Ethernet. If you have multiple Ethernet devices, such as Wi-Fi, these are listed. Figure 12-5 shows the Performance tab with disk 0 selected. There are three volumes on Disk 0, and these are aggregated as a single disk. In the lower pane, below the graphics, you see additional information such as read/write speed, capacity, and average response time. If you are connected to Wi-Fi and click Ethernet, you see the adapter name, Service Set Identifier (SSID), Domain Name Service (DNS) name, connection type, IPv4 and IPv6 addresses, and signal strength.

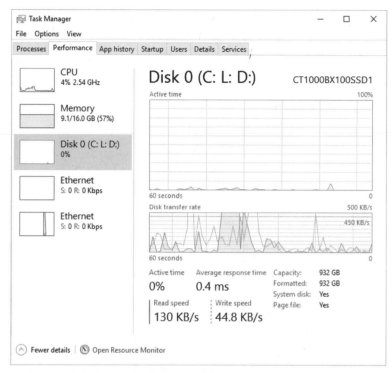

FIGURE 12-5 Task Manager Performance view

At the bottom of the Performance tab is an Open Resource Monitor link to the management console.

App History tab

The App History tab shows a list of all modern apps that are installed on the device. The table format lists the app usage for the previous month, and columns include CPU Time, Network, Metered Network, and Tile Updates. Where an app has related apps, such as the Messaging + Skype item, the results show aggregated usage totals for Skype Video and Messaging. The grid uses color to highlight the items that are using the most resources within each column.

If you right-click the name of an app, you can select Switch To, which launches the app.

Startup tab

The Startup tab displays which apps start when Windows 10 launches. The information appears in a table, and the columns include Name, Publisher, Status, and Startup Impact.

Under each column is displayed the status or setting for each app. You can enable or disable each app to allow or prevent it from starting when Windows starts. The startup impact caused by the app is an indication of what resources the app is using and how long it takes to initialize; it's categorized by None, Low, Medium, or High.

If you right-click one of the app names, the context menu allows you to:

- Toggle the Disable/Enable status for the app.
- Open File Location for the app.
- Search Online for details of the app.
- Launch the app Properties.

Users tab

All users currently logged on interactively or remotely are displayed on the Users tab. The information is displayed in table format, and the default columns include User, Status, CPU, Memory, Disk, and Network. You can right-click the column heading and select additional information to be displayed.

If the user signed on using a Microsoft account, the user name is the email address associated with the Microsoft account. On shared devices, such as a home computer on which users may access HomeGroup or still be logged on concurrently, you can review the impact on the computer resources for each active user.

If you right-click a user, you can expand the tree to view the active processes for the user. You can terminate any process in this list by selecting a single process and then clicking End Task.

If you want to end the session that the user has on the computer, you can disconnect a user by right-clicking the user and clicking Disconnect. The user will be informed by a pop-up window that they have been disconnected.

Details tab

All running processes are displayed on the Details tab. The information is displayed in table format, and the default columns include Name, Process ID (PID), Status, User Name, CPU, Memory (private working set), and Description.

You can right-click the column heading and select additional information to appear, including Package Name, Session ID, CPU Time, Page Faults, Threads, and many more. The information displayed is the same as was reported on the Windows 7 Task Manager Processes tab.

If you right-click a process, you can then select several options, including End Task, End Process Tree, Set Priority, Set Affinity, UAC Virtualization, Create Dump File, Open File Location, Search Online, Properties, and Go To Services.

Services tab

The last tab displays all services that are available on the device. These include the status of Running or Stopped. If you right-click a service, you can then select from the context menu to Start, Stop, Restart, Open Services, Search Online, and Go To Details for each service. Some options are only available for services that are running. At the bottom of the Services tab is a link to open the Services management console.

Skill: Monitor performance using Resource Monitor

The Resource Monitor displays more information and activity statistics relating to your system resources in real time. It is similar to Task Manager but also enables you to dive deeper into the actual processes and see how they affect the performance of your CPU, disk, network, and memory subcomponents.

Open Resource Monitor by using the link on the Performance tab of Task Manager or search for Resource on the Start button. The executable for Resource Monitor is Resmon.exe, which you can run from a Run dialog box or command prompt.

When you open Resource Monitor, you see an overview of your system with graphs for each area of the system subcomponent. Four further tabs are available, for CPU, Disk, Network, and Memory. The statistics tracked on the Overview tab include the following.

- % CPU Usage
- CPU Maximum Frequency
- Disk I/O Bytes Per Second
- Disk % Highest Active Time
- Network I/O Bytes Per Second
- % Network Utilization
- Memory Hard Faults Per Second
- % Physical Memory Used

Review each tab; each subcomponent offers additional components, as shown in Table 12-4.

TABLE 12-4 Resource Monitor components

System Component	Additional subcomponents
CPU	Processes Services Associated Handles Associated Modules
Memory	Processes Physical Memory
Disk	Processes With Disk Activity Disk Activity Storage
Network	Processes With Network Activity Network Activity TCP Connections Listening Ports

In each data collector, you can sort the output by clicking the column title. If you select one or more processes in the topmost section, selecting the check box on the left side creates a filter for the items across all four tabs. The selected item is highlighted in an orange color so that you can see how the item compares to the overall output, as shown in Figure 12-6.

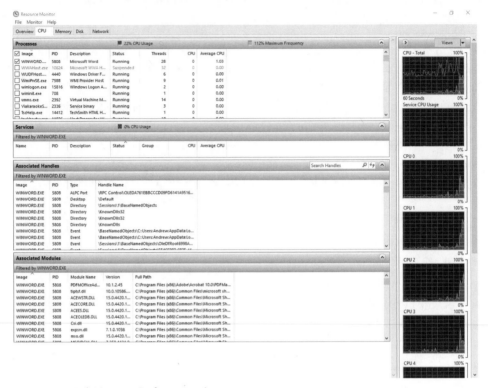

FIGURE 12-6 Task Manager Performance view

Resource Monitor is useful for troubleshooting performance issues that relate to high resource usage, and you need to establish which process is using a more than normal amount of resource such as memory.

For more advanced analysis, you can right-click any column and choose additional columns by choosing Select Columns. Each tab has associated columns; the CPU panel offers the following additional columns.

- **Average Cycle**   Average percentage of CPU cycle time for the process (over a 60-second interval)

- **Cycle**   Current percentage of CPU cycle time the process is using

- **Elevated**   Elevation status of the process. (If this is Yes, it is an elevated process.)

- **Operating System Context**   The operating system context in which the process is running

- **Platform**   Platform architecture that the process is running
- **User Name**   Name of the user or service that is running the process

If you want to freeze the screen so that you can analyze the display or capture an image, you can click the Monitor menu item and select Stop Monitoring.

Skill: Monitor performance using Performance Monitor and Data Collector Sets

You can use the Performance Monitor Microsoft Management Console (MMC) snap-in to monitor and track your device for the default set of performance parameters or a custom set you select for display. These performance parameters are referred to as counters. Performance Monitor graphically displays statistics and offers real-time monitoring and recording capabilities. By default, the update interval for the capture is set to one second, but this is configurable.

You can use the tool to record performance information in a log file so that it can be played back and used as part of your overall benchmarking process on a system being tested, or when collecting information to help you troubleshoot an issue. You can also create alerts that notify you when a specific performance criterion, such as a threshold or limit, has been met or exceeded.

The easiest way to learn how to use Performance Monitor is to run one of the two built-in collector sets and review the results.

- **System Diagnostics**   Data Collector Set collects the status of local hardware resources and configuration data, together with data from the System Information tool.
- **System Performance**   Data Collector Set reports the status of local hardware resources, system response times, and processes.

> **This section covers how to:**
> - Run the Performance Monitor data collector
> - Use Performance Monitor

Run the Performance Monitor data collector

To run the System Performance data collector and view the report, follow these steps.

1. Type **Performance** into Start and click Performance Monitor in Control Panel.
2. On the navigation pane, select Data Collector Sets\System and click System Performance.
3. On the toolbar, click the Run icon (green triangle).

   The collector runs for 60 seconds and then stops.

4. In the navigation pane, select Reports and expand System.

5. Click the chevron arrow next to System Performance and then click the report icon.

   The System Performance Report appears in the results pane.

6. Review the System Performance Report and then close Performance Monitor.

When you review the report, as shown in Figure 12-7, you can see how extensive and detailed the monitoring is. The report is saved and can be printed and refreshed to provide an up-to-date report.

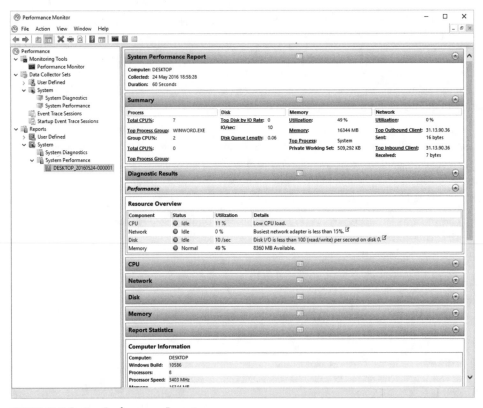

FIGURE 12-7 System Performance Report

The diagnostic or performance-monitoring data collector sets are very useful when identifying the cause of performance deterioration that might be a warning sign of potential malfunction or failing hardware.

You can manually configure Performance Monitor to report on one or many parameters you select for display. You choose the counters that relate to the hardware and software installed on your system. If you add new hardware, such as a new network card, Performance Monitor updates the set of performance counters for the new resource.

Use Performance Monitor

To use Performance Monitor, you start with a blank canvas and add items that you want to monitor. There are three components that you can add as follows.

- **Performance objects** These relate to any system component that enables monitoring such as:
  - *Physical*: The memory, the processor, or the paging file.
  - *Logical component*: For example, a logical disk or print queue.
  - *Software*: For example, a process or a thread.
- **Performance object instances** These represent single occurrences of performance objects. You can choose individual instances or track all instances of an object.
- **Performance counters** These are the measurable properties of performance objects, such as the Bytes Sent/Sec for the Ethernet Controller as shown in Figure 12-8.

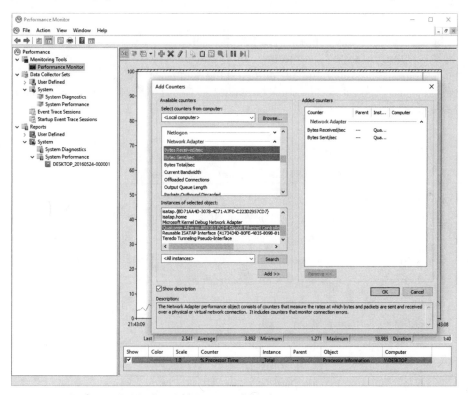

FIGURE 12-8 Performance Monitor Add Counters dialog box

After some counters have been selected, a moving graphical display shows the activity relating to the counters selected. You can locate the color of the line from the key at the base of the graph and hide/show any counter by clearing the check box on the left of the counter.

A selection of the most common performance objects that you might want to monitor are summarized in Table 12-5.

TABLE 12-5 Commonly tracked performance objects

Performance Object	Description
Memory	Monitors memory performance for system cache, physical memory, and virtual memory
IPv4	Monitors IPv4 communications
LogicalDisk	Monitors the logical volumes on a computer
Network Interface	Monitors the network adapters on the computer
PhysicalDisk	Monitors hard disk read/write activity and data transfers, hard faults, and soft faults
Print Queue	Monitors print jobs, spooling, and print queue activity
Processor	Monitors processor idle time, idle states, usage, deferred procedure calls, and interrupts

Because the monitoring is real-time, the effect of monitoring many counters can have an impact on the host system performance, which could distort the usefulness of the performance information. You should therefore test the number of counters and the frequency of data collection and witness the impact. To add new values to the Performance Monitor chart, follow these steps.

1. Click the Start button and type **perfmon**.

   Performance Monitor opens.

2. Click the Performance Monitor node in the left pane.

   The default counter for % Processor Time appears.

3. On the toolbar, click the plus (+) symbol to add an additional counter.

4. In the Available Counters area, expand PhysicalDisk and click % Idle Time.

5. In the Instances Of Selected Object box, click 0 C:, click Add, and click OK.

6. Right-click % Idle Time and then click Properties.

7. In the Color box, click blue, and then click OK.

8. Leave Performance Monitor open.

To create a new Data Collector Set based on a template, in Performance Monitor, follow these steps.

1. In the left pane, expand Data Collector Sets and then click User Defined.

2. Right-click User Defined, click New, and then click Data Collector Set.

3. On the Create New Data Collector Set page, type Disk Activity and click Next.

4. In the Template Data Collector Set box, click Basic and click Next.

5. Click Next to accept the default storage location.

6. Select Open Properties For This Data Collector Set and click Finish.

The Disk Activity Properties dialog box appears and has six tabs.

7. Review the General, Directory, Security, Schedule, Stop Condition, and Task tabs and click OK.

8. In the right pane, double-click Disk Activity.

   Three types of logs are shown in the right pane:

   - Performance Counter collects data, viewable in Performance Monitor.
   - Configuration records change to registry keys.
   - Kernel Trace collects detailed information about system events and activities.

9. In the right pane, double-click Performance Counter.

10. Select the Processor Counter and click Remove.

11. Click Add and then click PhysicalDisk in Available Counters.

12. Click Add and then click OK.

13. In the left pane, right-click Disk Activity and then click Start.

14. On the Disk Activity node, a small play icon appears for 60 seconds.

15. When Data Collector Set has stopped recording, right-click Disk Activity and then click Latest Report.

16. Review the report, which shows the data that the data collector set collected.

17. Close Performance Monitor.

In the troubleshooting section of this chapter, review some of the performance bottle-necks that can occur on a system and the performance counters that can be useful when diagnosing the cause and choosing remediation.

Skill: Monitor system resources

Every computer system has a performance threshold that, if pushed beyond this level, will cause the system to struggle to perform optimally. If you overload the system, it eventually slows down as it attempts to service each demand with the available resources. Most systems include a capable processor and sufficient amount of RAM for everyday or general needs. Memory is automatically reclaimed from apps that are closed. However, when apps or web browser tabs are left open, and more apps are then opened, the overall ability for the system to perform is degraded.

> **This section covers how to:**
> - Understand baseline performance vs. real-time monitoring
> - Create a performance baseline

Understand baseline performance vs. real-time monitoring

You have seen that with tools such as Performance Monitor, Resource Monitor, and Task Manager, you can monitor your system activity and understand how demands on processor, RAM, networking, and disks affect your computer system. Real-time monitoring information is useful for instant diagnosis, whereas creating a baseline for your computer's performance can generate a system-specific report that can be useful to show what your performance statistics look like during normal or heavy use.

If you intend to ship a device to a user who will use the device extensively for system-intensive tasks, such as video editing or computer-aided design, it might be useful to create a performance baseline for the device so that you can establish how the system performs normally and when under heavy load. This will be useful to confirm that the device specification is suitable for the user, but also if the user reports performance issues, you can run another performance baseline and compare the two baselines to evaluate whether the system environment has changed, for example, if the user regularly multitasks with additional new apps on the system that use additional memory.

In this scenario, when an issue or symptom occurs, you can compare your baseline statistics to your real-time statistic and identify differences between the two instances. When you can diagnose the issue, you can recommend a solution, such as to add more memory.

The most appropriate tool to record a baseline in Windows 10 is Performance Monitor; it will help you review and report on the following areas in your system.

- Evaluate your system workload.
- Monitor system resources.
- Notice changes and trends in resource use.
- Help diagnose problems.

Create a performance baseline

To create a performance baseline that monitors key system components you can use to measure against a future performance baseline, follow these steps

1. Click the Start button and type **perfmon**.

    Performance Monitor opens.

2. Click the Data Collector Sets node in the left pane.

3. Click User Defined, right-click User Defined, click New, and then click Data Collector Set.

4. In the Create New Data Collector Set Wizard, on the How Would You Like To Create This New Data Collector Set page, in the Name box, type **Initial PC Baseline**.

5. Click Create Manually (Advanced) and then click Next.

6. On the What Type Of Data Do You Want To Include page, select the Performance Counter check box and then click Next.

7. On the Which Performance Counters Would You Like To Log page, in the Sample Interval box, type **1** and then click Add.

8. Include the following counters.
   - Memory > Pages/Sec
   - Network Interface > Packets/Sec
   - PhysicalDisk > % Disk Time
   - PhysicalDisk > Avg. Disk Queue Length
   - Processor > % Processor Time
   - System > Processor Queue Length

9. Click OK and then click Finish.

10. Right-click Initial PC Baseline and then click Start.

11. Simulate load on the system by starting several programs, including Internet Explorer, Word 2016, Microsoft Excel 2016, and Microsoft PowerPoint 2016.

12. Close all Microsoft Office apps and Internet Explorer and stop the Initial PC Baseline data collector set.

13. To view the baseline report, in Performance Monitor, expand the Reports\User Defined node\Initial PC Baseline and click the report to open it.

14. Print the report or view the report and record the values for the following counters.
   - Memory > Pages/sec
   - Network Interface > Packets/Sec
   - PhysicalDisk > % Disk Time
   - PhysicalDisk > Avg. Disk Queue Length
   - Processor > % Processor Time
   - System > Processor Queue Length

Skill: Monitor and manage printers

Windows 10 provides some additional options for you to manage your printing compared to previous versions of Windows. A new Print Management desktop app and the new Printers & Scanners options in the Settings app provide basic printer management such as Add, Remove, and Set As Default Printer.

You still have previous printer tools, in the Devices And Printers section of Control Panel or from the link at the bottom of the Printers & Scanners options in the Settings app. The Devices And Printers Control Panel item is the same interface as in previous versions of Windows 7. This section focuses on the new features relating to Printer With Windows 10, but for the exam, you should also review the older printer tools.

> **This section covers how to:**
> - Manage printers by using Print Management
> - Manage printers by using Windows PowerShell
> - Manage Default Printer behavior

Manage printers by using Print Management

A new Print Management console is available for you to manage your device printers from a single management console. Print devices connected to your PC can be shared, and you can manage the properties of the device. The Print Management MMC, as shown in Figure 12-9, is included in the Administrative Tools of Windows 10 Pro and Enterprise editions and lists all printers, drivers, and other print servers that you are connected to.

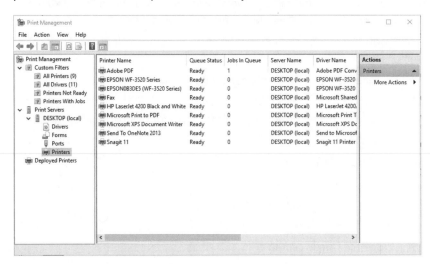

FIGURE 12-9 Print Management MMC

You can also launch the Print Management console by typing **Printmanagement.msc** in the Start menu.

The Print Management console offers you a single location to perform the following printer-related management tasks.

- Add and delete print devices
- View printers and print servers
- Add and remove print servers
- Add and manage print drivers
- Deploy printers using Group Policy
- Open and manage printer queues

- View and modify status of printers
- Use the filter feature to view printers based on filters

If you right-click a printer, you are presented with a list of some action items that can be performed on the selected printer. These can include the following tasks.

- Open Printer Queue
- Pause Printing
- List In Directory
- Deploy With Group Policy
- Set Printing Defaults
- Manage Sharing
- Print Test Page
- Enable Branch Office Direct Printing
- Properties
- Delete
- Rename
- Help

> *NOTE* **REMOTE PRINTERS**
>
> **You can use the Print Management console to manage both local and remote printers. Devices And Printers in Control Panel can only manage locally connected printers.**

Manage printers by using Windows PowerShell

More than 20 Windows PowerShell cmdlets can be used to manage printers. Some of the most common cmdlets are shown in Table 12-6.

TABLE 12-6 Windows PowerShell printer cmdlets

Cmdlet	Description
Add-Printer	Adds a printer to the specified computer
Add-PrinterDriver	Installs a printer driver on the specified computer
Add-PrinterPort	Installs a printer port on the specified computer
Get-PrintConfiguration	Gets the configuration information of a printer
Get-Printer	Retrieves a list of printers installed on a computer
Get-PrinterDriver	Retrieves the list of printer drivers installed on the specified computer
Get-PrinterPort	Retrieves a list of printer ports installed on the specified computer
Get-PrinterProperty	Retrieves printer properties for the specified printer

Cmdlet	Description
Remove-Printer	Removes a printer from the specified computer
Remove-PrinterDriver	Deletes printer drivers from the specified computer
Remove-PrintJob	Removes a print job on the specified printer
Rename-Printer	Renames the specified printer
Restart-PrintJob	Restarts a print job on the specified printer
Resume-PrintJob	Resumes a suspended print job
Set-PrintConfiguration	Sets the configuration information for the specified printer
Set-Printer	Updates the configuration of an existing printer
Set-PrinterProperty	Modifies the printer properties for the specified printer

To list all the available cmdlets, type the following command into a Windows PowerShell console.

```
Get-Command -Module PrintManagement
```

Default printer behavior

Whenever you print to your printer, Windows 10 sets the last used printer as the default printer. This saves you some time if you take your device between the office and home and, therefore, the default printer attempts to follow you. When you often print to different printers, such as a color, or print files to the PDF format, this feature is less useful.

To review the setting and configure the behavior you require, open the Printers & Scanners settings in the Settings app as follows.

1. Open Start and click Settings.

2. In the Settings app, click Devices.

   The Printers & scanners item is highlighted.

3. The Let Windows Manage My Default Printer setting is below the Printers & Scanners list, as shown in Figure 12-10.

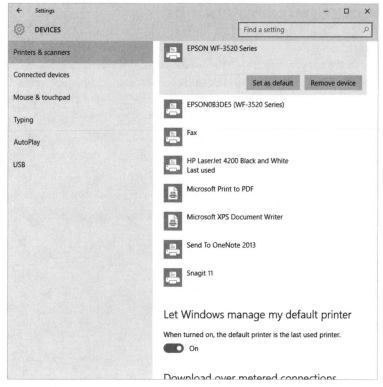

FIGURE 12-10 Managing default printer settings

If this setting is turned on, the last-used printer becomes the default printer until you select a different printer.

4. When the setting is set to Off, you configure which printer is the default by selecting a printer and then choosing Set As Default.

> **NOTE   DEFAULT PRINTER**
>
> The Let Windows Manage My Default Printer is a new feature in Windows 10 version 1511. The default configuration is set to On, and Windows 10 will configure the default printer to be the most recently used one.

At the bottom of the Printers & Scanners screen is an option to configure the behavior to determine whether Windows 10 should allow the downloading of drivers, info, and apps for new drivers when on a metered connection. This is set to Off by default and, therefore, won't download while you're on a metered Internet connection.

Skill: Configure indexing options

To maintain the performance of Windows 10 search, the system automatically indexes data on your computer in the background. This data includes user-generated files, folders, and documents. Most users will never modify the default indexing settings, but you can add new areas to be indexed and exclude others. Common locations include your user profile areas and app data that you access frequently, such as Office apps.

If you store a lot of data in a storage space or a removable drive, you can add this location to Indexing Options to speed up the performance of future searches in this location significantly.

To view your existing indexing locations, type **Index** on the Start screen and click Indexing Options in Control Panel to see the Indexing Options dialog box shown in Figure 12-11.

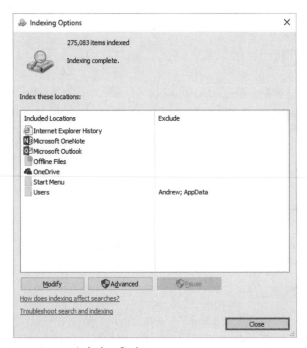

FIGURE 12-11 Indexing Options

You can use the Modify button to add or remove locations. In the Indexed Locations dialog box, you see the summary of locations. If you click Show All Locations, Windows 10 displays all the hidden locations, and this enables you to fine-tune the indexing to specific subfolders, if necessary. To select the Downloads and Documents folders within your profile, select the arrow next to the Users folder and then locate and select Downloads and Documents in your user profile.

After you apply changes to indexing, the indexing process doesn't happen immediately; rather, it runs as a background task whenever your machine is running but not being used.

While the indexing process is incomplete, the message in the dialog box indicates that Indexing Speed Is Reduced Due To User Activity. When the process has finished, the message states Indexing Complete.

Be careful not to index everything on your disk. A large index can affect the search performance negatively.

In the Indexing Options dialog box, the Advanced button enables you to configure Index Settings and specify File Types to be excluded. You can include or exclude encrypted files, treat similar words as different words, delete and rebuild the index (useful if you suspect search is not working), and change the index location from the default C:\ProgramData \Microsoft.

On the File Types tab, you can exclude file types from the index and configure whether the index searches in the file contents or just in the file properties. You can also manually add new file types that have not been automatically included to index.

Skill: Manage client security by using Windows Defender

Most organizations use an enterprise malware solution, often unaware that the Windows Defender antimalware software that is included with Windows 10 offers fully featured antimalware protection against viruses, spyware, rootkits, and other types of malware. Compared to earlier versions of Windows Defender, the solution is significantly improved in Windows 10.

Malware is a major problem for most computer users; therefore, Microsoft includes Windows Defender to monitor, protect, and if necessary, help remove malware from your computer.

Windows Defender also works with the Internet Explorer SmartScreen Filter that protects your web browsing activity and prevents downloading or installing malware. The signature-based antimalware technologies used in both SmartScreen Filter and Windows Defender are updated regularly, often daily, to provide the most comprehensive protection.

> **This section covers how to:**
> - Understand malware
> - Monitor for malware

Understand malware

Malicious software, or malware, can do many things to your computer, such as allowing unauthorized parties remote access to your computer or collecting and transmitting information that is sensitive or confidential to unauthorized third parties.

Some types of malware include:

- **Computer viruses** Replicating malware, normally with email attachments or files.
- **Computer worms** Replicate, without direct intervention, across networks.
- **Trojan horses** Tricks the user into providing an attacker with remote access to the infected computer.
- **Ransomware** Harms the user by encrypting user data. A ransom (fee) needs to be paid to the malware authors to recover the data.
- **Spyware** Tracking software that reports to the third party how a computer is used.

The most common attack vector for malware is still by email, although attacks from websites, pirated software, video, and music files are becoming increasingly common.

You can help protect against malware infection by following these guidelines.

- All software should be from a reputable source.
- All software and operating system updates are applied.
- Antimalware software is installed and enabled on your devices.
- Antimalware definitions are up to date.
- Avoid using or accessing pirated software or media sharing sites.
- Be suspicious of out-of-the-ordinary email attachments, and don't open links in spam or phishing email.

Although no antimalware solution can provide 100 percent safety, modern solutions can reduce the probability that malware compromises your device.

Windows Defender can help protect your device by actively detecting spyware, malware, and viruses both in the operating system and on Windows 10 installed on Hyper-V virtual machines. Windows Defender runs in the background and automatically installs new definitions as they are released, often on a daily basis.

You can use Windows Defender manually to check for malware with various scan options listed in Table 12-7.

TABLE 12-7 Windows Defender scan options

Scan options	Description
Quick	Checks the most likely areas that malware, including viruses, spyware, and software, commonly infect
Full	Scans all files on your hard disk and all running programs
Custom	Enables users to scan specific drives and folders to target specific areas of your computer such as a removable drive

Monitor for malware

You should routinely check your system for malware. If it becomes infected or you suspect malware is on your system, you can run a Full scan. To configure and use Windows Defender, follow these steps.

1. Type **Windows Defender** into Start and select Windows Defender Desktop App.

2. On the Home tab, verify that Real-Time Protection is On and the Virus and Spyware definitions are up to date. (You'll see a check mark on a green background.)

3. Under Scan Details, review the last scan date, time, and type, as shown in Figure 12-12.

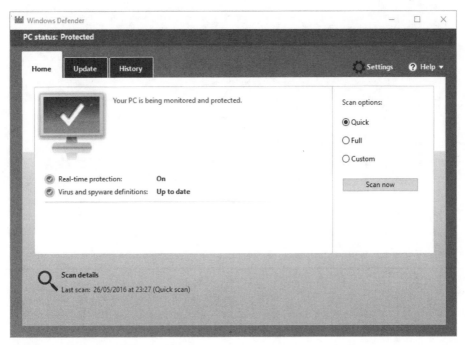

FIGURE 12-12 Windows Defender Home screen

4. Click the Update tab and verify that the definitions are up to date. If they are not, ensure that you are connected to the Internet and click Update Definitions.

5. Click the History tab, click View Details (allowing UAC if prompted), and then review the results of any quarantined items that were prevented from running on your PC.

    If items have been detected, they appear in the results area as shown in Figure 12-13, which shows a trojan has been detected and quarantined.

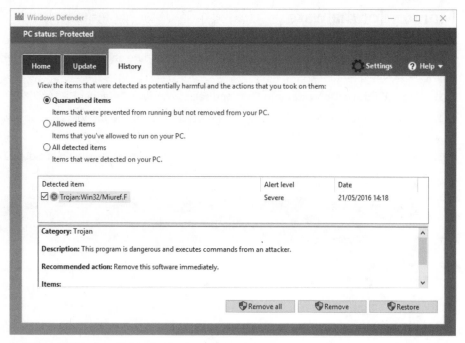

FIGURE 12-13 Windows Defender History screen

6. You can highlight each item and choose Remove All, Remove (to remove a single item), or Restore (to restore the file if you believe this is not malware).

7. When it is removed, the item is deleted, and the Detected Item list is cleared.

8. Close Windows Defender.

By default, Windows Defender telemetry automatically sends some user data to Microsoft, which helps improve security. You can customize this option to turn off the feature that sends data to Microsoft by selecting Turn Off Telemetry Options in the Settings app, using these steps.

1. Open Start and click Settings.

2. In the Settings app, click Update & Security and click Windows Defender.

3. Set Cloud-Based Protection to Off.

4. Set Automatic Sample Submission to Off.

You can also configure these settings by using Group Policy. The settings are found in the following node: Computer Configuration\Administrative Templates\Windows Components \Windows Defender\MAPS.

The Microsoft Active Protection Service (MAPS) is the cloud service that Microsoft uses to collect and analyze key telemetry events and suspicious malware queries from users running Windows 8 or later. The service also provides real-time blocking responses back to client devices for suspicious items that do not match published definitions.

Skill: Evaluate system stability by using Reliability Monitor

Members of the desktop support team often report that it is difficult to ascertain the precise nature of calls that relate to poor performance or system instability. Reliability Monitor is an excellent tool for these situations because it enables you to review a computer's reliability and problem history and offers both the help desk and you the ability to explore the detailed reports and recommendations that can help you identify and resolve reliability issues. Changes to the system such as software and driver installations are recorded, and changes in system stability are then links to changes in the system configuration.

To launch Reliability Monitor, type **reliability** in the Start screen and click View Reliability History in Control Panel, or type **perfmon /rel** at a command prompt. The tool displays a summary of the reliability history for your system, as shown in Figure 12-14.

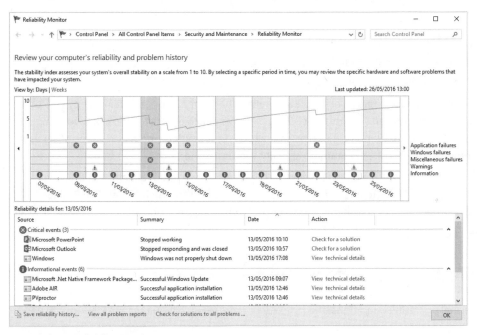

FIGURE 12-14 Reliability Monitor

The top half of the Reliability Monitor screen shows a line graph with a scale of 1 to 10 and date timeline along the bottom axis. You can toggle the view from weeks to days. The graph rises and sinks over time, and at the low points are colored markers in red, blue, or yellow. Below the graph are the details that relate to system configuration changes, such as software and driver installations. When system changes result in a negative system stability, such as an app crashing or a service stopping, there might be a relationship between the two, and these can be further explored. The graph gradually reaches the maximum level of 10 if the system does not experience negative system stability over a prolonged period.

Reliability Monitor is enabled by default in Windows 10 and requires the Microsoft Reliability Analysis task, RacTask, to process system reliability data, which is a background process that collects reliability data. RacTask can be found in the Task Scheduler library under the Microsoft\Windows\RAC node.

The Reliability Monitor main features include:

- **System stability chart**   Provides summary of annual system stability in daily/weekly increments. The chart indicates three levels of stability data: information, warning messages, and critical errors.

- **Records key events in a timeline**   Tracks events about the system configuration, such as the installation of new apps, operating system patches, and drivers.

- **Installation and failure reports**   Provides information about each event shown in the chart, including:

  - Software Installs/Software Uninstalls.

  - App Failures.

  - Hardware & Driver Failures.

  - Windows Operating System Failures.

  - Miscellaneous Failures.

Because the tool offers a rolling view of reliability history, you can retain a copy of a point-in-time report. You can save this by clicking the Save Reliability History link to save complete details at periodic time points, such as annually. System builders and repair shops often use the report to demonstrate computer stability for future reference.

At the bottom of the Reliability Monitor screen are two additional links that list all computer problems and attempt to locate problem solutions from the Internet. The Problem Reports And Solutions tool helps you track problems that are reported and check for all available solution information to problems.

Skill: Troubleshoot performance issues

In normal operating conditions, the majority of users rarely experience performance issues with their device after it has been configured with the necessary security, antimalware, productivity, and specialist software. Out of the box, Windows 10 is optimized for general user environments.

Over time, the device might gradually seem to become slower. If the user notices this decreased system performance, they might request help from the help desk.

You can avoid some performance degradation by performing regular maintenance such as using the Disk Cleanup utility to remove temporary or unwanted files. Windows 10 does a good job at self-healing and maintaining the system and schedules many maintenance tasks to run automatically for you.

If poor performance occurs, investigate and troubleshoot the reason to establish whether there is a bottleneck, perhaps a memory-hungry app, multiple startup programs, or even malware. Another gradual but common occurrence is when a system runs out of disk space, especially because the majority of devices are now using solid-state drives (SSDs) that are typically smaller capacity.

When looking at the factors that might influence your PC, consider some of the following.

- Windows 10 architecture: x86 or x64
- Processor speed, processor quantity, onboard cache memory, cores
- Physical hard disks input/output speed, buffer size, and defragmentation state
- Memory: capacity, speed, and type
- Graphics card: throughput, memory, onboard processing speed, quantity, and drivers
- Network interface throughput, onboard processing capability, quantity, and drivers
- Application number, type, available optimizations, architecture
- System, peripheral, and application drivers

Understand how system bottlenecks can occur, how to diagnose a system that is suffering from a performance bottleneck, and how to respond and recover from the problem. Some common performance bottlenecks that are useful to know about when troubleshooting are shown in Table 12-8.

TABLE 12-8 Performance bottlenecks

Performance Counter	Bottleneck
LogicalDisk\% Free Space	If this is less than 15 percent, you risk running out of free space for Windows 10 to use to store critical files.
PhysicalDisk\% Idle Time	If this is less than 20 percent, the disk system is overloaded. Consider replacing with a faster disk.
PhysicalDisk\Avg. Disk Sec/Read	If the number is larger than 25 milliseconds (ms), the disk system is experiencing read latency; suspect drive failure (or a very slow/old disk).
PhysicalDisk\Avg. Disk Sec/Write	If the number is larger than 25 milliseconds (ms), the disk system is experiencing write latency; suspect drive failure (or a very slow/old disk).
PhysicalDisk\Avg. Disk Queue Length	If the value is larger than 2 times the number of drive spindles, the disk might be the bottleneck.
Memory\% Committed Bytes in Use	If the value is greater than 80 percent, it indicates insufficient memory.
Memory\Available Mbytes	If this value is less than 5 percent of the total physical RAM, there is insufficient memory, which can increase paging activity.
Processor\% Processor Time	If the percentage is greater than 85 percent, the processor is overwhelmed, and the PC might require a faster processor.
System\Processor Queue Length	If the value is more than twice the number of CPUs for an extended period, you should consider a more powerful processor.
Network Interface\Output Queue Length	There is network saturation if the value is more than 2. Consider a faster or additional network interface.

Sometimes you might experience poor performance with the physical memory that is installed on a computer. Memory is generally very reliable, but it can suffer from overheating or from degrading performance with age. If the device is still under warranty, you could use a diagnostic tool to verify the problem and then return the device or memory for replacement. If the device is not under warranty, the diagnosis is useful for identifying whether faulty memory is the cause of the problem.

For pinpointing memory failures, use the Windows Memory Diagnostic tool by typing **mdsched.exe** into a command prompt and following the instructions on the Windows Memory Diagnostic tool, as shown in Figure 12-15.

Select either Restart Now And Check For Problems or Check For Problems The Next Time I Start My Computer; the Windows Memory Diagnostics tool runs when your computer restarts.

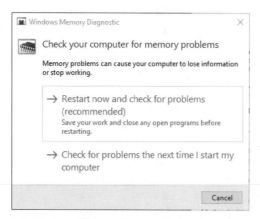

FIGURE 12-15 Windows Memory Diagnostic tool

Summary

- Event logs automatically record system activity such as logons, application errors, and services stopping and starting.

- You can pull event logs from remote computers by using event subscriptions if you enable remote management.

- Windows 10 includes several tools to view system performance, including Task Manager, Performance Monitor, and Resource Monitor.

- In Performance Monitor, you can create benchmarking reports by creating your own user-defined collector sets and running them to generate a performance baseline.

- Windows 10 provides the Print Management console, which provides a consolidated view of print-related activities, including print devices, drivers, and print queues.

- Windows 10 introduces the option to print to the last printer you used rather than to a fixed default printer.

- The built-in Search feature uses the background indexing service to index areas of your hard drive automatically, including files stored in your user profile.

- Windows Defender provides a comprehensive antimalware solution that automatically runs and updates itself to protect your system.

- Reliability Monitor provides a graphical history of your computer's reliability and offers solutions to resolve issues.

Thought experiment

In this thought experiment, demonstrate your skills and knowledge of the topics covered in this chapter. You can find answers to this thought experiment in the next section.

Your company has recently upgraded half of its computers from Windows 7 to Windows 10 Pro. Staff members use Office and a web-based line-of-business application. The help desk manager has received several complaints from users, who state a variety of problems following the upgrade, including that:

- Their computers are slow.

- Apps stop responding.

- Websites are slow to load.

The remaining Windows 7–based computers do not exhibit the same issues. You need to offer the help desk some advice on how to diagnose these problems and recommend how to resolve them as soon as possible.

Answer the following questions from the help desk.

1. Why might the computers be slow after the upgrade?

2. Which tool could you recommend to help the help desk support members verify which apps are freezing?

3. You suspect that the network card could be a performance bottleneck. How could this suspicion be tested?

4. How would a network card bottleneck present itself?

Thought experiment answer

This section contains the solution to the thought experiment.

1. Answers might vary. Several potential areas need to be investigated. The original computers should have met the minimum specification for Windows 10 to upgrade from Windows 7. The computers might be quite old and contain components that are slow in comparison to modern hardware, such as older hard drives without cache, or slow

RAM memory. The BIOS or motherboard firmware might be old and need updating. The hardware device drivers might not have been updated to the latest versions for Windows 10.

2. Recommend to the help desk that it suggest using Reliability Monitor to review the stability history of the computers that are reporting app freezing. The Reliability Monitor report should identify the failing app and how often it is failing. You should also be able to see whether other failures are occurring that might relate or contribute to the app failure.

3. Answers might vary. You could review the network card driver version and see whether there are any known issues relating to the network card and Windows 10 on the manufacturer's website. You could use Performance Monitor to review the performance for the Network Interface counter and monitor the Output Queue Length.

4. Network-related activities such as web browsing and opening and saving resources across the network would be slower than normal. If there is network saturation, the report indicates that the queue length is more than 2, meaning that the network card cannot process network packets quickly enough.

CHAPTER 13

Configure system and data recovery

In this chapter, you review how to configure system and data recovery options for Windows 10. If you have experience with an earlier version of Windows, you might be familiar with many of the options because some are included in Windows 10. To prepare for the exam, it is recommended that you work through all the wizards and tools to ensure that you're comfortable with each process, paying special attention to the newer options.

Skills covered in this chapter:

- Configure a recovery drive
- Configure system restore
- Perform a refresh or recycle
- Perform recovery operations using Windows Recovery
- Configure restore points
- Use Windows Backup and Restore
- Perform a backup and restore with WBAdmin
- Configure File History
- Restore previous versions of files and folders
- Recover files from OneDrive

> **NOTE OVERLAP IN SKILLS**
> You have already covered the skills relating to performing a driver rollback, resolving hardware and device issues, and interpreting data from Device Manager in Chapter 3, "Configure devices and device drivers."

Skill: Configure a recovery drive

When you install Windows 10, it does not include a separate recovery partition by default. However, if you purchase a new device, the original equipment manufacturer (OEM) might create one instead of providing Windows 10 installation media. You can create a USB recovery drive that enables you to recover your system. If Windows 10 becomes corrupted, your recovery drive can help you troubleshoot and fix problems with your PC when it won't start.

To do so, open Control Panel and click Recovery. Several advanced recovery tools are listed, including Create A Recovery Drive. You need a USB drive with a minimum capacity of 8 GB, which you should label as your system recovery drive.

> **NOTE   SECURE DIGITAL HIGH-CAPACITY MEMORY CARDS**
>
> If your device supports the use of Secure Digital High-Capacity (SDHC) memory cards, you can use one as an alternative to a USB flash drive when creating the recovery drive.

To create a recovery drive, follow these steps.

1. Click the Start button, type **Recovery,** and click Create A Recovery Drive.

2. Accept the User Account Control (UAC) prompt and provide the necessary credentials if required.

3. In the Recovery Drive dialog box, select the Back Up System Files To The Recovery Drive check box and click Next, as shown in Figure 13-1.

FIGURE 13-1 Recovery Drive tool

Windows 10 creates a recovery image, which can take a while.

When the image is prepared, the Connect An USB Flash Drive dialog box appears, and you're prompted to connect a USB drive with at least 8 GB of space to your PC.

4.   On the Select The USB Flash Drive page, confirm the USB drive to be used from the list and click Next.

5.   On the Create The Recovery Drive page, click Create.

The tool formats the USB drive and copies the recovery image files to the USB drive, which can take a while—in excess of an hour, depending on the performance of the PC and the media.

6.   On The Recovery Drive Is Ready page, click Finish.

The last page of the wizard advises you that you can delete the recovery partition stored on your PC and provides a link to do this, which will free up disk space.

Test that the recovery drive was successful by booting to the drive. It is good practice to label your USB flash drive as your recovery drive.

If you need to use the recovery USB, you can boot from the USB drive and access the advanced recovery tools to recover your computer.

EXAM TIP

The recovery drive is architecture-specific; therefore, a 64-bit (x64) recovery drive can only be used to reinstall a device with 64-bit architecture. Windows 10 Recovery Drive cannot be used to repair earlier versions of Windows.

Skill: Configure system restore

System Restore has been available in previous versions of Windows. It is useful when a computer becomes unstable and you need to restore the operating system to one of the restore points created during a period of stability.

System Restore is not enabled by default in Windows 10. To turn on System Restore and manually create a system restore point, follow these steps.

1.   Click the Start button, type **system,** and click System Control Panel.

2.   On System, select the System Protection link in the left pane.

The System Properties dialog box appears with the System Protection tab open.

3.   Highlight the drive you want to protect and click Configure.

4.   In the System Protection For Local Disk dialog box, select Turn On System Protection.

5.   Under Disk Space Usage, move the slider for Max Usage to allow room on the restore points to be saved (5 percent is a reasonable amount), as shown in Figure 13-2.

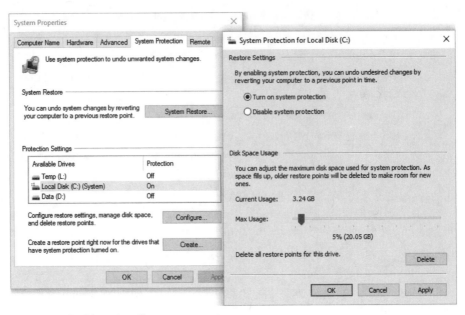

FIGURE 13-2 Enable and configure system restore

6. Click OK.

7. In the System Protection dialog box, click Create, provide a name, and then click Create.

8. After the restore point is created successfully, click Close.

9. Click OK to close the System Properties dialog box.

When System Restore is enabled, it automatically creates restore points at these times:

- Whenever System Restore–compliant apps are installed.
- Whenever Windows 10 installs Windows updates.
- Based on the System Restore scheduled task.
- When you create a system restore manually from the System Protection screen.
- When you use System Restore to restore to a previous restore point. Windows 10 automatically creates a new restore point.

> **NOTE   TASK SCHEDULER**
>
> The scheduled task that automatically creates system restore points is located at the Task Scheduler Library\Microsoft\Windows\SystemRestore location in the Scheduled Tasks feature.

Many users prefer to use the graphical user interface (GUI), but you can use Windows PowerShell to configure System Restore. This is useful if you need to configure the settings on a large group of computers and do not use Group Policy. Some of the available Windows PowerShell commands include:

- **Enable-ComputerRestore**   Enables the System Restore feature on the specified drive
- **Disable-ComputerRestore**   Disables the System Restore feature on the specified drive
- **Checkpoint-Computer**   Creates a new system restore point
- **Get-ComputerRestorePoint**   Gets the list of restore points on the local computer

Use the following command to enable System Restore on the C drive of the local computer.

```
PS C:\> enable-computerrestore -drive "C:\"
```

> **NOTE   SYSTEM RESTORE REQUIREMENTS**
>
> The System Restore feature requires drives that are formatted with the NTFS and uses the Volume Shadow Copy Service (VSS) in the background.

For systems with a small hard drive, you can still use System Restore, but you might want to reduce the amount of space allocated for the restore points to limit the number of historic maintained restore points. When the allocated space becomes full, System Restore deletes the oldest restore point and reuses the space.

To recover your system by using System Restore, start the process from System Restore in System Protection in Windows 10. If you cannot log on to your system, you can launch the wizard from Advanced Options, as shown in Figure 13-3.

Prior to launching the System Restore tool, the wizard offers to show you whether any apps and files will be affected by performing a specific System Restore based on the date and time of the restore point you select. To use System Restore to restore your PC to an earlier time, follow these steps.

1. Click the Start button, type **system,** and click System Control Panel.
2. On System, select the System Protection link in the left pane.

    The System Properties dialog box appears with the System Protection tab open.
3. Click System Restore.
4. On the Restore System Files And Settings page, click Next.
5. On the Restore Your Computer To A State It Was In Before The Selected Event page, choose the restore point that you want to be restored.
6. After you select a restore point, click Scan For Affected Programs and then click Next.
7. On the Confirm Your Restore Point page, click Finish.

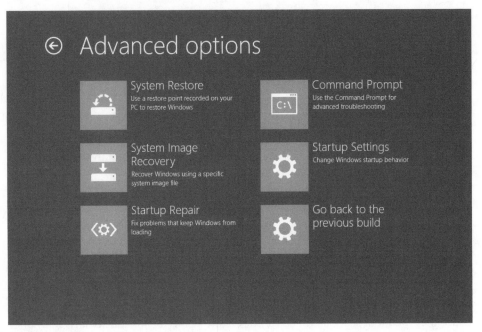

FIGURE 13-3 Advanced startup options

8. On the warning screen, click Yes.

    The System Restore prepares your computer and restarts. The System Restore process can complete in a few minutes or longer.

    When the process is complete, the system restarts, and you can sign in to Windows.

    You are presented with a summary of the system restore status and a confirmation that your documents have not been affected.

9. Click Close.

> **NOTE   PASSWORD PROTECTED**
>
> If you started System Restore from the Advanced startup options rather than from Windows 10, the Advanced startup options prompt you to log on to your account before allowing the System Restore process to complete.

Skill: Perform a refresh or recycle

With earlier versions of Windows, you might have manually reinstalled Windows from removable media following a system failure. This could involve reinstalling all apps, settings, and user data and could take many hours to complete. In Windows 10, if other methods of recovering your system fail, you can return your computer to its original state when you purchased it or when Windows 10 was first installed.

You have the option to refresh or recycle your computer in Windows 10. This feature was first introduced in Windows 8, and Windows 10 has improved the speed and reliability of the process. When referring to recovering a system by using this new quick method, the terms *refresh* and *recycle* are often used interchangeably. These terms refer to the recovery process that you access in Recovery in the Settings app.

To start the recovery process, follow these steps.

1. Open the Settings app, click Update & Security, and select Recovery.

2. On the Reset This PC page, click Get Started.

   The background screen is dimmed, and you are presented with three options:

   - **Keep My Files**   Removes all apps and settings but retains your personal files.

   - **Remove Everything**   Removes all apps, settings, and your personal files and offers two levels of cleaning: Just Remove My Files and Fully Clean The Drive.

   - **Restore Factory Settings**   This option is only available on systems purchased from an OEM. It removes personal files, apps, and settings and reinstalls the version of Windows that came with the PC together with any pre-installed apps and settings.

> **IMPORTANT   REMOVING ALL SETTINGS**
>
> If you choose to remove all settings, user accounts, apps, and personal files, Remove Everything restores the operating system to the initial state—that is, the state of the computer when you first installed or upgraded to Windows 10. With this option, you can clean the disk by fully erasing the hard disk prior to reinstallation of Windows 10. This option is useful if you are recycling your PC and need to make the recovery of any data on the computer, such as your personal files, nearly impossible. This is similar to performing a low-level full format of the disk, whereas the normal operation uses quick formatting.

3. Select Keep My Files. Choose one of the following options.

   - **Just Remove My Files**   Initiates a quick drive format

   - **Remove Files And Fully Clean The Drive**   Performs a complete drive format

   A warning appears, informing you that your apps will be removed; it lists any apps that will need to be reinstalled, as shown in Figure 13-4. After the process has completed, a new text file is created on the desktop that contains this list of apps.

4. Click Next.

   On the Ready To Reset This PC page, you are reminded that resetting the PC removes apps and resets all settings to defaults.

5. Click Reset to restart the PC and allow the reset process to begin.

6. Your PC will be reset, and after a short time, you are presented with the logon screen.

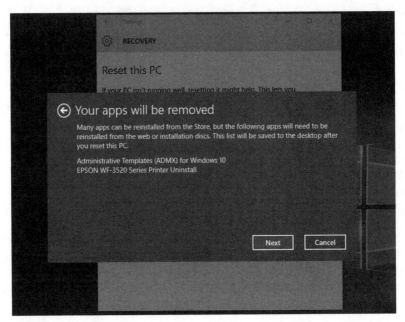

FIGURE 13-4 Reset this PC

If you are using a PC in an enterprise environment, the Recovery options might be disabled. Often, enterprises use image deployment solutions such as Microsoft Deployment Toolkit (MDT) or System Center Configuration Manager to deploy a customized image directly to a networked computer. This method is often the quickest way to provide a fully configured computer to a user on the local network. As administrators become familiar with the Windows Imaging and Configuration Designer (ICD) and DISM tools mentioned in an earlier chapter, there might be more deployments of Windows 10 using these tools together with provisioning packages.

EXAM TIP

The Refresh Your PC and Reset Your PC options that were available in Windows 8 and Windows 8.1 have been consolidated into Reset This PC.

At the end of the reset process, Windows 10 offers you the normal out-of-box experience (OOBE), and you must configure the device, add users, install any apps, and modify any settings that you need.

If the refresh or recycle process fails to complete for any reason, the system will not be modified, and after logon, a notification declares that the process could not complete and no changes were made to your computer.

EXAM TIP

In earlier versions of Windows, you could use a Recimg.exe utility to capture an image of your computer. This was useful to create a custom recovery image. This utility has been deprecated and is not available in Windows 10.

Skill: Perform recovery operations using Windows Recovery

Windows 10 includes a comprehensive recovery environment that enables you to trouble-shoot issues relating to the boot process and retains most of the functionality that was available in previous versions of Windows.

The Windows Recovery Environment (Windows RE) enables you to boot Windows 10 into safe mode or use other advanced troubleshooting tools. There are several ways to start Windows 10 in advanced troubleshooting mode, including:

- Boot from a Recovery Drive.
- Click Settings, select Update & Security, select Recovery, and then, under Advanced Startup, click Restart Now.
- Press the Shift key and select Restart on the Start menu.
- Restart the computer by running the Shutdown.exe /r /o command.
- Use installation media and select Repair.

After Windows 10 boots to the advanced troubleshooting mode, you can select Troubleshoot and then click Advanced Options. On the Advanced Options screen, shown in Figure 13-5, the primary recovery tools are listed.

You can choose one of the following options.

- **System Restore** To restore Windows from a System Restore point.
- **System Image Recovery** To recover Windows by using a system image file.
- **Startup Repair** To attempt to fix startup issues automatically that prevent Windows from loading.
- **Command Prompt** To start advanced troubleshooting.
- **Startup Settings** To change Windows startup behavior. This is similar to the F8 menu options in earlier versions of the operating system.
- **Go Back To The Previous Build** To revert your system to a previous Windows build.

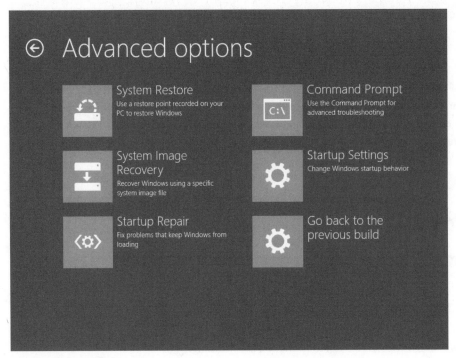

FIGURE 13-5 Advanced Options

If your system has a UEFI motherboard, you are also offered an additional option:

- **UEFI Firmware Settings**   Modify UEFI motherboard settings.

If you want to start Windows by using one of the earlier startup options, such as Enable Safe Mode or Enable Low-Resolution Video Mode, select Startup Settings on the Advanced Options screen. This instructs you to click Restart, and Windows 10 loads into a special troubleshooting mode that you might be familiar with if you have used previous versions of Windows.

After clicking Startup Settings and restarting, the troubleshooting mode presents you with a choice of startup options, as listed in Table 13-1.

TABLE 13-1 Startup settings

Startup Setting	Description
Enable Debugging Mode	Restarts Windows 10 to monitor and debug the behavior of device drivers to help troubleshoot device driver issues.
Enable Boot Logging Mode	Restarts Windows 10 and creates a file named Ntbtlog.txt, which records all device drivers installed and loaded during the startup process.
Enable Low-Resolution Video Mode	Starts Windows 10 in a low-resolution graphics mode.

Startup Setting	Description
Enable Safe Mode	Restarts Windows with a minimal set of drivers, services, and applications, enabling you to troubleshoot the system by using the GUI but without third-party drivers and services running.
Enable Safe Mode With Networking	Restarts Windows with a minimal set of drivers, services, and applications and enables network connectivity.
Enable Safe Mode With Command Prompt	Restarts Windows with a minimal set of drivers, services, and applications by using a command prompt window rather than the GUI.
Disable Driver Signature Enforcement	Enables you to bypass the requirement to load device drivers with a digital signature.
Disable Early-Launch Anti-Malware Protection	Restarts Windows and disables the Early Launch Anti-malware (ELAM) driver, useful if you suspect issues with Secure Boot or if you are modifying Windows boot configuration or anti-malware settings.
Disable Automatic Restart On System Failure	Prevents Windows 10 from automatically restarting after a system failure occurs. This allows the information screen to be reviewed.

> **NOTE   LAST KNOWN GOOD CONFIGURATION**
>
> **Windows 10 no longer supports the Last Known Good Configuration startup option that was present in Windows 7 and other versions of Windows.**

While on the Startup Settings screen, you can press Enter if you want to exit and restart your system normally. To choose a Startup Settings boot option from the list in Figure 13-6, press the number key or F1–F9 function key that corresponds to the item in the list.

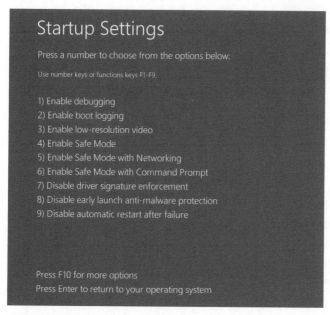

FIGURE 13-6 Windows 10 Startup Settings

If you press F10, a screen appears with a single option, Launch Recovery Environment, which returns you to a menu screen that offers you these three options:

- **Continue**   Exit And Continue To Windows 10
- **Troubleshoot**   Reset Your PC Or See Advanced Options
- **Turn Off Your PC**

> **NOTE   F8 NO LONGER LAUNCHES ADVANCED BOOT OPTIONS MENU**
>
> In previous versions of Windows, during the boot phase, you could press the F8 key to launch the advanced boot options menu. This is no longer available by default in Windows 10. To make the boot process quicker, the boot process no longer waits for you to press F8. You can reinstate this functionality, which will slow the booting of Windows 10, by opening an elevated command prompt and typing **bcdedit /set {default} bootmenupolicy legacy.**

Skill: Configure restore points

You reviewed how to enable System Restore earlier in this chapter. You also need to make sure you understand how to configure the amount of disk space that restore points occupy and how to remove old restore points manually to recover disk space.

The Recovery item in Control Panel contains the advanced recovery tools. Configure System Restore enables you to perform the several tasks relating to restore points that this section covers in more detail.

> **This section covers how to:**
> - Change restore settings
> - Manage disk space
> - Create or delete restore points

Change restore settings

On the System Protection tab of System Properties, if you have administrative privileges, you can modify the protection settings for your system.

Most users configure just the system drive for system protection. If you use additional drive volumes and store any data on them, consider using system protection for these drives also. The system protection feature helps prevent permanent data loss when you accidentally change or delete files, or files become corrupted.

To modify the drives that you currently protect using restore points, follow these steps.

1. Open Control Panel and click Recovery.

2. Click Configure System Restore.

3. If prompted by UAC, click Yes.

4. Under Protection Settings, select the drive on which you want to modify protection and click Configure.

5. In Restore Settings, you can select Turn On or Disable System Protection.

6. Click OK.

Manage disk space

With system protection enabled, your computer regularly creates and saves restore points containing your computer's system files and settings. Even if you do not perform any significant system events, such as install software or upgrade a device driver, a restore point is created automatically. A scheduled task every seven days creates a restore point if no restore point was created during the past week. You can create restore points manually, but this is unlikely to be practical for most users.

For each drive that you want to use system protection, you can adjust the maximum disk space reserved for the feature. Over time, this allocation will be consumed. When the space is full, older restore points are automatically deleted to make room for new ones.

To resize the maximum storage space that system protection uses for a drive, sign in as an administrator and follow these steps.

1. Open Control Panel and click Recovery.

2. Click the Configure System Restore link.

3. If prompted by UAC, click Yes.

4. Under Protection Settings, select the drive and click Configure.

5. In Disk Space Usage, adjust the Max Usage slider to the percentage of the total drive that you want to allocate and click OK.

To perform the same process by using the command prompt, use the vssadmin command-line tool as detailed in these steps.

1. Right-click Start and select Command Prompt (Admin); accept UAC.

2. To show you the current maximum usage size for all drives that use system protection, type **vssadmin list shadowstorage** and press Enter.

3. To resize the space allocated for system protection to 5 percent of the total volume size, type **vssadmin resize shadowstorage /for=C: /on=C: /maxsize=5%** and press Enter.

4. Close the command prompt.

> **NOTE SPECIFY THE UNIT MEASUREMENT**
> For the disk space size, you can use either a percentage of the drive or one of the following units: KB, MB, GB, TB, PB, or EB. If you do not specify a unit, the value defaults to bytes.

Create or delete restore points

You have reviewed how restore points are created both manually and automatically. To create a restore point manually, you must have administrator privileges. When you create a restore point, the feature creates a restore point that includes all drives that are protected.

If you find that not many restore points are available, you can increase the space used for system protection.

> **NOTE SAFE MODE**
>
> You cannot create a restore point if you started Windows 10 in Safe Mode.

To view the amount of space that system protection currently uses, you can use the **vssadmin list shadowstorage** command within an elevated command prompt or view the Current Usage amount in the System Protection For Local Disk dialog box, as shown in Figure 13-7. This usage information is reported on a per volume basis.

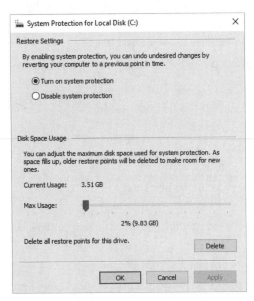

FIGURE 13-7 System Protection current usage

If you want to delete all restore points for a specific volume, click Delete in the System Protection For Local Disk (C:) dialog box, as shown in Figure 13-7. After you click Delete, you receive a warning message that you cannot undo the deletion. After it is deleted, the current drive usage for the selected drive is zero.

Another method of removing restore points is to use the Disk Cleanup feature, which removes all restore points except the most recently created one. In Disk Cleanup, click the More Options tab and choose Clean Up in System Restore And Shadow Copies, as shown in Figure 13-8.

FIGURE 13-8 System Protection current usage

You can remove all or selected restore points from the command prompt, using the **vssadmin** command. You need to use an elevated command prompt to use this feature.

When you use the vssadmin command-line tool, you see for each restore point the volume drive letter and a Shadow Copy ID number. This ID number is useful if you need to delete specific restore points. Examples using the vssadmin command-line tool to delete restore points are shown in Table 13-2.

TABLE 13-2 Deleting restore points using vssadmin

Command Line	Description
vssadmin list shadows	List restore points are currently stored on all drives.
vssadmin delete shadows /all	This deletes all restore points on all drives.
vssadmin delete shadows /all /quiet	This deletes all restore points on all drives, without confirmation.
vssadmin delete shadows /For=C: /all	Delete All Restore Points On C: Drive.
vssadmin delete shadows /For=C: /oldest	Delete Oldest Restore Point On C: Drive.
vssadmin delete shadows /Shadow={ 3e6d99a8-4242-4a29-abcd-9887cd8aa911 }	Delete Specific Restore Point, using Shadow Copy ID.

Skill: Use Windows Backup And Restore

Windows 10 includes the Backup And Restore (Windows 7) tool, which allows the creation of backups of your data. This backup feature was not included in Windows 8, but it has returned in Windows 10 to enable users who might have upgraded from Windows 7 to this version to restore data contained in Windows 7 system image backups.

In addition to restoring files and folders, you can also use this tool to create backups of files contained in folders, libraries, and whole disk volumes.

Backups can't be saved to the disk on which Windows 10 is installed, so you must provide another location such as an external USB drive, network drive, or non-system local disk. To launch the Backup And Restore (Windows 7) tool in the GUI, open the System And Security section of Control Panel or use the Backup And Restore (Windows 7) item listed in the Settings app.

To create a backup of your files and folders and a system image, follow these steps.

1. Open Settings and click Update And Security.
2. Click Backup and then click Go To Backup And Restore (Windows 7).
3. On the Backup And Restore (Windows 7) page, click Set Up Backup.
4. On the Select Where You Want To Save Your Backup page, choose the location and click Next.
5. On the What Do You Want To Back Up page, click Let Windows Choose (Recommended) and click Next.
6. On the Review Your Backup Settings page, click Change Schedule.
7. On the How Often Do You Want To Back Up page, leave the Run Backup On A Schedule (Recommended) check box selected and, if necessary, modify the backup schedule.
8. Click OK.
9. On the Review Your Backup Settings page, click Save Settings And Run Backup.

   The backup begins, and you see the progress bar as shown in Figure 13-9.

> **NOTE BACKUP TIME**
>
> The first backup takes the longest time because it is a full backup. Subsequent backups are incremental and can take only a few minutes to complete.

When the backup is complete, use the links on the Backup And Restore (Windows 7) page to see the size of the backup on disk, edit the schedule, and manage the disk space the Backup And Restore (Windows 7) tool uses.

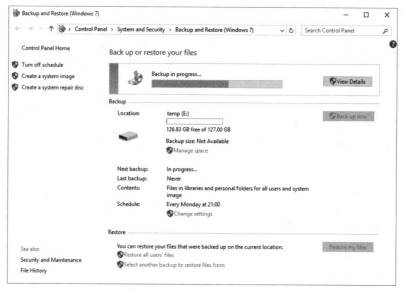

FIGURE 13-9 Backup And Restore (Windows 7)

When backing up your system, you can opt for the recommended settings, which create a backup of all files and folders in your user profile (including libraries) as well as a system image. The system image files are large, likely to be approximately 10 GB in size. You can specify the frequency and time when Windows 10 performs backups or retain the default backup schedule of Sunday at 7 P.M. every week.

If you require more specific scheduling, you can modify the triggers in the AutomaticBackup job in Task Scheduler after you have enabled scheduled backups. Available options to trigger a scheduled backup include:

- On A Schedule.
- At Logon.
- At Startup.
- On Idle.
- On An Event.
- At Task Creation/Modification.
- On Connection/Disconnect To A User Session.
- On Workstation Lock/Unlock.

If you want to choose specific libraries and folders for the backup manually, select Let Me Choose on the What Do You Want To Back Up page when initially setting up the backup. Although you cannot select individual files for backup, you can clear the check box to include a system image of the drive.

The Backup And Restore (Windows 7) tool uses the Volume Shadow Copy Service (VSS) to create the backups. The initial backup creates a block-level backup of the files to the backup file and uses the virtual hard disk (.vhdx) file format. VSS greatly enhances the performance of the backup operation because subsequent backups only copy the data that has changed since the previous backup, which is typically a smaller amount of data, thus creating the incremental backup much faster.

Each time you run a backup, the Backup And Restore (Windows 7) tool creates a new restore point, which the Previous Versions feature in File Explorer can use (and is covered later in this chapter).

> **NOTE BACK UP NTFS ONLY**
>
> The Backup And Restore (Windows 7) tool can only be used to back up data that is stored on file system volumes formatted as NTFS.

To restore libraries, folders, or files from a backup, you can use the Restore My Files link in the lower right of the Backup And Restore (Windows 7) screen. You can select which backup set to use and restore items to their original locations or to different locations. To restore data from a backup, use these steps.

1. On the Backup And Restore (Windows 7) page, click Restore My Files.

2. The Restore Files dialog box presents you with access to the latest backup. If you want to choose an alternative backup, click Choose A Different Date, select the correct backup, and click OK.

3. Locate the files or folders you intend to restore by using one of the three options for you to find your files to recover.

   - **Search** Type part of the name of the file you intend to restore. Click the file or Select All to restore all the found files. Click OK. (The search speed is very fast.)

   - **Browse For Files** Click the backup name with the correct date and time stamp and browse to the folder that contains the items you want. Select the items and click Add Files.

   - **Browse For Folders** Click the backup name with the correct date and time stamp and browse to the folder that you want. Select the folder and click Add Folder.

   You can choose multiple files and folders and use any of the three options or combinations of the options to locate the items you want.

4. Click Next.

5. On the Where Do You Want To Restore Your Files page, choose to restore to the original location or browse and select a different location.

6. If you restore an item to a location that contains the same item name, you are prompted to choose one of the following.

- **Copy And Replace**   The item restored from the backup overwrites the item in the destination location.
- **Don't Copy**   Nothing changes and no item is restored.
- **Copy, But Keep Both Files**   The original items remain as is, and the file name of the restored item is modified to show it is a version of the same item.
- **Do This For All Conflicts**   If you're restoring multiple items, you can apply the same choice to each conflict.

7. When the restoration is complete, the Your Files Have Been Restored page appears, and you can click the link to View Restored Files.

8. Click Finish.

Skill: Perform a backup and restore with WBAdmin

In addition to the Backup And Restore (Windows 7) tool, Windows 10 includes another backup tool, the Windows Backup tool that you can use from a command line. This tool is also found in Windows Server and is useful if you need to automate or create a backup job on several computers. Use the WBAdmin.exe command to create, configure, and restore backup jobs. In this section, you review some of the commonly used applications for WBAdmin.

> **This section covers how to:**
> - Back up using WBAdmin
> - Restore data by using WBAdmin

Backing up using WBAdmin

The Windows 10 version of WBAdmin is a simplified version of the utility that is available with the Microsoft Server operating systems and offers some of low-level features such as the generation of index listings of all files and folders within an image data file. To perform a recovery using WBAdmin, you must be a member of the Backup Operators group or the Administrators group, or have been delegated the appropriate permissions. You must also run WBAdmin from an elevated command prompt. A number of the subcommands are not supported in Windows 10, and you must boot to Windows RE to perform a restore operation of data that was created using the WBAdmin Start Backup subcommand.

Table 13-3 lists the command-line syntax of WBAmin.exe.

TABLE 13-3 WBAdmin.exe command-line syntax

Command	Description
Wbadmin get versions	Lists the details of backups available from the local computer or from a specified computer
Wbadmin enable backup	Configures and enables a regularly scheduled backup
Wbadmin start backup	Runs a one-time backup; if used with no parameters, uses the settings from the daily backup schedule
Wbadmin get items	Lists the items included in a backup
Wbadmin start recovery	Runs a recovery of the volumes, applications, files, or folders specified. Supported only in a Windows Recovery Environment (RE)

> **NEED MORE REVIEW?   WBADMIN TECHNET RESOURCE**
>
> You can find additional detailed information relating to WBAdmin by typing **WBAdmin /?** at the command prompt. The content provided in this section should be sufficient for your exam preparation, and if required, you can find a detailed TechNet resource at *https://technet.microsoft.com/library/cc754015(v=ws.11).aspx.*

For example, if you connect a removable hard drive to your computer, which uses the drive letter E, the following examples guide you through the process of performing a backup and restore using the WBAdmin command-line tool.

To back up the entire contents of the C drive to a backup drive located on E, follow these steps.

1. Right-click Start and select Command Prompt (Admin); accept UAC.

2. Type the following command.

```
WBadmin start backup –BackupTarget:E: –Include:C:
```

3. Type **Y** to begin the backup operation.

   The tool creates a shadow copy of the volume and then creates a block copy of the volume, as shown in Figure 13-10. A simple log file relating to the operation is created, and this is stored in C:\Windows\Logs\WindowsBackup\.

The WBAdmin utility saves the image backup in a WindowsImageBackup folder on the target drive.

After you have created a backup, you can list backup images created on the system by using the following command.

```
wbadmin get versions –backupTarget:E:
```

FIGURE 13-10 WBAdmin command-line tool

Restoring data using WBAdmin

To recover from a backup that you have previously created with WBAdmin, boot to a
Windows RE and type **wbadmin get versions** to provide the version information of the available backups. For example, to recover a backup of volume E from May 31, 2016, at 17:12, type
the following command at a command prompt and then press Enter. You receive the output
shown in Figure 13-11.

```
wbadmin start recovery -version:05/31/2016-17:12 -itemType:Volume -items:\\?\
Volume{a6f2e427-0000-0000-0000-501f00000000}\ -BackupTarget:D: -RecoveryTarget:E:
```

> **EXAM TIP**
>
> The Wbadmin start recovery command is only supported in Windows RE and not in a
> normal Windows 10 administrative command prompt. Be careful because the drive letters
> of the mounted volumes can be different in Windows RE from those in Windows 10. You
> might need to replace the drive letters in your wbadmin start recovery options.

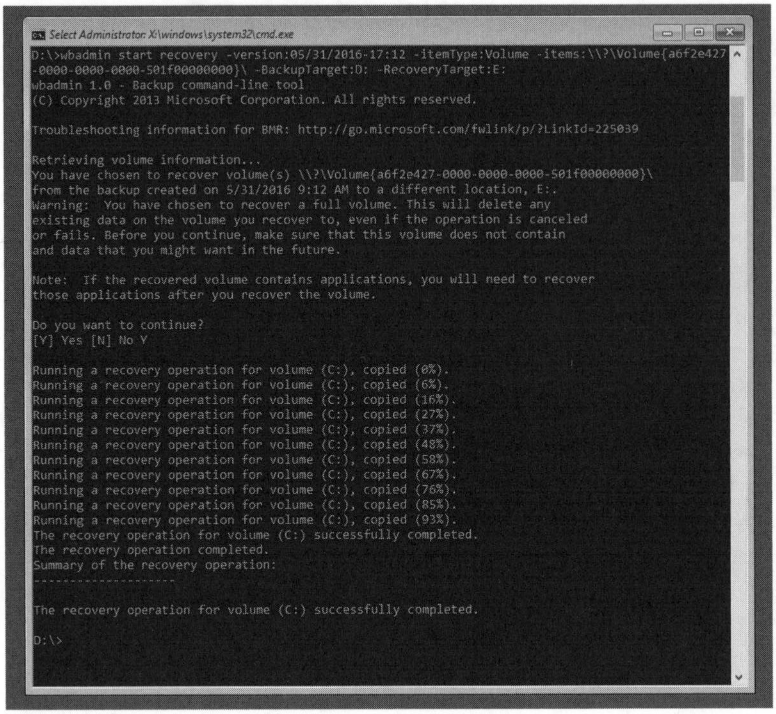

FIGURE 13-11 Recovering backed up volume with WBAdmin

Skill: Configure File History

The File History feature protects your data by backing it up periodically to a local or network drive. You can easily recover files that have been accidently deleted or modified, in a simple and user-friendly method. When it's enabled, File History automatically creates a backup on an hourly schedule, but this can be modified. As long as the backup destination location does not become full, File History continues to store changes made to your data indefinitely.

> **This section covers how to:**
>
> - Configure File History
> - Recover Files using File History
> - Consider using File History in an enterprise

Configuring File History

File History was introduced in Windows 8; the current version has an enhanced user interface and new improvements and is the recommended backup solution that Windows 10 offers.

To turn on File History for the first time, follow these steps.

1. Open Settings, click Update & Security, and select Backup.

2. Click the Plus (+) icon labeled Add A Drive.

   File History searches for available drives.

3. In the Select A Drive dialog box, select the external or local hard drive that you want to use for File History.

4. On the Back Up Using File History page, verify that the Automatically Back Up My Files toggle is On.

When it's enabled, File History saves copies of your files for the first time. This is a background operation, and you can continue to work normally while it completes.

File History saves the files from your user profile and all the folders located in your libraries, including data synced to your device from your OneDrive. You can modify what is saved by including or excluding folders. To manage the folders File History monitors, perform the following steps.

1. Open Settings, click Update & Security, and select Backup.

2. Click More Options.

3. In the Backup Options page, as shown in Figure 13-12, click Add A Folder.

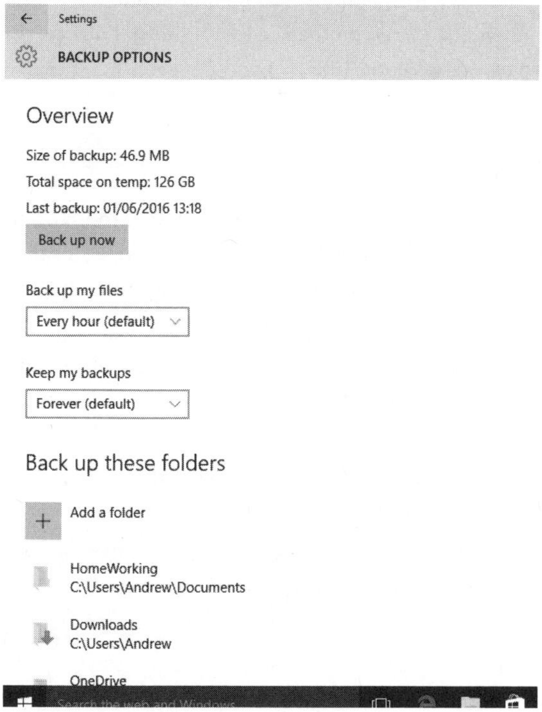

FIGURE 13-12 Configuring File History Backup Options

4. Select the folder that you want to be backed up and click Choose This Folder.

5. Ensure that the folder appears in the list of folders under Back Up These Folders.

6. If you scroll down to the bottom of the screen, you can also use Exclude These Folders to remove folders explicitly from File History.

7. Close the Backup Options page.

Some advanced settings are available in File History. Some of these can be configured through the Settings app or from the Advanced Settings link in File History in Control Panel. For example, you can configure the following.

- Modify the frequency of how often File History saves copies of files from every 10 minutes to daily.

- Share the backup drive to other HomeGroup members.

- Open File History event logs to view recent events or errors.

- Define the length of time to keep saved versions of your files.

- Manually clean up older versions of files and folders contained in the backup to recover space on the backup drive.

EXAM TIP

For the exam, it might be useful to know that the FhManagew.exe command-line tool enables you to delete file versions based on their age stored on the File History target device from the command line, such as: FhManagew.exe -cleanup 180.

Recovering Files by using File History

After it's enabled, File History monitors the files and folders you choose and backs them up to your backup storage. If you need to restore a folder or files that have been deleted, you can begin a restore operation by launching File History file recovery, as shown in Figure 13-13, in several ways, including the following.

- **History icon**   Open File Explorer and navigate to the folder that contains a modified or deleted file and then click History on the Home ribbon. The File History page opens, and you can view the recoverable files at this location.

- **Restore Personal Files**   Open File History in Control Panel and select the Restore Personal Files link on the left side. This screen displays all recoverable items.

- **Restore Files From A Current Backup**   The Restore Files From A Current Backup link is at the bottom of the Backup Options page in the Settings app.

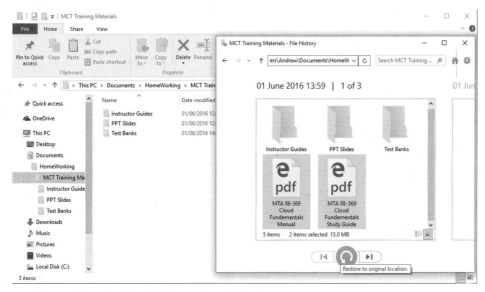

FIGURE 13-13 Restoring deleted files by using File History

When the File History page is in view, you can navigate through each restore point by using the arrow buttons at the bottom of the screen. In Figure 13-13, three restore points relate to items in the selected folder. Each restore point has a date and time to help you decide which version of the file or files to restore. You can select one or more files in the center pane, as in Figure 13-13, to revert, and select which version of the file by navigating through the numbered backups that File History has made. If you right-click the file, you can preview the file to view the contents. If you want to proceed to recover the file, click the large green button on the File History screen. The file or files selected are automatically restored; File Explorer opens the folder and displays the restored files.

> **NOTE   FILE HISTORY BACKUP LOCATION**
> You can easily navigate to the backup files that File History creates. They are stored on the backup drive in a logical folder hierarchy. The files backed up in Figure 13-13 are found at E:\FileHistory\Andrew\DESKTOP\Data\C\Users\Andrew\Documents\HomeWorking \Training Materials.

In the upper-right corner of the File History screen is a cog icon that displays links relating to the restore operation, view options, File History setup, and Help. The Restore To option enables you to select another location on your hard disk to restore the file.

If you experience a hard-drive failure, you can use the File History backup contained on your external hard disk to recover the most recent versions of all your files to your new system by following these steps.

1. On your new system, connect your external hard disk.

2. Launch File History in Control Panel.

3. On the Keep History Of Your Files page, allow Windows to complete the search and display the existing backup drive.

4. Ensure that I Want To Use A Previous Backup On This File History Drive is selected.

5. Select the previous File History backup from the list retrieved from the drive that contains your previous File History backups, as shown in Figure 13-14.

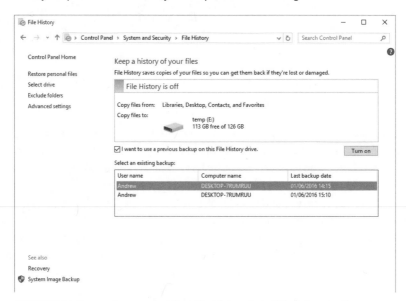

FIGURE 13-14 Connecting your existing File History to a different computer

6. Click Turn On.

   File History is now active.

7. Restore your files and folders by using the Restore Personal Files link.

Enterprise considerations for using File History

In an enterprise environment, you might configure File History to use removable USB drives for staff members who work away from the office. Removable drives containing data backups should to be secured.

File History supports backing up files that are encrypted using Encrypting File System (EFS) if you use Windows 10 Pro, Education, or Enterprise. The removable USB drive must be formatted with NTFS to allow either File History or EFS.

If you have Windows 10 Pro, Education, or Enterprise, you can use BitLocker Drive Encryption to protect your data on your PC, but this will not protect the backed-up files stored externally. If you want to use BitLocker technology to protect data stored on a portable drive, consider enabling BitLocker To Go on the removable drive, which will protect the contents.

If you want to disable File History from use on a device, you can configure the Group Policy Object (GPO) relating to File History located at Computer Configuration \Administrative Templates\Windows Components\File History\ Turn Off File History. When enabled, users can't turn on File History.

Skill: Restore previous versions of files and folders

Restoring files from a regular backup can take several hours or even longer if the backup is stored offsite; it typically requires administrator-level resources to accomplish the task. To reduce the administrative effort, you can enable the Previous Versions feature on Windows 10, which uses the Volume Shadow Copy Service (VSS) to generate local shadow copies, and then you can restore previous versions of files and folders within seconds.

The Previous Versions feature enables users to view, revert, or recover files and folders that have been modified or deleted. Previous Versions requires either the File History feature or restore points that the Backup And Restore (Windows 7) tool created. One of these features must be configured for you to be able to use the Previous Versions feature.

After you have enabled File History or created a backup by using Backup And Restore (Windows 7), your system will have created a shadow copy (or a snapshot) of your data, such as the files and folders located in your user profile. The snapshot tracks the changes to the files and folders on the drive, but it should be seen as complementary to the existing backup solution that is in use. Because the snapshot data is not a complete copy of files and is typically stored on the same drive as your data, it is not considered a replacement for traditional backups.

By default, Previous Versions monitors special folders, including AppData (Roaming), Desktop, Documents, Pictures, Music, Videos, Favorites, Contacts, Downloads, Links, Searches, and Saved Games. With Previous Versions, you can browse in File Explorer to a location where your files and folders have been modified or deleted, and when you open the item properties, a Previous Versions tab lists the available restore points for your data. If the Previous Versions tab is empty, it might be that the file has not been modified, or the shadow copy has not yet made a snapshot.

EXAM TIP

Do not confuse System Restore points and File History. The Previous Versions feature uses restore points that are created by either File History or the Backup And Restore (Windows 7) tool and not the restore points that System Restore creates.

If you configure both File History and Backup And Restore (Windows 7), you benefit from the creation of multiple restore points that will be available to Previous Versions.

To revert files using Previous Versions, use the following steps.

1. Ensure that File History is turned on.

2. Create a folder on your computer—for example, This PC\Documents\HomeWorking—and then create or save a text file in the folder.

3. In File History, click Run Now.

4. Open the text file and modify the contents, save them, and exit the file.

5. Right-click the text file and select Restore Previous Versions.

   The Text file has one previous version listed, which is the original file. If you modify the file again, another Previous Version is automatically created when File History creates the next Restore Point.

6. To create a new Restore Point manually, return to File History and click Run Now. Return to the Text file and notice that two file versions are now listed, as shown in Figure 13-15.

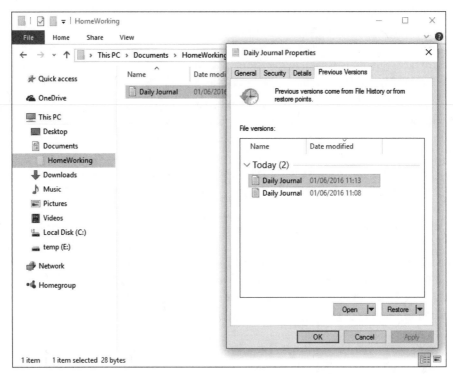

FIGURE 13-15 Viewing Previous Versions of files

7. Delete the Daily Journal.txt file.

8. To recover the last version of the file that File History saved, right-click the This PC\Documents\HomeWorking folder and select Restore Previous Versions.

9. Click the HomeWorking folder and click Restore.

10. Verify that the Daily Journal.txt file has been restored to the This PC\Documents \HomeWorking folder and that the latest version has been recovered.

11. Close File Explorer.

In a corporate environment, an administrator can enable shadow copies for folders shared over the network. This can be useful because, normally, when a user deletes a file contained in a shared folder, the files are permanently deleted and are not moved to the local Recycle Bin. Before the introduction of VSS technology, the only way to recover deleted files on a network share was from a backup, which is not very efficient. With shadow copying in place, the Previous Versions feature enables users to recover deleted files instantaneously without needing assistance from an administrator.

The VSS command-line tool vssadmin can be useful to review or troubleshoot VSS, for ex-ample, if you want to review the space that shadow copies use, create a new volume shadow copy, or suspect shadow copies are not working properly.

Some of the volume shadow commands available with vssadmin are listed in Table 13-4.

TABLE 13-4 VSSAdmin commands

Command	Description
Vssadmin add shadowstorage	Adds a volume shadow copy storage association
Vssadmin create shadow	Creates a new volume shadow copy
Vssadmin list providers	Lists registered volume shadow copy providers
Vssadmin list shadows	Lists existing volume shadow copies
Vssadmin list shadowstorage	Lists all shadow copy storage associations on the system
Vssadmin list volumes	Lists volumes that are eligible for shadow copies
Vssadmin list writers	Lists all subscribed volume shadow copy writers on the system
Vssadmin delete shadows	Deletes volume shadow copies
Vssadmin delete shadowstorage	Deletes volume shadow copy storage associations
Vssadmin resize shadowstorage	Resizes the maximum size for a shadow copy storage association

Skill: Recover files from OneDrive

Microsoft OneDrive enables you to store your files online, sync files between your PC and OneDrive, and access files directly by a web browser located at OneDrive.com. You need to understand how you can recover files from OneDrive that you have deleted.

This section covers how to:

- Recover files from OneDrive
- Use Previous Versions in OneDrive

Recovering files from OneDrive

If you accidentally delete a file stored in your OneDrive account, you can recover it by using Recycle Bin, which is available with OneDrive.com and on the local desktop of your PC. OneDrive automatically empties files from Recycle Bin after 30 days. If you delete a file by mistake, to prevent losing a deleted file, make sure you restore it within 30 days.

When you delete a file in OneDrive from one device, OneDrive deletes the file from all your OneDrive locations everywhere, including the OneDrive folder synced to File Explorer. If you move a file out of OneDrive to a different location, such as a local folder on a device, this removes the file from your OneDrive.

The OneDrive Recycle Bin can retain deleted items for a minimum of 3 days and up to a maximum of 30 days. The actual retention period is normally 30 days, but this depends on the size of Recycle Bin, which is set to 10 percent of the total storage limit by default. If you are running low on available OneDrive space or if Recycle Bin is full, old items will be deleted to make room for new items as they are added to Recycle Bin, and this might have an impact on the 30-day retention period.

To recover deleted files from your OneDrive.com, follow these steps.

1. Browse to your OneDrive.com or right-click the cloud icon in the notification area and click Go To OneDrive.com.
2. On the left side of the page, select Recycle Bin.
3. If Recycle Bin is not visible, click the three horizontal lines in the top left corner of the screen and select Recycle Bin.
4. Select the items that you want to recover.
5. Click Restore on the menu.
6. OneDrive restores the items, and they are removed from Recycle Bin.

> **NOTE RECYCLE BIN SIZE**
> There is no setting for you to modify the size of Recycle Bin. If you increase the OneDrive space by freeing up space or purchasing additional OneDrive storage space, the 10% allocation for Recycle Bin will be increased.

When you delete files by using the web interface or directly from your OneDrive folders in File Explorer, the deleted files are automatically synchronized to OneDrive.com Recycle Bin and File Explorer Recycle Bin.

Just as with Recycle Bin in File Explorer, if you select items in Recycle Bin and delete them, you are warned that they will be permanently deleted, as shown in Figure 13-16.

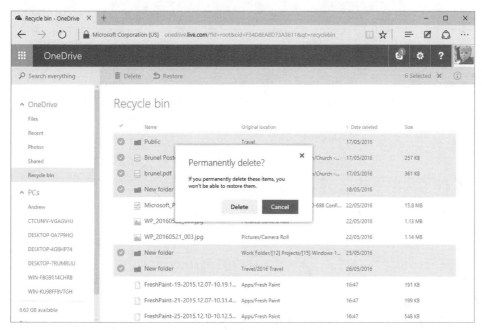

FIGURE 13-16 Permanently deleting items from OneDrive Recycle Bin

Take care also when using Restore All or Empty Recycle Bin because these tasks are irreversible.

The Search Everything feature in OneDrive.com is a very powerful method of locating files stored in your OneDrive because it searches the file name and metadata. However, OneDrive search results do not include items in OneDrive Recycle Bin or File Explorer Recycle Bin.

Using Previous Versions in OneDrive

Earlier in this chapter, you reviewed the Previous Versions feature in File Explorer. A similar feature exists when you use OneDrive. Whenever you store and modify Microsoft Office documents in OneDrive.com, OneDrive maintains a version history of these documents, similar to how Previous Versions behaves.

To view the available versions stored in OneDrive, navigate to and select a Microsoft Office file and then choose Version History from the context menu. OneDrive opens the file in a new browser tab, and you see the list of available versions in the left pane. You can review the contents of each file, as shown in Figure 13-17. If you open the document in Word Online, you can select Previous Versions from the settings menu on the right side.

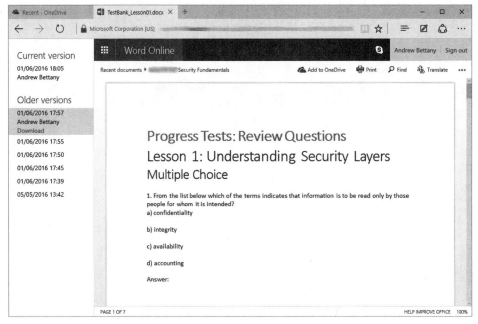

FIGURE 13-17 Older Microsoft Office versions available in OneDrive

The older versions are listed together with the date and time of when the file was last saved. If you edit the document online, OneDrive automatically saves the file when you make changes. If you select an older version of the document from the list of older versions in the left pane, OneDrive opens the older file into the tab. You can click the Download link under this older version.

Summary

- A recovery drive can be stored on a USB drive or SDHC memory card and used to boot to Windows RE to access the advanced recovery tools.

- System Restore can provide you with an effective method of recovering your system after a corrupt device driver or malware infection.

- When resetting your device, you can remove everything and return your device to the OOBE state or keep your files and reset the operating system.

- Windows 10 provides additional tools in the advanced troubleshooting mode and still supports many older options such as booting in Safe Mode.

- You should configure System Protection to safeguard your computer's system files, settings, and data on a regular schedule.

- Windows 10 provides multiple backup tools, including File History and Backup And Restore (Windows 7).

- WBAdmin enables you to perform backups from the command line and restore data from Windows RE.

- File History provides a continuous backup of your personal data files, offering a high level of recovery granularity.

- The Previous Versions feature is included in Windows 10 and offers users a simple method of recovering deleted or accidentally modified files from File Explorer.

- You can recover deleted files in OneDrive by using Recycle Bin in OneDrive.com or File Explorer for up to 30 days before they are automatically removed.

Thought experiment

In this thought experiment, demonstrate your skills and knowledge of the topics covered in this chapter. You can find answers to this thought experiment in the next section.

Your company is upgrading its operating system from Windows 7 Pro to Windows 10 Pro for its 500 users. The Sales team members will be provided with new Surface 4 Pro tablets with Windows 10 Pro. The remaining members of the staff use desktop PCs. The Sales team members work away from the office and are required to create a local backup of data contained on their tablets to an external USB hard drive on a weekly basis.

The networked file server in the head office is available for all staff to use, either through the local network or by using VPN technology. Office users do not create backups because backups are performed on the file server.

You need to ensure that the users of the Surface tablets can create backups and access files contained in previous backups as necessary.

Answer the following questions for your manager.

1. Which Windows 10 backup tool will you implement for the Sales team members?

2. One of the Sales team members needs to access a file saved on their old laptop. How will you advise this user?

3. All users need to be able to restore files without contacting the help desk. How can this be achieved?

Thought experiment answer

This section contains the solution to the thought experiment.

1. The Sales team members should use the File History feature in Windows 10, which will back up their data to a removable drive.

2. The Windows 7 laptop devices were regularly backed up. The Backup And Restore (Windows 7) tool allows access to the backups created with Windows 7. The user

should be able to restore the required file from the backup created with the Backup And Restore (Windows 7) tool.

3. Previous Versions is the preferred method for users to restore files that have been deleted or accidentally modified from File Explorer. The Sales team members can use Previous Versions, which is enabled by their use of the File History feature. For office staff, the Previous Versions feature will need to be enabled on the file server.

CHAPTER 14

Configure authorization and authentication

Authentication is the process of verifying the identity of a security principal: a user, a group, a computer or other device, a service or process. Authorization takes place after a security principal has been authenticated and is the process of granting access to a resource for an identified security principal.

In Windows 10, you can implement authentication in a number of ways. It is important to understand the various authentication methods and to know how to enable and configure them to help ensure that your network and connected devices remain secure. As a result, the 70-698 Installing and Configuring Windows exam contains questions that relate to authentication methods, account and credential management, and device security.

Skills covered in this chapter:

- Configure user accounts
- Configure Microsoft Passport and Windows Hello
- Manage credential security
- Manage device security
- Configure HomeGroup, workgroup, and domain settings

> ***NOTE*** **HOMEGROUP**
>
> The list of skills measured for the exam includes HomeGroup in this section. To avoid repetition, this topic isn't covered here. You'll find information about configuring HomeGoup in Chapter 6, "Configure networking," under "Skill: Connect to a network," and in Chapter 8, "Configure data access and usage," under "Skill: Configure HomeGroup connections."

Skill: Configure user accounts

Before you can sign in to your Windows 10–based computer, you must create a user account. Windows 10 supports the ability for you to sign in using local accounts, Active Directory Domain Services (AD DS) domain accounts, and Microsoft accounts.

After you are signed in, it is important to ensure that your user account operates as a standard user account and is only elevated to an administrative level when needed. User Account Control (UAC) can help you control administrative privilege elevation in Windows 10.

> **This section covers how to:**
> - Configure local accounts
> - Configure a Microsoft account
> - Configure User Account Control behavior

Configure local accounts

Local accounts, as the name suggests, exist in the local accounts database on your Windows 10 device; it can only be granted access to local resources and, where granted, exercise administrative rights and privileges on the local computer.

When you first install Windows 10, you are prompted to sign in using a Microsoft account or to create a local account to sign in with. Thereafter, you can create additional local user accounts as your needs dictate.

Default accounts

In Windows 10, three user accounts exist by default in the local accounts database. These are the Administrator account, DefaultAccount, and the Guest account. All of these are disabled by default.

When you install Windows 10, you create an additional user account. You can give this account any name. This initial user account is a member of the local Administrators group and therefore can perform any local management task.

You can view the installed accounts, including the default accounts, by using the Computer Management console, as shown in Figure 14-1. You can also use the net user command-line tool and the get-wmiobject -class win32_useraccount Windows PowerShell cmdlet to list the local user accounts.

EXAM TIP

In Windows 10 Home edition, you cannot use Computer Management to view or edit user accounts because the Local Users And Groups node does not exist.

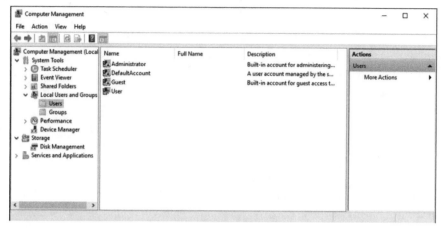

FIGURE 14-1 Viewing built-in user accounts

Managing local user accounts

You can manage local user accounts by using Computer Management (except with Windows 10 Home edition), the Settings app, Control Panel, and Windows PowerShell.

USING COMPUTER MANAGEMENT

To manage user accounts by using Computer Management, right-click Start and then click Computer Management. Expand the Local Users And Groups node and then click Users. To create a new user, right-click the Users node and click New User.

In the New User dialog box, configure the following properties, as shown in Figure 14-2, and then click Create.

FIGURE 14-2 Adding a user with Computer Management

- User Name
- Full Name
- Password
- User Must Change Password At Next Logon
- User Cannot Change Password
- Password Never Expires
- Account Is Disabled

After you have added the new user account, you can modify more advanced properties by double-clicking the user account. On the General tab, you can change the user's full name and description and password-related options. On the Member Of tab, you can add the user to groups or remove the user from groups. The Profile tab, shown in Figure 14-3, enables you to modify the following properties.

FIGURE 14-3 Modifying the profile properties for a user

- **Profile path** The path to the location of a user's desktop profile. The profile stores the user's desktop settings, such as color scheme, desktop wallpaper, and app settings, including the settings stored for the user in the registry. By default, each user who signs in has a profile folder created automatically in the C:\Users*Username* folder. You can define another location here, and you can use a Universal Naming Convention (UNC) name in the form of *Server**Share**Folder*.

- **Logon script** The name of a logon script that processes each time a user signs in. Typically, this will be a .bat or .cmd file. You might typically place commands to map network drives or load apps in this script file. It is not usual to assign logon scripts in this way. Instead, Group Policy Objects (GPOs) are used to assign logon and startup scripts for domain user accounts.

- **Home folder** A personal storage area where users can save their personal documents. By default, users are assigned subfolders within the C:\Users*Username* folder for this purpose. However, you can use either of the following two properties to specify an alternate location.

  - **Local path** A local file system path for storage of the user's personal files. This is entered in the format of a local drive and folder path.

  - **Connect** A network location mapped to the specified drive letter. This is entered in the format of a UNC name.

USING CONTROL PANEL

You can manage user accounts from Control Panel. Open Control Panel and click User Accounts and then click User Accounts again. From here, you can:

- **Make Changes To My Accounts In PC Settings** Launches the Settings app to enable you to make user account changes

- **Change Your Account Name** Enables you to change your account name

- **Change Your Account Type** Enables you to switch between Standard and Administrator account types

- **Manage Another User Account** Enables you to manage other user accounts on this computer, as shown in Figure 14-4

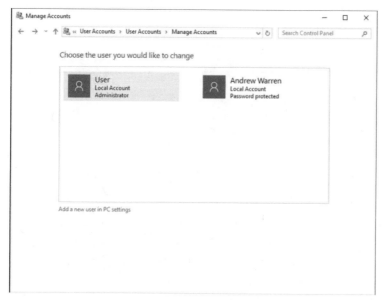

FIGURE 14-4 Managing user accounts in Control Panel

- **Change User Account Control Settings** Launches the User Account Control Settings dialog box from Control Panel

You cannot add new accounts from this location. If you want to add a new account, use Computer Management, the Settings app, or Windows PowerShell.

USING THE SETTINGS APP

The preferred way to manage local accounts in Windows 10 is by using the Settings app. From Settings, click Accounts. As shown in Figure 14-5, on the Your Email And Accounts tab, you can modify your account settings, including:

- Assigning a picture to your account.
- Adding accounts for email, calendar, and contacts.
- Adding a Microsoft account.
- Adding a workplace or school account, such as a Microsoft Office 365 account.

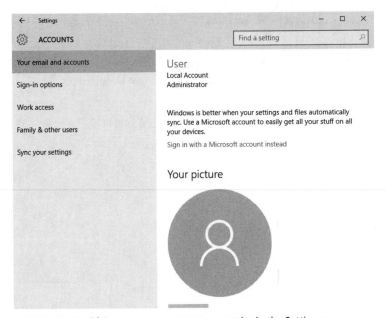

FIGURE 14-5 Modifying your user account properties in the Settings app

If you need to add a new account, click the Family & Other Users tab and then click Add Someone Else To This PC. You must then enter that person's email address, typically the address they use to sign in to Office 365, OneDrive, Skype, Xbox, or Outlook.com.

If you want to add a local account by using the Settings app, use the following procedure.

1. In the Settings app, click Accounts.
2. On the Family & Other Users tab, under Other Users, click Add Someone Else To This PC.
3. In the How Will This Person Sign In dialog box, click I Don't Have This Person's Sign-In Information.

4. In the Let's Create Your Account Dialog Box, click Add A User Without A Microsoft Account.

5. On the Create An Account For This PC page, type the user name, type a new password twice, and then click Next to create the local account.

USING WINDOWS POWERSHELL

Before you can manage local user accounts, you must install the Windows PowerShell local account module. You can do this by running the following cmdlet from an elevated Windows PowerShell command.

```
Find-Module localaccount | Install-Module
```

You can then use the following cmdlets to manage local user accounts.

- Get-LocalUser
- New-LocalUser
- Remove-LocalUser
- Rename-LocalUser
- Disable-LocalUser
- Enable-LocalUser

For example, to add a new local user account called Sales 02 with a password that expires in one month, run the following cmdlet.

```
New-LocalUser -Name "Sales02" -Description "Sales User account" -PasswordExpires (Get-Date).AddMonths(1)
```

> **NEED MORE REVIEW? LOCAL ACCOUNTS CMDLETS**
>
> To review further details about using Windows PowerShell to manage local accounts, refer to the Microsoft TechNet website at *https://technet.microsoft.com/library/mt651682.aspx.*

Configure Microsoft accounts

A Microsoft account provides you with an identity that you can use to sign in on multiple devices and access online services. You can also use the account to synchronize your personal settings between your Windows-based devices.

If Windows 10 detects an Internet connection during setup, you are prompted to specify your Microsoft account details. However, you can link your Microsoft account to a local or AD DS domain account after setup is complete.

After you connect your Microsoft account with your local account, you can:

- Access personal Microsoft cloud services, including OneDrive, Outlook.com, and other personal apps.
- Use the Microsoft account to access Microsoft Intune, Microsoft Office 365, and Microsoft Azure.

- Download and install apps from the Microsoft Store.
- Sync your settings between devices that are linked to your account.

EXAM TIP
You can browse the Windows Store even if you do not sign in using a Microsoft account.

Signing up for a Microsoft account

To sign up for a Microsoft account, use the following procedure.

1. Open a web browser and navigate to *https://signup.live.com.*

2. To use your own email address for your Microsoft account, type it into the web form. If you choose this option, you must verify the address later.

3. If you want to create a Hotmail or Outlook.com account, click Get A New Email Address and then complete the email address line, specifying whether you want a Hotmail or Outlook suffix.

4. Press Tab to verify that the name you entered is available.

5. Complete the rest of the form and then agree to the privacy statement by clicking I Accept.

After you have created your Microsoft account, you can connect it to your local or domain account.

Connecting your Microsoft account to your device

To connect your Microsoft account to your local or domain user account, use the following procedure.

1. In Settings, click Accounts.

2. On the Your Email And Accounts page, in the details pane, click Sign In With A Microsoft Account Instead, as shown in Figure 14-5.

3. On the Make It Yours page, enter the email address and password associated with your Microsoft account and then click Sign In, as shown in Figure 14-6.

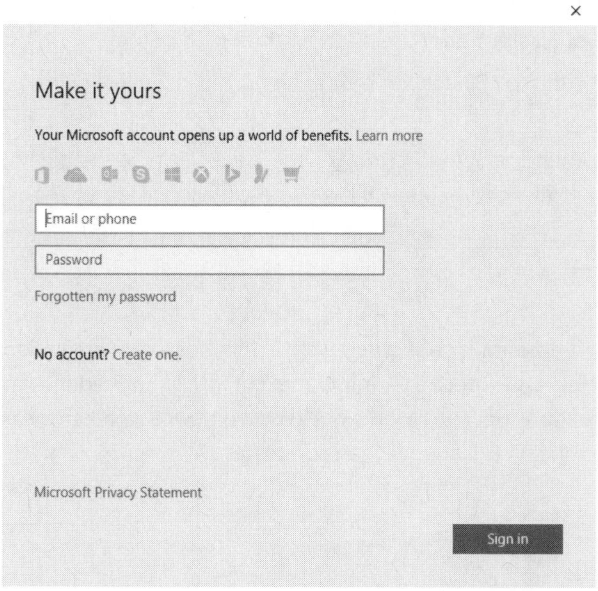

FIGURE 14-6 Enter the Microsoft account credentials

4. On the Sign In To This Device Using Your Microsoft Account page, in the Old Password box, type the password for your local user account and then click Next.

5. On the Set Up A PIN page, click Set A PIN, as shown in Figure 14-7.

Set up a PIN

Using a PIN is faster and more secure than a password – we think you'll love it.
How can a PIN be safer than a long password?

Skip this step

Set a PIN

FIGURE 14-7 Setting up a PIN for authentication

This is optional, but using a PIN is more secure than a password because it is only relevant on this device. If you prefer to not use a PIN, click Skip This Step.

6. When prompted, in the Set Up A PIN dialog box, enter your chosen PIN twice and click OK.

7. You are returned to the Your Email And Accounts page. Click Verify to enable Microsoft to verify that you have permission to connect this Microsoft account to your device.

Depending on your Microsoft account options, you can receive an email to a designated account for confirmation purposes, or you might choose to receive a text message to your cell phone.

In this instance, the Microsoft account is configured with a cell phone for verification, as shown in Figure 14-8. On the Help Us Protect Your Info page, enter the required information, click Next, and follow the instructions on your Windows 10–based device to enter the code that you receive on your cell phone. Verification is then complete.

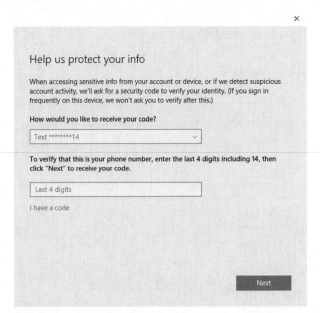

FIGURE 14-8 Performing verification by using a cell phone

NEED MORE REVIEW? **SETTING UP ACCOUNTS**

To review further details about setting up Microsoft accounts, refer to the Microsoft TechNet website at *http://windows.microsoft.com/en-us/windows-10 /getstarted-set-up-accounts.*

Configure User Account Control

In earlier versions of Windows, it was necessary to sign in using an administrative account to perform administrative tasks. This often led to users signing in with administrative accounts at all times, even when performing standard user tasks, such as running apps or browsing Internet websites.

However, being signed in with administrative privilege at all times poses a security risk because it provides for the possibility of malicious software exploiting administrative access to files and other resources. Windows 10 provides UAC to help mitigate this threat.

When you sign in using an administrative account, UAC inhibits the account's access to that of a standard user, only elevating the account's privileges to administrative level when required, and only after prompting the user for permissions to do so. In addition, if a user signs in with a standard user account and attempts to perform a task requiring administrative privileges, UAC can prompt the user for administrative credentials.

Standard users can perform the following tasks without requiring elevation.

- Change their user account passwords.
- Configure accessibility options.
- Configure power options.
- Install updates by using Windows Update.
- Install device drivers included in the operating system or by using Windows Update.
- View Windows 10 settings.
- Pair Bluetooth devices.
- Establish network connections, reset network adapters, and perform network diagnostics and repair.

However, the following tasks require elevation.

- Install or remove apps.
- Install a device driver not included in Windows or Windows Update.
- Modify UAC settings.
- Open Windows Firewall in Control Panel.
- Add or remove user accounts.
- Restore system backups.
- Configure Windows Update settings.

> **NOTE**
>
> This is not an exhaustive list of tasks but, merely, an indication of the types of tasks requiring or not requiring elevation.

When a user performs a task requiring elevation, depending on settings, UAC can prompt the user in two ways for elevation.

- **Prompt for consent** This appears to administrators in Admin Approval Mode when they attempt to perform an administrative task. It requests approval to continue from the user.

- **Prompt for credentials** This appears to standard users when they attempt to perform an administrative task.

Admin Approval Mode is the process whereby a user signed in with an administrative account operates in the context of a standard user until a task is attempted that requires administrative privilege. At that time, the user receives the configured prompt—by default, a prompt for consent.

UAC is enabled by default, but you can configure and, if necessary, disable UAC by using Control Panel or Group Policy Objects (GPOs) in an AD DS domain environment. To configure UAC by using Control Panel, use the following procedure.

1. From Control Panel, click System And Security.

2. Click Change User Account Control Settings.

   As shown in Figure 14-9, you can use the slider bar in the Choose When To Be Notified About Changes To Your Computer dialog box to adjust the UAC settings.

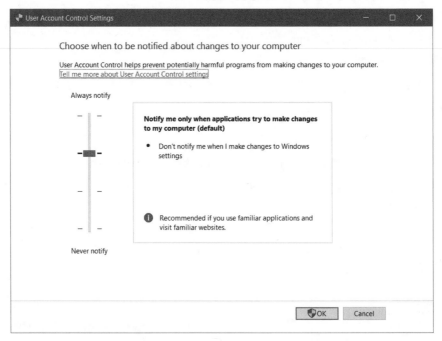

FIGURE 14-9 Configuring User Account Control prompts

The available settings are:

- **Never Notify Me When** In this setting, UAC is disabled. This means that users signing in with Standard accounts cannot perform administrative tasks because there is no means to prompt for credentials with which to perform those tasks. Users signing in with administrative accounts can perform any task requiring elevation, without a prompt for consent.

- **Notify Me Only When Apps Try To Make Changes To My Computer (Do Not Dim Desktop)** In this mode, users are prompted, but Windows does not switch to Secure Desktop while awaiting user consent. This is less secure.

- **Notify Me Only When Apps Try To Make Changes To My Computer (Default)** In this mode, users are prompted, and Windows switches to Secure Desktop while awaiting user consent. This is more secure.

- **Always Notify Me When** This is the most secure but most intrusive setting. Users are prompted not only for application installations, but also any time they make Windows settings changes.

> **NEED MORE REVIEW? HOW USER ACCOUNT CONTROL WORKS**
>
> To review further details about configuring UAC, refer to the Microsoft TechNet website at *https://technet.microsoft.com/itpro/windows/keep-secure/how-user-account-control-works*.

In addition to configuring UAC settings locally, you can also use GPOs in an AD DS environment. On a domain controller, open Group Policy Management and locate the appropriate GPO. Open the GPO for editing and navigate to Computer Configuration \ Policies \ Windows Settings \ Security Settings \ Local Policies \ Security Options and then locate the settings in the details pane that have the User Account Control prefix.

> **NEED MORE REVIEW? UAC GROUP POLICY SETTINGS AND REGISTRY KEY SETTINGS**
>
> To review further details about configuring UAC by using GPOs, refer to the Microsoft TechNet website at *https://technet.microsoft.com/library/dd835564(v=ws.10).aspx*.

Skill: Configure Microsoft Passport and Windows Hello

Traditional computer authentication is based on user name and password exchange with an authentication authority. Although password-based authentication is acceptable in many circumstances, Windows 10 provides for a number of additional, more secure methods for users to authenticate with their devices, including multifactor authentication.

Multifactor authentication is based on the principle that users who wish to authenticate must have two (or more) things with which to identify themselves. Specifically, they must have knowledge of something, they must be in possession of something, and they must be something. For example, a user might know a password, possess a security token (in the form of a digital certificate), and be able to prove who they are with biometrics, such as fingerprints.

> **This section covers how to:**
> - Configure Windows Hello
> - Configure Microsoft Passport and biometrics
> - Configure picture passwords

Configure Windows Hello

Windows Hello is a biometric authentication mechanism built into Windows 10 to address the requirement that users must be able to prove who they are by something they uniquely have. When you implement Windows Hello, users can unlock their devices by using facial recognition or fingerprint scanning.

Windows Hello works with Microsoft Passport to authenticate users and enable them to access your network resources. It provides the following benefits.

- It helps protect against credential theft. Because a malicious person must have both the device and the biometric information or PIN, it becomes more difficult to access the device.
- Employees don't need to remember a password any longer. They can always authenticate using their biometric data.
- Windows Hello is part of Windows 10, so you can add additional biometric devices and authentication policies by using GPOs or mobile device management (MDM) configurations service provider (CSP) policies.

To implement Windows Hello, your devices must be equipped with appropriate hardware. For facial recognition and iris scanning, suitable cameras must be present in the Windows 10 device. For fingerprint recognition, your devices must be equipped with a fingerprint scanner.

After you have installed the necessary hardware devices, to set up Windows Hello, open Settings, click Accounts, and then, on the Sign-in Options page, under Windows Hello, review the options for face, fingerprint, or iris. If you do not have Windows Hello–supported hardware, the Windows Hello section does not appear on the Sign-in Options page.

> ***NEED MORE REVIEW?*** **WINDOWS HELLO BIOMETRICS IN THE ENTERPRISE**
>
> To review further details about using Windows Hello in the enterprise, refer to the Microsoft TechNet website at *https://technet.microsoft.com/itpro/windows/keep-secure /windows-hello-in-enterprise.*

Configure Microsoft Passport and biometrics

To avoid authentication with passwords, Microsoft provides an authentication system called Microsoft Passport. This enables secure authentication without sending a password to an authenticating authority, such as an AD DS domain controller.

Microsoft Passport uses two-factor authentication based on Windows Hello–based biometric authentication (or a PIN) together with the ownership of a specific device. Using Microsoft Passport provides a number of benefits for your organization.

- **User convenience**   After your employees set up Windows Hello, they can access enterprise resources without needing to remember user names or passwords.
- **Security**   Because no passwords are used, Microsoft Passport helps protect user identities and user credentials.

To set up Microsoft Passport, after users have configured Windows Hello and signed in using their biometric features (or PIN), they register the device. The registration process is as follows.

1. The user creates an account on the device; this can be a local account or a domain account.
2. The user signs in using the account.
3. The user sets up PIN authentication for the account.

EXAM TIP

Signing in with a Microsoft account on a Windows 10–based device automatically sets up Microsoft Passport on the device; users do not need to do anything else.

After a user has completed the registration process, Microsoft Passport generates a new public–private key pair on the device known as a *protector key*. If installed in the device, the Trusted Platform Module (TPM) generates and stores this protector key; if the device does not have a TPM, Windows encrypts the protector key and stores it on the file system. Microsoft Passport also generates an administrative key that is used to reset credentials if necessary.

NOTE **PAIRING OF CREDENTIALS AND DEVICES**

Microsoft Passport pairs a specific device and a user credential. Consequently, the PIN the user chooses is associated only with the active account and that specific device.

The user now has a PIN *gesture* defined on the device and an associated protector key for that PIN gesture. The user can now securely sign in to their device using the PIN and then add support for a biometric gesture as an alternative for the PIN. The *gesture* could be facial recognition, iris scanning, or fingerprint recognition, depending on available hardware in the device. When a user adds a biometric gesture, it follows the same basic sequence as mentioned earlier. The user authenticates to the system by using the PIN and then registers the new biometric. Windows generates a unique key pair and stores it securely. The user can then sign in using the PIN or a biometric gesture.

NEED MORE REVIEW? MICROSOFT PASSPORT GUIDE

To review further details about Microsoft Passport, refer to the Microsoft TechNet website at *https://technet.microsoft.com/itpro/windows/keep-secure/microsoft-passport-guide*.

You can use MDM policies or GPOs to configure settings for Microsoft Passport in your organization. For example, you can configure a policy that enables or disables the use of biometrics on devices affected by the policy. You can also impose rules on PINs so that, for example, a PIN must consist of five characters, including digits and lowercase letters.

To implement GPOs to configure Microsoft Passport settings in your organization, open the appropriate GPO for editing and navigate to Computer Configuration / Policies / Administrative Templates / Windows Components / Microsoft Passport For Work. Edit and configure the appropriate values.

NEED MORE REVIEW? IMPLEMENTING MICROSOFT PASSPORT

To review further details about implementing Microsoft Passport by using GPOs or MDM policies, refer to the Microsoft TechNet website at *https://technet.microsoft.com/itpro /windows/keep-secure/implement-microsoft-passport-in-your-organization*.

Configure picture passwords

In addition to using PINs and biometric gestures to sign in, users can also choose to use a picture password. This is configured in the Settings app. As shown in Figure 14-10, select Accounts and then select the Sign-In Options tab.

EXAM TIP

If you do not see the Picture Password heading, your display is not touch-enabled. Picture passwords are associated with an image and a touch gesture on the screen.

To set up picture passwords, complete the following procedure.

1. On the Sign-in Options tab, under Picture Password, click Add.

    You are prompted to verify your account information.

2. Reenter your account password.

3. You are provided with an initial picture. If you want, click Select Picture to choose another.

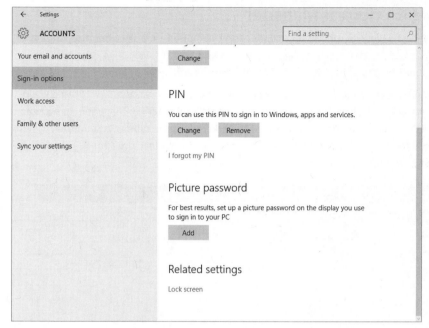

FIGURE 14-10 Configuring a picture password

4. Draw three gestures directly on your screen.

 Remember that the size, position, and direction of the gestures are stored as part of the picture password.

5. You are prompted to repeat your gestures. If your repeated gestures match, click Finish.

Skill: Manage credential security

After you have configured sign-in options, it is important to understand how user credentials are stored and protected. Users must sign in not only to Windows 10 but to websites and on-line services, most of which do not use the user's Windows 10 credentials. To help users access these websites and services, Windows stores the credentials and provides two features to help protect users' credentials.

This section covers how to:

- Configure Credential Manager
- Configure Credential Guard

Configure Credential Manager

When users access a website, online service, or server computer on a network, they might need to provide user credentials to access those sites and services. Windows can store the credentials to make it easier for users to access those sites and services later.

These credentials are stored in secure areas known as *vaults*. To access the stored credentials, open Control Panel, click User Accounts, and then click Credential Manager. As shown in Figure 14-11, you can then browse the list of stored credentials. Windows separates the list into those used for websites, listed under Web Credentials, and those used for Windows servers, listed under Windows Credentials.

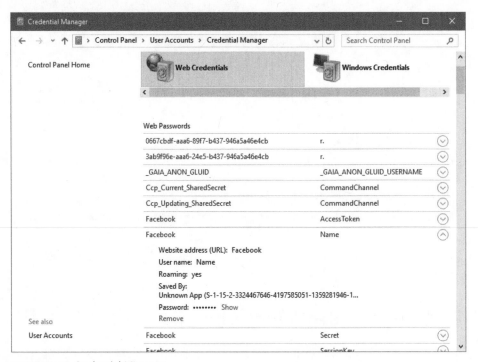

FIGURE 14-11 Credential Manager

To view stored credentials, select the appropriate website or online service from the list and expand the entry by clicking the Down Arrow. Click Show to view the stored password and click Remove if you no longer want to store the entry. You are prompted to reenter your user account password before you can perform either of these actions.

Configure Credential Guard

When a user signs in to an AD DS domain, they provide their user credentials to a domain controller. As a result of successful authentication, the authenticating domain controller issues Kerberos tickets to the user's computer. The user's computer uses these tickets to establish sessions with server computers that are part of the same AD DS forest. Essentially, if a server receives a session request, it examines the Kerberos ticket for validity. If valid in all respects, and issued by a trusted authenticating authority, such as a domain controller in the same AD DS forest, a session is allowed.

These Kerberos tickets, and related security tokens such as NTLM hashes, are stored in the Local Security Authority, a process that runs on Windows-based computers and handles the exchange of such information between the local computer and requesting authorities. However, it is possible for certain malicious software to gain access to this security process and, hence, exploit the stored tickets and hashes.

To help protect against this possibility, 64-bit versions of both Windows 10 Enterprise and Windows 10 Education editions have a feature called Credential Guard, which implements a technology known as *virtualization-assisted security*; this enables Credential Guard to block access to credentials stored in the Local Security Authority.

In addition to requiring the appropriate edition of 64-bit editions of Windows 10, the following are the requirements for implementing Credential Guard.

- Unified Extensible Firmware Interface (UEFI) 2.3.1 or greater
- Secure Boot
- Virtualization features: Intel VT-X, AMD-V, and SLAT must be enabled
- A VT-d or AMD-Vi input–output memory management unit
- A TPM: Windows 10 version 1511 supports both TPM 1.2 and TPM 2.0, but earlier versions of Windows 10 support only TPM 2.0
- Firmware lock

After you have verified that your computer meets the requirements, you can enable Credential Guard by using GPOs in an AD DS environment. Open the appropriate GPO for editing and navigate to Computer Configuration \ Policies \ Administrative Templates \ System \ Device Guard. Enable Turn On Virtualization Based Security, as shown in Figure 14-12.

> **NEED MORE REVIEW?** **PROTECT DERIVED DOMAIN CREDENTIALS WITH CREDENTIAL GUARD**
>
> To review further details about how Credential Guard works, refer to the Microsoft TechNet website at *https://technet.microsoft.com/itpro/windows/keep-secure/credential-guard*.

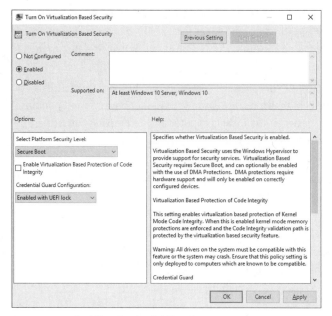

FIGURE 14-12 Enabling Credential Guard

Skill: Manage device security

It is important that when users attempt to connect their devices to your organization's network, you can determine that those devices are secure and conform to organizational policies regarding security settings and features.

Microsoft provides two features in Windows 10 that can help you meet the goal of allowing only secured devices to connect to your organization's network. These features are Device Guard and Device health attestation.

> **This section covers how to:**
> - Configure Device Guard
> - Configure Device Health Attestation

Configure Device Guard

With malicious software (malware) changing daily, the ability of organizations to keep up to date with emerging threats is challenged. Device Guard is an attempt to mitigate this challenge. Rather than allow apps to run unless blocked, Device Guard only runs specifically trusted apps.

The requirements for Device Guard are as for Credential Guard. These are:

- 64-bit version of Windows 10 Enterprise.
- UEFI 2.3.1 or greater.
- Secure Boot.
- Virtualization features: Intel VT-X, AMD-V, and SLAT must be enabled.
- A VT-d or AMD-Vi input–output memory management unit.
- A TPM: Windows 10 version 1511 supports both TPM 1.2 and TPM 2.0, but earlier versions of Windows 10 support only TPM 2.0.
- Firmware lock.

To enable Device Guard in your organization, you must first digitally sign all the trusted apps that you want to allow to run on your devices. You can do this in a number of ways.

- **Publish your apps by using the Windows Store** All apps in the Windows Store are automatically signed with signatures from a trusted certificate authority (CA).
- **Use your own digital certificate or public key infrastructure (PKI)** You can sign the apps by using a certificate issued by a CA in your own PKI.
- **Use a non-Microsoft CA** You can use a trusted non-Microsoft CA to sign your own desktop Windows apps.
- **Use the Device Guard signing portal** In Windows Store For Business, you can use a Microsoft web service to sign your desktop Windows apps.

NEED MORE REVIEW? DEVICE GUARD SIGNING

To review further details about digital signing for Device Guard, refer to the Microsoft TechNet website at *https://technet.microsoft.com/itpro/windows/manage /device-guard-signing-portal*.

After digitally signing the trusted apps, you must enable the required hardware and software features in Windows 10. Assuming your devices meet the hardware requirements, and you have enabled the required software features in Windows 10 (Hyper-V Hypervisor and Isolated User Mode), using Control Panel, you can use GPOs to configure the required Device Guard settings. Open the appropriate GPO for editing and navigate to Computer Configuration \ Policies \ Administrative Templates \ System \ Device Guard.

Configure Device Health Attestation

It is important to consider the question, "What is device health?" before looking at how Windows 10 helps to ensure that only healthy devices can connect to corporate network resources.

Generally, a Windows 10 device might be considered healthy if it is configured with appropriate security features and settings. For example, a Windows 10–based device might have the latest antivirus patterns and antimalware signatures installed, be up to date with important Windows updates, and have Device Guard and Credential Guard enabled and configured.

Windows 10 Enterprise includes the Device Health Attestation feature, which can help you determine the health of devices connecting to your corporate network. The requirements for Device Health Attestation are the same as for Device Guard with the exception that TPM 2.0 is required. However, you also require a cloud-based service such as Microsoft Intune to enable the necessary MDM features and device policies to enforce health attestation on your users' devices.

After determining what constitutes a healthy device, you must next consider how to evaluate device health and what to do when devices fail health evaluation. Windows 10 contains features that enable device health determination during startup, and Device Health Attestation to be stored in the device's TPM. The process is as follows.

1. Hardware startup components are measured.

2. Windows 10 startup components are measured.

3. If Device Guard is enabled, the current Device Guard policy is measured.

4. The Windows 10 kernel is measured.

5. Antivirus software is started as the first kernel mode driver.

6. Boot start drivers are measured.

7. The MDM server through the MDM agent issues a health check command by using the Health Attestation configuration service provider (CSP).

8. Startup measurements, now stored in a log, are sent to and validated by the Health Attestation Service.

The following process describes how health startup measurements are sent to the Health Attestation Service.

1. The device initiates a request with the remote device Health Attestation Service, usually a Microsoft cloud service such as Microsoft Intune.

2. The client sends the startup log with associated digital certificates.

3. The remote device Heath Attestation Service then:

■ Verifies that the certificate is valid.

■ Verifies the integrity of the submitted log.

■ Parses the properties in the TCG log.

■ Issues a device health token that contains the health information, the device ID, and the boot counter information. The device health token is encrypted and signed.

4. The device stores the health token locally.

NEED MORE REVIEW? **CONTROL THE HEALTH OF WINDOWS 10–BASED DEVICES**

To review further details about Device Health Attestation, refer to the Microsoft TechNet website at *https://technet.microsoft.com/itpro/windows/keep-secure /protect-high-value-assets-by-controlling-the-health-of-windows-10-based-devices*.

Skill: Configure HomeGroup, workgroup, and domain settings

There are a number of ways you can connect your users' devices to your organization's network infrastructure, depending on your requirements. In small networked environments, the simplicity of creating and using a workgroup is usually sufficient. In larger organizations, the desirability of centralizing security settings for connected devices means that using an AD DS domain is the logical option. Understanding when to use workgroups and domains is important, and you must know how to connect your users' devices to these environments.

This section covers how to:

■ Configure workgroups

■ Configure AD DS domain settings

■ Configure Device Registration

NOTE **HOMEGROUP**

The list of skills measured for the exam includes HomeGroup in this section. To avoid repetition, this topic isn't covered here. You'll find information about configuring HomeGoup in Chapter 6, "Configure networking," under "Skill: Connect to a network," and in Chapter 8, "Configure data access and usage," under "Skill: Configure HomeGroup connections."

Configure workgroups

A workgroup is a small collection of computer devices that can share resources. Unlike a HomeGroup, which is discussed in Chapter 6, "Configure networking," setup and sharing resources in a workgroup requires significant manual intervention. Unlike a domain, there is no centralization of user accounts and related security policies and settings.

A workgroup is sometimes described as a peer-to-peer network, in which each device has its own set of user and group accounts, its own security policy, and its own resources that can be shared with others.

To establish a workgroup, you must define the workgroup name. You do this on each computer that will be part of the workgroup. Use the following procedure to define the workgroup.

1. Open Control Panel.
2. Click System And Security and then click System.
3. Click Change Settings, as shown in Figure 14-13.

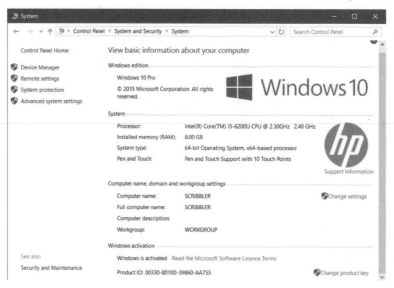

FIGURE 14-13 System settings

4. In the System Properties dialog box, on the Computer Name tab, click Change.
5. In the Computer Name/Domain Changes dialog box, in the Workgroup box, as shown in Figure 14-14, type the name of the new workgroup and click OK twice. Restart your computer.

FIGURE 14-14 Change the workgroup name

After you have defined the workgroup name, configure all other devices to use the same workgroup name; this makes browsing for network resources easier for users. Next, set up user accounts on each computer. This is necessary because there is no centralization of user accounts in a workgroup. When a user maps a network drive to a folder that you have shared on your computer, they must provide credentials to connect to the resource; these credentials are held on the sharing computer.

For more information about sharing resources, refer to Chapter 8, "Configure data access and usage."

Configure AD DS domain settings

In most organizations, using an AD DS domain environment provides the best management experience. In a domain environment, you can centralize administration, security, and application policies and provide a more managed approach to sharing and accessing resources.

To join a computer to an AD DS domain, use the following procedure.

1. Open Control Panel.
2. Click System And Security.
3. Click System.
4. Click Change Settings, as shown in Figure 14-13.
5. In the System Properties dialog box, on the Computer Name tab, click Change.

6. In the Computer Name/Domain Changes dialog box, under Member Of, in the Domain box, type the domain name and click OK.

7. In the Windows Security dialog box, shown in Figure 14-15, enter the credentials of a domain account that has the required permission to join computers to the domain. Typically, this is a domain administrator account.

FIGURE 14-15 Adding a computer to an AD DS domain

8. Click OK.

   The computer attempts to connect to the domain, create an object for the computer in the AD DS domain, and then update the local computer's configuration to reflect these changes.

9. When prompted, click OK twice.

10. Click Close and restart your computer.

    You can now sign in using domain user accounts. After you have added your computer to the domain, it becomes a managed device and is affected by domain GPO settings and security policies.

To use the preceding procedure to add a computer to a domain, the computer you are adding must be online and must be able to communicate with a domain controller. It is possible to add a computer to a domain if the computer you want to add is offline; this process is known as *offline domain join*.

Offline domain join is useful when you are adding computers to a domain from a regional data center that has limited connectivity to the main data center where domain controllers reside. To add a computer to a domain by using the offline domain join procedure, use the Djoin.exe command-line tool.

> **NEED MORE REVIEW?** **OFFLINE DOMAIN JOIN (DJOIN.EXE) STEP-BY-STEP GUIDE**
>
> To review further details about using offline domain join, refer to the Microsoft TechNet website at *https://technet.microsoft.com/library /offline-domain-join-djoin-step-by-step(v=ws.10).aspx*.

Configure Device Registration

If a Windows 10–based device is joined to your AD DS domain, users can access your organization's resources by using the same credentials they signed in to their device with, without needing to reenter them. Users who are using devices that are not domain-joined that connect to resources in your organization must enter credentials for each resource to which they attempt a connection. This can be frustrating for users that want to use their own devices.

Device Registration enables you to facilitate a single sign-on (SSO) experience for these users, negating the need to enter credentials repeatedly or add the device to the domain. The main reasons to implement Device Registration are:

- To enable access to corporate resources from non-domain-joined devices.
- To enable SSO for specific apps and/or resources in your internal network.

After you enable Device Registration, users can register and enroll their devices in your organizational network. After they have enrolled their devices:

- Enrolled devices are associated with a specific user account in the AD DS directory.
- A device object is created in AD DS to represent the physical device and its associated user account.
- A user certificate is installed on the user's device.

Requirements

Establishing Device Registration can require complex infrastructure. Table 14-1 shows the infrastructure requirements.

TABLE 14-1 Infrastructure requirements for Device Registration

Requirement	Explanation
AD DS	You must implement an AD DS forest. One of the domain controllers must run at least Windows Server 2012. You must extend the AD DS forest schema to Windows Server 2012 R2 level.
PKI	Devices require digital certificates, so you must implement a PKI in your organization to manage the process of issuing and revoking certificates. All devices that use Device Registration must trust the CAs in your PKI, and that is not necessarily automatic, because these devices are not domain members. You might need to configure the devices manually for them to trust the CA.
Active Directory Federation Services (AD FS)	You require AD FS to implement Device Registration. The AD FS server requires a certificate from your CA.
Device Registration Service	This service is required for you to perform the registration of the devices in AD DS.
DNS	You must add appropriate records in DNS so that devices can locate the components for Device Registration. A host record for Enterpriseregistration is required.
Supported client operating systems	You can only implement Device Registration on devices running Windows 10, Windows RT 8.1, Windows 8.1, and iOS operating systems.

Enabling Device Registration

Assuming that your organization's network infrastructure meets the prerequisites listed in Table 14-1, you can use the following procedure to register devices.

1. Open Settings and then click Accounts.

2. In Accounts, click the Work Access tab, as shown in Figure 14-16.

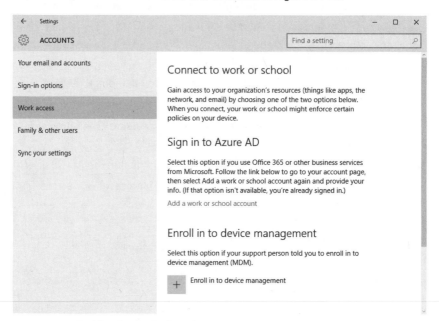

FIGURE 14-16 Enabling Device Registration

3. In the details pane, under Enroll In To Device Management, click Enroll In To Device Management.

4. On the Connect To Work Or School page, in the Email Address box, type the user ID with which you want to register the device.

5. When prompted, enter the domain credentials to begin Device Registration.

   You must use a domain account for this purpose, even if your Windows 10–based device is in a workgroup.

   The device attempts to communicate with the Enterpriseregistration host and continues the process of Device Registration.

EXAM TIP

Each device must be configured with the necessary network settings to enable the device to locate servers in your organization. The device must also trust the company CA. If you used a public certificate on the server with the Enterpriseregistration address, this trust is implicit. If you did not, you must export the root certificate from your CA and import it on all devices that you want to register.

NEED MORE REVIEW? **JOIN TO WORKPLACE FROM ANY DEVICE FOR SSO AND SEAM-LESS SECOND FACTOR AUTHENTICATION ACROSS COMPANY APPLICATIONS**

To review further details about Device Registration, refer to the Microsoft TechNet website at *https://technet.microsoft.com/library/dn280945.aspx*.

Summary

- You can use either local or Microsoft accounts for authentication in Windows 10.
- You can use Windows Hello, Microsoft Passport, and picture passwords to improve authentication security.
- You can use Credential Manager and Credential Guard to help protect authentication.
- Device Guard and Device Health Attestation can help secure Windows 10 devices.
- Devices can access domain resources by belonging to that domain or by using Device Registration.

Thought experiment

In this thought experiment, demonstrate your skills and knowledge of the topics covered in this chapter. You can find answers to this thought experiment in the next section.

You work in support at A. Datum Corporation. You are implementing authentication and authorization. Your manager has some concerns about security of devices, and you must investigate and then configure features in Windows 10 that can help allay your manager's concerns.

As a consultant for A. Datum, answer the following questions about authentication and authorization in the A. Datum organization.

1. Your manager asks you about the benefits of using Microsoft accounts over those of using local accounts on your users' Windows 10 devices. What are these benefits?

2. Your manager wants to know why entering a four-digit PIN is more secure than using a complex password. How would you answer?

3. Windows 10 implements a feature called User Account Control. What is the default prompt that a user receives when they attempt to perform a management task requiring elevation when they are signed in using a standard user account?

4. What are the requirements of Device Guard in Windows 10?

5. What is the purpose of Device Registration?

Thought experiment answer

This section contains the solution to the thought experiment. Each answer explains why the answer choice is correct.

1. Microsoft accounts offer the following benefits to users of Windows 10 devices.

   A. Access to personal Microsoft cloud services, including OneDrive, Outlook.com, and other personal apps

   B. Access to Microsoft Intune, Microsoft Office 365, and Microsoft Azure

   C. The ability to download and install apps from the Microsoft Store

   D. The ability to sync user settings between devices that are linked to your account

2. A PIN is more secure because it is based on two-factor authentication: knowledge of the PIN and possession of the device where that PIN is registered as an authentication gesture. A password can be used on any device, and only knowledge of the password is required.

3. A standard user receives the prompt for credentials when they attempt elevation to perform an administrative task.

4. To implement Device Guard, your device requires a 64-bit version of Windows 10 Enterprise; a UEFI version 2.3.1 or greater; Secure Boot; virtualization features: Intel VT-X, AMD-V, and SLAT; a VT-d or AMD-Vi input–output memory management unit; a TPM; and firmware lock.

5. Device Registration enables users with their own devices to access corporate network resources by using SSO. From the organization's perspective, these devices can be managed as part of an MDM policy.

CHAPTER 15

Configure advanced management tools

Windows 10 provides you with a number of tools with which to manage the operating system. You can use any or all of these tools, depending on your needs. This chapter explores how to use these tools to manage your users' Windows 10 devices efficiently.

Skills covered in this chapter:

- Configure services
- Configure Device Manager
- Configure and use the MMC
- Configure Task Scheduler
- Configure automation of management tasks using Windows PowerShell

Skill: Configure services

A service can best be described as a software component that interacts at one level with device drivers and, at another level, with app-level components. In a sense, services sit between apps and hardware devices and are considered a core part of the operating system, controlling user requests, through apps, to hardware resources.

These operating system services provide discrete functions in Windows 10 and require no user interaction.

This section covers how to:

- Manage services
- Use the System Configuration tool

Manage services

You can manage services in a number of ways, including from the command-prompt, by using Windows PowerShell, and by using the management console.

Using the Services management console snap-in

The most straightforward way to manage services is to use the Services management console snap-in, shown in Figure 15-1.

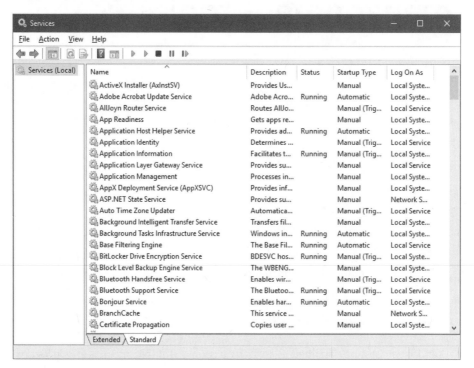

FIGURE 15-1 Services management console snap-in

You can use this console to view and manage services in the operating system. For example, to manage the status of a service (assuming it is not running), right-click the service and then click Start. If you want to stop or restart a running service, right-click the running service and then click either Stop or Restart.

You can also manage the settings of a service by double-clicking the desired service. In the Properties dialog box for the named service, as shown in Figure 15-2, you can then configure the properties shown in Table 15-1.

FIGURE 15-2 Managing the properties of a service

TABLE 15-1 Configurable options for a Windows 10 service

Tab	Options and explanation
General	Service name. You cannot change this value, but it is useful to know what name Windows assigns to the service so that you can reference it when using a command-line tool or Windows PowerShell. Startup type: Disabled, Manual, Automatic, Automatic (Delayed Start). This option enables you to determine the startup behavior of the service. Start parameters. You can add properties to configure the service behavior when it starts.
Log On	Log on as Local System Account or This Account. Some services run in the context of the Local System Account. Others must be configured to use a specific, named account, for example, when communicating across the network with another service. You can create special local user accounts for the purpose of running services. When you define a specific user account and change the user password, you must update the password information on the Log On tab for the services that use that account.
Recovery	You can configure what happens when a service fails to start. Specifically, you can configure Windows 10 to attempt a restart of a service if it fails to start on the first attempt. On second attempts, you can choose another option, such as Restart The Computer. Available options for failures are Take No Action, Restart The Service, Run A Program, and Restart The Computer. If you select Run A Program, you can configure additional options for the path and name of the program, plus any runtime switches you want to apply.
Dependencies	Some services depend on other services, or groups of services, to run. In this way, Windows 10 can start efficiently by making sure only the required services are in memory. You cannot make changes on this tab, but it is informative to know whether a service has dependencies, especially when a service is failing to start properly.

Using Event Viewer

As you can see in Figure 15-1, the status column in the Services snap-in shows whether a service is running. If a service is shown as not running, and you feel that it should be running, you can investigate further by using tools such as Event Viewer. You can see service startup information in the System log. Look for Service Control Manager source events, as shown in Figure 15-3.

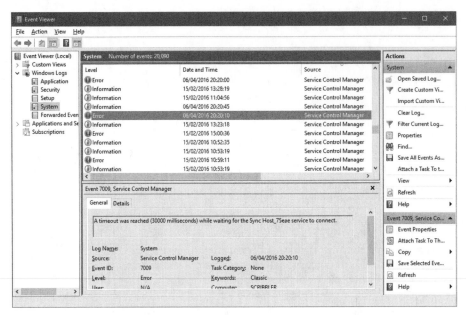

FIGURE 15-3 Service failures listed in Event Viewer

Using command-line tools

You can also use the command line to investigate and troubleshoot service startup. Table 15-2 shows some of the more common command-line tools you can use to work with services. To use these commands, open an elevated command prompt.

TABLE 15-2 Managing services from the command line

Command	Explanation
Net start	When used without arguments, lists the running services. When used with the name of a service, the service, if not running, is started. For example, net start workstation starts the Windows workstation service.
Net stop	Must be used with the name of a running service. For example, net stop workstation will stop the Windows workstation service.
Sc query	Displays a list of services.

Command	Explanation
Sc stop	Enables you to stop a named service. For example, to stop the spooler service, run: Sc stop spooler.
Sc start	Enables you to start a named service. For example, to start the spooler service, run: Sc start spooler.

You can also use Windows PowerShell to manage services. This is particularly useful because you can use Windows PowerShell to administer other computers remotely, including their services. In addition, you can script Windows PowerShell cmdlets, enabling you to store common administrative tasks for future use. Table 15-3 shows the cmdlets you can use to manage services in Windows 10. Open an elevated Windows PowerShell window to use these cmdlets.

TABLE 15-3 Managing services with Windows PowerShell

Cmdlet	Explanation
Get-service	Lists available services. To get a list of running services, use the following cmdlet: Get-Service | Where-Object {$_.status -eq "running"}
Stop-service	Enables you to stop the named service(s). For example: Stop-service – name spooler
Start-service	Enables you to start the named service(s). For example: Start-service – name spooler
Restart-service	Enables you to stop and start the named service(s). For example: Restart-service – name spooler
Set-service	Enables you to reconfigure the startup and other properties of the named service. For example, to change the display name of the Workstation service, use the following cmdlet: set-service -name lanmanworkstation -DisplayName "LanMan Workstation"

> **NEED MORE REVIEW? MANAGING SERVICES**
>
> To review further details about using Windows PowerShell to manage services, refer to the Microsoft MSDN website at *https://msdn.microsoft.com/powershell/scripting/getting-started /cookbooks/managing-services*.

Use the System Configuration tool

If you are experiencing problems with starting your Windows 10 device, and you suspect a service might be the cause of the problem, you can control which services start when you start your computer by using Safe Mode. This reduces the set of services that start to the minimum required to run Windows.

You can force your computer into Safe Mode during startup or use the System Configuration tool, Msconfig.exe, as shown in Figure 15-4. To access the System Configuration tool, run **msconfig.exe**. You can then configure your computer's startup behavior. Configurable options are described in Table 15-4.

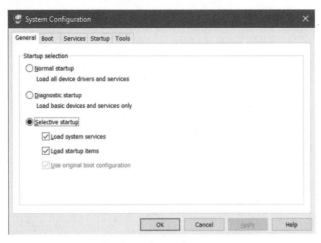

FIGURE 15-4 System Configuration tool

TABLE 15-4 System configuration options

Tab	Options and explanation
General	Select Normal Startup to configure normal operations on your computer. Choose Diagnostic Startup to load a minimal set of devices and services. Choose Selective Startup to be more selective about what is initialized during startup.
Boot	You can enable Safe Mode by clicking Safe Boot. Then you can choose additional options: Minimal, Alternate Shell, and Network. You can also start without the GUI, enable a boot log, and configure startup to use a base video driver and configuration. The Advanced Options button enables you to restrict Windows to using fewer logical processors and a reduced amount of memory. These options are useful for re-creating a computer configuration in which a specific problem was experienced. If multiple operating systems are installed on your computer, they are listed on this tab, enabling you to select between the available operating systems. You can choose to make your boot selections permanent, but you should exercise caution with this option in case the settings you have selected are inappropriate.
Services	The Services tab displays the available operating system services and enables you to configure their startup behavior. For example, you can disable any services that you suspect might be causing issues with your computer. To disable a service, clear the check box next to its name.
Startup	The Startup tab enables you to access the Start-up tab in Task Manager to control the startup behavior of apps.
Tools	The Tools tab provides a consolidated list of available system tools, including: Change UAC Settings, System Properties, Computer Management, Device Manager, and the Registry Editor.

Skill: Configure Device Manager

Devices are hardware components, either built in to your device or connected as a peripheral device. The operating system interacts with devices by using device drivers, specialist pieces of software generally developed by the hardware vendor.

You can manage devices and the associated drivers by using the Device Manager management console snap-in.

You can access Device Manager from the Computer Management tool or by right-clicking Start and then clicking Device Manager, as shown in Figure 15-5.

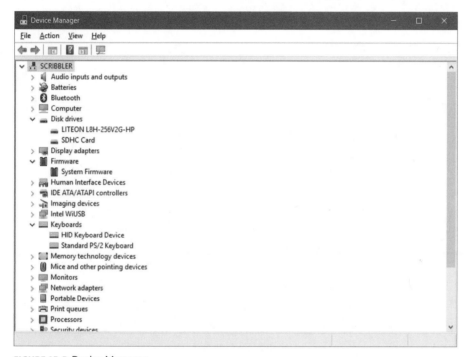

FIGURE 15-5 Device Manager

If there is a problem with a device, it is shown with an exclamation mark in Device Manager. You can then manage the device by right-clicking it and then choosing:

- **Update Driver Software**   Use this to update the driver software for your device. You can choose to use a device driver that you have obtained and stored locally or have Windows try to detect and download the latest driver.

- **Disable**   You can stop the device from running. This option leaves the device configured in Windows for possible later use.

- **Uninstall**   This option enables you to remove the device and its driver from Windows. When you restart, Windows might detect the device and install the default driver for it.

- **Scan For Hardware Changes** Windows normally detects changes in hardware and might reconfigure devices to accommodate such changes. For example, adding additional hardware might force Windows to reconfigure existing devices. If you suspect Windows has not properly adapted to a change in hardware, you can force it to scan for hardware changes.

- **Properties** You can configure advanced options by using the Properties option for a device, as shown in Figure 15-6. Table 15-5 describes the configurable options.

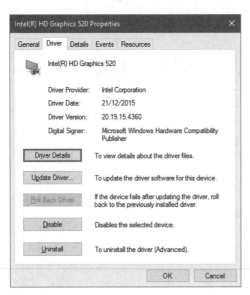

FIGURE 15-6 Properties of a device

TABLE 15-5 Device Manager device properties options

Tab	Options and explanation
General	Shows the current status of the device. No configurable options.
Driver	Current driver information appears: Driver Provider, Driver Date, Driver Version, and Digital Signer. You can also view driver details, update the driver, roll back the driver (if previously updated), and disable or uninstall the driver.
Details	Enables you to view advanced properties for the device. No configurable options.
Events	Provides a useful history of events that relate to the device, for example, when the device was installed, updated, or reconfigured. No configurable options.
Resources	Displays the hardware resources the device uses. Conflicts with other devices are shown, where they exist. No configurable options. Note: This tab is not always present.
Power Management	Enables you to configure two power-related settings: ■ Allow The Computer To Turn Off This Device To Save Power ■ Allow This Device To Wake The Computer Note: This tab is not always present.

Skill: Configure and use the MMC

Most of the administrative and management tools built in to Windows 10 are based on Microsoft Management Console. This tool is a framework into which you can plug management tools. You can also set the focus of the tool to be local or remote, enabling you to manage not just your own Windows 10–based device.

> **This section covers how to:**
> - Configure the management console
> - Customize your console by using Taskpad views

Configure the management console

You can add management tools, or snap-ins, to the console by clicking the File menu and then choosing Add/Remove Snap-in, as shown in Figure 15-7. You can then choose one or more snap-ins to add to your console.

When you add a snap-in, you are asked whether the focus for the snap-in will be the local computer or a remote computer. Make this selection and then click Finish. If you want, you can add additional snap-ins to the console. When you have added all the required snap-ins, click OK.

After you have added your snap-ins, you can save the console. Click File and then click Save. Specify a suitable name and location for the console. Click Save.

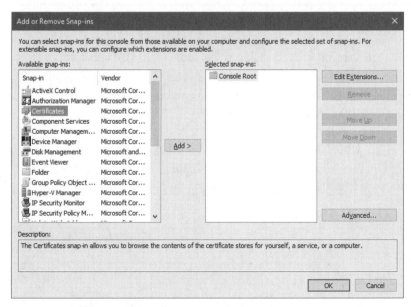

FIGURE 15-7 Adding snap-ins to the management console

Customize your console by using Taskpad views

You can further customize your console by using Taskpad Views. Taskpad enables you to create a task-focused version of your console. This is particularly useful for when you want to designate a particular subset of management tasks to a user. To create a Taskpad view, click Action and then click New Taskpad View. As shown in Figure 15-8, you have the option to display Taskpad as a vertical or horizontal list or use no list. Give your Taskpad a name and then click Finish.

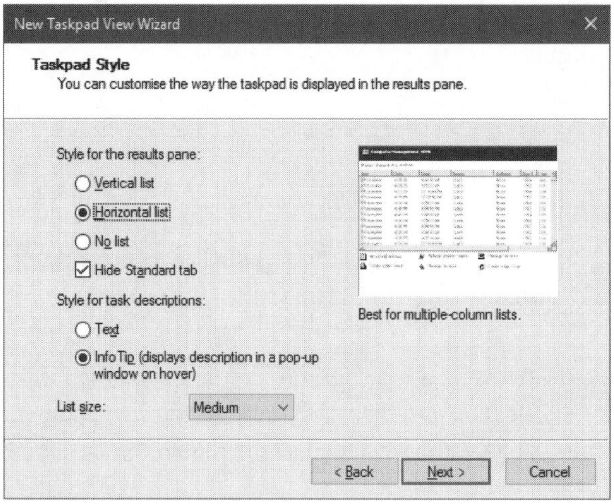

FIGURE 15-8 A Taskpad view

You are prompted to launch the Add New Tasks Wizard. This enables you to add specific tasks to the Taskpad view. In the New Task Wizard, you can add menu commands, shell commands, or navigation options. You can run through the wizard as many times as you need to set up the individual tasks that you want to enable in Taskpad.

Finally, you must restrict a user to use only the Taskpad view you have created. This is achieved by clicking the File menu and then the Options menu. In the Options dialog box, in the console mode list, click User Mode—Limited Access, Single Window. Clear the Allow The User To Customize Views check box and then click OK. Save your console.

For example, as shown in Figure 15-9, tasks for viewing user properties, deleting users, and setting user passwords have been added to a Taskpad view. Note that the user still requires administrative rights to perform the management tasks that the console facilitates.

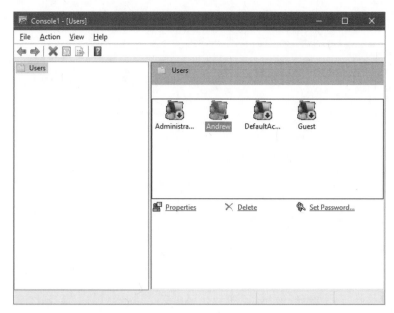

FIGURE 15-9 A Taskpad view

After you have created the console with its Taskpad view, you can distribute it to users that have the appropriate management rights to perform the task.

Skill: Configure Task Scheduler

Often, there will be tasks that you must perform at specific times, or on a repeated basis. Task Scheduler can help you. You can use it to schedule simple or complex tasks, either on the local computer or on a remote computer.

You can access Task Scheduler from All Apps, under the Windows Administrative Tools node. In fact, Task Scheduler is a management console snap-in and can be added to any custom console using the procedure outlined earlier.

To create a task, load Task Scheduler and, from the Action pane, click Create Basic Task, as shown in Figure 15-10.

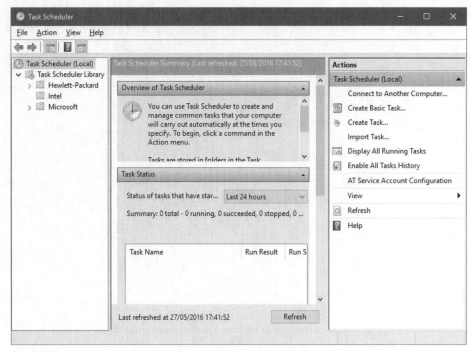

FIGURE 15-10 Task Scheduler

The Create A Basic Task Wizard starts. Use the following procedure to create a task.

1. On the Create A Basic Task page, type a name and description for your task and then click Next.

2. On the Task Trigger page, specify when you want the task to start. Choose from Daily, Weekly, Monthly, One Time, When The Computer Starts, When I Log On, and When A Specific Event Is Logged. Click Next. If you chose a time trigger, you must then specify the time. For example, if you chose Weekly, you must define when during the week. Click Next.

3. On the Action page, choose Start A Program.

4. On the Start A Program page, specify the name and location of the program and any command-line switches for the program. Click Next.

5. On the Summary page, click Finish. You can select the Open The Properties Dialog For This Task When I Click Finish check box to review your task settings.

To review or reconfigure your scheduled task, in the navigation pane, click Task Scheduler Library and, in the center pane, locate and double-click your task. You can then use the tabbed dialog box to reconfigure the properties, as shown in Figure 15-11.

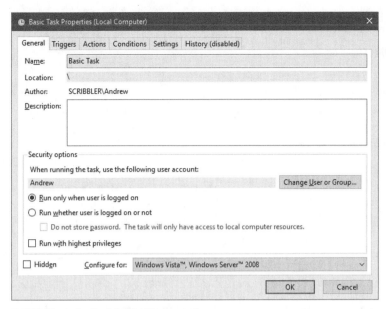

FIGURE 15-11 A scheduled task's properties

Skill: Configure automation of management tasks with Windows PowerShell

You have already seen in this book how useful Windows PowerShell can be and how pervasive this management tool in Windows 10 is. However, it's worth considering the benefits of using Windows PowerShell to automate common or repetitive administration or management tasks.

Building complex scripts in Windows PowerShell can be daunting and is beyond the scope of this book. However, there is no reason you cannot begin to gain skills with Windows PowerShell and save your frequently used cmdlets to .ps1 files for subsequent reuse.

> **This section covers how to:**
> - Create simple scripts
> - Enable scripts to run
> - Use Windows PowerShell ISE

Create simple scripts

Windows PowerShell cmdlets are constructed of verbs and nouns. The nouns are always singular. For example, you have seen in this chapter that you can use the get-service cmdlet to retrieve information on Windows 10 services; "get" is the verb, "service" is the noun.

You can also add parameters to most cmdlets. So, for example, to retrieve information about the service called LanmanWorkstation, add the -name parameter to the get-service cmdlet:

```
get-service -name lanmanworkstation
```

You can pass the results of one cmdlet to another for additional processing. This is known as piping. For example, you can retrieve a list of services with the get-service cmdlet and then pipe the result (a list of all services) and look for those services that are running, as shown in the following code.

```
Get-Service | Where-Object {$_.status -eq "running"}
```

In the preceding command, you search through the list of all returned services and look for those services for which the status value equals running. You could just as easily use the same approach to look for services that are not running and then pipe that on to another cmdlet that might start those services or query why they're not running.

You can see that a few simple cmdlets joined together begin to create a powerful script. Your script can contain any Windows PowerShell cmdlet that you have used in the Windows PowerShell window. You can also use variables and gather input from an operator and provide output to the monitor to let the operator know what's happening in the script.

To create a simple script, you merely need to store your cmdlets in a text file with a .ps1 file extension. Then, to run the script, double-click the file in File Explorer or type the path and name of the file in a Windows PowerShell window.

Enable scripts to run

To protect you from unsafe scripts, Windows 10 prohibits running unsigned scripts. Unless you can sign your scripts, you must enable your computer to run unsigned Windows PowerShell scripts. You can do this by using the Set-executionpolicy cmdlet in an elevated Windows PowerShell window.

To enable your computer to run any scripts that you create locally, but only digitally signed scripts from remote sources, run the following cmdlet.

```
Set-ExecutionPolicy RemoteSigned
```

> **NEED MORE REVIEW? MICROSOFT SCRIPT CENTER**
>
> To review further details about using Windows PowerShell scripts, refer to the Microsoft TechNet website at *https://technet.microsoft.com/scriptcenter/default*.

Use Windows PowerShell ISE

Windows PowerShell ISE, shown in Figure 15-12, provides command-completion functionality. This feature enables you to learn about cmdlet syntax as you use them. You can also create and edit scripts in Windows PowerShell ISE and then run the scripts step by step in the script window. This procedure can help you debug your scripts to ensure that they are running as intended.

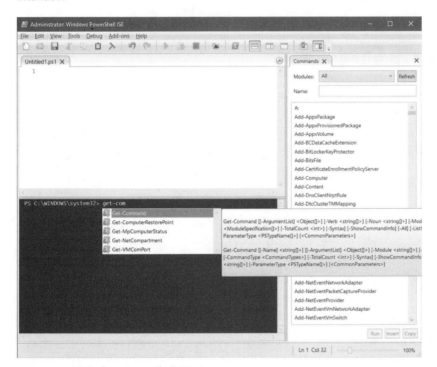

FIGURE 15-12 Windows PowerShell ISE

Summary

- Operating system services can be controlled from the Services snap-in, from the command prompt, and with Windows PowerShell.

- The System Configuration tool enables you to control aspects of system startup behavior, including minimal services startup.

- You can use Device Manager to view and manage device drivers and the underlying hardware devices, including updating drivers, disabling devices, and uninstalling devices.

- You can customize the management console to your needs with whichever snap-ins you need and use Taskpad views to create a specific, restricted tool for delegated administrators.

- Windows 10 enables you to create and manage a schedule of automated tasks by using Task Scheduler.

- By saving commonly used administrative Windows PowerShell cmdlets in a .ps1 file, you can easily automate routing management tasks with scripts.

Thought experiment

In this thought experiment, demonstrate your skills and knowledge of the topics covered in this chapter. You can find answers to this thought experiment in the next section.

You work in support at A. Datum Corporation. Your Windows 10 deployment is complete, and you are now busy supporting your users. As a consultant for A. Datum, answer the following questions about using advanced management tools and techniques in the A. Datum organization.

1. You find that you are repeatedly performing the same management task on multiple computers. At the moment, you use the management console to perform the required tasks. How could you achieve this more easily?

2. A number of users are experiencing problems with their computers. You determine that the issue relates to a service that occasionally stops and is restarted. Where can you track information about this service?

3. What command-line tools can you use for managing services?

4. You decide to delegate administration of resetting user passwords to a specific user in each department. You have already assigned the appropriate users the required management rights to perform this task. You want to provide a management tool for this task, and only this task. What could you do?

Thought experiment answer

This section contains the solution to the thought experiment. Each answer explains why the answer choice is correct.

1. You could create a Windows PowerShell script that contains the required management cmdlets. Because Windows PowerShell supports remoting, it is easy to run the script against remote computers. You must, however, ensure that the execution policy for each computer supports scripts. You must also ensure that Windows PowerShell remoting is enabled.

2. Use the System log in Event Viewer. You can group events based on source; in this instance, the source is Service Control Manager.

3. You can use Windows PowerShell, but also the SC.exe and Net.exe command-line tools.

4. You could create a custom Taskpad view for the required task.

Index

Numbers and Symbols

6to4 protocol, 178
16-bit applications, 17
32-bit architecture
  device drivers, 76
  Windows 10 versions, 17
64-bit architecture
  device drivers, 76
  Windows 10 versions, 17
802.11x wireless standards, 190

A

access control entry (ACE), 257
access control list (ACL), 50, 257, 260
accessibility options, 115–116
ACE (access control entry), 257
ACL (access control list), 50, 257, 260
ACT (Application Compatibility Toolkit), 7–9
Action Center
  about, 108–109
  notifications area, 111–112
  Quick Action tiles, 109–111
Action menu (Device Manager), 80
activation
  about, 137–138
  selecting method, 138–139
  volume activation, 140–142
  for Windows 10, 142–144
Active command (DiskPart), 210
Active Directory
  configuring, 148–151
  volume activation, 140
Active Directory Administrative Center (ADAC), 148,
152–154
Active Directory Domain Services (AD DS)
  activation support, 138, 140
  blocking Windows Store Apps, 288
  configuring domain settings, 443–444
  configuring firewall settings, 300
  configuring Start with GPOs, 104
  configuring UAC, 146–147

configuring Windows Update, 324
Device Registration requirement, 445
disabling UACs, 430
distributing fixes via GPOs, 9
dynamic access control, 269
HomeGroups feature and, 174, 243
implementing DirectAccess, 178–179
installing desktop apps, 274, 276
network location profiles, 180
remote connections, 314
volume licensing, 140
Active Directory Federation Services (AD FS), 445
Active Directory Users And Computers snap-in, 148, 152
active styluses, 19
ActiveX controls, 121
AD DS (Active Directory Domain Services)
  activation support, 138, 140
  blocking Windows Store Apps, 288
  configuring domain settings, 443–444
  configuring firewall settings, 300
  configuring Start with GPOs, 104
  configuring UAC, 146–147
  configuring Windows Update, 324
  Device Registration requirement, 445
  disabling UACs, 430
  distributing fixes via GPOs, 9
  dynamic access control, 269
  HomeGroups feature and, 174, 243
  implementing DirectAccess, 178–179
  installing desktop apps, 274, 276
  network location profiles, 180
  remote connections, 314
  volume licensing, 140
AD DS server role, 150
AD FS (Active Directory Federation Services), 445
ad-hoc mode (wireless networking), 190
ADAC (Active Directory Administrative Center), 148,
152–154
Add-AppxPackage cmdlet, 289
Add command (DiskPart), 210
Add Hardware Wizard, 81–82
Add Mirror Wizard, 234
Add New Tasks Wizard, 458
Add-PhysicalDisk cmdlet, 225
Add-Printer cmdlet, 371

W

X

Z

About the authors

ANDREW BETTANY is a Microsoft Most Valuable Professional (MVP), recognized since 2012 for his Windows expertise, and author of several publications including Windows exam certification prep and Microsoft official training materials. A Microsoft Certified Trainer, Andrew has taught many IT pros a wide range of technical skills in a variety of areas, including Windows client, Server, and cloud. Andrew enjoys creating and delivering "IT Masterclasses," a series of short intensive technical courses, and is passionate about helping others learn technology. He is a frequent speaker and proctor at TechEd and Ignite conferences worldwide. In 2011 and 2013, he delivered classes in earthquake-hit Haiti to help the community rebuild its technology skills. Andrew can be found on *www.itmasterclasses.com*, LinkedIn, Facebook, and Twitter. He lives in the countryside close to the beautiful city of York in Yorkshire in the UK.

ANDREW WARREN has more than 30 years of experience in the IT industry, many of which he has spent teaching and writing. He has been involved as a subject matter expert in many of the Windows Server 2016 courses and as the technical lead in many Windows 10 courses. He also has been involved in developing TechNet sessions about Microsoft Exchange Server. Andrew is based in the United Kingdom, and lives in rural Somerset where he runs his own IT training and education consultancy.

Now that you've read the book...

Tell us what you think!

Was it useful?
Did it teach you what you wanted to learn?
Was there room for improvement?

Let us know at http://aka.ms/tellpress

Your feedback goes directly to the staff at Microsoft Press, and we read every one of your responses. Thanks in advance!

 Microsoft